RELIGION AND POLITICS IN AMERICA

RELIGION AND POLITICS IN AMERICA

Faith, Culture, and Strategic Choices

Third Edition

ROBERT BOOTH FOWLER
University of Wisconsin—Madison

ALLEN D. HERTZKE
University of Oklahoma

LAURA R. OLSON
Clemson University

KEVIN R. DEN DULK
Grand Valley State University

Westview
PRESS

A Member of the Perseus Books Group

To our students

Published in the United States of America by Westview Press, A Member of the Perseus Books Group, 5500 Central Avenue, Boulder, Colorado 80301–2877, and in the United Kingdom by Westview Press, 12 Hid's Copse Road, Cumnor Hill, Oxford OX2 9JJ.

Find us on the world wide web at www.westviewpress.com

Westview Press books are available at special discounts for bulk purchases in the United States by corporations, institutions, and other organizations. For more information, please contact the Special Markets Department at the Perseus Books Group, 11 Cambridge Center, Cambridge, MA 02142, or call (617) 252-5298, (800) 255-1514 or email special.markets@perseusbooks.com.

A Cataloging-in-Publication data record for this book is available from the Library of Congress.
ISBN-10: 0-8133-4229-5   ISBN-13: 978-0-8133-4229-0

Interior design by Lisa Kreinbrink
Set in 11.5-point Adobe Garamond by the Perseus Books Group

The paper used in this publication meets the requirements of the American National Standard for Permanence of Paper for Printed Library Materials Z39.48–1984.

CONTENTS

INTRODUCTION

Religion and politics and the dynamic interactions between them are visible everywhere in the United States—and they are the focus of this book. Eminently evident is the vigorous presence of the conservative religious movement, which concerns itself with abortion, pornography, sex education, prayer in public schools, and family breakdown. We also see the growing assertiveness of the Roman Catholic Church, which allies itself with evangelical Protestants on abortion and educational choice and with mainline Protestants on foreign policy and social welfare issues. We note the increasing politicization of African American and Latino religion. We continue to observe vigorous lobbying efforts by liberal religious groups, both Protestant and Catholic. We consider the prominent role played by Jewish groups in American politics, especially regarding support for Israel; their involvement contrasts sharply with the fitful efforts of the growing Muslim population to gain a modicum of political influence, especially in the wake of the attacks on September 11, 2001. We watch the rising flood of cases in the American judicial system, especially cases brought by religious minority groups. Everywhere one looks, religion and politics appear to be intertwined in American public life.

The aim of this book is to understand the politics of religion in the United States and to appreciate the strategic choices that politicians and religious participants make when they participate in politics. We try to make sense of how religion and politics come together in the voting booth, Congress and the state legislatures, the executive branch, the courts, the interest group system, and the larger culture of the United States. The subject is large and complex, and it features fascinating and often contradictory currents. It is a topic of great importance, since we believe one can understand American politics and society today only with an appreciation of religion's role in them.

We have attempted to make this book accessible. Our goal was to produce a readable and informative text, not a scholarly tome. We have thoroughly updated the content of the second edition to reflect current trends and important changes in the relationship between religion and politics. One of the challenges we have faced in preparing this edition relates to the very nature of American religion—its real and ever growing pluralism, its diverse regional and ethnic bases, and its tendency to change rapidly. These characteristics preclude the possibility of any single definition of religion. Moreover, we are not especially attracted to elaborate philosophical or linguistic attempts to define such a changing and fluid concept as religion. Rather, we define religion phenomenologically. That is, we discuss the politics of religion in the United States with the understanding that what the culture generally treats as religion (or as a religion), we do too—from Protestantism in all of its varieties, to Judaism, Roman Catholicism, Islam, the LDS Church, and innumerable other faiths. Despite the great religious diversity of American culture, religion is ordinarily assumed to involve the acknowledgment and worship of a transcendent god or gods, spirit, or force. Usually it is more specific than the alternate definition, which would suggest that any general system of meaning is a religion.

We endeavor to strike a balance between providing enough information and cluttering the narrative with endless nuance. Historical background, we believe, is an essential part of this context, so we devote an entire chapter to historical roots, in addition to providing historical details elsewhere in the text. As we present the big picture, we may oversimplify at times or give short shrift to some subjects. For example, there are plenty of complexities today in the relationship between evangelical Protestants and Roman Catholics, and we discuss many of them in various chapters. But the most significant development may be their emerging cooperation—a fact that can be appreciated only if one understands the deep historical antipathy between these two groups.

Our book also depicts the arena of struggle and strategic calculation, of the clashing ideals and necessary compromise that mark all of politics, a concept we define as conflict and agreement in public life. We shift back and forth between describing practical politics, religious traditions, and theology. We try to illuminate religious politics as it operates in government, among clashing interest groups, and in American voting behavior. At the same time, we explore the nature of citizens' and churches' faiths and the personal values that have so much effect on their political beliefs and behaviors. Only by doing both tasks may the dynamics of religion in American politics today be appreciated.

Chapter 1 of this book begins with a thematic interpretation of religion and politics in American history. We avoid presenting a merely chronological review because we are more interested in broad themes that resonate with current issues. We move to the contemporary scene in Chapter 2, where we describe the status of religion in America today. Here we examine the religious affiliations of the American people, their religious practices, and the theological and political outlooks of major Christian religious traditions in America—Catholic, evangelical Protestant, and mainline Protestant. In Chapter 3 we turn to the politics of Judaism, Islam, the LDS Church, and other smaller religious traditions in the United States. Not only do such traditions highlight important themes in religion and politics, but they also often have a tangible impact (especially through the courts) on politics in the United States. In the next three chapters we turn to practical politics: voting and party politics in Chapter 4, lobbying in Chapter 5, and political elites in Chapter 6. As a case study of the intersection of religion and politics, we devote Chapter 7 to an exploration of the contrasting roles of various religious groups, especially those associated with the "Christian Right," in both domestic and international affairs.

This brings us to the legal and constitutional arenas, which are the subject of Chapters 8 and 9. Here we consider clashing views about the meaning of the First Amendment's provision for religious free exercise and its prohibition of official religious establishment. We explore crucial court cases that have defined church-state law; we also examine various legal interest groups involved in the relevant court battles. We then explore several important topics that merit focused treatment, including Latino and African American religion in Chapter 10 and gender, religion, and politics in Chapter 11. Finally, in Chapter 12 we discuss several broad theories that attempt to explain religious politics in America today. Looking at the big picture helps us to understand the fascinating, ever-changing world of politics and religion in America.

Several individuals helped immeasurably in the preparation of this book. We would like to thank Sarah Warner, our editor at Westview, for her advice and patience. John Green and Corwin Smidt generously shared their useful data (collected in conjunction with Lyman Kellstedt and James Guth) on the 2000 elections. Clarke Cochran shared a wealth of information about the Catholic Church and healthcare policy. Alice Honeywell graciously read through the entire book and her comments and suggestions helped to improve it in every instance. We also benefited greatly from the excellent research assistance of Scott Templin at the University of Oklahoma and Jaime Greene at Grand Valley State University. To all, we are very grateful.

RELIGION AND POLITICAL CULTURE IN AMERICA: THE HISTORICAL LEGACY

It would be hard to understand American politics today without knowing something about American religion. And it would be equally difficult to understand either without a sense of history, a sense of how the interplay among religion, politics, and culture has shaped the story of the United States. Since colonial days, religion has played a profound role in molding American culture, directly and indirectly, in ways that no one could have imagined or predicted. In order to sort out the complex history of the relationships among religion, politics, and culture, we have organized this chapter around four themes: the Puritan temper, pluralism, the evangelical dimension, and populism.

THE PURITAN TEMPER

The United States was born of religious zeal. Its colonization coincided with, and was fueled by, vast upheavals in Europe that had been unleashed by the Protestant Reformation. None of these was so important as the Puritan revolution, which shook England and inspired many to emigrate to the New World. Today the term *puritanical* connotes a narrow-minded, self-righteous rejection of anything pleasurable. But the Puritan legacy is something quite different. The Puritans bequeathed to Americans strong civic institutions, a sense of national mission, and a reformist impulse that continues to shape American society and political culture.

The Puritans earned their name from their desire to "purify" the Church of England and, more broadly, society itself in the late 1500s and early 1600s. Inspired by Calvinist Reformed theology, Puritans reacted vehemently against what they saw as laxity and corruption in Christian churches. Infused with a sense of moral urgency, Puritans threatened established political and religious elites, and they often suffered persecution when they agitated. But if the encrusted Old World of Europe resisted renovation, the American colonies offered a fresh start. Thus the Puritans (along with other religious dissenters) found their way to the American seaboard in the early 1600s.[1]

Though the American colonies were characterized by religious diversity from the beginning, the Puritans brought with them such a powerful vision that they exercised a disproportionate influence for a century and a half before the Revolutionary War. Many people at the time, regardless of their denominational affiliation, embraced the central tenets of Puritanism, and several of the leading colonial intellectuals were Puritan ministers.[2]

To the Puritans, the new land was not just a place where they could freely exercise their religion. It was literally the New Israel, the promised land on which the faithful could build a holy commonwealth unencumbered by Old World corruption. They called their mission an "Errand in the Wilderness" and saw it as divinely ordained. In the celebrated Puritan phrase, America was to be "a city upon a hill," a light to the nations. This sense of the nation's providential destiny continues to fascinate, mystify, and sometimes horrify people in other countries. From the "manifest destiny" of westward expansion, to Abraham Lincoln's determination to preserve the Union, to Woodrow Wilson's quest to "make the world safe for democracy," to John Kennedy's Peace Corps, to George W. Bush's "war or terrorism," Americans have continued the Puritan legacy by acting on a sense of special mission and destiny. Understanding this legacy is especially important now that the United States, as the only surviving superpower, strives to define its global responsibilities.

Puritan doctrine also helped to nurture self-government in the new land.[3] Puritans articulated a "covenant theology" that rejected the idea of the divine right of kings. As the Puritans saw it, political leaders do not derive their authority directly from God; instead they favored government based on a community's covenant with God. Puritan churches were organized around the congregational model, on the basis of the autonomous, self-governing parish. This tradition gave rise to a similar political practice of community self-governance. To be sure, this was not democracy as we know it today. Only the religious "elect," or church members, were allowed to participate. People could become church members only by persuading the church fathers that they were most likely predestined to be saved by God (understood to be only a small percentage of the population). But even if the Puritan colonies were more theocracies than democracies, a form of self-government was fostered from the start. Christian colonists had become outraged by 1775 as England and its established church continued to assert authority over the colonies. The colonists had governed themselves for more than a century, and their religious doctrine, they believed, justified their action.[4]

The Puritan emphasis on all humans' tendency to sin also affected American politics, though scholars disagree on the extent. Certainly it contributed to the American fear of concentrated governmental power. If leaders are as tempted by sin as other human beings, then precautions against abuse must be built into the system. Thus some see evidence of the residual cultural influence of Puritan doctrine in James Madison's concern with diffusing and checking power in the national Constitution. Others note that early Americans largely avoided romantic and utopian thinking of the kind that led to the excesses of the French Revolution. A deeply ingrained understanding of sin thus tempered the practice of popular democracy.[5]

In addition, throughout the nation's history, many Americans have based their social practices on the Puritan understanding of the need to restrain individual sin for the good of the community. As the French observer Alexis de Tocqueville noted in the 1830s, the majority of Americans shared the Puritan conviction that freedom did not mean license to do anything one pleased, but rather the ability to do that which is good and right. Tocqueville found Americans remarkably faithful to that idea in their organization of churches, schools, communities, and families. Powerful socialization restrained those human impulses deemed destructive to the community.[6] Thus morally intrusive laws and practices that may seem suffocating today were actually viewed as helpful in early America, as they would liberate the individual from "slavery to sin."[7]

And many Americans continue to share these views. When popular radio commentator and psychologist James Dobson argues that Satan uses human appetites, greed, and lust to destroy us, he is echoing the basic Puritan understanding of the world. So is the Rev. Jesse Jackson when he argues that the moral laws contained in the Ten Commandments protect the individual from self-destructive behavior and are thus "liberating."[8]

Puritans emphasized community's central role in nurturing and restraining the individual. This aspect of their outlook is receiving renewed attention today. The Puritans and their heirs could be harsh, but their focus on community meant that people were not isolated. Women were not abandoned if they became widows; orphans were cared for; people did not suffer from rootlessness. Religious mores and strong communities restrained the atomizing tendencies unleashed by modern political freedom. Most Americans continue to align themselves at least nominally with religious groups, even if their attendance is sporadic, in part just because they see in churches at least vestiges of this sense of community.[9]

Finally, Puritanism bequeathed to the nation a mighty store of moral zeal that often did not recognize that shades of gray are needed in a political system whose lifeblood is compromise. Critics note how Puritan clergy moved with equal stridency from depicting the French as anti-Christian during the French and Indian War to viewing the British in similar terms only a decade later during the American Revolution.[10] More sympathetic voices note that politics sometimes cries out for an infusion of religious conviction and fervor. Where would the nation be, they ask, without the uncompromising zeal of the abolitionists in the nineteenth century or the reformist energies of suffragists?

Whether for good or ill, we see evidence of this zeal among religionists across the political spectrum today. When such figures as Rev. Pat Robertson and Rev. Jesse Jackson prophesy against the evils of society and equate their political struggles with God's cause, they are exemplifying the American Puritan tradition.

RELIGIOUS FREEDOM AND PLURALISM

Important as the Puritan legacy was and is, religious pluralism played an equally strong role in shaping the nation's history. The roots of the dominant characteristic of American religion today—its almost bewildering multiplicity of religions, denominations, theologies, and organizational styles—can be traced to early colonial patterns. Moreover, the American break with the 1,500-year European tradition of a state-established church, as well as the eventual constitutional protection for religious freedom, combined to allow religious pluralism to flourish in the New World.

No one planned this turn of events. Most colonies, in fact, did follow the European practice of establishing a state church, which meant that citizens had to pay a tax to support the colonial church and had to be married by a government-supported minister. Such practices were commonplace.[11] The New England colonies established the Congregational (or Puritan) Church, whereas most southern colonies established the Anglican Church (the Church of England, which later became the Episcopal Church in the United States).

Despite the existence of some established churches, dissenting religious people—Jews, Quakers, Baptists, and Catholics from Protestant countries—all found more room to practice their faiths in the New World than they had in Europe. If one found Massachusetts too suffocating, there was always Rhode Island, home to a host of dissenters, or New York, which had numerous Jewish settlers by the late seventeenth century. Then there were the middle colonies, which more than the others provided a model of religious tolerance for the new nation. And there was always the seemingly endless wilderness, which became a haven to nonconformists and religious visionaries. So Catholics settled in Maryland and tolerated Protestants; Quakers settled in Pennsylvania and tolerated Lutherans; Baptists agitated for their own freedom in a number of colonies. The idea of a society in which each faith tolerated all others in order to enjoy its own freedom began to sprout.[12]

Religious tolerance was strengthened in the late eighteenth century when the Constitution and the Bill of Rights were drafted and adopted, officially forming the United States. The framers of the American Constitution faced an enormous challenge: knitting together thirteen colonies with different cultures, religions, economies, and climates. The solutions were born of necessity and compromise, as we can see in the religion clauses of the First Amendment, which attempted to address the complexities of religious pluralism. Those clauses read: "Congress shall make no law respecting an establishment of religion, or prohibiting the free exercise thereof."

Then as now, the idea of religious freedom meant different things to different people. Some of the framers, such as Benjamin Franklin, Thomas Jefferson, and James Madison, hoped to reduce clerical interference with politics, which to them represented a vestige of the corrupt and oppressive European world. Some were Enlightenment deists who believed in a God who had set the universe on course with natural laws and then left it alone. They saw a chance to create an enduring United States free of the intense religious squabbles that infected the Old World.

Jefferson, a religious skeptic who had written his own version of the New Testament in which he did not affirm Christ as God, authored the Virginia Statute of Religious Freedom (a precursor to the First Amendment). James Madison shared Jefferson's belief that leaving individual conscience unfettered by the state was the best guide in religion and morality. He therefore fought to disestablish the state church in Virginia.

But this is not the full story. Fervent Baptists, along with other religious dissenters, strongly supported constitutional protection of religious freedom and an end to state support for the established church. Persecuted by Anglican authorities in the southern colonies and Congregational Church leaders in New England, Baptists remembered the times when they had been jailed for seeking marriages outside the established church or for refusing to pay the church tax. As a result they were natural allies of separationists such as Jefferson and Madison.

Even for those Christians who initially favored state-established churches, the sheer necessity of protecting their own faiths ultimately led them to support religious freedom. Given the pluralism among the thirteen colonies, no one could ensure that any particular church would be the one established by the new national government. All believers wanted freedom for themselves, but they concluded that the "only way to get it for themselves was to grant it to all others."[13]

The bold national experiment, as embodied in the First Amendment, did set the stage for an end to established religion. While the language of the Religion Clauses was understood to prohibit only establishment by the national government, the national model eventually swept through the states, which acted on their own to end the practice. Massachusetts was the last, disestablishing the Congregational Church in 1833.[14]

This ideal of church-state separation and religious freedom is deeply ingrained in American culture today. It is also one of the central contributions of the United States to the world. To understand the uniqueness of the American experiment, it is necessary only to observe that from the time of the Emperor Constantine in the fourth century to the founding of the colonies in the seventeenth century, European practice and doctrine had been to establish an official religion by state law. So embedded is this practice that government support for religion continues to this day in the largely secular nations of Europe. Yet the United States has never had a state-established national religion.

By the nineteenth century in the United States, state governments continued to help organized religion in a few ways, but religious institutions were mostly on their own. Cut off from the paternalistic hand of government and largely freed from persecution, churches became voluntary associations, dependent upon the continued support of their members for survival. And contrary to what some thought might happen, churches thrived. Indeed, in the wake of disestablishment, remarkable religious growth occurred in the nineteenth century, spurred by those denominations—especially Baptists and Methodists—that adapted best to the new conditions. Unsupported by the state and facing the vastness of the frontier, "volunteerist churches" sprang up as circuit-riding ministers traveled west to preach the gospel.

A new kind of entrepreneurial climate fostered a multiplicity of worship styles and faith interpretations. If you did not like the local minister or if you held unorthodox views, you could always form a new congregation. Churches blossomed and new denominations sprouted as religious entrepreneurs competed with one another for the loyalty of the faithful. Religious practice, in turn, adapted endlessly to changing economic and social circumstances. The peculiar vitality of American religion today (in contrast to the relatively moribund state churches of Europe) owes its origin to this blend of religious freedom, evangelical fervor, and frontier life.

The fruit of this religious culture was a proliferation of religious experiments, from utopian communities to the practice of transcendentalism. Another development was the rise of millennial sects. Convinced they could divine the coming of the end times prophesied in scripture, charismatic leaders of the nineteenth century forged new denominations and contributed to the eschatological theology of modern fundamentalism. A host of movements and sects today can trace their lineage to this time. The popularity of writer Hal Lindsey, whose books and videos on the signs of the imminent second coming of Christ have sold millions, as well as the remarkable success of Timothy LaHaye with his *Left Behind* book series, show the continuing appeal of millennial religion in America today. So does the charismatic revival of large proportions that began in

1995 in Pensacola, Florida, at Rev. Stephen Hill's Brownsville Assembly of God, where it has continued to the present day.[15]

This God-intoxicated culture also produced religious movements in the nineteenth century that the Protestant-dominated society viewed as threats. The most important of these was the Church of Jesus Christ of Latter-day Saints (LDS Church), whose adherents are called Mormons. Its story illustrates the limits of tolerance and how religious clashes in America sometimes took violent turns. The Mormon story also illustrates how the American experience can give rise to a popular new faith, one with worldwide membership that is continuing to grow rapidly in the twenty-first century.

Mormons trace their origins to the vision of Joseph Smith Jr. of Palmyra, New York, who claimed to have found sacred tablets describing how the lost tribe of Israel migrated to the New World. A farmer's son with limited formal education, Smith published in 1830 his translations of the sacred tablets, thereby creating what became known as the Book of Mormon. Within a few years of the book's publication, Smith's following became a serious religious movement.[16]

But the new religious movement Smith fashioned, which was fervent, disciplined, and situated outside of the mainstream with its practice of polygamy, aroused the enmity of neighbors. Smith's followers were chased successively out of New York, Ohio, Missouri, and Illinois. Smith himself fled a near war in Missouri (where the governor issued an extermination order against Mormons); after founding the city of Nauvoo, Illinois, he was arrested by the Illinois state militia. Before Smith could stand trial, a lynch mob stormed the jail in Carthage, Illinois, and killed him. Smith's successor, Brigham Young, then led the faithful to safety in the Salt Lake Valley, where he founded what amounted to a theocratic nation.[17]

The safe haven was short lived, however, because the territory of Utah came under United States control in 1848, following the Mexican War. To Protestant culture the Mormon practice of polygamy was repugnant, and politicians responded aggressively. President James Buchanan ordered troops to besiege Salt Lake City in 1857, and Congress followed suit by passing a series of laws outlawing polygamy in the territories. Penalties included the confiscation of church property and the loss of citizenship privileges. These actions, which were upheld by the U.S.

Supreme Court, ultimately succeeded in forcing Mormons to conform to the norms of mainstream American culture. The leaders of the LDS Church issued a declaration late in the nineteenth century against plural marriages and pledged loyalty to the laws of the United States. Only then could Utah be admitted to the Union, in 1890.[18]

In addition to homegrown pluralism, of course, immigration also fueled religious diversity and continues to do so. By far the most important legacy of the nineteenth century was the dramatic expansion of the Roman Catholic population. From the mid–1800s on, successive waves of immigrants from Catholic countries such as Ireland, Italy, and Poland poured into the United States. This phenomenon produced a long enduring cultural divide in American history—the Catholic-Protestant split—which shaped partisan political loyalties for over a century and a half. Indeed, one cannot understand the significance of John Kennedy's election in 1960 or of alliances between Catholics and evangelical Protestants today without appreciating how much the divide between Protestants and Catholics once shaped American political history.

The first large wave of Roman Catholics came in the 1840s and 1850s, as Irish immigrants settled in American cities and built a vigorous and public Catholic Church. A second group came from Germany in the second half of the nineteenth century. A third came at the turn of the century, this time from southern, central, and eastern Europe. As the Catholic presence grew, some political issues took on overtones reflecting religious division. Temperance was in part a Protestant attempt to discipline Catholic drinkers; campaigns against "corrupt" big city machines also were partly a reaction against the political power of Catholic immigrants and their descendants. Even before the Civil War there were occasional Catholic-Protestant skirmishes. Civil War draft riots in New York, in which Irish Catholics protested military conscription, reflected their resistance to the evangelical Protestant tendency to view the Civil War as a holy crusade.

Political parties, which were much stronger in the late nineteenth century than they are in the twenty-first, naturally channeled this cultural combat, especially in the North. There, Protestant voters were disproportionately Republican, whereas most Catholics became loyal Democrats. Something of this division lingers to this day. As we will see in Chapter 4, white Protestants as a group are still more Republican than are Catholics.

One of the most graphic examples of the Catholic-Protestant split concerned education. Though church and state institutions were constitutionally separated in nineteenth-century America, Protestant domination of society produced an unofficial, cultural Protestant establishment. Public schools frequently used texts—from the Protestant King James Bible to the McGuffey Readers—that promoted Protestant values. Catholics developed their own parochial school system and, where they were strong enough, pushed for state aid for it. Protestants fought against such efforts.

After the Civil War, Catholics intensified their effort to secure public support for their church-run schools. Protestant fealty to the Republican Party produced its response: the Blaine Amendment, an attempt by the Republican administration of Ulysses S. Grant to amend the U.S. Constitution to prohibit any state governmental aid to parochial schools. Introduced in the House of Representatives by James G. Blaine of Maine in 1875, the amendment became a symbol of anti-Catholic sentiment among the Protestant majority (Blaine, a Republican, became associated with the charge that the Democrats were the party of "Rum, Romanism, and Rebellion"). The proposed constitutional amendment passed the House but fell short of the two-thirds vote needed in the Senate. Republican platforms from 1876 to 1892, however, continued to call for an end to government aid to sectarian schools.

These kinds of battles continued to be fought at the state level. Many states passed a version of the Blaine amendment in their own constitutions, but state-level responses to parochial education did not end there. In the 1920s, for example, Catholics had to take their case all the way to the U.S. Supreme Court when the state of Oregon decreed that all children had to attend public schools—in effect making parochial systems illegal. Catholics won and the Oregon law was overturned.[19] With that victory, however, the battle shifted once again to state public support, which remains a major issue today.

THE EVANGELICAL DIMENSION

Intimately linked with both the Puritan heritage and the American experiment in religious freedom is the strong evangelical dimension of American religion. We mean "evangelical dimension" in two senses. First, we mean the branch of Protestantism that teaches traditional tenets of Christian faith, is deeply committed to the Bible as the only authoritative source of God's revelation, and stresses the adult conversion ("born-again") experience and vigorous evangelizing (seeking converts). A driving force for much of American history, evangelicalism was the dominant strain of Protestantism in the nineteenth and early twentieth centuries, and it accounts for much of the revivalism and religiously motivated activism of that time (as well as today).

Second, the evangelical dimension also refers to the fact that all major churches, to some extent, had to adopt evangelizing strategies to survive in the American religious marketplace. Because evangelical Protestants have been assertive about seeking converts, evangelical Protestantism has become the paradigm of successful church life in America. But whether Protestant or Catholic, Mormon or Muslim, any faith must evangelize to thrive. And given the link between culture and politics, this sense of evangelicalism often produces political fallout.

These two senses of the evangelical dimension are strongly related. In a major study of church growth and decline from the revolutionary era to today, Roger Finke and Rodney Stark contend there is a consistent pattern in which disestablishment, religious freedom, and the frontier have combined to produce a "religious marketplace."[20] In this marketplace churches thrive or decline on the basis of how well they serve the needs of existing and potential members. And contrary to what we might expect, thriving churches are often more conservative, more evangelical, and more in tension with the broader culture than declining churches.[21]

This study supports what others have argued: Sometimes the overall intensity of the religious experience a church offers wanes; this is usually due to the fact that the church's members have become comfortable and worldly. Clergy also contribute to this decline in intensity when they grow complacent and accommodating. As a result the church's message becomes watered down, and the church itself becomes unable to convey a powerful message about the meaning of life. People yearning for such meaning will therefore leave and seek it in other religious settings. And there is ample evidence that the United States today is a nation of seekers; in fact many people who do not profess any particular faith attend religious services in search of answers to life's questions.[22] As Dean Kelley notes, the "business of religion is meaning," and strict evangelical faiths convey that they really mean what they preach with their often demanding style. Churches that do not convey such conviction cannot expect to flourish.[23] Religious communities must distinguish themselves by conveying clear, consistent, and meaningful messages.

In American history we do see this pattern of rising sects and the decline of once-dominant churches. For example, Puritan sects of the seventeenth century, which were otherworldly and severe, were eventually transformed into the comfortable Congregational churches of the eighteenth century. When they did become more comfortable, these churches lost a good share of their members to new evangelical congregations born of revivals in the 1730s and 1740s. As these churches in turn became comfortable with the world and less distinct from the mainstream culture, upstart Methodist and Baptist congregations, which had grown dramatically since the founding era, eclipsed them. The cycle continued: As Methodism became the home of an increasingly settled membership and its ministers grew less strict about enforcing traditional rules in the late nineteenth century, a fervent Holiness religious movement drew away a significant portion of its membership (Box 1.1).

This dynamic occurs because many people turn to religion in part to get something distinct and different from what can be found in the broader culture. When churches become too accommodating and worldly, they offer a less unique experience and therefore cease to address this need. Some measure of sectlike tension with the world, along with an evangelical zeal, is a key to continued church success.

The great religious movements in American history have often stimulated significant political upheaval. Consider several major examples of political fallout from Protestant evangelical revivalism, beginning in the eighteenth century and continuing into the twentieth.

Special Case:
Evangelicals, Slavery, and the Civil War

One of the characteristics of evangelicalism in America has been its Puritan tendency to view politics at times as an unambiguous, cosmic struggle between good and evil. We see this evangelical temper in one of the most momentous, religiously infused movements in the nation's history: the crusade against slavery. No issue so tormented the young nation as

---

**BOX 1.1 ARE HIGHLY PAID MINISTERS
THE SIGN OF A DECLINING CHURCH?**

Yes, say Roger Finke and Rodney Stark. In their book *The Churching of America*, Finke and Stark demonstrate that there has been an inverse ratio between clergy salaries and church vitality throughout American history. Upstart churches with few material resources depend on ministers, who are willing to make extraordinary sacrifices for their cause.

Low-paid circuit-riding clergy transformed the Methodist Church from a tiny sect in the mid-1700s into the largest denomination in the United States a century later. The Methodist Church grew rapidly in relation to Congregational, Episcopal, and Presbyterian churches, which paid their ministers far more. But as the Methodist Church became more affluent and comfortable with the world—and paid its member's accordingly—it began to lose its vigor, ceased making high demands on its members, and slipped into decline. Methodism thus has lost its "market share" to Baptist and Pentecostal churches, both of which have an abundance of low-paid clergy.

SOURCE: Roger Finke and Rodney Stark, The Churching of America, 1776-1990: Winners and Losers in Our Religious Economy (New Brunswick, NJ: Rutgers University Press, 1992), 115.

---

slavery, America's "original sin." Black people came to the New World in bondage with the first colonists. It was a contradiction with both professed political ideals and Christian beliefs from the beginning. Some early leaders such as George Washington and Thomas Jefferson acknowledged this contradiction. Quakers expelled slaveholding Friends in 1776, and antislavery societies sprouted among churchgoing people. But the practice of slavery was so entrenched that the Constitution itself made a "pact with the devil" by accepting servitude and allowing southern states to count, for purposes of allocating members in the House of Representatives, three-fifths of the enslaved population.

A revolution against slavery began in northern thinking in the early 1800s, as antislavery societies sprang up in the wake of religious revivals. These revivals awakened Christian consciences against slavery, and churches increasingly became the fulcrum of antislavery agitation through the decades leading up to the Civil War. Many great revivalists and preachers eventually joined the cause. During debate over the Kansas-Nebraska bill, which allowed the extension of slavery into new territories, Congress was presented with a petition from 3,000 New England ministers who opposed the bill.[24]

This heightened northern agitation served only to harden southern attitudes. White southern evangelicals came to view the defense of their land and institutions as divinely ordained, and biblical justifications for slavery became common.[25] The evangelical tendency to see political clashes as spiritual struggles between good and evil increasingly characterized both sides. Thus the irreconcilable conflict was, in some sense, a clash of evangelicals.

When war came, preachers in both camps depicted their cause in religious terms. From the pulpits of both the North and South came invocations of God's wrath toward the other side in martial prayers of vivid and bloody mien. Hymns similarly carried an almost apocalyptic message, as this stanza of Julia Ward Howe's "Battle Hymn of the Republic" shows:

> I have read a fiery gospel, writ in burnished rows of steel.
>   "As ye deal with my contemners, so with you my grace shall deal";
>   Let the Hero, born of woman, crush the serpent with his heel,
>   Since God is marching on.

But how could both sides invoke God? And how could anyone find God's will in the carnage of the Civil War? These questions deeply vexed Abraham Lincoln, whose story is central to the religious and political history of America.[26] His thinking on the meaning of the Civil War reveals a great deal about the potential of religiously inspired politics.

The Second Inaugural Address (1865) was perhaps Lincoln's greatest speech. Reflecting on the bloodthirsty prayers of partisans, Lincoln observed that "both North and South read the same Bible, and pray to the same God. . . . The prayers of both could not be answered; that of neither has been answered fully. The Almighty has his own purposes." Perhaps, pondered Lincoln, God had prolonged the war as the means to eradicate slavery, something neither side had expected. Perhaps the war was also God's punishment of *both* North and South for the sin of slavery.

Lincoln prayed for a speedy end to the war but accepted that God might will that it last until "every drop of blood drawn with the lash, shall be paid by another drawn with the sword." For Lincoln, this decision was God's. The same God expected him to articulate a forgiving vision of reconstruction and reunification once the war was over: "with malice toward none, with charity for all."

Special Case: Evangelicals and the
Crusade Against Alcohol

The crusade against intoxicating drink constitutes another example of evangelical politics, and it provides some important practical lessons for religious partisans today. The crusade, which began in the early 1800s and lasted well into the twentieth century, was one of the landmark efforts by churches to affect American politics. Led by Protestant ministers and laity, it attained a remarkable public following. The Temperance Movement was in large part rooted in patterns of extraordinary alcohol consumption that had begun in the colonial period and continued long afterward. Alcohol use in the colonies was widespread and included the consumption of hard liquor by youth. Spurred by the difficult life on the frontier, consumption rose to extraordinary levels. Alcoholism was a pervasive problem, especially among men. Given the role of the male as breadwinner at the time, this posed an enormous threat to women and children and was debilitating to community life as well.

To understand the central role of churches in the Temperance Movement, it is helpful to trace the history of one of the most effective pressure groups in American political history, the Anti-Saloon League. Founded in 1895 by Rev. Howard Hyde Russell, the League united Protestant pietists across denominational lines in a brilliantly conceived strategic approach that led to political success. Because of its close ties to Protestant churches, which served as the precinct bases for local organization, the League became a formidable national force, able to field 20,000 speakers nationwide for the cause.[27]

What made the Anti-Saloon League successful was its relentless pressure and clear strategic calculation. Knowing that state legislatures would resist, League leaders realized they would win only through ceaseless education, lobbying, and electioneering. The organization overcame the multitude of divisions within Protestantism with a simple message of democratic appeal: Fight for the right of local communities to regulate or close down saloons. League organizers compromised when necessary, formed alliances, flooded wavering legislators with mail, and played hardball with opponents. Where they could expand on Protestant fears of Catholic immigrants, they did. Where they could form alliances with Catholics, they would. State after state fell into line.

Moreover, once local option laws passed, the League moved to get local communities in line. Where they were not powerful enough to close down saloons, they fought to regulate their hours, gambling, and locations. As more and more local communities acted, remaining wet areas became isolated, and most of a state went dry. Then organizers fought to repeal local option laws in favor of stricter statewide prohibition.[28]

The strategy of beginning a political effort in states before acting nationally worked beautifully. In 1900, five states were dry and four held down the amount of drinking by enacting high license fees from sellers. The others allowed local communities to regulate alcohol, but wet areas still predominated in many of them. The Anti-Saloon League increasingly began to avoid state legislatures, which were often responsive to beer and alcohol interests. They moved instead to get voters to decide about alcohol policy directly through state referenda. State after state enacted prohibition in this manner. Swept by a mood of optimism, the League finally turned to the federal government, where Congress passed the Eighteenth Amendment to the Constitution banning the production and sale of intoxicating beverages. Only the heavily Catholic states of Connecticut and Rhode Island refused to ratify the amendment. Prohibition became the law of the land in 1920.

Though the common understanding today is that this effort to legislate morality failed, evidence suggests that the diverse efforts to curb alcohol consumption—from voluntary temperance to legal prohibition—succeeded in changing drinking habits. One study argues that per capita yearly consumption of alcohol went from an astonishing ten gallons of alcohol in the 1830s to a little over two gallons by 1850. With westward expansion, alcohol consumption went up again. But the prohibition movement succeeded in changing that pattern also. Even after Prohibition was repealed, consumption remained below the 1910 level.[29]

Prohibition represented the high-water mark of the popularity and political clout of evangelical Protestantism. But its success helped lead to its downfall. Evangelicals faced increasing opposition throughout the 1920s. One reason is that while Prohibition reduced drinking, it also fueled political corruption and gangsterism and made lawbreakers out of millions of otherwise law-abiding citizens. Moreover, during the Roaring Twenties, the culture itself was changing. Catholics and Jews grew in number and clout, and the religious pluralism of the nation expanded.

Evangelical Protestant domination of the culture eroded. The Great Depression was the final straw, making pietist moral concerns far less pressing than economic ones. Though many Protestant churches vigorously fought the repeal of Prohibition, the nation moved on, and the Eighteenth Amendment was repealed in 1933.

Nevertheless, much of the same energy continues to exist today and serves as a catalyst for modern-day religious reformers who wish to engage the world and redeem it. As we will see throughout this book, many citizens understand their work against smoking, crime, gambling, abortion, poverty, drunk-driving, and myriad other social issues as an urgent religious response to a world marked by immorality and suffering.

THE POPULIST DIMENSION OF AMERICAN RELIGION

Churches in America, as we have seen, depend upon the voluntary support of the faithful to survive, let alone thrive. But thrive many do. Churches were, and are, the most common means (apart from work and family) by which ordinary Americans meet voluntarily in large numbers. To a great extent religion in America is popular religion—and the churches that succeed understand this reality. Thus popular religion is often a way for people to discover and express their common hopes and concerns. It can be, therefore, a conservative force, helping to preserve traditions people cherish. It can also be a radical force, however, channeling mass discontent and challenging elites with prophetic denunciations of injustice. Whatever its specific directions, however, popular religion often fosters populist politics that focus on mass-based democracy and hold elites accountable to the people.

This populist dimension was evident in the religious Great Awakening of the eighteenth century, which fostered grassroots evangelism and prepared colonists for the Revolution. It was present in the crusades against slavery and alcohol. It is alive today in black churches that serve as vital social and political centers for many African Americans, directing both their hopes and their challenges. There is also a kind of populism alive today among Christian conservatives who lash out against the hegemony of "cultural elites." To understand this form of contemporary religious politics it is helpful to survey some important chapters in the evolution of popular democracy and populist politics.

The drafters of the Constitution did not view direct democracy or majority rule favorably at all. Such figures as James Madison feared popular demagogues and knew that the "demos" could trample on liberty just as easily as a single tyrant could. The resulting Constitution, as well as standard suffrage restrictions (the exclusion of women and African Americans, for example) and the absence of strong political parties combined to ensure that politics in early American history remained far from fully democratic.

As Nathan Hatch suggests, however, a continuing democratization of Christianity advanced political democracy in the early 1800s. At the forefront of democratized religion were itinerant and often untutored grassroots preachers (especially Baptists and Methodists) who understood the special needs of people on the frontier.[30] Tent revivals, which brought souls to Christ by the thousands, originated in this period (Rev. Billy Graham later updated the setting and technology). Clergy who arose from among the common people dominated religious life on the frontier because, as George Whitefield observed, Harvard and Yale divinity schools did not prepare their elite students "to spend half their days in the saddle going from one rural hamlet to another."[31]

Circuit-riding preachers endured real hardships to spread their message to the masses and brought with them a democratic faith that all are equal before God. Many people were profoundly moved by this populist Christianity and began refusing to see themselves as inferior to others. They pushed for elimination of property restrictions on voting and other measures that advanced democratization. By the late 1820s mass democracy (among white males only, however) had come to America, propelled in part by Protestant evangelical forces in the young nation.

This link between popular religion and popular democracy emerged again toward the end of the nineteenth century, the era from which the term "populist" derives.[32] This was a time when industrialists garnered wealth while millions of farmers and workers struggled to survive as industrial capitalism dawned. Along with rapid economic growth and ferment came a new set of ideas—especially the gospel of wealth, conspicuous consumption, and social Darwinism. In 1859 biologist Charles Darwin had shocked religious sensibilities with the publication of *The Origin of Species*, with its central argument that life-forms developed by a natural process of evolution. Herbert Spencer and William Graham Sumner popularized a social counterpart to this theory, with a competitive "survival of the fittest" model of human social evolution. Some saw captains of industry as the "fittest" by virtue of their success and wealth. To critics, this new doctrine provided a suspicious justification for the plunder perpetrated by nineteenth-century robber barons.

This new age and its justifying doctrine clashed sharply with rural Christian life, where more traditional, communal norms of barter, shared work, and extended families still operated. This clash of worldviews turned into a fierce political struggle when hard times settled over much of agricultural America for a decade beginning in the 1880s.

For our purposes, what is notable about the populist movement was its religious overtone. Many populists were evangelical Protestants. The crusade took on a distinct revivalist flavor, complete with camp meetings and stirring speeches. The crusade was "a pentecost of politics in which a tongue of flame sat upon every man."[33] Populists sought a series of religiously connected goals aimed at a moral structuring of society, which was also reflected in the Protestant-led temperance movement (many populists were also "temperance men"). They concluded that the threat posed by industrialists required that government act with vigor and authority to protect the people. They proposed a variety of radical ideas, from inflationary monetary policies to outright state ownership of the railroads and the telegraph.

In the presidential election of 1896, Democrats nominated William Jennings Bryan, a fiery speaker who shared the populist repugnance for the emerging industrial society. Bryan could sound like a socialist one minute and a pietist preacher the next. For Bryan, as for many populists, the gospel of the New Testament was the proper basis for a good and caring society.[34]

To be sure, many other pietist Protestants branded the populists and Bryan dangerous radicals. But careful voting studies suggest that Bryan, as a Democrat, did better than expected among pietist Republican voters in the West. At the same time, he fared relatively poorly among many Democrats, especially Catholics and Lutherans who were uncomfortable with his brand of evangelical politics. Indeed, the two parties, for a time, seemed to have swapped characteristics. Many Republicans shifted from pietist concerns to embrace emergent entrepreneurial capitalism, whereas Bryan Democrats lauded the pietist idea of creating a Bible-based moral social order, insisting, like Bryan, that "you shall not crucify mankind on a cross of Gold."[35]

Bryan's crusade was inherently limited, however, because it created an urban-rural cleavage and undercut traditional Democratic support among Catholics and some Protestants. But Bryan's legacy lived on. We even hear echoes of Bryan and populism today—from across the political spectrum—as religious and political leaders denounce the "business as usual" of elites and demand that the "people," especially those with economic or cultural discontent, be heard.[36]

CONCLUSION

Threads of America's religious history are so intimately woven into the social and political fabric of the United States that they continue to shape public life in the present day. To switch metaphors, as the historian Mark Noll puts it, America's religious past "frames" its future. He points to numerous developments in the twentieth century that have had a surprising impact: the rise of charismatic religious movements in the United States and abroad, the remarkable explosion of religious diversity combined with the membership losses in some of the older Protestant denominations, increased Catholic-Protestant interaction, and a heightened role of ethnicity within Christianity.[37] To varying degrees, these developments are the legacies of the Puritan, pluralist, evangelical, and populist dimensions of American religion that we have emphasized in this chapter. In later chapters, we will see how these themes, along with some new ones, help us understand politics and religion today.

FURTHER READING

Ahlstrom, Sydney. *A Religious History of the American People.* New Haven, CT: Yale University Press, 1972. The standard history of religion in the United States.

Butler, Jon. *Awash in a Sea of Faith: Christianizing the American People.* Cambridge, MA: Harvard University Press, 1990. A bold reinterpretation of the history of Christianity in America.

Butler, Jon, Grant Wacker, and Randall Balmer. *Religion in American Life: A Short History.* New York: Oxford, 2002. A brief examination of religion in American history.

Clark, Norman H. *Deliver Us from Evil: An Interpretation of American Prohibition.* New York: Norton, 1976. A thoughtful modern history of the Prohibition experience.

Eck, Diana L. *A New Religious America: How a "Christian Country" Has Become the World's Most Religiously Diverse Nation.* San Francisco: Harper, 2002. A recent history with a central theme of religious diversity in the United States.

Finke, Roger, and Rodney Stark. *The Churching of America, 1776–1990: Winners and Losers in Our Religious Economy.* New Brunswick, NJ: Rutgers University

Press, 1992. Pioneering work on a market interpretation of the history of American religion.

Gaustad, Edwin S., and Leigh E. Schmidt. *The Religious History of America: The Heart of the American Story from Colonial Times to Today.* Rev. ed. San Francisco: Harper, 2002. A recent update of one of the leading historical treatments of religion in America.

McLoughlin, William. *Revivals, Awakening, and Reform: An Essay on Religion and Social Change in America, 1607–1977.* Chicago: University of Chicago Press, 1978. Especially useful discussion of the Great Awakening.

Marty, Martin E. *Pilgrims in Their Own Land: 500 Years of Religion in America.* Boston: Little, Brown, 1984. Sweeping history by one of the nation's foremost church historians.

Miller, Perry. *Errand into the Wilderness.* Cambridge, MA: Belknap Press of Harvard University Press, 1956. The classic intellectual history of Puritanism.

Morgan, Edmund. *The Puritan Dilemma: The Story of John Winthrop.* Boston: Little, Brown, 1958. A readable introduction to Puritan religion and politics.

Reichley, A. James. *Faith in Politics.* Washington, D.C.: Brookings Institution, 2002. A superb historical introduction to its subject.

NOTES

1. See Perry Miller, *Errand into the Wilderness* (Cambridge, MA: The Belknap Press of Harvard University Press, 1956); and Edmund Morgan, *The Puritan Dilemma: The Story of John Winthrop* (Boston: Little, Brown, 1958).

2. A. James Reichley, *Faith in Politics* (Washington, D.C.: Brookings Institution, 2002), 54–73.

3. John Witte, Jr., "How to Govern a City on a Hill: The Early Puritan Contribution to American Constitutionalism," *Emory Law Journal* 39 (1990), 41–64.

4. Sydney Ahlstrom, *A Religious History of the American People* (New Haven, CT: Yale University Press, 1972); and Reichley, *Faith in Politics.*

5. This point is made by Barry Allen Shain, *The Myth of American Individualism: The Protestant Origins of American Political Thought* (Princeton, NJ: Princeton University Press, 1994).

6. Alexis de Tocqueville, *Democracy in America,* trans. George Lawrence and ed. J. P. Mayer and A. P. Kerr (Garden City, NY: Doubleday/Anchor, 1969).

7. Shain, *The Myth of American Individualism.*

8. See Allen D. Hertzke, *Echoes of Discontent: Jesse Jackson, Pat Robertson, and the Resurgence of Populism* (Washington, D.C.: CQ Press, 1993), chap. 3.

9. Robert Booth Fowler, *Unconventional Partners: Religion and Liberal Culture in the United States* (Grand Rapids, MI: Eerdmans, 1989).

10. Mark Noll, ed., *One Nation Under God? Christian Faith and Political Action in America* (San Francisco: Harper, 1988).

11. Ahlstrom, *A Religious History of the American People*; Leonard Levy, *The Establishment Clause: Religion and the First Amendment,* 2nd ed. (Raleigh: University of North Carolina Press, 1994).

12. Andrew Greeley, *The Denominational Society: A Sociological Approach to Religion in America* (Glenview, IL: Scott, Foresman, 1972); Ahlstrom, *A Religious History of the American People*; Will Herberg, *Protestant-Catholic-Jew* (New York: Doubleday, 1955).

13. Sydney Mead, *The Lively Experiment: The Shaping of Christianity in America* (New York: Harper and Row, 1963), 35. For an excellent general discussion of the theological and political ideas that presaged the Religion Clauses, see John Witte Jr., *Religion and the American Constitutional Experiment: Essential Rights and Liberties* (Boulder, CO: Westview Press, 2000), ch. 2.

14. Witte, *Religion and the American Constitutional Experiment*, ch. 4; Michael Malbin, *Religion and Politics: The Intentions of the Authors of the First Amendment* (Washington, D.C.: American Enterprise Institute, 1978); Gary Glenn, "Forgotten Purposes of the First Amendment Religion Clause," *Review of Politics* 49 (1987), 340–366.

15. See http://www.brownsville-revival.org. See also Steve Rabey, "Pensacola Outpouring Poised to Cover the Globe," *Christianity Today* (February 8, 1999), 12–13.

16. Ahlstrom, *A Religious History of the American People*, 501–509.

17. Ibid.

18. Anson Phelps Stokes, *Church and State in the United States*, vol. 2 (New York: Harper, 1950), 275–285.

19. *Pierce v. Society of Sisters*, 268 US 510 (1925).

20. Roger Finke and Rodney Stark, *The Churching of America, 1776–1990: Winners and Losers in Our Religious Economy* (New Brunswick, NJ: Rutgers University Press, 1992).

21. Donald E. Miller, *Reinventing Protestantism: Christianity in the New Millennium* (Berkeley: University of California Press, 1997).

22. Robert N. Bellah, Richard Madsen, William M. Sullivan, Ann Swidler, and Steven M. Tipton, *Habits of the Heart: Individualism and Commitment in American Life* (New York: Harper and Row, 1985); Jack Miles, "Religion Makes a Comeback (Belief to Follow)," *New York Times Magazine* (December 7, 1997), 56–59.

23. Dean M. Kelley, *Why Conservative Churches Are Growing: A Study in Sociology of Religion* (San Francisco: Harper, 1972).

24. Luke Eugene Ebersole, *Church Lobbying in the Nation's Capital* (New York: Macmillan, 1951).

25. Ahlstrom, *A Religious History of the American People*, 653–654.

26. On Lincoln and religion, see Allen C. Guelzo, *Abraham Lincoln: Redeemer President* (Grand Rapids, MI: W.B. Eerdmans, 1999); Richard J. Carwardine, *Lincoln* (New York: Longman, 2003).

27. Norman H. Clark, *Deliver Us from Evil: An Interpretation of American Prohibition* (New York: Norton, 1976).

28. Ibid.

29. Ibid.

30. Nathan O. Hatch, *The Democratization of American Christianity* (New Haven, CT: Yale University Press, 1989).

31. As quoted in Finke and Stark, *The Churching of America*, 86.

32. The literature on the populist movement, including its religious dimensions, is extensive and growing. It is summarized by Hertzke, *Echoes of Discontent*, chap. 2.

33. As quoted in John D. Hicks, *The Populist Revolt: A History of the Farmers' Alliance and the People's Party* (Lincoln: University of Nebraska Press, 1961).

34. This point is developed more fully in Hertzke, *Echoes of Discontent*, chap. 2.

35. Paul Kleppner, *The Cross of Culture: A Social Analysis of Midwestern Politics, 1850–1900* (New York: Free Press, 1970).

36. Hertzke, *Echoes of Discontent*.

37. Mark A. Noll, "How the Religious Past Frames America's Future," in Charles Dunn, ed., *Faith, Freedom, and the Future: Religion in American Political Culture* (Lanham, MD: Rowman and Littlefield, 2003), 19–40.

CHRISTIANITY AND
ITS MAJOR BRANCHES

In this chapter and the next we analyze the status of religion in America and chart its impact on the nation's political culture. We focus in this chapter on the most prominent traditions of Christianity in the United States and their enduring yet changing roles in shaping public life. In Chapter 3 we examine Judaism, Islam, and other religious expressions that, despite size constraints and pressures from the broader culture, exercise a significant voice in American society and politics. At one level there has always been great continuity in religion's vitality in the United States. But the picture is complex. Religious pluralism continues to grow while secular forces, especially at the elite level, increasingly make their mark. To understand the political ramifications of these forces, we must examine the status of religion in contemporary American society.

THE STATUS OF RELIGION IN THE UNITED STATES

American religion today is alive, thriving, and diverse. Some 95 percent of Americans profess a belief in God or a universal spirit,[1] with over 60 percent claiming never to doubt God's existence.[2] More than six in ten say that religion is "very important" in their everyday lives and that "religion can answer all or most of today's problems."[3] Ninety percent associate with one of the many religious traditions present in the United States.[4] While there is a small but growing segment of secular Americans,[5] the vast majority of Americans continue to make religious faith an important part of their lives.

One way to understand the significance of faith in the United States is to compare Americans with citizens of other nations. The comparison lends some credence to the description of American culture as "exceptional."[6] On every measure—belief in God, spiritual experiences, attendance at religious services, and daily prayer or meditation—Americans consistently express far more religious faith than citizens of Canada and most European and Pacific Rim nations. Only 69 percent of citizens in Great Britain, 52 percent in France, and 57 percent in the Netherlands share a belief in God, which is nearly universal in the United States.[7] Twice as many Americans say that religion is very important in their lives as Canadians (60 versus 30 percent, respectively), and the percentages are even lower in Italy (27 percent), Germany (21 percent), Russia (14 percent), Japan (12 percent), and France (11 percent).[8] Similarly, while nine in ten Americans express a specific religious preference, the religious affiliation rate in Britain is approximately 55 percent; in France it is 53 percent; and in the former East Germany it is only 32 percent.[9] Over 80 percent of Americans express belief in life after death, but only 56 percent in Great Britain, 51 percent in France, and 41 percent in Denmark have the same confidence.[10] In the United States, nearly eight in ten citizens believe that miracles happen today; only 39 percent of Germans, 42 percent of the British, and 37 percent of the French agree.[11]

On the other hand, among nations outside Europe and the Pacific Rim, the United States is not so exceptional. We see evidence of religion's continuing strength, and often its resurgence, from the Middle East to Latin America to Africa. Unlike Europe and Southeast Asia, where the average citizen rates the importance of God in everyday life less than a 5 on a 1-to-10 scale (10 denotes a belief that God is "very important"), Latin Americans rate God's importance as 8.7 and West Africans a remarkable 9.7.[12] Such data hint at the future prospects of religion across the globe. If demographic trends continue, well over 50 percent of the world's Christians will be in Africa, Latin America, and parts of Asia within twenty-five years—a clear shift from Christianity's traditional home in Europe and North America.[13] In addition, the Islamic faith, with an estimated billion adherents, is the dominant faith in the Middle East, northern Africa, and many other regions of the world.[14] From this perspective, the United States is hardly unusual; it is Europe and the Pacific Rim that are the exceptions.

Another useful comparison is between groups of citizens within the United States itself. Faith is especially important to women and nonwhites, for example. Nearly two-thirds of women in the United States say religion is a significant guide in their day-to-day lives, compared with less than half of all American men.[15] Well over three-quarters of African Americans, compared with 55 percent of whites, agree.[16] In fact, African Americans have often scored the highest average in their responses to questions about the importance of God of any group the Gallup organization has surveyed around the world.[17] This high salience of religion is the basis for the tremendous political role of black churches, which we explore in later chapters.

Despite growing religious diversity, the U.S. population remains decidedly Christian. Over 80 percent of Americans associate with some form of the Christian faith.[18] As many as eight in ten Americans claim to accept the traditional Christian view of God as a Trinity—Father, Son, and Holy Spirit[19]—and three-quarters say that "forgiveness of sins is only possible through faith in Jesus Christ."[20] Three-quarters believe in heaven (and most of those say they believe their chances of getting to heaven are good), though fewer believe in hell.[21] Most Americans have a high view of Christian scripture as well, with over 80 percent saying the Bible should be understood as the word of God; only 14 percent explicitly reject any divine role in writing of scripture.[22]

A sizable portion of Americans say they have had extraordinary spiritual experiences, often through intense religious awakenings that change their lives. At least a third claim to be "born-again" Christians who have had a profound, once-in-a-lifetime experience of repentance and commitment to Jesus Christ.[23] Experiences with hearing God's voice and being filled with the gifts of the Holy Spirit—e.g., faith healing, speaking in tongues, prophecy—are also commonly reported. When sociologist and Catholic priest Andrew Greeley looked at the evidence, he proclaimed the United States a "nation of mystics."[24] This was an exaggeration, but for a notable portion of the population these religious experiences are part of life.

Americans invest considerable trust in their religious institutions and clergy. For years, Americans have expressed confidence in organized religion, more so than in many other private and public institutions. Moreover, clergy consistently rank highest among sets of social leaders in terms of public regard for their ethics and honesty. Confidence in clergy dropped briefly in the wake of the televangelist scandals of the late

1980s, however, and has fallen sharply for Catholic clergy in the wake of child abuse accusations over the past few years.[25] Still, the public expresses more confidence in organized religion than it does in the U.S. Supreme Court, Congress, the health care system, banks, public schools, the press, organized labor, and big business.[26] Here again, Americans are distinct from those in other Western nations. Whereas Americans express more confidence in churches than they do in the public schools, for example, these confidence figures are reversed in Germany, France, Great Britain, and many other European countries.[27]

Many Americans are also churchgoing Christians; in fact, 25 percent say they attend weekly, and another 30 percent say they attend almost weekly or at least once or twice a month.[28] Some scholars, however, argue that people are less than truthful in responding to surveys about church attendance.[29] It is quite possible that many Americans have in fact become more secular in their habits but are unwilling to admit it. Yet even if attendance figures are inflated, the fact remains that church participation is the single most common group activity in America. Among Christian traditions, evangelical Protestants attend services most frequently, followed by Roman Catholics, with mainline Protestants trailing behind. As we will see in Chapter 4 when we discuss voting behavior, this pattern has increased the political clout of evangelical voters while reducing that of mainline Protestants.

On balance, the portrait of religious America is one of enduring faith. How much difference this makes in the daily lives of Americans, let alone in their politics, is another matter. Critics suggest that religion in America is like the proverbial prairie river: a mile wide and an inch deep. They note an obvious gap between high levels of apparent faith and considerable business dishonesty, tax fraud, sexual promiscuity, marital infidelity, family breakdown, cheating in school, crime, violence, and vulgarity in the popular culture. George Gallup Jr., whose surveys demonstrate the widespread appeal of religion in the United States, has concluded that much of American faith is indeed shallow and marked by a gap between faith and ethics.[30] On the one hand, Gallup's findings are not too surprising given the powerful secular forces at play in the popular culture. A society that celebrates the individual pursuit of happiness, unrestrained popular culture, and unfettered capitalism, some suggest, will produce pervasive hedonism and materialism that compete with religious socialization.[31]

On the other hand, we have evidence that religious belief and practice do make a difference in people's lives. Research suggests that religious conviction and practice are correlated with personal happiness, physical health, and general life stability.[32] But it is the salience and authenticity of religious conviction that matters more than nominal affiliation: the greater the faith or practice, the more intense the benefits, irrespective of denomination. Thus strong religious commitment apparently contributes to longer, happier lives, speedier recovery from injuries, fewer psychological illnesses, and a lowered risk for depression and suicide.[33] On the social and civic level, religious people are more likely than the secular to contribute to charities, vote, and become otherwise involved in the community.[34]

Religious institutions also play an important role in helping to sustain a healthy American civic life. In a huge study of civic voluntarism, a team of scholars headed by Sidney Verba found that churches provide a crucial venue in which people may develop "civic skills." The argument is that people are more likely to participate in politics when they have done things that occur frequently in church settings, such as organizing meetings, writing letters, and speaking in public. People who are deeply involved in churches or synagogues, therefore, may be expected to possess substantial civic skills.[35]

In a slightly different vein, a variety of scholars have argued that places of worship facilitate interactions among people that contribute to what Robert Putnam has termed "social capital."[36] Social capital, which refers to networks of relationships and trust among citizens, has been shown to contribute to the effectiveness of government and even the economy. Churches are well suited to developing the networks that build social capital, especially those churches that have turned to the increasingly popular use of small group ministries (such as Bible studies, prayer fellowships, and 12-step programs).[37] And social interactions in places of worship help shape political attitudes as well, as both Christopher Gilbert and Kenneth Wald and their colleagues have demonstrated.[38]

Religious commitment also translates frequently into activism. This often comes in the form of evangelism—the effort to win converts or bring new members to one's religion. This is a must for churches in the competitive environment of American religion, where some churches grow and others decline. For example, the conservative denomination Assemblies of God has grown rapidly in the past decade, partly because of remarkable outreach to Latinos, whose numbers in the denomination during that time period have grown by 60 percent.[39] The thriving LDS Church illustrates well the importance of active evangelism. Mormons send out an estimated 50,000 young missionaries each year worldwide, and the LDS Church's remarkable growth rates and aggressive missionary activity have led some to predict that it could be one of the major world religions by the middle of the twenty-first century.[40]

Churches are very active in American society. A large share of the charitable giving in the United States is done by churches; indeed, citizens who attend church regularly give money to social causes and volunteer to do charitable work at a dramatically higher rate than those who rarely or never attend religious services.[41] People of modest means are particularly likely to donate almost exclusively through religious outlets. This generosity enables churches to operate an impressive array of social organizations, hospitals, schools, universities, charitable agencies, and international relief organizations.[42] At least three-quarters of church members participate through their congregations in social service or community development activities;[43] one recent survey even suggests that the average American congregation is more likely to provide its members with basic social outreach opportunities (such as cash or food assistance programs) than with prayer or theological study groups.[44] Even small denominations make their presence felt. The Seventh-day Adventists, with about 900,000 members in the United States, support ten liberal arts colleges, two universities, a seminary, a medical school, and numerous K–12 schools and welfare agencies (Box 2.1).[45]

Private education, of course, is a major activity of many religious groups. The Catholic Church operates the largest religious educational system, with over 8,000 elementary and secondary schools attended by at least 2.5 million students. Evangelical and other Christian schools enroll over 1.5 million children in nearly 12,000 smaller schools.[46] The growing world of homeschoolers, nearly 40 percent of whom cite religious reasons for their choice to educate in the home, has also relied heavily on the resources of religious institutions.[47] In addition, various Christian denominations have established their own colleges and universities, including over 270 Catholic institutions of higher learning.

Social involvement by churches has clear political ramifications. Church-run charities, adoption agencies, educational institutions, and in-

---

**BOX 2.1 PARACHURCH GROUPS
IN PUBLIC LIFE**

Many religious associations are parachurch organizations, groups that are intimately connected with and supported by a religious tradition yet have no formal ties to a specific religious denomination. For example, with a great deal of support from various Christian churches and individuals, evangelist Charles Colson has led the most visible movement for prison reform in the 1990s and 2000s. Colson is a former "hatchet man" for President Richard Nixon who went to jail for his Watergate crimes. After experiencing a religious conversion, Colson created Prison Fellowship, a worldwide program that not only spreads the Christian gospel among prisoners but fights for reform of inhumane prisons. Lauded by conservatives and liberals alike, Colson's evangelical quest to redeem prisoners and prisons is yet another chapter in a long history of Christian reform efforts.

Habitat for Humanity is another contemporary example. Through this organization, Jimmy Carter and many others imbued with religious faith work to build houses with and for poor people in the United States and abroad. For them, the need to minister to a suffering and limited world is urgent, and their faith provides the reforming energy to make a difference in people's lives.

SOURCES: http://www.pfm.org; http://www.habitat.org

---

ternational relief programs operate in a milieu that is heavily influenced by government. Interaction between these institutions and government is inevitable. A large number of the religious social services and hospitals, for example, receive government money to perform their services, and no major healthcare changes can succeed without the participation of religious hospitals.[48] Most recently, President George W. Bush established the White House Office of Faith-Based and Community Initiatives as part of his administration's broader efforts to expand public support for religious social services. Although such efforts can be intensely controversial— indeed, Bush's initiatives have met stiff resistance—throughout American history government has frequently partnered with organized religion to shape and implement public policy. Religious institutions fully understand the importance of these inevitable interactions.[49]

A less widespread, but more controversial, activity of religious groups is political activism. Political efforts that grow out of a church's charitable or educational ministries are common. So is public testimony on issues by church leaders, as are ministerial exhortations to vote. It is also common for clergy to speak to social and political issues from the pulpit. Far less common is overt involvement by congregations in partisan politics. Most ministers are not comfortable endorsing candidates from the pulpit or raising money for them. Such efforts are often divisive and threaten a church's tax-exempt status.[50] In some cases, however, active lay members (or ministers) use their church as an organizational base for political efforts. In the 1950s and 1960s, the civil rights movement was based in African American churches, leaving a legacy of church-centered political mobilization that continues today.[51] The antiabortion movement and the Christian Right have also depended on a base of churches over the past three decades.

One reason American religion has so much vitality is its pluralism. In Europe, people who become alienated from the established church simply drift away from it; in America people often form or join a new church. A bewildering diversity of religious expression continues unabated in the United States and remains one of its primary defining characteristic. A constitutional doctrine that protects religious freedom, a relative openness to immigration, and a tradition of individualism that promotes the continual formation of new sects combine to foster American religious pluralism.

Part of this pluralism within Christianity, of course, is reflected in the division of people into the familiar categories of Protestant and Roman Catholic. Moreover, diversity within these broad traditions increases the pluralism of American religion. The United States is home to virtually every Protestant denomination or sect in existence, some of which are very diverse in their own right. Consider the Baptists. There are black Baptist denominations and white ones, fundamentalists and moderates, northern branches and southern ones. Indeed, there are several hundred Baptist groupings, a pluralist reality that nonetheless exaggerates Baptist unity because every one of these groupings considers itself autonomous. There are also myriad independent evangelical churches, some affiliated with national organizations, others entirely separate (or "nondenominational"). Even the hierarchical Catholic Church is pluralistic. There are liberal and conservative Catholics, a host of religious orders from Jesuits to Maryknolls, and numerous religious lay groups from the most traditional to the decidedly radical. The patchwork of American pluralism also includes small pacifist churches, such as the Quakers, Brethren, Mennonites, and Amish, as well as Mormons, Jehovah's Witnesses, black Muslims, Native American religionists, viewers of television ministries,

TABLE 2.1   A Profile of Current Religious Affiliations, 2002

	Percentage of U.S. Population
Protestant	
Baptist	16 percent
Church of Christ	2 percent
Episcopalian	2 percent
Lutheran	6 percent
Methodist	8 percent
Pentecostal	4 percent
Presbyterian	5 percent
Other Protestant	13 percent
Roman Catholic	26 percent
Jewish	2 percent
Mormon	1 percent
Other	4 percent
None	11 percent

Source: National Election Studies 2002.

pre- and postmillennial fundamentalists, Pentecostals and charismatics, evangelical Presbyterians, high church Episcopalians, and members of gay churches—not to mention people who join the host of new religious movements that sprout with regularity.[52]

Protestant Christianity remains the faith of a majority of Americans (roughly 60 percent), with Catholics accounting for a sizable 26 percent, and the remaining population comprising Jews, Eastern Orthodox Christians, Mormons, Muslims, adherents of other faiths, the unaffiliated, and those who do not believe at all (Table 2.1).[53]

Getting a good handle on actual church membership is harder than it might seem. Churches keep their own records and they tend to count *members* according to their own, often differing, methods; independent opinion surveys of people's *religious preferences* look at another, broader picture of self-identification and do not always arrive at the same results. Nonetheless, the general outlines of affiliation provide a basic sketch of American religious pluralism.

The tremendous diversity that characterizes American religion has frequently given rise to cultural clashes. Roughly one-fourth of the American population is Catholic, one-fourth white evangelical Protestant, less than one-fourth mainline Protestant, and nearly one-tenth African American

Protestant.[54] When we categorize people by religious affiliation, evangelicals are the most numerous. Also, liberal denominations claim more conservative members than conservative denominations claim liberal adherents.

The political significance of religious pluralism within Christianity is manifold. Pluralism acts as a check on the political influence of any religious group. No one group dominates, nor can it—a pluralist reality often ignored by those who fear that any single religious group could establish a "theocracy" or otherwise use government for widespread oppression. Religious pluralism also requires a willingness on the part of activists to overcome theological differences in the interest of coalition building, which is a must for successful political endeavors. Deeply held convictions must sometimes be modified if effective political alliances are to result.

THE MAJOR CHRISTIAN TRADITIONS AND POLITICS

The broad traditions of Christianity—Catholics and evangelical, mainline, and African American Protestants—are in many ways distinctive in their history, theology, and ethnic makeup. Moreover, these traditions are politically distinct, although, to be sure, the boundaries sometimes become blurry. The theological orientations of many African American Christians, for example, are firmly planted within the evangelical world, yet because of the American legacy of slavery and segregation, black churches developed in directions that diverge from white evangelical churches. We discuss the African American church tradition only briefly here; Chapter 10 is devoted primarily to it. In addition to these major American Christian groupings, of course, are the Mormons, who do not fit neatly into any category, along with a host of other small religious traditions, which we treat more fully in Chapter 3.

Evangelical Protestantism

As we saw in Chapter 1, much of American history has been influenced by evangelical Protestant culture. By the 1920s that evangelical presence seemed to be in retreat, but it re-emerged decades later with considerable vigor.

An important watershed for modern evangelicals was the year 1976, when presidential candidate Jimmy Carter proclaimed himself a "born-again Christian." It was at that time that evangelicals burst onto the pages of the elite press and into academic consciousness; a bevy of journalists made pilgrimages to the South to discover just what evangelicalism was. Then George Gallup Jr. stunned the literati by announcing that fully one-third of Americans claimed to be born-again evangelicals. Conservative churches were evidently offering precisely what their members found lacking as the society rushed headlong into modernity: strong faith, concrete answers to life's challenges, and community. One example of the incredible growth in evangelicalism in the United States has been the presence of active evangelical student organizations on college campuses. InterVarsity Christian Fellowship, founded in 1941, had more than 35,000 student and faculty participants in 2003, and Campus Crusade for Christ, founded in 1951, served 44,000.[55]

But this evangelical phenomenon would have remained of limited political interest had the Christian Right not burst onto the scene as a political force in the late 1970s. It began with isolated protests by parents against public school texts in the mid–1970s; gained momentum through the movement to defeat the Equal Rights Amendment led by Phyllis Schlafly; hit stride with the creation of the Moral Majority and other national groups in 1979; and became an established political player with the role of the Christian Coalition in the 1994 congressional elections and beyond.[56] Ronald Reagan acknowledged white evangelical voters in the 1980s and embraced their concerns, at least rhetorically, and to varying degrees presidents Clinton and George W. Bush followed suit.[57] By the early twenty-first century white evangelicals had become one of the most loyal and important Republican constituencies.[58]

What does it mean to be an evangelical? That question may be answered by self-identification or by a statement of beliefs and characteristics. It is revealing, for example, that so many Americans (including a majority of African Americans) answer "yes" to the question, "Do you consider yourself a born-again or evangelical Christian?" This question taps a central tenet of Protestant evangelical Christianity—the need for a once-in-a-lifetime adult conversion, or a "born-again" experience. Evangelicals also hold a highly respectful view of scripture, and for some this means they interpret the Bible literally. Evangelicals also accept the orthodox tenets of the Christian faith (Christ's divinity, his atoning death and resurrection, everlasting salvation or damnation) and are committed to Jesus' "great commission" to evangelize others by spreading the good news.

Evangelicals also share a common language and basic assumptions. Evangelicals ask others, "Are you saved?" or, "When did you commit your life to Christ?" Though a number of denominations are heavily evangelical (the Southern Baptist Convention, the Lutheran Church–Missouri Synod, the Church of the Nazarene, the Assemblies of God, the Presbyterian Church in America, and most of the major African American denominations), born-again Christians are scattered throughout the Protestant world. Indeed, evangelical "renewal" groups occur within mainline denominations and some evangelically oriented local Presbyterian and Methodist congregations. George W. Bush illustrates the point: he identifies strongly with evangelicalism, but he is a member of the United Methodist Church, a mainline denomination.

By far the most important distinction within the evangelical world is a racial one. Normally when scholars and commentators speak of evangelicals, they are referring to white evangelicals. Yet many black Baptists and Pentecostals are also fervent evangelicals. Moreover, decreased segregation and increased racial tolerance have brought increased interaction between white and black evangelicals. The Southern Baptist Convention, for example, now trumpets its growing black membership, and many Pentecostal and charismatic congregations are truly interracial. White religious conservatives have been modestly successful in building alliances with black clergy on such issues as school prayer, abortion, school choice, and pornography, and some white evangelicals have called for greater attention to racial justice among their brethren.[59]

Nonetheless, a considerable gulf remains between black and white evangelicals.[60] African American churches feature a unique blend of theological conservatism and political liberalism; piety is combined with prophetic witness. In black churches one hears the "liberationist" messages of the Bible about God's mercy toward the poor and the captive, his harsh judgment of the rich and powerful, and considerable confidence in government as the temporal means to change.[61] This combination lends itself naturally to political liberalism, at least on economic and civil rights issues. The vast majority of evangelical African Americans are also Democrats, which is just another indication of how they continue to exist in a world apart from their white evangelical brothers and sisters.

Beyond race, a number of theological and cultural divisions also exist within the evangelical world. Pluralism reigns here, just as it does elsewhere in religious America. There are "mainstream" evangelicals who believe humans must interpret scripture and are ambivalent, rather than simply hostile, toward the broader culture. Fundamentalists, biblical literalists, are suspicious of those who want to "interpret" God's word, and highly critical of the "fallen" culture around them.[62] There are premillennialists who expect certain biblical prophecies to come true before Jesus returns for a thousand-year reign on Earth (the enormously popular writer Hal Lindsey or the best-selling *Left Behind* book series fit this category). Postmillennialists believe a Christian reign will precede Jesus' second coming. This group includes the small but influential group of Christian Reconstructionists, who hold that believers should structure society as a theocracy on the basis of Old Testament law. And there are Pentecostals and charismatics who stress the availability of gifts of the spirit—such as speaking in tongues, faith healing, and prophecy.[63] Though Pentecostals and charismatics are fervent believers in traditional values, fundamentalists and other evangelicals remain skeptical of them because of their strong emphasis on personal spiritualism.

We see this diversity reflected in leading evangelical personalities. Such diverse figures as Rev. Billy Graham, Rev. Jerry Falwell, Rev. Pat Robertson, Charles Colson, and Rev. Bob Jones III are all evangelicals, but so are the African American preachers Rev. E. V. Hill and Bishop T. D. Jakes and Mississippi community developer John Perkins.[64] Both evangelical Democrats and Republicans serve in Congress and in state governments, as we discuss in Chapter 6.[65]

One way to clarify this diversity is to think of the evangelical world as a tree with several main branches and numerous smaller ones. We have already spoken of the African American branch. Another main branch is represented by the National Association of Evangelicals (NAE), an umbrella group for numerous evangelical churches and denominations. This group says it wishes to transform the world spiritually and is generally conservative politically, but not militant. Another branch is fundamentalism, which has historically been separatist, biblically literalist, and more militantly opposed to the secular world.[66] Finally, there is the fast-growing Pentecostal or charismatic branch, whose members share many of the political views of fellow evangelicals, but whose vibrant religious practice and emphasis on spiritual gifts set them apart. Whereas a fundamentalist church service usually features traditional Bible reading and preaching, charismatic congregations enjoy contemporary music, speaking in tongues, and a free-form worship style.[67] Though some of these distinctions may seem trivial to outsiders, to evangelical leaders they present a very serious challenge to political unity.

A major recent change in the evangelical world involves attitudes about political participation. Evangelicals have long viewed politics with distaste; political activity constituted an engagement with the sinful world God meant them to eschew. To be sure, many evangelical churches have always stressed the civic duty of voting, but beyond occasional local issues involving gambling or alcohol, not much effort was expended on politics. That left the political field open for mainline churches, which rode the crest of civil rights and antiwar activism in the 1960s.[68] But by the 1970s all of that began to change. Many evangelical leaders came to believe that the government and the broader culture had become dangerously secular and intrusive, so they felt they had to fight back. Others felt inspired to rekindle the nineteenth-century evangelical commitment to bringing the gospel message to all corners of society. Moreover, evangelical congregations were growing. Their members were becoming better educated and more affluent, and their television and radio ministries were becoming more popular. They had the motivation to fight and the increasing resources to do so.

Not all evangelicals, however, agree with each other politically. Many evangelicals oppose the tactics and even the aims of the so-called "Religious Right"—some vigorously so. Some fundamentalists oppose the turn to national politics, because such a turn means engaging with the fallen world. Fundamentalist pastor Bob Jones Jr. once called Jerry Falwell the most dangerous man in America because he thought Falwell's political efforts would undermine the fundamentalist aim of separating from the broader (sinful) society. In recent years, more moderate evangelical voices, including commentator Cal Thomas and preacher Ed Dobson, have also suggested that Christian conservatives lost their religious moorings in the political conflicts of the past two decades.[69] Television preachers, moreover, are by no means universally popular among the born again. Southern Baptists, for example, voted heavily against Pat Robertson (who is a Pentecostal) in the 1988 presidential primaries, and at least some voted for fellow Southern Baptist Bill Clinton in 1992 and 1996.

One evangelical branch provides a left-wing political witness. Represented by sociologist and Baptist pastor Tony Campolo, Jim Wallis of the radical group Sojourners, and Ronald Sider, founder of Evangelicals for Social Action, this branch exercises some influence in religious circles. Evangelicals for Social Action was founded in 1978 and focused on the poor, gender equality, and the preservation of God's natural creation. It says it views injustice in all forms as an "affront to the Creator who made persons to bear the very image of God."[70]

As a group, evangelicals are conservative politically, but real fissures belie the depiction of a disciplined army marching to take over America. Still, as we show in Chapter 4, most white evangelical voters have realigned into the Republican Party and now constitute a key GOP voting bloc in both national and local politics. Beneath the diversity of theologies and traditions, therefore, lies a broad and growing consensus in support of conservative politics. How political leaders deal with this constituency will shape a key dimension of American politics in the years to come.

Mainline Protestantism

In the twentieth century mainline Protestantism evolved into a tradition distinct and separate from evangelicalism (which held such influence in the previous century). This tradition carries the label "mainline" because historically its denominations represented the dominant expression of organized Protestantism in the United States, a position that translated into exceptional political access. Mainline churches remain among the oldest and wealthiest in American religion. In terms of lay numbers and contemporary influence, however, the "mainline" nomenclature does not fit as easily as it used to, because the Protestant center of gravity has shifted toward the evangelical community.

Some scholars refer to the tradition as "liberal Protestantism," the adjective coming from theology, not politics. As theological liberals mainline Protestants view the Bible as inspired by God but by no means literally true. They also argue that scripture must be read in the context of history and modern science. In fact, the mainline-evangelical split crystallized in the 1920s when mainline Protestants embraced modernity and scientific theories, such as Darwinism, of which evangelicals were wary.[71] This does not mean mainline Protestants abandon the central tenets of Christian faith, but they do place more emphasis on the goal of gradual, reflective spiritual development and less on the "born-again" conversion experience. Mainline Protestants are skeptical of the literalism of fundamentalists, the emotionalism of Pentecostals, or the claims of faith healing among charismatics.

Here, too, considerable variation exists from church to church. Mainline Lutherans (adherents of the Evangelical Lutheran Church in America, or

ELCA) maintain their distinct liturgical tradition founded in ethnic roots; Methodists still stress doing good works in the world as a manifestation of faithfulness; Episcopalians often treasure a formal high mass; and some denominations, such as the United Church of Christ, are far more theologically liberal than most others. Despite these differences, however, mainline Protestants have a lot in common, not only in theology but in worship style. In mainline Protestant churches one rarely hears sermons about hell or personal sin. More common are scholarly discussions of the meaning of divine incarnation or the ethical insights of Jesus' teachings. Services are orderly and often include well-prepared choral and organ music. Mainline Protestant churches are also more accepting of skepticism about portions of the Bible than are their evangelical counterparts. Bible discussions, therefore, are likely to focus on the moral precepts contained in the Bible and to welcome examinations of the context of biblical times. This is not to say that there are no traditional religionists sitting in the pews of mainline churches—there are many indeed—but most mainline church leaders do not reinforce their outlook.[72]

In many mainline churches, there is an emphasis on a general call to love one's brother or sister. Moreover, Christian love is often interpreted in collective ways as well as individual ones. Mainline clergy in particular argue that Christians must address the world's injustices not merely by individual charity but by collective efforts to change societal structures. Mainline seminaries, liberal both in theological and political terms since the early twentieth century, became radicalized during the civil rights movement in the 1960s, leading an entire generation of clergy to have some exposure to liberal politics.[73] It is in seminary that many clergy learn that, unless one changes political and economic structures, injustice and oppression will continue irrespective of personal acts of mercy and love.[74]

For mainline clergy and denominational leaders this theological liberalism often correlates with activist liberal politics. Among their parishioners, however, no clear link exists between liberal theology and liberal politics.[75] Indeed, though their partisan loyalties are diminishing, a majority of mainline Presbyterians, Methodists, and Episcopalians have traditionally voted Republican. Theological liberalism does correlate, however, with liberal attitudes among parishioners on such issues as abortion and gay rights.[76] When this liberal theological orientation became the dominant force in the major Protestant seminaries, fundamentalists split off and formed their own churches.

The well-established Protestant denominations were still the clearly dominant force in American religion through the 1950s. Methodists, Presbyterians, Episcopalians, Congregationalists, many Lutherans, and northern (American) Baptists, as well as their shared organizational arm, the National Council of Churches (NCC), represented the core culture. From Main Street to Wall Street to Washington, mainline Protestants were well entrenched. When radical social movements gathered steam in the 1960s, influential mainline leaders voiced their solidarity with activists and many mainline Protestants became foot soldiers in the movements.

The 1960s exercised a strong influence on mainline Protestant leaders. They embraced—and continue to embrace—issues of poverty, racism, sexism, and oppression—and the unjust structures they see as incorporating these evils.[77] If one were to summarize how mainline church leaders view their work, it would be as champions of "peace and justice."[78] By this phrase they mean their mission is to fight for justice as they understand it, especially for the poor. As they have seen it, this goal requires expanded government funding for welfare at home and economic assistance for developing nations abroad. They also work for world peace (sometimes from a pacifist perspective) and frequently fault American foreign policy as too militaristic and too oriented toward gain for the U.S. economy. For example, the United Methodist Church ran a series of highly visible television advertisements preceding the 2003 war with Iraq, in which church leaders stated, "We are President Bush's church, and we oppose war in Iraq."

Two significant challenges confront mainline clergy. First, many lay members do not share the ideological orientations of their national leaders and activist local pastors. As an illustration of this phenomenon, consider the recent schisms within mainline denominations and congregations over homosexuality.[79] Indeed, because of the structure of political decision-making in these large denominations, lay members are not always consulted as political positions are developed.[80] Critics thus speak of "generals without armies" in liberal denominations.[81]

A second challenge is that mainline Protestantism has faced membership declines in recent decades. From 1990 to 2000, for example, the United Methodist, United Church of Christ, and Presbyterian USA denominations lost 6.7, 14.8, and 11.6 percent of their memberships, respectively.[82]

Explanations abound, including the assertion that by turning to politics the mainline churches turned off their parishioners.[83] But Dean Kelley offers the most convincing explanation when he argued that because the "business of religion is meaning," stricter and more demanding churches, especially conservative evangelical congregations, offer more of what many people desire from religion. As we saw in Chapter 1, this theme echoes throughout American history; whenever churches relax their firm beliefs, they decline in proportion to more demanding churches. Theological liberalism, then, not political activism, may undermine the ability of mainline churches to compete in the religious marketplace.[84]

Despite their decline, however, mainline churches still possess a wealth of inherited capital in the form of buildings, institutions, and endowments, as well as the loyalty of a considerable number of parishioners. Local churches continue to operate a host of food banks and day-care centers, and national church organizations operate large hospitals, charitable agencies, and highly respected international development organizations. Mainline Protestant churches are also key players in city coalitions designed to alleviate poverty and injustice.[85] Thus extensive community involvement continues to thrive in mainline Protestantism.[86] Mainline Protestants continue to exercise what Robert Wuthnow terms "quiet" but significant influence in American political and religious life.[87]

Roman Catholicism

In Chapter 1 we observed that the Catholic-Protestant split played an important role in shaping American political culture for a century and a half. Catholics were seen as profoundly "other" in American society, living in ethnic neighborhoods and sustaining separate institutions to shield themselves from the dominance of Protestant culture. The result by the 1950s was a tremendously vibrant Roman Catholic Church dominated by an ethic of cultural separatism with an impressive number of Catholic churches, schools, hospitals, and social service agencies staffed by large numbers of priests and sisters.

This cleavage lingers in a few places, but it is mostly a memory. Modern suburban Roman Catholics are hardly outsiders anymore. Indeed, complaints are heard among Catholics themselves that the distinctive Catholic culture has been lost amid a homogenized mass society. Still, Catholics remain theologically distinct, preserving a sacramental approach to the "mysteries" of the faith and a unique intellectual tradition.[88]

Today, Catholics inhabit a strategic place in American politics. Catholics are key swing voters, and both mainline Protestants and evangelicals frequently seek political alliances with Catholic elites. Catholic bishops make news whenever they speak on political issues. But Catholics, especially at the parish level, do not speak with a single political voice; here pluralism reigns just as it does elsewhere in religious America. This lack of unity can hamper Catholic political clout, though the size of the Catholic population and the institutional strength of the Church ensure that Roman Catholics are important players in the American system.

Some historical perspective is helpful in appreciating the place of Catholics in America today. The Catholic Church is literally the oldest institution in the world; it is a truly global church with a distinct hierarchical structure headquartered at the Vatican in Rome. This adds a unique dimension to Catholic politics. One cannot focus merely on the American church; one must consider the pope and his relationship to church officials. The structure of the church hierarchy is rooted in two millennia of history. Priests belong to a diocese or archdiocese (a geographic area) headed by a bishop or archbishop, who receives his appointment from the pope. A few of these archbishops around the world become cardinals, the elite officials of the church responsible for electing a new pope each time the "bishop of Rome" dies.

At the heart of Church structure is the doctrine of apostolic succession, the idea that the pope is literally the successor of the apostle Peter. Though hierarchy remains a defining characteristic of the Catholic Church, American Catholicism is also characterized by pluralism. Diverse holy orders of monks and nuns, each with a distinct focus and élan, exist alongside the traditional structure. Thus one finds left-wing Jesuits, feminist nuns, and Maryknoll missionaries spreading liberation theology alongside more conservative orders and groups of Catholic traditionalists (such as Opus Dei) that are fiercely loyal to orthodoxy (and to Rome).

One of the distinctive features of the Catholic Church is its appreciation of politics. Throughout European history, for example, the Roman Catholic Church was deeply enmeshed in statecraft. Politics was not alien to church leaders then, nor is it today. Catholics have been intensely involved in politics around the globe, from the Philippines to Latin America, from Eastern Europe to the United States. In one sense this political comfort level is an asset: the Church and its activists do not need to overcome as much resistance to politics as do some evangelical Protestants. On the other hand, for much of American history the Catholic Church was seen as a suspect institution. The church's roots in the medieval world of kings and princes, along with its skepticism about democracy and religious freedom, placed it at odds with the American liberal tradition. Well into the twentieth century, for example, the Catholic Church resisted many liberal democratic reforms and allied itself with authoritarian governments.

These tendencies created a huge problem for American Catholics, whom many Protestants and others viewed as lacking a fundamental commitment to American democracy and liberal freedoms.[89] Though Catholics in fact embraced the American creed of democracy and individual liberty and were often ardent patriots and anti-communists. Yet the question of whether or not their embrace of American liberal democracy was compatible with their religious tradition remained into the 1950s.[90]

What changed all that was a profound revolution within the Catholic Church itself, a revolution in which the United States and its church leaders played a pivotal role. In 1961 Pope John XXIII declared that the church needed to open its windows and get some fresh air. For only the second time in Roman Catholic history the pope called for a meeting of the world's bishops to modernize the church. Vatican II, as this meeting came to be called, lasted from 1962 to 1965. It was an earthquake for the church, and its effects are still being felt. Through it the church embraced democracy and ordered liberty, and for the first time Protestants were accepted as fellow Christians rather than as apostates. The Mass, which had always been said in Latin, would thereafter be in the vernacular. And the bishops in each country were given greater authority to speak on behalf of the church in their respective lands. One worldwide impact of the church's change, as Samuel Huntington shows, was to help lead a wave of democratization in formerly authoritarian and largely Catholic nations.[91]

In the United States, Vatican II legitimated the Catholic accommodation with liberal democracy and accelerated the mainstreaming process for Catholics. Even before Vatican II, leaders of the American church had begun to assert themselves politically. After Vatican II the bishops were joined by many others in the Catholic Church in political engagement. Nuns and priests marched in civil rights demonstrations, and Philip and

Daniel Berrigan, radical antiwar priests, poured blood on the Pentagon to protest U.S. involvement in Vietnam. Catholic Charities and the Campaign for Human Development sponsored antipoverty projects in inner cities and rural backwaters. The Catholic Church also lent support to the farm worker movement led by César Chávez.

Ultimately Vatican II led to an increased role for the bishops' national organization, known today as the United States Conference of Catholic Bishops, or USCCB (the bishops changed the organization's name from the National Conference of Catholic Bishops after restructuring in 2001). Headquartered in Washington, D.C., and composed of approximately 260 leaders of Catholic dioceses in the United States, the USCCB leads the church's social and political efforts. The politics of the bishops are not easily categorized, which is why the bishops are sought after by conservatives and liberals alike today. On social welfare, labor, civil rights, and military policies the bishops have taken a rather liberal posture. At least some of this agenda stems from the church's historical concern that untrammeled industrial capitalism exploits workers and undermines the dignity of work and the vitality of community and family. However, the church's positions on abortion, divorce, and sexual ethics are conservative, while their support of "school choice" is libertarian in spirit.

Liberals celebrated when the bishops drafted their "pastoral letters" on nuclear arms and the economy; conservatives applauded the bishops when they condemned abortion. Similarly, liberal activists welcomed the support of Catholics who lobbied against Reagan's support for the Nicaraguan Contras or George W. Bush's push for war in Iraq,[92] and conservative Republicans embraced the cause of Catholics fighting for day-care vouchers and school choice.[93] The church is thus strategically placed as a sort of bridge between evangelical and mainline Protestants.

Ironically, at the very time that the Catholic Church is poised to exercise influence in American society and politics, it faces serious problems and shows signs of the same malaise found in mainline Protestantism. Since Vatican II, attendance rates at Mass have declined and about one-third of all confirmed Catholics pay little or no attention to the Church. While another third are deeply involved, most post-Vatican II American Catholics practice what is called "cafeteria-style Catholicism" in that they pick and choose what to take from the faith and what to leave.[94] Moreover, the number of people willing to become priests and nuns is very low. Many orders of nuns will die out within twenty-five years, in fact, unless recruiting patterns change dramatically. Already there is a major shortage within the aging priesthood and the prospect for an even greater shortage in the near future.[95]

Of course many of the Roman Catholic Church's challenges derive from the clash between its values and American norms. Thus it defends celibacy for priests, an all-male priesthood, a hierarchical church authority structure, opposition to divorce, and even opposition to "artificial" birth control. These stances have led not only to divisions within the church, but to portrayals of the church in the movies, elite media, and popular music that sometimes border on anti-Catholic bigotry.[96] Other challenges, though, come from its own leaders, above all the evidence that some priests and bishops engaged in sexual abuses, especially in the decades before the 1980s. Others have ignored their celibacy vows and taken part in sexual relations. This behavior has damaged the church's credibility within and without its ranks.

But perhaps the most penetrating long-run explanation for the church's challenges today is its evolution into a mainstream denomination. As we saw in Chapter 1, church growth and decline in the American religious marketplace operate with a seemingly ineluctable logic. To the extent that the Catholic Church has become a mainstream institution in the United States, it has become subject to the profound encounter with the outside world that often leads to church decline.[97] Many Catholics, for example, have been leaving the church in favor of evangelical Protestantism, particularly in its Pentecostal incarnations. In fact, sociologist Andrew Greeley reports that one in seven Hispanic Catholics left the church between 1970 and 1995,[98] and a recent study suggests that large numbers of second- and third-generation Hispanic Catholics are leaving for Protestant churches.[99]

This should not surprise us. Catholics today are no longer found disproportionately among the working classes, as was the case at the turn of the twentieth century. Now Catholics and white Protestants have equal educational levels and are equally represented in professional and managerial occupations. And herein lies a paradox. When American Catholics resided at the lower end of the socioeconomic scale they represented a distinct and much more unified constituency that tended to accept the authority of the church. Today many Catholics, especially highly educated ones, do not feel bound by the dictates of the church, let alone its political efforts. The Catholic Church, as a consequence, does not exercise the clout that it once did. Nonetheless, with its relatively large size, impressive organization, and long-standing openness to politics, it remains a major player.[100]

CONCLUSION

Christian religion in America flourishes with pluralism and vitality, yet it does so amid contrary secular forces. Thus we have something of a paradox. On the one hand, professed faith seems to be strong and churches remain heavily involved in society. On the other hand, moral and ethical problems abound and many powerful institutions—such as the mass media, government, business, public schools, and universities—seem to operate with a secular logic that is relatively independent of religious influence.

One of the perennial questions, therefore, is why such an apparently thriving religious community does not exercise more political influence. The major reason lies in America's religious pluralism. Politicians hear a babel of competing religious voices on most issues. When religious groups do form a united front, they can be quite effective. But those instances are rare enough to prove the rule: Pluralism dilutes any group's power.

Religious influence is also checked by the nature of the American system. As we discuss in Chapters 8 and 9, the First Amendment's requirement of religious disestablishment has fostered a separatist tradition and ethic in the United States that includes a wariness—even suspicion—of interaction between religious traditions and politics. This wariness is especially pronounced among secular elites, many of whom occupy positions of influence and power in government, media, and business.

The framers of the Constitution constructed a political order designed to disperse, fragment, and check power. A majority is required to pass national legislation, which can then be diluted or nullified by the actions of states, bureaucracies, or the courts. To achieve real clout, therefore, a movement or group must work successfully on a number of fronts—from the states to the national government, from Congress and the president to the courts and bureaucracies, from lobbying and electoral mobilization to the shaping of public opinion through the mass media. The challenge is formidable, and continuing success is rare. Though the American political system cannot be dominated by a single movement, it is open enough to provide access to the smallest group. Thus our political structure ensures many religious groups the chance to have some political influence and blocks each one from achieving dominance.

FURTHER READING

Corbett, Julia Mitchell. *Religion in America*, 4th ed. Englewood Cliffs, NJ: Prentice-Hall, 2000. A good introduction to the sociology of religion in the context of the United States.

Gallup, George H., Jr., and D. Michael Lindsay. *Surveying the Religious Landscape: Trends in U.S. Beliefs.* Harrisburg, PA: Morehouse, 1999. A helpful data source on religion in America.

Gaustad, Edwin Scott, and Philip L. Barlow. *New Historical Atlas of Religion in America.* New York: Oxford, 2001. A valuable information resource that focuses on the geographical distribution of religion in America.

Hammond, Phillip. *The Protestant Presence in Twentieth-Century America: Religion and Political Culture.* Albany, NY: State University of New York Press, 1992. Argues that religious pluralism has cost mainline Protestantism its sovereignty over America.

Kelley, Dean. *Why Conservative Churches Are Growing: A Study in Sociology of Religion.* San Francisco: Harper, 1977. The classic work on the rise of evangelical Protestantism and the decline of the mainline.

Morris, Charles R. *American Catholic.* New York: Random House, 1997. A history of American Catholicism.

Steinfels, Peter. *A People Adrift: The Crisis of the Roman Catholic Church in America.* New York: Simon and Schuster, 2003. Examines the contemporary challenges facing the Roman Catholic Church.

Wuthnow, Robert. *The Quiet Hand of God: Faith-based Activism and the Public Role of Mainline Protestantism.* Berkeley: University of California Press, 2002. Argues that the mainline's political and social influence, though "quiet," nevertheless continues to be important.

———. *The Restructuring of American Religion: Society and Faith Since World War Two.* Princeton, NJ: Princeton University Press, 1988. A thoughtful book reflecting on the evolution of religion in the United States.

NOTES

1. George H. Gallup, Jr., "Public Gives Organized Religion Its Lowest Rating," *Gallup Poll Tuesday Briefing* (January 7, 2003).

2. Pew Research Center, *Evenly Divided and Increasingly Polarized: 2004 Political Landscape* (Washington, D.C.: Pew Research Center, 2003), 65.

3. George Gallup Jr., *The Gallup Poll: Public Opinion 2002* (Wilmington, DE: Scholarly Resources, 2003), 397–398.

4. Gallup, "Public Gives Organized Religion Its Lowest Rating."

5. Andrew Kohut, John C. Green, Scott Keeter, and Robert C. Toth, *The Diminishing Divide: Religion's Changing Role in American Politics* (Washington, D.C.: Brookings, 2000), 112–113.

6. Seymour Martin Lipset, *American Exceptionalism: A Double-Edged Sword* (New York: W.W. Norton, 1997).

7. International Social Survey Programme (ISSP), *Religion II: ISSP 1998 Codebook* (Cologne: Central Archive for Empirical Social Research, 2001), available at http://www.issp.org/data.htm. These results are discussed in Andrew M. Greeley, *Religion in Europe at the End of the Second Millennium* (New Brunswick, NJ: Transaction, 2003), 3.

8. Pew Research Center, "Among Wealthy Nations, U.S. Stands Alone In Its Embrace of Religion," *The Pew Global Attitudes Project* (December 19, 2002). Report available at http://www.people-press.org.

9. ISSP, *Religion II,* as discussed in Greeley, *Religion in Europe,* 8.

10. ISSP, *Religion II,* 55–56.

11. ISSP, *Religion II,* as discussed in Greeley, *Religion in Europe,* 3.

12. Marita Carballo, "Religion in the World at the End of the Millenium," *Gallup International Millennium Survey* (Washington, D.C.: Gallup International, 1999). The report is available at http://www.gallup-international.com.

13. Philip Jenkins, *The Next Christendom: The Coming of Global Christianity* (New York: Oxford, 2003).

14. For a fascinating cartographic description of global Islam, see Ninian Smart, *Atlas of the World's Religions* (New York: Oxford, 1999), 168–197.

15. Center for Political Studies, *National Election Studies 2002* (Ann Arbor, MI: University of Michigan / Center for Political Studies, 2002). Data from the NES' biannual surveys are available at http://www.umich.edu/~nes/. See also Albert L. Winseman, "Religion and Gender: A Congregation Divided," *Gallup Poll Tuesday Briefing* (December 3, 2002).

16. Center for Political Studies, *National Election Studies 2002.*

17. Robert Bezilla, ed., *Religion in American 1992–1993* (Princeton, NJ: Princeton Religion Research Center, 1993).

18. Pew Research Center and Pew Forum on Religion and Public Life, "Religion and Politics: Contention and Consensus," available at http://www.people-press.org/reports (July 24, 2003), 42.

19. Barna Research Group, "Americans Draw Theological Beliefs from Diverse Points of View," *Barna Research Online,* http://www.barna.org (October 8, 2002).

20. Barna Research Group, "Beliefs: Salvation," *Barna Research Online,* http://www.barna.org (n.d.)

21. Barna Research Group, "Americans Describe Their Views About Life After Death," *Barna Research Online,* http://www.barna.org (October 21, 2003).

22. NORC, General Social Survey 2002.

23. Center for Political Studies, *National Election Studies 2000.* Other surveys put the number as high as 47 percent. See Gallup, *The Gallup Poll: Public Opinion 2002,* 398.

24. Andrew Greeley, *The Denominational Society: A Sociological Approach to Religion in America* (Glenview, IL: Scott, Foresman, 1972).

25. NORC data, as reported in Tim O'Neil, "Scandal Rocks Church, But Faith Remains," *St. Louis Post Dispatch,* June 22, 2003, A1.

26. George H. Gallup, Jr., *Gallup/CNN/USA Today Poll* (June 19, 2003).

27. ISSP, *Religion II,* 26–27, 30–31.

28. Center for Political Studies, *National Election Studies 2002.*

29. Figures on church attendance are disputed by C. Kirk Hadaway, Penny Long Marler, and Mark Chaves, "What the Polls Don't Show: A Closer Look at U.S. Church Attendance,"

American Sociological Review 58 (1993), 741–752. See also C. Kirk Hadaway and Penny Long, "Did You Really Go to Church This Week? Behind the Poll Data," *Christian Century* (May 6, 1998), 472–475.

30. George Gallup Jr., "Religion in America: Will the Vitality of the Churches be the Surprise of the Next Century?" *The Public Perspective* 6 (October/November 1995), 1–8. See also Barna Research Group, "Survey Shows Faith Impacts Some Behaviors But Not Others," *Barna Research Online*, http://www.barna.org (October 22, 2002).

31. This argument is made by Allen D. Hertzke, *Echoes of Discontent: Jesse Jackson, Pat Robertson, and the Resurgence of Populism* (Washington, D.C.: CQ Press, 1993). See also Benjamin Cheever, "God or BMW," *New York Times Magazine* (December 7, 1997), 42–44.

32. Hampton Sides, "The Calibration of Belief," *New York Times Magazine* (December 7, 1997), 92–95.

33. Medical researchers and social scientists have only begun seriously delving into the impact of religion on health in the last decade, though the literature on the subject is growing fast. For journalistic discussions of the topic, see Claudia Kalb, "Faith and Healing," *Newsweek* (November 10, 2003), 44–56 and Bill Broadway, "Putting Spirituality to the Test," *Washington Post* (November 1, 2003), B9.

34. Kohut et al, *Diminishing Divide*, 109–117; Arthur C. Brooks, "Religious Faith and Charitable Giving," *Policy Review* 121 (October/November 2003); Mark Regnerus, Christian Smith, and David Sikkink, "Who Gives to the Poor? The Role of Religious Tradition and Political Location on the Personal Generosity of Americans toward the Poor," *Journal for the Scientific Study of Religion* 37 (1998), 481–493.

35. Sidney Verba, Kay Lehman Schlozman, and Henry E. Brady, *Voice and Equality: Civic Voluntarism in American Politics* (Cambridge, MA: Harvard University Press, 1995). See also Paul Djupe and J. Tobin Grant, "Religious Institutions and Political Participation in America," *Journal for the Scientific Study of Religion* 40 (2001), 303–14.

36. Robert D. Putnam, *Making Democracy Work: Civic Traditions in Modern Italy* (Princeton, NJ: Princeton University Press, 1993).

37. On the trends toward small group ministry, see Robert Wuthnow, ed., "I Come Away Stronger": How Small Groups Are Shaping American Religion (Grand Rapids, MI: Eerdmans, 1994) and Wuthnow, *Sharing the Journey: Support Groups and America's New Quest for Community* (New York: Simon and Schuster, 1996).

38. Kenneth D. Wald, Dennis E. Owen, and Samuel S. Hill Jr., "Churches as Political Communities," *American Political Science Review* 82 (June 1988), 531–548; Kenneth D. Wald, Dennis E. Owen, and Samuel S. Hill Jr., "Political Cohesion in Churches," *Journal of Politics* 52 (March 1990), 197–215; Christopher P. Gilbert, *The Impact of Churches on Political Behavior: An Empirical Study* (Westport, CT: Greenwood Press, 1993).

39. Data from the Commission on Ethnic Relations, Assemblies of God, USA, available at http://www.ethnicrelations.ag.org/ethnicrelations/stats.cfm.

40. Rodney Stark, "Modernization and Mormon Growth: The Secularization Thesis Revisited," in Marie Cornwall, Tim B. Heaton, and Lawrence A. Young, eds., *Contemporary Mormonism: Social Science Perspectives* (Urbana, IL: University of Illinois Press, 2001).

41. Brooks, "Religious Faith and Charitable Giving."

42. Ram A. Cnaan, *The Invisible Hand of Caring: American Congregations and the Provision of Welfare* (New York: New York University Press, 2001).

43. Based on data from the National Congregations Study, available at http://www.saint-denis.library.arizona.edu/natcong. For a discussion of the data and methods used in this large study of religious congregations, see Mark Chaves et al., "The National Congregations Study: Background, Methods, and Selected Results," *Journal for the Scientific Study of Religion* 38 (1999), 458–476.

44. Carl S. Dudley and David A. Roozen, *Faith Communities Today: A Report on Religion in the United States Today* (Hartford, CT: Hartford Seminary, 2001), 46–47.

45. Office of Archives and Statistics, Seventh-Day Adventist Church, *Adventist Online Yearbook 2003,* available at http://www.adventistyearbook.org.

46. National Center for Education Statistics, *Private School Universe Survey: 1999–2000* (Washington, D.C.: US Department of Education, 2001), 6.

47. National Center for Education Statistics, *Homeschooling in the United States: 1999* (Washington, D.C.: US Department of Education, 2000), 10.

48. Stephen V. Monsma, *When Sacred and Secular Mix: Religious Nonprofit Organizations and Public Money* (Lanham, MD: Rowman & Littlefield, 1996).

49. Amy E. Black, Douglas L. Koopman, and David K. Ryden, *Of Little Faith: The Politics of George W. Bush's Faith-Based Initiatives* (Washington, D.C.: Georgetown University Press, 2004). For a wide-ranging discussion of the values in the debate over faith-based social services, see E.J. Dionne Jr. and Ming Hsu Chen, eds., *Sacred Places, Civic Purposes: Should Government Help Faith-Based Charity?* (Washington, D.C.: Brookings, 2001).

50. For an extensive discussion of the choices clergy make about political participation in one American city, see Laura R. Olson, *Filled with Spirit and Power: Protestant Clergy in Politics* (Albany: State University of New York Press, 2000). See also Sue E.S. Crawford and Laura R. Olson, eds., *Christian Clergy in American Politics* (Baltimore: Johns Hopkins, 2001) and James L. Guth, John C. Green, Corwin E. Smidt, Lyman A Kellstedt, and Margaret M. Poloma, *The Bully Pulpit: The Politics of Protestant Clergy* (Lawrence, KS: University of Kansas, 1997).

51. Aldon D. Morris, *The Origins of the Civil Rights Movement* (New York: Free Press, 1984).

52. On the religious experiences of gay men, see Brian Bouldrey, ed., *Wrestling with the Angel: Faith and Religion in the Lives of Gay Men* (New York: Free Press, 1995).

53. The Pew Research Center puts the Catholic population at 23 percent (Pew Research Center, "Religion and Politics," 34), and other surveys (e.g., National Election Studies 2002) put it as high as 27 percent, so elsewhere in the text we simply say that Catholics comprise approximately a quarter of the American population. The figures for total Protestants in many surveys may also contain a number of only nominally religions individuals, as we suggest in Chapter 4.

54. Based on denominational affiliations in National Election Studies 2002. See also the electoral breakdown in James L. Guth, Lyman Kellstedt, John C. Green, and Corwin Smidt, "American Fifty/Fifty," *First Things* (October 2001), 19–26. For a discussion of methodological uses of denominations as indicators of religious traditions, see Lyman A. Kellstedt and John C. Green, "Knowing God's Many People: Denominational Preference and Political Behavior," in David C. Leege, Lyman A. Kellstedt, eds., *Rediscovering the Religious Factor in American Politics* (Armonk, NY: M.E. Sharpe, 1993), 53–69 and Lyman A. Kellstedt, John C. Green, James L Guth, and Corwin E. Smidt, "Grasping the Essentials: The Social Embodiment of Religion and Political Behavior," in John Green, James Guth, Corwin Smidt, and Lyman Kellstedt, *Religion and the Culture Wars* (Lanham, MD: Rowman and Littlefield, 1996), 174–192.

55. On InterVarsity, see http://www.gospelcom.net/iv; on Campus Crusade, see http://www.uscm.org. Religion on college campuses also reflects the tremendous pluralism of American religion in general. See Diane Winston, "Campuses Are a Bellwether for Society's Religious Revival," *The Chronicle of Higher Education* (January 16, 1998), A60.

56. For a fine discussion of the Christian Right, see Clyde Wilcox, *Onward Christian Soldiers? The Religious Right in American Politics,* 2nd ed. (Boulder, CO: Westview, 2000).

57. See, e.g., Reagan's *Abortion and the Conscience of the Nation* (Nashville: Thomas Nelson, 1984). On the symbolic use of religion by political elites, see Laura R. Olson, "Bill Clinton's Strategic Use of Religious and Family Rhetoric: The Co-Optation of Partisan Symbolism" (paper presented at the annual meeting of the Midwest Political Science Association, Chicago, 1997).

58. Geoffrey Layman, *The Great Divide: Religious and Cultural Conflict in American Party Politics* (New York: Columbia University Press, 2001).

59. Chris Rice, *Grace Matters: A True Story of Race, Friendship, and Faith in the Heart of the South* (Indianapolis, IN: Jossey-Bass, 2002); James W. Skillen, "Evangelical Cooperation in the Cause of Racial Justice," in Gary Oldfield and Holly J. Lebowitz, eds., *Religion, Race, and Justice in a Changing America* (New York: Century Foundation Press, 1999), 115–136.

60. Michael O. Emerson and Christian Smith, *Divided by Faith: Evangelical Religion and the Problem of Race in America* (New York: Oxford, 2001).

61. Fredrick C. Harris, *Something Within: Religion in African-American Political Activism* (New York: Oxford University Press, 1999).

62. Joel A. Carpenter, *Revive Us Again: The Reawakening of American Fundamentalism* (New York: Oxford University Press, 1997); Mark Dalhouse, *An Island in the Lake of Fire: Bob Jones University, Fundamentalism, and the Separatist Movement* (Athens: University of Georgia Press, 1996).

63. For a detailed discussion of Pentecostalism, see Edith Blumhofer, *Restoring the Faith: The Assemblies of God, Pentecostalism, and American Culture* (Urbana, IL: University of Illinois, 1997); Grant Wacker, *Heaven Below: Early Pentecostalism and American Culture* (Cambridge: Harvard University Press, 2001).

64. For profiles of some emerging evangelical and other religious leaders, see Jo Renee Formicola and Hubert Morken, *Religious Leaders and Faith-Based Politics: Ten Profiles* (Lanham, MD: Rowman and Littlefield, 2001).

65. James L. Guth and Lyman Kellstedt, "Religion and Congress," in Corwin Smidt, ed., *In God We Trust? Religion and American Political Life* (Grand Rapids, MI: Baker, 2001), 213–233.

66. For a fine historical discussion of fundamentalism in the United States in the 1930s and 1940s, see Carpenter, *Revive Us Again*.

67. See Kenneth L. Woodward, "Living in the Holy Spirit," *Newsweek* (April 13, 1998).

68. On this topic, see James F. Findlay Jr., *Church People in the Struggle: The National Council of Churches and the Black Freedom Movement, 1950–1970* (New York: Oxford University Press, 1993).

69. Cal Thomas and Ed Dobson, *Blinded by Might: Can the Religious Right Save America?* (Grand Rapids, MI: Zondervan, 1999).

70. http://www.esa-online.org; see also Ronald J. Sider, *Rich Christians in an Age of Hunger: Moving from Affluence to Generosity* (Dallas, TX: Word Publishing, 1997).

71. H. Richard Niebuhr, *Christ and Culture* (New York: Harper and Row, 1951); Robert Wuthnow and John H. Evans, eds., *The Quiet Hand of God: Faith-Based Activism and the Public Role of Mainline Protestantism* (Berkeley: University of California Press, 2002).

72. Guth et al., *The Bully Pulpit*; Robert Wuthnow, *The Restructuring of American Religion: Society and Faith Since World War II* (Princeton, NJ: Princeton University Press, 1988).

73. Harold E. Quinley, *The Prophetic Clergy: Social Activism Among Protestant Ministers* (New York: Wiley, 1974).

74. Jackson W. Carroll, Barbara G. Wheeler, Daniel O. Aleshire, and Penny Long Marler, *Being There: Culture and Formation in Two Theological Schools* (New York: Oxford University Press, 1997).

75. Sue E. S. Crawford and Laura R. Olson, "Clergy as Political Actors in Urban Contexts," in Crawford and Olson, *Christian Clergy in American Politics*.

76. Kenneth D. Wald, *Religion and Politics in the United States*, 4th ed. (Lanham, MD: Rowman and Littlefield, 2003), chap. 4.

77. James F. Finley, Jr., *Church People in the Struggle: The National Council of Churches and the Black Freedom Movement, 1950–70* (New York: Oxford University Press, 1993); Michael

B. Friedland, *Lift Up Your Voice Like a Trumpet: White Clergy and the Civil Rights and Antiwar Movements, 1954–1973* (Chapel Hill, NC: University of North Carolina Press, 1998).

78. Guth et al., *The Bully Pulpit.*

79. See Wendy Cadge, "Vital Conflicts: The Mainline Protestant Denominations Debate Homosexuality," in Wuthnow and Evans, *The Quiet Hand of God.*

80. Jeffrey Hadden, *The Gathering Storm in the Churches* (Garden City, NY: Doubleday, 1969); A. James Reichley, *Faith in Politics* (Washington, D.C.: Brookings Institution, 2002), 264; James L. Adams, *The Growing Church Lobby in Washington* (Grand Rapids, MI: Eerdmans, 1970); Quinley, *The Prophetic Clergy.*

81. Hadden, *The Gathering Storm in the Churches.*

82. Dale Jones et al., *Religious Congregations and Membership: 2000* (Nashville, TN: Glenmary Research Center, 2002). Data available at http://www.glenmary.org.

83. Phillip Hammond, *The Protestant Presence in Twentieth-Century America: Religion and Political Culture* (Albany: State University Press of New York, 1992).

84. Dean M. Kelley, *Why Conservative Churches Are Growing: A Study in Sociology of Religion* (San Francisco: Harper, 1977); Roger Finke and Rodney Stark, *The Churching of America, 1776–1990: Winners and Losers in Our Religious Economy* (New Brunswick, NJ: Rutgers University Press, 1992); Robert Wuthnow, *The Crisis in the Churches* (New York: Oxford University Press, 1996).

85. Stephen Hart, *Cultural Dilemmas of Progressive Politics: Styles of Engagement Among Grassroots Activists* (Chicago: University of Chicago Press, 2001); Olson, *Filled with Spirit and Power*; Jim Rooney, *Organizing the South Bronx* (Albany, NY: State University of New York Press, 1995); James K. Wellman, *The Gold Coast and the Ghetto: Christ and Culture in Mainline Protestantism* (Urbana, IL: University of Illinois Press, 1999).

86. Wuthnow and Evans, *The Quiet Hand of God;* Ram A. Cnaan, *The Newer Deal: Social Work and Religion in Partnership* (New York: Columbia University Press, 1999).

87. Wuthnow and Evans, *The Quiet Hand of God.*

88. Richard John Neuhaus, *The Catholic Moment: The Paradox of the Church in the Postmodern World* (San Francisco: Harper and Row, 1987).

89. See, e.g., Paul Blanshard, *American Freedom and Catholic Power* (Boston: Beacon Press, 1949).

90. See John Courtney Murray, *We Hold These Truths: Catholic Reflections on the American Proposition* (New York: Sheed and Ward, 1960). Murray concluded that the American experiment, properly understood, was compatible with Church teachings.

91. Samuel Huntington, *The Third Wave: Democratization in the Late Twentieth Century* (Norman: University of Oklahoma Press, 1991).

92. Bumiller, "Religious Leaders Ask. . . "

93. Hugh Morken and Jo Renee Formicola, *The Politics of School Choice* (Lanham, MD: Rowman and Littlefield, 1999).

94. Peter Steinfels, "When is a Catholic Not a Catholic?" *New York Times Magazine* (December 7, 1997), 63–65.

95. On the priest shortage in the Catholic Church, see Richard A. Schoenherr, *Goodbye Father: The Celibate Male Priesthood and the Future of the Catholic Church* (New York: Oxford University Press, 2002).

96. Philip Jenkins, *The New Anti-Catholicism: The Last Acceptable Prejudice* (New York: Oxford University Press, 2003).

97. Finke and Stark, *The Churching of America.*

98. Andrew Greeley, "Defection Among Hispanics (Updated)," *America* (September 27, 1997), 12–14.

99. Gaston Espinosa, Virgilio Elizondo, and Jesse Miranda, "Hispanic Churches in American Public Life: Summary of Findings," *Interim Reports* 2 (January 2003), 15.

100. Two important books on the contemporary Roman Catholic Church are Peter Steinfels, *A People Adrift: The Crisst of the Roman Catholic Church in America* (New York: Simon and Schuster, 2003); and David Gibson, *The Coming Catholic Church: How the Faithful are Shaping a New American Catholicism* (San Francisco: HarperSanFrancisco, 2003).

JUDAISM, ISLAM, AND OTHER EXPRESSIONS OF RELIGIOUS PLURALISM

Most of the discussion of religion and politics in the United States concentrates on the political activity of large, familiar, and well-established Christian groups: Catholics and various Protestant denominations. This focus makes sense, since these groups are the most prominent of the complex and pluralistic mix of religions in the United States. But these major religious groups hardly constitute the entire story of religion—or religion and politics—in the United States.

After all, the United States has literally hundreds of religions and thousands of religious communities and churches. Every one of them is a part of the larger nation, and that simple fact affects each of them by necessity. Of course, each American religious group has political objectives—even if it simply wishes to be left alone. And each exercises political influence, however small, indirect, or unintended. Smaller religions have important lessons to teach about what they do, how they protect themselves, and how they advance their values. Their stories will be ever more relevant as the pluralism of American religion continues to grow.

It is not obvious how to study the political dimensions of these kinds religious groups in the United States. Few have done so, and as we proceed we are acutely aware that our approach represents only one possible method. We approach smaller religions with respect—not as strange phenomena. Religious movements deserve to be taken seriously, both on their own terms and for their political implications.

In this chapter we divide small religious movements into three groups: Judaism and Islam, both of which present major alternatives to Christianity in American public life; religious traditions that have maintained a clear separation from politics and the mainstream culture; and non-separatist traditions that have reached beyond their own walls and engaged the broader culture. For each category we give attention to their attitudes toward, and involvement in, political life. We argue that distinctive religious beliefs and behaviors combine with a host of other factors—geography, relative size, and so on—to explain differences in how these groups approach public life.

MAJOR ALTERNATIVE RELIGIONS

Judaism and Islam, both in terms of their size and public exposure, are the most prominent non-Christian religious traditions in America (later in this chapter we discuss the LDS Church, which has a more ambiguous relationship to the Christian faith). Jews have lived in the United States from before the founding and have carved out a highly successful niche in American society. Islam, by contrast, is a relative newcomer and is struggling to address unique political and social challenges.

Jews and Judaism

On almost any measure Jews are the most successful minority group in America. After suffering persecution for centuries throughout the world, Jews have found the United States, with its doctrine of religious tolerance, a remarkably hospitable place. This is not to say that they have not faced serious disadvantages; many Jews have been subjected to outright discrimination and cultural hostility. But the constitutional protection of religious liberty, combined with a social system that rewards strong families, hard work, and education, has enabled Jews to prosper in the United States. By every measure—education level, income, professional status—Jews are disproportionately well off. They have moved into positions of prominence in business, law, higher education, politics, journalism, and entertainment. In all of these areas they exercise considerable influence.[1]

However, we need to avoid reinforcing unfair stereotypes of Jewish cabals ruling the world. In fact, their influence is sometimes exaggerated. Constituting less than 2 percent of the population, their voting strength makes an impact only in cities and states where their numbers are concentrated, and migration patterns suggest increasing vote dilution as Jewish Americans disperse across the United States.[2] And Jews are influential on some issues—backing for Israel, for example—because they enjoy broad support from Christians. Still, Jews in the United States, through their activism and major role in the Democratic Party, have had an impact on American politics that is more profound than their relatively small size would suggest.

Most Jews who are formally associated with a synagogue fall into one of three major groupings—Reform (39 percent), Conservative (33 percent), and Orthodox (21 percent)—that reflect the diversity within American Judaism.[3] Yet many Jews are in fact largely secular and committed to a secular approach to life. As a result, one dimension of the politics of religion, the conflict between secular forces and religious ones in the American public square, attracts many Jewish voices strongly opposed to government interaction with religion.

Among Jewish Americans, synagogue attendance rates are low—only a quarter attend on a monthly basis[4]—and many Jews admit to agnostic views. Nevertheless, there is a cultural dimension to Judaism that ties even the least religious Jews together out of a sense of shared history. Many Jews proudly describe themselves as Jewish even though they never set foot in a synagogue. One of the serious issues in Jewish circles today is the challenge of maintaining a Jewish culture without much of a religious dimension.[5] The intermarriage rate among American Jews since 1996 is 47 percent, and children are often raised with only a vague sense of their Jewish heritage.[6] Moreover, birthrates for Jewish women are lower than the rate needed to replace the population.[7] The myriad calls to reclaim Jewish heritage only confirm the concern.[8]

Jews have a well-deserved reputation for political liberalism that derives from a combination of several factors. The majority of religious American Jews are adherents of the two largest theologically liberal branches of Judaism—Conservative and Reform. Reform Jews in particular have roots in the liberal Enlightenment and are assertive champions of civil liberties and church-state separation. Moreover, because of their historical experience of persecution, most Jews believe in the need to maintain a society that tolerates minorities and cares about the disadvantaged. Support for progressive taxation, civil rights, and other liberal causes often places Jews in the vanguard.[9]

Jews exercise political power through a host of robust organizations. The oldest of these is the American Jewish Committee, which was formed in 1906. These organizations exercise influence because they have thriving local chapters, seasoned leaders, and a clear political agenda. Though the common agenda is undeniably liberal, there is pluralism in American Jewish politics.[10] Indeed, Orthodox Jews and the Ultraorthodox (see Box 3.1) often oppose abortion, support government aid to religious schools, applaud the enforcement of antipornography laws, back various measures to check the advance of secular culture, and vote Republican. But this is not the extent of Jewish pluralism. A highly influential group of intellectuals, including former liberals Norman Podhoretz and Irving Kristol, were leaders of the neoconservative movement, helping to formulate the reaction against perceived excesses of the 1960s and 1970s.[11] Who was it that wrote Dan Quayle's famous family values speech that blasted Murphy Brown, to the applause of conservative Christians? It was none other than a Jewish man, William Kristol. Kristol is the son of Irving Kristol and historian Gertrude Himmelfarb and now heads the conservative magazine *The Weekly Standard*. Kristol and other "neocons" made waves again in 2002 and 2003 by advocating military action against Iraq. A key link between the neocons and the Bush administration was Paul Wolfowitz, the Deputy Secretary of Defense and another Jewish American.[12]

Support for Israel, of course, is a major cause for most American Jews, since the connection between American Jews and Israelis traditionally has been deep. No other nation has as many Jews as the United States; in fact, more Jews are in the United States than in Israel itself. There is a great deal of contact between Jews in both lands. But for many American Jews, Israel is more than a familiar land where close friends and relatives often live. It is also the Jewish homeland and has been a place of refuge (off and on) for several millennia. This is another reason for the strong commitment to the preservation of Israel, despite plenty of disagreements with particular Israeli leaders and policies. Thus many American Jews support Israel both politically and financially. In turn, Israeli leaders keep in close contact with Jewish leaders and organizations in the United States.

Islam

Islam today receives a great deal of media attention, especially as observers finally discovered its presence in the United States in the wake of the Sep-

---

BOX 3.1 THE HASIDIM IN AMERICA

The largest single group within the Ultraorthodox community are Hasidic Jews, who are concentrated in New York City and the surrounding areas. It is important to note that the Hasidim are not a thoroughly unified group; they are in fact divided into several tight subgroups, each organized under a *rebbe* (master) and devoted to the laws and teachings of ancient scripture. Unlike many other Ultraorthodox Jews, however, the Hasidim do not single-mindedly study the scriptures. For the Hasidim, such an approach is much too formal and scholarly; it downplays the essential importance of emotion in their worship of God.

The political tradition of the Hasidim has been mostly one of political withdrawal from larger, usually Christian societies. Hasidic Jews are similar to many fundamentalist Protestant groups in that they seek distance from societies they judge as corrupting or otherwise dangerous to the faithful. At the same time, however, the Hasidim do sometimes participate in politics. In the United States this has included regular voting. Because the Hasidim are usually socially conservative, it has also meant voting Republican in many instances. Moreover, the Hasidim have on occasion tried to elect their own candidates in local and state contests where they perceive crucial issues to be at stake and where they have a chance to win (as in parts of New York City).

SOURCES: Jack Wertheimer, *A People Divided* (New York: Basic Books, 1993); Samuel C. Heilman and Steven M. Cohen, *Cosmopolitans and Parochials: Modern Orthodox Jews in America* (Chicago: University of Chicago Press, 1989); William M. Kephart and William W. Zellner, *Extraordinary Groups* (Worth Publishing, 2000), ch. 6.

---

tember 11, 2001, attacks on the World Trade Center and the Pentagon. The precise number of Muslims living in the United States is unknown; even the best estimates range from 2 to 6 million.[13] The counting problem is complicated because surveys must be adjusted for the fact that many American Muslims today are immigrants who sometimes do not speak English well or at all. A reasonable estimate is that about 1 percent of the U.S. population is now Muslim. The number of Muslims is growing; as recently as fifty years ago no more than 20,000 Muslims lived in the United States. The numbers of Muslim places of worship have also risen. In the early 1930s, only one mosque could be found in the United States, but by 2001 there were at least 1,200 Islamic religious centers with as many as 2 million members.[14] There is no reason to think that this growth will not continue.[15]

Though many American Muslims are first- or second-generation immigrants, a sizable proportion are African American. Most African American

Muslims adhere to mainstream Islam, though assorted splinter groups exist, including the much discussed Nation of Islam led by Louis Farrakhan (see Chapter 10). Perhaps the most influential black Muslim leader in the United States today is Warith Deen Muhammed, the son of Elijah Muhammad, who was the leader of the Nation of Islam in the mid-twentieth century. Until his retirement from the American Society of Muslims in 2003, Warith Deen Muhammed led his followers toward mainstream Islam and away from Farrakhan's racially separatist theories.

The ethnic diversity that characterizes other American Muslims is remarkable. Muslim immigrants have come to the United States in considerable numbers, especially from Pakistan, Iran, Bangladesh, Nigeria, Egypt, the Philippines, Indonesia, and various Middle Eastern countries. Good estimates suggest about 24 percent of American Muslims are African American, 25 percent originated in South Asia, and 26 percent come from Arabic countries in the Middle East, with the remainder arriving from East Asia and other regions.[16] Ethnic diversity also means that immigrant Muslims represent both major traditions of Islam, Sunni and Shi'ite. These tradition differ primarily over the question of who succeeded the Prophet Mohammad after his death. Although there is a sizable Shi'ite population in Southern California today, Sunni Muslims predominate in the United States, as they do in the Islamic world as a whole.

Today there are signs of organization that may lead to political influence for American Muslims. The basic federation of Islamic groups in the United States is the Islamic Society of North America. The Muslim Public Affairs Council (MPAC) is emerging as an active participant in U.S. politics, vigorously promoting Muslim civil liberties and rights, especially since September 11, 2001, as homeland security matters have begun to affect American Muslims.[17] September 11 also led CAIR, the Council on American-Islamic Relations, founded in 1974, to the forefront. It focuses specifically on protecting civil liberties and rights of U.S. Islamic citizens and actively protects against perceived violations. Since September 11, these and other organizations have been spending much of their time confronting and debunking the false perception that most Muslims are terrorists or even anti-American. Islamic leaders understand that such stereotypes must be dismantled if Muslims are to gain political influence in the United States. Another way these myths will be debunked is through the growing visibility of some younger Muslims, who are assimilating into American culture with relative ease.[18]

Before September 11, given the racial and ethnic divisions inherent in American Islam—divisions that are especially keen between black Muslims and the large numbers of immigrant Muslims—collective Muslim political muscle seemed unlikely to develop.[19] That is changing now as Muslims of all backgrounds worry about their future in the United States. Security issues aside, however, Muslims come in every political persuasion and do not yet agree on the appropriate political agenda for the Islamic community in the United States. Many, however, tend to be conservative on social and moral issues such as abortion, women's rights, and sexual behavior. Indeed, many people who convert to Islam from other religions are attracted to its confident discipline and clear boundaries. It is possible that as adherence to Islam in the United States grows and as it becomes more organized, it may become something of a partner in the conservative movement in American religion, which today includes evangelical Protestants and Orthodox Jews. The 2000 elections showed signs of a potential partnership in the endorsement of George W. Bush by several of the most prominent Muslim groups[20] and the victory of Bush over Al Gore among Muslim voters (unlike Bob Dole, the Republican candidate in 1996, who lost the Muslim vote handily to Bill Clinton).[21] Still, there are many obstacles to such a partnership, including deep-seated religious differences and the fact that as a disadvantaged minority group, Muslims seem to feel some affinity for the Democratic Party.[22]

Another possibility, of course, is that policy concerns affecting Islamic countries will become a political agenda for Muslims in the United States, at least in the near future. Such an agenda would mirror American Jews' concern for Israel. To some extent this is true already, though it has not necessarily led to a single set of policies, given the diversity both of Islamic nations and of Muslims in America. The exception is strong, universal support among Muslims for the Palestinian cause. And when in 2003 the United States went to war with Iraq, many Muslim groups spoke out against military action.[23]

It may turn out that Islam will never achieve substantial political leverage in the United States regardless of what agenda or agendas it pursues. Certainly the 2001 terrorist attacks did not help. Perhaps Islam will remain divided and subdivided along ethnic and racial lines, which may undercut the development of any serious Islamic political agenda in the United States. In the short run we suspect that this is what will happen. But in time assimilation may render ethnicity less important in defining and dividing American Muslims. In that event, a more unified Islam could well emerge. How might an organized Islam proceed if its believers do move toward greater engagement in American politics? For this to happen several things need to occur: a serious effort must be made to fashion a more positive image of Islam in America; a focused political agenda is a must; improved relations with American Jews would also be beneficial.

Features of Islam that clash with mainstream American culture, however, pose difficulties.[24] This is true, for example, of Islam's distinctly patriarchal attitudes toward women.[25] More broadly speaking, Islam is not well understood in most parts of the United States, a reality that must be acknowledged and overcome. But these difficulties can be addressed. Other groups, including both Roman Catholics and Jews, have overcome similar obstacles in American history.

SEPARATIST RELIGIONS AND POLITICS

Many religions in the United States have relatively few members and have adopted a distinctly separatist orientation toward the broader culture. By the term "separatist" we mean that these religious communities set stricter moral boundaries for their members than do mainstream religions, and that these boundaries necessarily separate their members from the larger society to some degree. Most of these groups are deeply critical of the larger society, which they portray as immoral, evil, or wrongheaded. Some have an interest in reaching out to the larger society to gain converts, but many enjoy only limited success in such efforts due to the heavy demands required of group members.

It is also helpful to subdivide small, separatist religions into two types. Some have a membership who share a common history or ethnic origin. Such characteristics provide a powerful basis for community, but they also limit growth. Other groups have no such basis for unity, so they substitute some other foundation for their tightly bounded community.

The Amish are a good example of a religious group whose community is based on a shared history. Most Amish originally came from the sixteenth-century Anabaptist movements that began during the Protestant Reformation in Switzerland. The Amish broke away from one Anabaptist branch over issues that are now dusty with time. They began their formal existence as a separate religious group in 1693, though it was not until the eighteenth century that Amish people began migrating to the United States. Today there are nearly a hundred thousand Amish residing in many states, but their most well-known communities are located in southern Pennsylvania.[26]

The Protestant religious beliefs of the Amish are reasonably familiar in the American context. After all, the Amish constitute a fragment of the larger Protestant Reformation, the descendants of which now form the Protestant majority of the United States. At the same time, however, the Amish are not a part of mainstream American religion or culture. Their focus on maintaining a tightly knit and separatist religious community, as well as their buggies, plain clothes, and rejection of electricity in the home, make this obvious. This separatism is particularly clear to the Amish themselves as they struggle to maintain their way of life against an indifferent and occasionally hostile American culture.

The Amish have traditionally displayed little interest or faith in politics or government. Their numbers are tiny and their chances of having much political influence are extremely modest. In the United States the Amish have usually had only the most minimal contact with the government. Some Amish citizens vote, and there have been some Amish efforts to lobby state legislatures over issues of urgent importance to them. In 1972, they were involved in a noted U.S. Supreme Court case in which they won the right not to send their teenagers to high school *(Wisconsin v. Yoder)*. Mostly, though, the Amish have turned away from politics. Their politics are really the politics of noninvolvement and withdrawal.

Because it is dictated by a sense of religious and cultural separatism, political disengagement has worked well for the Amish. They have acquired a reputation as a quaint and inoffensive people who should be left in peace. This is why they have escaped significant persecution and interference. The broader U.S. culture seems to accept the Amish as a charming expression of a past and a people who pose no threat (with perhaps the small exception of some local drivers who find slow-moving Amish buggies an annoyance). Amish separatism has turned out to be a form of politics that has provided protection from the broader society.

Unlike the Amish, new religious movements, or "cults," are the prime illustration today of small, separatist religions that reach into the society for converts but more often receive opprobrium. Every year or two, television, radio, and newspapers seem to be full of reports of one "cult" religion or another and the seemingly strange, dangerous, or fanatical activities of its members.[27] Use of the term "cult" is prejudicial, since its meaning is always negative. The terms "alternative religion" or "unconventional religion" might be better, but there are many kinds of alternative or unconventional religions that are very unlike "cults." This is why we reluctantly continue to use the term "cult" for a specific type of highly dissident alternative religion organized into a tight community that exists in great tension with the broader culture. Often such religious groups are headed by a single charismatic leader whom the community members are willing to follow—sometimes to death, as was the case with Marshall Applewhite and his Heaven's Gate followers in 1997.

Estimates range from as many as 5,000 or as few as 700 cults in the United States, depending on how strictly one interprets the definition. Few are, or have been, as well known as Heaven's Gate, the Branch Davidians, or the equally deadly People's Temple cult, which was led to mass death in Guyana in 1978 by their leader, Jim Jones. Most cults are nonviolent and shun both politics and the public eye. Perhaps the largest cult in America today is the Los Angeles–based International Churches of Christ (ICOC), which is said to have as many as 185,000 members. It is known for its very close guidance (called shepherding) of its adherents, though it understandably resists the label "cult." The ICOC has grown dramatically since its beginning in the 1970s, in part due to its outreach to college students. Recent leadership conflicts, however, as well as charges of abusive treatment of wayward members, leaves the group's continued vitality in some doubt.[28]

In recent years few cults have had much political influence, but some have locked horns with the government. The fiery April 1993 demise of David Koresh and the Branch Davidian community outside Waco, Texas, demonstrated this fact. The Branch Davidian community was a breakaway group of another breakaway group of the Seventh-day Adventists. Under Koresh, the Branch Davidians soon became a classic illustration of a strictly separatist community led by a charismatic leader. Its eventual destruction had a definite political impact, especially on the Bureau of Alcohol, Tobacco, and Firearms and the FBI, while dramatically demonstrating the Branch Davidians' own lack of political influence.[29]

On the extreme fringe of American religious life is the tiny but noteworthy Christian Identity movement, which is made up of small separatist organizations whose leaders preach hate through religion. Most Christian Identity groups are very hostile toward racial and ethnic minorities and people who practice faiths other than Christianity. They embrace what they term the "Israel message" that white people are chosen by God and that Jews and persons of color are subhuman. In the view of Christian Identity followers, an apocalyptic holy war will destroy all people except white Christians. As postmillennialists, Christian Identity followers see this battle as imminent, so they often arm themselves heavily and live together in remote compounds. The Christian Identity movement's political approach is sometimes violent; convicted Oklahoma City bomber Timothy McVeigh had links to the movement.[30]

There is little doubt that the extent of the cult phenomenon gets exaggerated when sporadic outbursts of media attention flare up. This is doubly true if we think about cults in political terms, since most of their adherents stay out of politics as much as they possibly can. They know society does not like them and that the public eye can only be cruel to them. Though they seek converts, they also seek withdrawal. They may not want to let society alone, but they certainly want society to leave them alone.

The Unification Church of Rev. Sun Myung Moon presents an exception to cults' standard strategy of political avoidance. This movement—its followers are universally known, often derisively, as "Moonies"—is committed to being involved in politics. How influential the Unification Church is, however, is another matter. Though the membership, financial resources, and political influence of the Unification Church are not well understood, we do know that the church in the United States is part of a larger movement, based in South Korea, that has substantial financial resources. It has been willing to commit these resources, for example, to funding the politically conservative *Washington Times*, a newspaper that is the major alternative to the more liberal *Washington Post*.[31]

OTHER SMALL RELIGIONS

Some alternative religions are not especially separatist, though because of their size their political involvement and political impact is modest.

Nevertheless, religious expressions defined by ethnic characteristics or even sexual orientation can provide a means for smaller religious communities to build social capital, group solidarity, and civic skills.

Consider religion among Native Americans, a highly complex phenomenon. It includes diverse tribal practices, Indian Christian congregations, and a number of syncretic expressions that blend aspects of Christian worship with traditional native ritual. Most Native American religious groups today are fairly loosely organized and organic, though some are institutionalized in familiar senses.

Because of its use of the drug peyote as a part of worship, the Native American Church is one of the best known of the syncretic faiths. Influenced to some extent by Christianity, this religion shares with other Indian expressions a belief in a supreme being; the reality and power of spirits, visions, and ghosts; life after death; and the omnipresence of a spiritual aspect, usually unseen but of great significance in the empirical world. The church has developed a clergy and other signs of organization. Yet in most instances its formal religious organization and institutionalization are modest in comparison with other American religions.[32] Not surprisingly, the main political effort of this religion is defensive—going to court to defend peyote use, not always successfully.

While peyote use may grab the headlines, a more important expression of Native American spirituality takes place within Christian churches made up of Indian congregants. Both on reservations and off there are numerous such congregations, and many prominent Indian leaders have been members. Because Christian churches represented a legacy of conquest, many early political efforts by Native American activists were directed at the main Catholic and Protestant denominations themselves. This campaign to gain Indian self-determination within the churches contributed to the Red Power consciousness that bubbled up in the late 1960s and 1970s.

We see this in such figures as Vine Deloria, Jr., a Yankton Sioux and seminary graduate. His book *Custer Died for Your Sins* served as a "manifesto" of Indian activism.[33] While damning of the way Christian proselytizing divided people and undermined tribal ways, he nonetheless did not abandon the vision of a more ecumenical and truly Indian Christianity. In much the same way that black religious leaders developed fresh understandings of the Christian message, Deloria and others attempted to do the same for Indians.

The most tangible aspect of organizing through Christian churches involved the Indian Ecumenical Conference, founded in 1969. As James Treat shows, the Conference began as an effort to mend the divisions between tribal and Christian traditions throughout the nation. The vision was the same one that occupied Deloria—building unity across tribes. While focused mostly on religious matters, the thousands who gathered every summer for the next decade helped stimulate a kind of "cultural revival" among Native people that contributed to other political efforts.[34]

Native American groups have become more politically involved and sophisticated in recent times because of tribal involvement in the gaming industry and the high stakes politics surrounding it. The money and clout gaming provides are enabling tribes to defend their sovereignty and ways, sometimes with high powered lobbyists. To the extent that religion is woven together with tribal affairs, as it often is, Native American spiritual practices may benefit from the power and visibility this new era represents, though some remain dubious about the source of that clout.[35]

If Native American spirituality must overcome tribal and regional divisions, the Fellowship of Metropolitan Community Churches (MCC), a special ministry to gay and lesbian persons, faces other obstacles. It illustrates another way that a small religion can sometimes make a modest impact by fostering group solidarity and confidence, even if their larger political role is low. While these churches are Christian, and not "alternative" in that sense, their largely gay membership and focus has ensured that their version of Christianity has brought them much more controversy than acceptance in the broader Christian community. Even the liberal National Council of Churches has not agreed to admit the MCC as a member.

The Fellowship includes nearly three hundred affiliated churches, approximately 43,000 members worldwide, and a large headquarters in Los Angeles.[36] It has not progressed beyond the outsider role it plays as a gay church, because, of course, it approves of gay sexual activity (as few other religious groups do). Though the church itself has not been particularly influential in the broader society, it plays a role in various gay rights campaigns, most notably its recent "Marriage Equality Project" that seeks legal recognition of same-sex unions. It is on the local level, perhaps, where some gay congregations exercise a more distinct, if still modest, role. Debra St. John followed the activity of a small MCC congregation in a west Texas city. She observed how it fostered civic skills among formerly sheepish members who became more confident over time, to the point of engaging in a visible political campaign over the town's library policy on gay books.[37]

Such examples, though, illustrate the disparate character of the MCC's political impact. If the Fellowship of Metropolitan Community Churches wished to exert wider collective political clout, it would be hard-pressed to succeed because of its still-small numbers. The only way for small religious groups to exercise broad political clout is to work in a coalition with other, more powerful groups.

A CASE STUDY: MORMONS AND JEHOVAH'S WITNESSES

The example of the Church of Jesus Christ of Latter-day Saints (LDS Church), or the Mormons, seems to belie the picture of only modest political effectiveness of alternative religions. Mormons constitute a serious political force in American politics. In contrast, the Jehovah's Witnesses are a good case with which to illustrate our argument that smaller religions have little political sway. Comparing and contrasting these two religious communities sheds light on the problems and challenges politics presents for minority religions today in the United States.

Because of a unique combination of factors, Mormons are major players in modern American religion and politics. Two of these factors are their size and steady growth. The LDS Church reported approximately 5.4 million members as of the end of 2002, with another 6.3 million worldwide.[38] The church experienced nearly 20 percent growth from 1990 to 2000, and its numbers continue to increase steadily today.[39] But this growth in numbers and political influence has not come easily. The story of Mormonism presents a remarkable case study of an unconventional religion overcoming tremendous disadvantages. In their early days, the Mormons had no influence. Indeed, it can accurately be argued that no religious group in the United States has suffered more discrimination—often severe and deadly persecution—than the Mormons did in the nineteenth century.

Yet today the Mormons' situation has changed dramatically. Headquartered in Salt Lake City, the LDS Church is highly organized. Its members are engaged in local, state, and national politics all across the country, but especially in western states. The church itself is also involved in politics, but mostly behind the scenes.

Whether Mormonism is a form of Christianity or not is a contested matter. The church itself says it is; many traditional Protestant and Roman Catholic groups disagree.[40] These disagreements over its status as part of the Christian tradition have impeded Mormon efforts to reach out to the mainstream. LDS leaders have responded with more direct engagement with mass culture, most recently through their efforts to show LDS's mainstream credentials during the 2002 Winter Olympics in Salt Lake City.[41]

To be sure, both Christianity and Judaism inspired Joseph Smith in 1830, when he founded the LDS Church in western New York.[42] Yet his interpretations of those faiths inevitably clashed with the traditional Protestantism that dominated American culture of the time. Smith contended that the angel Moroni directed him to golden plates that translated into the Book of Mormon. The plates explained the history of a tribal branch of Israelites who came to the Americas after about 600 B.C. This tribe was visited by Jesus Christ and was eventually destroyed because its members failed to follow God's will. Mormons believe that in his earthly life, Moroni was the son of a prophet, Mormon, who repeatedly warned the tribe of its impending doom. They also hold that Mormon himself recorded most of the history recounted on the golden plates and that he buried them several thousand years before they were revealed to Joseph Smith.

The account of the Mormon religious community in the nineteenth century is an often heroic and always controversial story. From the founding of the LDS Church in 1830 to the murder of Joseph Smith in 1844 to the settlement of Utah a few years later, Mormons clashed with the broader American culture. The result was a great deal of pain and suffering for the Mormons—which intensified as people became aware of the Mormon practice of polygamy (which has long been officially abandoned).

Mormonism's belief system affirms the three persons of the Christian Trinity—the Father, Son, and Holy Spirit—but maintains that they are separate entities, not three persons in one. Mormons also believe that all people were with God before creation and that they move on after death to live with God. In the Mormon view, people who lived before Smith's revelation, and thus did not know the Mormon truth, may be saved by present-day Mormons. This is why Mormons have amassed the United

States' leading genealogical archive: They are seeking past relatives to help them toward salvation.

The socioeconomic profile of Mormons is fairly consistent with that of the U.S. population at large. There are some differences, however. Mormons in the United States are overwhelmingly white (94 percent) and have a higher than average marriage rate. Mormons are especially likely to vote, and they tend to be sharply more conservative than the population as a whole on almost every policy issue. They are also distinctly Republican in their party affiliation and voting behavior[43]; they are an even more reliable part of the GOP base than evangelical Protestants. In the 2000 presidential election, a remarkable 88 percent of all Mormon voters preferred George W. Bush over Al Gore.[44] Part of the explanation for these facts has to do with Mormon commitment to family life, individual responsibility, and moral conservatism. Another reason lies in their deep suspicion of government, which is rooted in the Mormon history of conflict with the U.S. government. This attitude can lead some Mormons to adopt liberal political causes, but more often it creates a consistent conservatism that is almost unrivaled among other religious groups.

The LDS Church contends that it is not really political. This is so in large part because the church does not take political stands unless its president, whom Mormons view as a prophet, experiences and shares a specific revelation. Like most religious associations in the United States, the LDS Church does not endorse candidates for office, nor does it contribute directly to candidate campaigns. Evident in this reticence is the fact that Mormons have learned from their tumultuous experiences in the nineteenth century, when popular and governmental hostility forced them to try to fashion a political theocracy—a nation of Zion. That effort brought Mormons only grief in the end. Though the LDS Church lost this political struggle, it learned how to have an effective political voice in the process.

The fact is that the LDS Church is very political—but works carefully and quietly within the American political system. The LDS Church is political in several senses: It encourages involvement in politics; it has created a setting where conservative values and politics are a way of life; and from time to time it quietly advances specific public policies. This is why in Utah, and other heavily Mormon areas, clashing with the LDS Church can be a serious political mistake.

Jehovah's Witnesses are quite another story. Though the Witnesses achieved some notable political victories through their use of the courts, at least in the 1940s, they have no political impact today. They are correctly cited as a prime example of the more normal pattern of small religious groups having no political power.[45]

Jehovah's Witnesses emerged in the United States in the 1870s under the leadership of their founder, Charles Russell. The movement has undergone a steady growth, despite a strict morality that rejects much of the conventional world around them. Their growth is due in good part to the group's well-known intensive evangelism and its communal ethics. Witnesses are unusually integrated racially and ethnically for a religion in America and continue to enjoy steady growth, now claiming 1,012,000 members.[46]

Witnesses declare that they are true followers of the Bible. They affirm Jehovah (God the Father) and acknowledge Jesus Christ as the son of God—indeed, as God's first creation. However, Witness theology contends that though Christ is the son of God, Christ is not God. This marks a crucial difference from Christian belief. Witnesses also believe that at the end of the world there will be 144,000 disciples who will be glorified with God. The rest of the dead will live again on an Earth that will have become a wonderful land of peace and happiness.

Their view is that the end of the world is near, so no one ought to waste time trying to help others via politics or government. Helping individuals to discover religious truth is the answer now. This is why Witnesses distance themselves from government, politics, and even the nation itself. They refuse to salute the flag, serve in the military, or otherwise do anything that might violate their beliefs or indicate that they value the nation. For them, loyalty must be to God, so they have opted for strict separatism.

Still, it would be inaccurate to say that Witnesses have made no political impact. Over the years their involvement in court cases to defend their religious freedom has expanded religious liberty for all kinds of small religious groups, especially against the government (see Chapters 8 and 9 for discussion). Realistically, minority religions may not be able to have any greater political success. In terms of day-to-day politics and policy making in the United States, however, Witnesses do not wish to play an important role. Although not all small religious groups share this goal of noninvolvement, most encounter the same political fate whether they like it or not.

POLITICAL ASSESSMENTS

Pluralism defines religion in the United States, but all religious groups are not politically equal, and the overall political strength of most non-Christian and unconventionally Christian religious groups in the United States is modest at best. Few of them have much political influence. Some have made a political mark in the courts by seeking to protect themselves, as has been the case with the Jehovah's Witnesses. The few exceptions, such as Jews and Mormons, are comparably large groups composed of members who are well integrated into American life and willing to undertake political action.

Of course size is a factor that can hardly be ignored in explaining why some religious groups play such a small role in American politics. We know that most alternative religions are small, comprising a tiny fraction of a country with nearly 300 million people. Many of these faith groups are not growing, either. Only a few, such as the LDS Church, are growing fast enough to increase their share of the nation's population. To be sure, numbers are not everything, but they matter in politics. They furnish activists, supporters, and much more. A group begins at a serious disadvantage without those numbers, even if the politics it practices is almost entirely defensive, as is the case with Jehovah's Witnesses or the Amish.

The issue of isolation is also important. Many smaller religious communities self-consciously choose withdrawal or isolation, as we know, because they fear the corrupting power of the larger culture (the Amish and Hasidim are examples). Sometimes this decision also reflects a realistic analysis of the slim chances these groups have to affect the broader culture. Often, however, disengagement is rooted in theological belief. Jehovah's Witnesses hold that the true believer should not be concerned with governments and nations, so political engagement becomes almost sacrilege.

Islam, like Judaism, may have an advantage politically, since its religious principles *encourage* political involvement. Islam holds that religion should pervade every aspect of life. Thus Muslim leaders have argued that politics and government are legitimate and important realms. This tenet should provide hospitable theological and ideological support for Muslims as they enter American politics.

Geography can also influence isolation. This has been true throughout Mormon history. It is still true today, at least to some extent, since the majority of American Mormons still reside in Utah and surrounding western states. Today Mormons are mostly integrated into the larger culture, but this is much less true of many Native Americans on reservations. For them, geography has played a major role in fostering separation. It can pose major problems for political influence, but does not for tribes generating large sums of money from the gaming industry, some of which they put into politics.

Socioeconomic isolation also has an effect. Many smaller religions have a high number of adherents who lack financial resources, sometimes because of restrictions imposed by their faiths. This situation limits their potential political influence. They have fewer resources, from money to highly educated members, to bring to bear on politics than do religious communities with affluent and well-educated memberships. A small religion of the poor faces daunting odds if it seeks to make a political impact. This has been the case for Jehovah's Witnesses. Judaism and Mormonism, many of whose members are affluent, conversely have a major advantage.

Something that also matters a great deal is what we call "respectability." Many alternative religions are unknown and thus not automatically respected by mainstream religions. In some cases they acquire a reputation as less than respectable groups, and for this they pay a considerable political price. Such has been the fate of cults. Fashion, though, can make unheralded groups and their religions popular, which benefits them. This is increasingly true of Native Americans in the United States—and thus of Native American religions. Native Americans and Native American spirituality are increasingly being celebrated, which could increase their political clout in the long run.

FURTHER READING

Bromley, David G., and Anson Shupe. *Strange Gods: The Great American Cult Scare*. Boston: Beacon, 1981. Cults in the United States.

Conklin, Paul K. *American Originals: Homemade Varieties of Christianity*. Chapel Hill, NC: University of North Carolina Press, 1997. Excellent account of Mormons, Jehovah's Witnesses, and Pentecostals, among others.

Esposito, John L. *The Oxford History of Islam*. New York: Oxford, 1999. A broad history of Islam.

Haddad, Yvonne Yazbeck, and Jane Idelman Smith, eds. *Muslim Communities in North America*. Albany, NY: State University of New York Press, 1994. The best book on American believers in Islam.

Heilman, Samuel C., and Steven M. Cohen. *Cosmopolitans and Parochials: Modern Orthodox Jews in America.* Chicago: University of Chicago Press, 1989. Very interesting discussion of Orthodox Jews.

Kephart, William M., and William W. Zellner. *Extraordinary Groups*, 7th ed. New York: Worth Publishers, 2001. Good study that considers a number of the same groups as does this chapter.

Maisel, L. Sandy, and Ira N. Forman, eds. *Jews in American Politics*, Lanham, MD: Rowman and Littlefield, 2001. An excellent collection of essays on many aspects of Jewish politics in America.

Ostling, Richard, and Joan K. Ostling. *Mormon America: The Power and the Promise.* San Francisco: Harper, 1999. A journalistic account of the LDS Church, past and present.

Treat, James. *Around the Sacred Fire: Native Religious Activism in the Red Power Era* New York: Palgrave Macmillan, 2003. A historical case study of the role of religion in Native American politics.

NOTES

1. L. Sandy Maisel and Ira N. Forman, eds., *Jews in American Politics* (Lanham, MD: Rowman and Littlefield, 2001); J. J. Goldberg, *Jewish Power: Inside the American Jewish Establishment* (Reading, MA: Addison-Wesley, 1996); Bernard M. Lazerwitz, *Jewish Choices: American Jewish Denominationalism* (Albany: State University of New York Press, 1988).

2. In 1966, 84 percent of American Jews lived in the East; by 2002, that percentage had declined to half of the Jewish population, with dramatic percentage increases in the South. See Linda Lyons, "Migration Patterns of Religion in America," *Gallup Poll Tuesday Briefing: Religion and Values* (January 21, 2003).

3. United Jewish Communities, *The National Jewish Population Survey 2000–01* (New York: United Jewish Communities, 2003), 7.

4. Ibid, 7.

5. Samuel G. Freedman, *Jew vs. Jew: The Struggle for the Soul of American Jewry* (New York: Simon and Schuster, 2000).

6. United Jewish Communities, *The National Jewish Population Survey*, 16.

7. Ibid, 4.

8. Ari Goldman, *Being Jewish: The Spiritual and Cultural Practice of Judaism Today* (New York: Simon and Schuster, 2000); Michael Lerner, *Jewish Renewal: A Path to Healing and Restoration* (New York: Putnam, 1994); Alan Dershowitz, *The Vanishing American Jew: In Search of Jewish Identity for the Next Century* (Boston: Little, Brown, 1997); Rodger Kamenetz, "Unorthodox Jews Rummage Through the Orthodox Tradition," *New York Times* (December 7, 1997), 84–86.

9. On the ideological commitments of American Jews, see Anna Greenberg and Kenneth D. Wald, "Still Liberal After All These Years: The Contemporary Political Behavior of American Jewry," in Maisel, ed., *Jews in American Politics*, 161–193.

10. On this point see Lazerwitz et al., *Jewish Choices.*

11. On Jewish conservatism, see Edward Shapiro, "Right Turn? Jews and the American Conservative Movement," in Maisel ed., *Jews in American Politics*, 195–211.

12. Bruce Murphy, "Neoconservative Clout Seen in U.S. Iraq Policy," *Milwaukee Journal Sentinel* (April 6, 2003), A1.

13. Bill Broadway, "Number of U.S. Muslims Depends on Who's Counting," *Washington Post* (November 24, 2001), A1; Howard Fienberg and Iain Murray, "How Many Muslims in the U.S.? Our Best Estimate," *Christian Science Monitor* (November 29, 2001).

14. Ihsan Bagby, Paul M. Perl, and Bryan T. Froehle, *The Mosque in America: A National Portrait* (Washington, D.C.: CAIR, 2001), 2.

15. For a straightforward introduction to Islam, see John Esposito, *The Oxford History of Islam* (New York: Oxford, 1999) and Ninian Smart, *Atlas of the World's Religions* (New York: Oxford, 1999), 168–197; on Muslims in America, see Jane I. Smith, *Islam in America* (New York: Columbia University Press, 2000); Yvonne Yazbeck Haddad and John Esposito, eds., *Muslims on the Americanization Path?* (New York: Oxford University Press, 2000); Yvonne Yazbeck Haddad and Jane I. Smith, eds., *Muslim Communities in North America* (Albany: State University of New York Press, 1994); Steven Barboza, *American Jihad: Islam After Malcolm X* (New York: Doubleday, 1993); Carla Power, "The New Islam," *Newsweek* (March 16, 1998), 35.

16. Zogby International, American Muslim Council Survey (August 2000). Affiliation reports from Islamic religious centers present slightly different numbers: 33 percent South Asian, 30 percent African American, and 25 percent Arab. See Ihsan Bagby et al., *The Mosque in America*, 3.

17. Peter Skerry, "Not Terrorists, Just Terrified," *Washington Post National Weekly Edition* (January 13–19, 2003), 23.

18. Carla Power, "The New Islam," *Newsweek* (March 16, 1998), 35.

19. "2 Gatherings Reflect U.S. Muslims' Divide," *New York Times* (August 30, 2003), A13.

20. Drummon Ayres, Jr., "The 2000 Campaign: Campaign Briefing" (October 24, 2000), A27.

21. James L. Guth, Lyman A. Kellstedt, John C. Green, and Corwin E. Smidt, "America Fifty/Fifty," *First Things* 116 (October 2001), 19–26.

22. Laurie Goodstein, "Seeing Islam as 'Evil' Faith, Evangelicals Seek Converts," *New York Times* (May 27, 2003), A1.

23. CAIR, "Even A Quick War Has Negative Consequences, Say Muslims," News Release (March 19, 2003); Muslim Public Affairs Council, "Statement on Brink of War," News Release (March 19, 2003).

24. Hannah Rosin, "To Be Arab and American," *Washington Post National Weekly Edition* (November 18–24, 2002), 9–10.

25. See Asma Gull Hasan, *American Muslims: The New Generation,* 2nd ed. (New York: Continuum, 2002).

26. The population figure is from Dale Jones et al., *Religious Congregations and Membership: 2000* (Nashville, TN: Glenmary Research Center, 2002). Data available at http://www.glenmary.org. See also Lucian Niemeyer and Donald Kraybill, *Old Order Amish: The Enduring Way of Life* (Baltimore, MD: Johns Hopkins University Press, 1993); William Kephart and William Zellner, *Extraordinary Groups*, 7th ed. (New York: Worth Publishers, 2001).

27. On cults and topics in the discussion that follows, see Robert Booth Fowler, *The Dance with Community* (Lawrence: University Press of Kansas, 1992), 147–153; David G. Bromley and Anson Shupe, *Strange Gods: The Great American Cult Scare* (Boston: Beacon, 1981), chap. 2; Willa Appel, *Cults in America: Programmed for Paradise* (New York: Holt, Rinehart and Winston, 1983); Ronald Enroth, ed., *A Guide to Cults and New Religions* (Downers Grove, IL: InterVarsity, 1983); Anthony Hoekema, *The Four Major Cults* (Grand Rapids, MI: Eerdmans, 1963); Walter Martin, *The Kingdom of the Cults* (Minneapolis, MN: Bethany, 2002); and J. Gordon Melton and Robert L. Moore, *The Cult Experience: Responding to the New Religious Pluralism* (New York: Pilgrim, 1982).

28. Timothy R. Callahan, "'Boston Movement' Founder Quits," *Christianity Today* (March 2003), 26.

29. "The Messiah of Waco," *Newsweek* (March 15, 1993), 56–58; David Gelman, "From Prophets to Losses," *Newsweek* (March 15, 1993), 62; "Adventists Disavow Waco Cult," *Christian Century* (March 17, 1993), 285–286.

30. The Christian Identity movement is monitored closely by the Southern Poverty Law Center. See *False Patriots: The Threat of Antigovernment Extremists* (Montgomery, AL: Southern Poverty Law Center, 1996); http://www.splcenter.org/intel/map/hate.jsp.

31. On the Unification Church, see Irving Louis Horowitz, ed., *Science, Sin and Scholarship: The Politics of Rev. Moon and the Unification Church* (Cambridge, MA: MIT Press, 1978); Eileen Barker, *The Making of a Moonie: Choice or Brainwashing* (New York: Basil Blackwell, 1984).

32. Lawrence E. Sullivan, ed., *Native American Religions: North America* (New York: Macmillan, 1987).

33. Vine Deloria, Jr., *Custer Died for Your Sins: An Indian Manifesto* (New York: Macmillan, 1969).

34. James Treat, *Around the Sacred Fire: Native Religious Activism in the Red Power Era* (New York: Palgrave Macmillan, 2003).

35. Dale Mason, *Indian Gaming: Tribal Sovereignty and American Politics* (Norman, OK: University of Oklahoma Press, 2000).

36. "Metropolitan Community Churches: Fact Sheet," available at www.mccchurch.org/mediaroom/index.htm.

37. Debra St. John, "Unexpected Participants in Democracy: Refuge, Community, and Activism in a Congregation of the Metropolitan Community Church," Ph.D. Dissertation, University of Oklahoma, 2001.

38. Church of Jesus Christ of Latter-day Saints, "Key Facts and Figures," available at http://www.newsroom.lds.org.

39. Jones et al., *Religious Congregations and Membership: 2000.*

40. For a brief survey of the debate, see Ostling and Ostling, *Mormon America,* chap. 19.

41. Kenneth L. Woodward, "A Mormon Moment," *Newsweek* (September 10, 2001), 44.

42. To begin an exploration of nonmainstream religions, we recommend Kephart and Zellner, *Extraordinary Groups*; and Catherine L. Albanese, *America, Religions and Religion*, 3d ed. (Belmont, CA: Wadsworth, 1998).

43. Andrew Kohut, John C. Green, Scott Keeter, and Robert C. Toth, *The Diminishing Divide: Religion's Changing Role in American Politics* (Washington, D.C.: Brookings, 2000), 152–153.

44. Guth et al., "America Fifty/Fifty."

45. On the Jehovah's Witnesses, see James A. Beckford, *The Triumph of Prophecy* (Oxford: Basil Blackwell, 1975); Robert M. Anderson, *Vision of the Disinherited* (New York: Oxford University Press, 1979); Martin, *The Kingdom of the Cults,* chap. 4; Kephart and Zellner, *Extraordinary Groups,* chap. 8.

46. "Statistics: 2002 Report of Jehovah's Witnesses Worldwide," at http://www.watchtower.org/statistics/worldwide_report.htm. See also Gaustad and Barlow, *New Historical Atlas of Religion in America,* 165–173.

VOTING AND RELIGION IN AMERICAN POLITICS

Throughout American history religious currents have flowed powerfully, defining partisan attachments and shaping voting behavior. In this chapter we chart the voting patterns of the key American religious groups and offer evidence for the existence of value- and religion-based cleavages in the American electorate. Differences among religious groups are as real and politically important now as they ever were in the past. But we caution against exaggerating them. Value conflict does not necessarily make for "culture wars." Some religious activists see themselves engaged in a Kulturkampf against mortal enemies, but most voters do not see things that way. White evangelicals, for example, now align strongly with the Republican Party, but many do not see themselves as members of the "Christian Right." Our overall analysis of religion and voting behavior suggests that the nature and intensity of religion-based cleavages in the electorate have varied widely throughout American history, often due to religion's interaction with a host of other influences on how people vote.

A HISTORICAL REVIEW

Religion has played an important role in national elections in the United States from the beginning. In the first contested presidential campaign (in 1800) Thomas Jefferson's Democratic-Republican Party challenged the Federalists under John Adams. Episcopalians and Congregationalists closely aligned with the status quo Federalists, while Jefferson gained support from Baptists, Methodists, and Presbyterians. Part of this alignment can be traced to the class profiles of these churches: Members of higher-status churches often supported the Federalists, whereas populist upstarts backed Jefferson.

Linked with class, however, was the debate over state establishment of religion. Even though the Constitution prohibited a national religion, several states retained legally established churches. Federalists generally backed such establishment, but the Jeffersonians did not. Religious minorities thus aligned with Jefferson, though he was not particularly religious. During the campaign, in fact, the Federalists mounted attacks accusing Jefferson of rejecting the Christian faith. But Jefferson's beliefs were less important to his supporters than the fact that he was committed to protecting religious minorities and ending government preferences for one faith over others at all levels. Thus Baptists, with their commitment to the separation of church and state, flocked to Jefferson.

After the demise of the Federalist party, a similar division persisted, manifesting itself particularly in the two elections of Andrew Jackson (in 1828 and 1832), who gained the support of more populist churches but not established ones. By 1833, however, all states had disestablished their churches, and the era of formal church establishment in the United States was over.[1]

Immigration of Catholics from Europe, which increased significantly in the 1830s and continued unabated until 1920, resulted in the softening of earlier cleavages between Protestant denominations and the development of something far more durable: a Catholic-Protestant divide. This division profoundly shaped political and voting patterns for more than a century. While Catholics became heavily Democratic, northern Protestants gravitated to their opponents: first the Whigs, then the Republicans. This alignment also shaped partisan positions on important issues. State aid to Catholic parochial schools, a perennial issue in American politics, found its strongest resistance among Republicans, who took their cues from Protestant activists. Moreover, the Republican Party platforms of the late nineteenth and early twentieth centuries contained "strict separationist" planks designed to block Catholic inroads.[2]

The Catholic-Protestant split was not the only way in which religious culture played itself out in nineteenth-century elections and politics. Careful studies by historians suggest that those Protestants least prone to evangelical pietism often joined Catholics in voting Democratic in the nineteenth and early twentieth centuries. Thus one way to understand the division of the electorate was that it pitted pietists against others (sometimes termed ritualists).[3] This religious division, which was also tied to ethnic differences, drew deep and enduring lines on the American political map. The pietists included evangelical Methodists, Baptists, Congregationalists, Presbyterians, and less ritualistic Lutherans. These groups were overwhelmingly Republican in nearly every region from California to Rhode Island. The ritualists included Roman Catholics as well as many Lutherans, who usually voted Democratic.

What distinguished pietists from ritualists were their incompatible visions of the "good life" and the role government ought to play in it. As heirs to the Puritan evangelical spirit, pietists stressed religion's connection with morality. They saw themselves as moral reformers, and they favored active government involvement through laws and policies designed to accomplish their moral ends. Whether the perceived evil was alcoholism, gambling, dueling, or the breaking of the Sabbath, pietists were comfortable bringing their desire to reform society into the public realm (just as modern-day religious moralists of several types favor government regulation of abortion, gambling, pornography, and television violence).

Ritualists, on the other hand, emphasized church liturgies and sacraments, as opposed to moral crusades, in their conception of religion. Compared to pietists, they were more tolerant regarding personal behavior and less likely to support government regulation of morals. This religious and cultural divide between pietists and ritualists was powerful enough to transcend class and immigrant status. In the North, Catholics were Democrats and Methodists were Republicans regardless of their socioeconomic status.[4]

In the South, of course, religious factors were often supplanted by the politics of race and regional pride. During post–Civil War Reconstruction (1865–1877) southern whites saw the Republican Party literally as a conquering army of occupation, and thus whites voted Democratic. African Americans voted overwhelmingly for Republicans, but when southern whites reasserted control of politics in their region, they disenfranchised and otherwise kept African Americans subordinate and made the South solidly Democratic. Thus, despite the fact that the white southern population was heavily Baptist and Methodist, these pietists voted Democratic—unlike their northern counterparts.

The contemporary movement of evangelical Protestants into the Republican fold (beginning in the 1960s and continuing today) represents a return to nineteenth-century patterns. In order to appreciate the significance of this trend, we must examine an important development of the 1930s—Franklin Delano Roosevelt's New Deal coalition. Its breakup has reconfigured religio-political alignments in contemporary America.

The economic upheavals of the Great Depression produced what scholars term a "critical election," resulting in a partisan realignment of voters and creating a relatively stable majority for the new Democratic coalition. Roosevelt's New Deal coalition rested on three interrelated factors: region, class, and religion.[5] A fourth dimension, race, was not a major factor during Roosevelt's time because the northern black electorate, though it became generally Democratic by the mid–1930s, constituted a very small percentage of the total voting population because of the disenfranchisement of southern black voters. Only later did African Americans, securely enfranchised by the Voting Rights Act of 1965, come to represent a major voting bloc.

Roosevelt received his highest vote margins in the solidly Democratic South. The Civil War legacy and the total dominance of the Democratic Party played key roles here. But so did Roosevelt's activist policies regarding the economy; these were popular among many white southerners, the majority of whom were poor evangelical Protestants. The kind of moral cleavages we see today were largely absent from national partisan politics at the time and thus presented few cross-pressures for southern Democrats.[6]

In the rest of the country, too, class cleavages were vital to Roosevelt's fortunes. He was popular with many poor and working-class voters, labor union members, and others of modest means. Much of his appeal to northern pietists (both traditional evangelicals and Pentecostals) flowed from the fact that many of them were far less affluent than their mainline Protestant counterparts. This same kind of appeal brought northern black voters into the New Deal coalition despite their previously longstanding loyalty to the party of Lincoln.

But religious groups were also quite cohesive elements of the New Deal coalition. Catholics at every socioeconomic level were far more likely to identify themselves as Democrats and vote that way than were similarly situated Protestants. Catholics, indeed, constituted one of the central New Deal constituencies.[7] Also solidly aligned with the Democrats under Roosevelt were Jewish voters. In earlier years, many Jews had been Republicans because they viewed the GOP as the more liberal party. With the Depression and Roosevelt, though, they gravitated heavily to the Democratic Party, where most have stayed ever since.[8]

Who, then, opposed Roosevelt? Northern white Protestants (especially those from mainline denominations), wealthier individuals, and traditional Yankee Republicans formed the core of his opposition. Many modest-income Protestants in the North remained loyal to the GOP, especially in more traditional rural areas. The problem for the Republicans, of course, was that this base was too narrow to mount a serious challenge to Democratic Party hegemony. Republican war hero Dwight Eisenhower interrupted that dominance at the presidential level, but Roosevelt's coalition enabled the Democrats to remain the clear majority party at all levels of government until at least 1968.

The point here is that religion was a key factor that combined with socioeconomic status and region to shape voting patterns and political outcomes in the Roosevelt years and for the decades after his death when his coalition remained intact. By the beginning of the twenty-first century, though, the New Deal coalition had crumbled, producing new alignments in which religion has taken a more decisive role.

CONTINUITY AND CHANGE
IN THE POSTINDUSTRIAL ERA

Since the 1960s much about American politics has been fluid and unpredictable. Cross-pressures have strained old loyalties, divisive new cultural issues have fractured the New Deal coalition, and politics itself has alienated an increasing number of American voters. Voting rates are down, partisan loyalties have weakened, and citizen discontent is far greater than in 1960. Some scholars attribute these phenomena to the nature of postindustrial society.[9] Traditional class-based and ethnic differences have given way to lifestyle differences and disputes over moral issues.[10] Religious currents, not surprisingly, play a large part in shaping the politics surrounding these issues. In order to understand how this is so, we analyze the evolving political attitudes and voting behavior of the major American religious groups.

Today about 50 to 55 percent of the adult population vote in a presidential election year; less than 40 percent vote in off-year congressional elections. The typical religious breakdown of the electorate is usually about 25 percent Catholic, 25 percent evangelical Protestant, 20 percent (and perhaps less) mainline Protestant, 15 percent (and probably more) secular, with the remaining 15 percent including black Christians, Jews, Mormons, Muslims, and other small groups. Some differences exist among religious groups in terms of their comparative levels of representation in the voting public. While 82 percent of Jews voted in the 2000 general elections, for example, only 53 percent of African American Protestants and 30 percent of Latino Christians turned out.[11] Hence some religious groups have clout in elections that may be out of proportion to their actual size.

ROMAN CATHOLICS: BELLWETHER GROUP

We know that from the middle of the nineteenth century through the 1960s Democrats could count on the votes of a large majority of Catholics. Indeed, white Catholics provided more than a third of the total Democratic presidential vote during the New Deal and in later eras.[12] The cultural divide between Catholics and Protestants continued to be a strong predictor of partisan voting through the early 1960s, especially when Catholic voters were directly mobilized. This happened most recently when Catholic John Kennedy received the Democratic presidential nomination in 1960. His candidacy electrified the Catholic world, and he received an overwhelming 80 percent of the votes of declared Roman Catholics. His candidacy also provoked some intense Protestant opposition. Both mainline and evangelical leaders expressed fears about having a Catholic in the White House. Would his loyalties be divided? Would he be under pressure to take directions from the Vatican? As a Catholic, how could he serve the entire American population? Anti-Catholic tracts appeared by the thousands, reminiscent of nineteenth-century broadsides against "Romanism" and "papists."[13]

In spite of Kennedy's adroit handling of the religious issue, his Catholicism nearly cost him the election. Gains among Catholic voters were more than offset by losses among the larger group of Protestant Democrats, particularly in border states, but also in places as different as Pennsylvania, New Mexico, California, and Wisconsin.[14] Kennedy probably lost about 1.5 million votes because of his religion.[15] His razor-thin margin of 100,000 votes could have vanished easily had he not personally blunted at least some anti-Catholic prejudice. In the end, however, Kennedy's presidency and assassination, coupled with changes in the Catholic Church after Vatican II, appear to have put to rest the deep cleavage between Catholics and Protestants that existed for over a century in American politics.

Kennedy's election represented the high-water mark for the loyalty of Catholic voters to the Democratic Party. This loyalty has trailed off notably since 1960. Catholics are now less Democratic for many of the same reasons that reduced Catholic-Protestant tension. Catholics today have largely integrated into the larger society and no longer feel the slightest tension with it or with the Protestant majority. Most Catholics are well educated, and most have joined the middle class. Most have moved out of ethnic enclaves to the suburbs, where they have often sent their children to public schools. Many are now Republicans. Moreover, cross-cutting issues—such as some Catholics' opposition to abortion—have chipped away at Catholic support for the Democratic Party. But Catholics have not rushed en masse into the Republican camp either. On a number of social welfare issues Catholics remain more liberal than either mainline Protestants or evangelicals. Often Catholic voters are clearly not happy with the direction of either the Democratic Party or the GOP. They have become the quintessential swing voters.

An evaluation of Catholic voting patterns over the last three decades confirms that the majority of the Catholic vote is up for grabs in any given election. In 1980 and 1984 Ronald Reagan won increasing shares of the white Catholic vote from his Democratic opponents; his 57 percent majority in 1984 led some commentators to believe that a permanent Catholic realignment was occurring, a belief reinforced by George Bush's 56 percent of the white Catholic vote in the 1988 election.[16] Republican presidential candidates, however, did worse among Catholic voters in 1992 and 1996, when Bill Clinton reversed the slide toward the Republicans. The picture was muddied in 1992 and 1996, however, by the independent candidacy of H. Ross Perot, who attracted 22 percent of the Catholic vote in 1992 and kept Clinton from winning a majority of the popular vote in either election. In the 2000 election, the white Catholic electorate nearly evenly split its vote in the head-to-head matchup of George W. Bush and Al Gore, with Bush getting a slight edge of 53 percent (Box 4.1).[17]

**BOX 4.1 MEASURING RELIGION AND
POLITICS: A SPECIAL CHALLENGE**

Although scientific surveys are a reasonably reliable way of gathering information about the ways religious believers think and believe politically, it is important to be aware that they are not always precise. There is some error in all surveys, and how social scientists determine whom to ask questions and what questions to ask can have a big impact on results.

Measurement of religion is especially challenging. The best ways to determine religious affiliation, religious commitment, and the role of religion in politics are matters of great debate among researchers. In addition, no survey could ever do full justice to the bewildering religious diversity in the United States. The point is that while vote choices and other beliefs and behaviors are often reported as cold, hard facts, there is good reason to be cautious about these results.

Clinton and then Gore won a majority of Catholic votes in some key states in the 1992, 1996, and 2000 elections, but that support did not approach New Deal levels, and it was complex and conditional. In 2000, for example, many Catholic voters were drawn to Gore's emphasis on issues that were also of interest to many voters in the electorate at large. On the other hand, three-quarters of white "traditionalist" Catholics—those who are most devout and who adhere to the teachings of the Vatican—supported George W. Bush.[18] Fifty-nine percent of Catholic clergy also voted for Bush, compared to 32 percent for Gore (even though 48 percent claim to be Democrats or at least lean in that direction, compared to 31 percent leaning or solidly Republican).[19] As we see in Table 4.1, generational cleavages are also evident among Catholics today that may presage the future of American Catholic voting behavior. Older Catholics were more likely to identify with the party of Roosevelt in 2000, while younger Catholics (especially males) turned to Bush in the presidential election and to Republican candidates for the House of Representatives. Gender also matters among Catholic voters. Catholic women are more likely than Catholic men to be Democrats.[20] Clearly, Catholics remain a voting constituency that cannot be taken for granted by either party at the presidential level.

One of the most important recent trends in Catholic America has been the growth of the nonwhite Catholic population (especially Hispanics, but also African Americans, 4 percent of whom are now Roman Catholic). In 1960 the Catholic electorate was largely white, but by the 2000s nonwhites constituted about one-quarter of all Catholic voters.

TABLE 4.1 Presidential Votes, Congressional Votes, and Party Identification of Catholics by Age, 2000

	Bush	Gore	Democratic House Vote	Republican Party ID	Democratic Party ID
All	54	46	45	39	42
18-39	65	35	33	47	40
40-58	51	49	46	33	43
59+	50	50	51	38	43

Source: University of Akron, 2000 National Survey of Religion and Politics. Analysis courtesy of John C. Green, University of Akron (via personal communication).

TABLE 4.2 Presidential Votes, Congressional Votes, and Party Identification of Catholics by Race, 2000

	Bush	Gore	Democratic House Vote	Republican Party ID	Democratic Party ID
All	49	51	51	35	46
White	54	46	45	39	43
Latino	24	76	72	25	57
Black	22	78	100	9	79

Source: University of Akron, 2000 National Survey of Religion and Politics. Analysis courtesy of John C. Green, University of Akron (via personal communication).

Nonwhite Catholics (with the exception of Asian Americans) are far more Democratic in their voting loyalties than are their white counterparts. Thus their growing numbers have masked a serious slide in white Catholic support for Democratic presidential and congressional candidates, as we see in Table 4.2.[21]

The significance here again is that white Catholics, once a mainstay of the Democratic Party, have become a critical swing constituency. They divide largely as the national population does in any given election. It is not surprising, then, that white Catholics have become something of a bellwether group in the American electorate. Comprising a quarter of the electorate, they are sandwiched between white Protestants, who are disproportionately Republican, and African Americans, Jews, and secular voters, who are disproportionately Democratic. White Catholics, at least for now, seem to be the median American voting group.

One of the reasons for the swing character of the Catholic vote is that many Catholic views do not fit neatly with those of either of the two major American political parties. Table 4.3 elaborates on the issue positions of Catholics (as well as other religious groups), giving us a sense of the distinctiveness of the Catholic electorate. Catholics are fairly liberal on a number of issues, no matter how often they attend church. Regularly attending Catholics are more likely to support government health insurance and policies to fight hunger and poverty than either mainline or evangelical Protestants. But on abortion, regularly attending Catholics are more conservative than their counterparts in mainline Protestant churches. Thus Republican policies on the economy and health care alienate many Catholics as do liberal Democratic views on abortion.

This leads us to question whether there is good reason to speak of the "Catholic vote" at all. As we have seen, there are Republican Catholics, Democratic Catholics, many swing voter Catholics, involved and uninvolved Catholics, Catholics very committed to their church's policy positions and those who oppose some or all of them, Catholics loyal to the institutional church and those disillusioned with it. It is not at all clear that there is any coherent group of "Catholics" by any standard except self-definition. The voting behavior of Catholics, which so clearly parallels the divisions in the larger electorate, appears to reflect this simple fact.[22]

EVANGELICAL PROTESTANTS: A PIETIST REVIVAL FOR THE GOP

Two momentous developments in the evangelical world have influenced the voting behavior and party alignment of evangelical Protestants. The first has been the growth of evangelical churches over the past several decades and the corresponding decline of mainline denominations. In 1960, over 40 percent of all white adults claimed membership in mainline denominations, compared with only 27 percent in evangelical churches. Today, however, mainline affiliation is barely equal to an evangelical membership that is one-quarter of the population. Moreover, since regular church attendance and other measures of commitment are lower in mainline churches than in evangelical ones, this estimate exaggerates the number of people who are actually in-

TABLE 4.3 Issue Positions by Religious Tradition and Frequency of Attendance at Religious Services, 2000

	Evangelical Protestant		Mainline Protestant		Black Protestant		Roman Catholic		Jews	Secular
	High	Low	High	Low	High	Low	High	Low		
Abortion: Solely woman's choice	12	39	34	41	30	54	11	19	58	51
Support equal rights for homosexuals	37	58	55	67	53	79	62	74	58	72
Government should do more to fight poverty / hunger	42	47	45	42	58	62	52	47	63	46
Support national health insurance	29	42	35	37	46	53	41	46	51	50
Need strict environmental rules	40	54	57	59	46	29	52	57	66	55
Government should provide school vouchers	48	42	33	32	49	51	53	41	29	33
Government should fund faith-based social services	40	49	40	37	63	68	52	46	29	37

Source: University of Akron, 2000 National Religion and Politics Survey. Analysis courtesy of Corwin Smidt, Calvin College (via personal communication).

volved in mainline church life. Evangelical Protestants are increasingly becoming the strategic center of American politics.

The second development has been the growing alignment of evangelical Protestants with the Republican Party—a development made all the more significant by their numerical growth. These two developments have altered the dynamics of internal GOP politics dramatically. The old Republican Party was an alliance of business interests and mainline Protestants, but the new GOP also relies heavily on evangelicals.[23] As a result, politics in the Democratic Party has also changed, particularly by solidifying Jewish and secular support for Democrats.[24]

For much of the twentieth century many Baptists, Pentecostals, and other evangelicals were Democrats, in spite of general Protestant loyalty to the Republican Party. Many evangelicals, especially conservative Baptists and Methodists, lived in the South, where loyalty to the Democratic Party reflected the Civil War legacy of opposition to the party of Lincoln. Second, a class dimension reinforced Democratic tendencies among evangelicals. During the New Deal era, for example, lower-status Protestants (who were usually evangelical) were more likely to vote for Roosevelt than upper-class Protestants, who tended to belong to the theologically liberal mainline denominations. Thus Pentecostals, independent Baptists, and other evangelicals were quite a bit more likely to be Democrats than were Presbyterians, Episcopalians, United Methodists, and Congregationalists.

Things began to change in the 1960s. Many southern Protestants began voting Republican at the presidential level at the same time that the Democratic Party was embracing new agendas. The 1960s and 1970s introduced a new kind of cultural politics, associated with the counterculture, the sexual revolution, newly legalized abortion, women's rights, and gay rights. As liberalism—and by extension the Democratic Party—became associated in some minds with alternative lifestyles, "loose morality," and indifference to traditional religion, Republicans made sizable gains among conservative Protestants.

Jimmy Carter, a born-again Baptist from the South, temporarily stalled the transition of evangelical voters into the Republican Party with his 1976 presidential victory. Analysts concluded that Carter probably did better at the polls among evangelicals than he did among mainline Protestants.[25] But many evangelicals later felt betrayed by Carter's liberal presidency, and simmering cultural forces combined to bring about the emergence of an activist "New Christian Right" on the eve of the 1980 presidential election. Ronald Reagan courted the evangelical constituency, and they proved a major factor in his 1980 victory over Carter.

The real story is the solidifying Republican alignment of evangelicals. Though the born-again vote was indistinguishable from the overall white Protestant vote in 1980, evangelicals have become increasingly more Republican since then. By 1988, George Bush garnered over 80 percent of the evangelical vote. In 1992 and 1996, a Southern Baptist, Bill Clinton, sat atop the Democratic ticket, as did his fellow Southern Baptist, Al Gore, in 2000. Yet neither Clinton nor Gore attracted much support at the polls from white evangelicals in any of their election campaigns. In fact, over three-quarters of white evangelicals voted for George W. Bush in 2000, with regular church-attenders giving him 85 percent of their votes.[26] Today the importance of the evangelical constituency to the Republican Party is well recognized and Republican get-out-the-vote drives target the evangelical constituency.

Evidence for evangelical realignment may be found in generational trends in voting and party affiliation, as we see in Table 4.4. It is younger evangelical voters who have become the most solidly Republican. Nearly two-thirds (64 percent) of all evangelical voters under 40 identify with the Republican Party, as do 54 percent of evangelical voters between the ages of 40 and 58. It is particularly noteworthy that only 46 percent of evangelicals over the age of 60 identify themselves as Republicans. Another indication of true realignment is voting behavior in races below the presidential level, starting with the 1994 elections.[27] In 2000, House Democrats received only 26 percent of the evangelical vote, with younger evangelicals providing only 19 percent and the over-60 group contributing 36 percent. As the older generation is gradually replaced, therefore, we expect to see even higher levels of Republican identification and voting loyalty among evangelicals.

It is important to note that the term "evangelical" is not synonymous with the "Christian Right." Indeed, many evangelicals do not support the rhetoric or agenda of today's major Christian Right interest groups, such as the Family Research Council, just as many did not align themselves with Rev. Jerry Falwell and the Moral Majority in the 1980s. Sometimes religious differences among evangelicals have made mobilization difficult. Many Southern Baptists, for example, look askance at Pentecostal practices and have not been thrilled to see Robertson's charismatic followers flooding Republican Party meetings. Realignment, therefore, has brought a series of different (and sometimes competing) evangelical groups into the Republican fold.

Although many contemporary evangelicals vote Republican for economic reasons, a strong element of cultural conservatism is clearly behind the evangelical-Republican marriage. Table 4.3 shows, for example, that evangelicals are conservative among American voters on a host of issues,

TABLE 4.4 Presidential Votes, Congressional Votes, and Party Identification of White Evangelicals by Age, 2000

	Bush	Gore	Democratic House Vote	Republican Party ID	Democratic Party ID
All	74	26	26	55	31
18-39	81	19	19	64	27
40-58	77	23	26	46	29
59+	63	38	36	55	41

Source: University of Akron, 2000 National Survey of Religion and Politics. Analysis courtesy of John C. Green, University of Akron (via personal communication).

from abortion and gay rights to healthcare reform and defense. Evangelical clergy, too, are most likely to be politically active (and Republican partisans) when they are cultural conservatives.[28] Unlike the electorate as a whole, evangelicals rank the social nexus of abortion and family values as more important than economic issues. Moreover, the salience of social issues is even higher for frequent church attendees and among middle-aged citizens, who are often involved in raising children—and who are most likely to vote.[29] The salience of these issues has only increased over time, and it will likely continue to do so. Indeed, the explosive issue of same-sex marriage, which cuts to the core of conservative evangelical concerns about the status of the family, may also reinforce evangelicalism's place within the Republican Party, which has been largely unified in opposition to legalizing gay marriage.[30]

MAINLINE PROTESTANTS: NO LONGER SOLIDLY REPUBLICAN

Unlike the realigned voting behavior of their evangelical counterparts, some continuity is evident in the voting behavior of white mainline Protestants. Methodists, Presbyterians, Episcopalians, Congregationalists, and northern Baptists continue to tilt toward the Republicans, just as they have for more than a century.[31] But this continuity is set in a context of three key changes. First, as we discussed in Chapter 2, a decline in membership and attendance in the mainline denominations have occurred. This decline has decreased the relative importance of the mainline to the Republican Party.

Second, the mainline's decline has paralleled an increase in the number of voters who may be considered almost entirely secular and who seldom attend church but who continue to identify nominally with a mainline denomination. As we discuss in the next section, the politics of such individuals are often different from those more religiously committed. Recent analysis suggests that although faithful mainline attendees remain more Republican than Democrat, many nominal mainline Protestants, like the growing secular segment of the electorate, lean Democratic.[32]

The third change has been an increase in Democratic adherence among even the committed mainline Protestants. While movement in this direction is strongest among mainline clergy, who are solidly Democratic and liberal across the range of issues, increases in Democratic affiliation have also been significant among ordinary mainliners as well, who now are becoming more liberal on social issues, even as they remain moderately conservative on economic issues.[33] Voting patterns in the presidential elections, as displayed in Table 4.5, reflect these changes in party affiliation. The 1992 presidential election, in which nearly of a quarter of the white mainline vote went to third party candidate Ross Perot, was a turning point. The GOP's share of the white mainline vote, which had not dipped below 60 percent in any of the six preceding elections, fell to just over 40 percent in 1992. Though nearly half of mainliners voted Republican in 2000, the percentage is still well below historical levels.

In a sense, like Catholic voters, mainline Protestants have become something of a swing constituency. The "traditionalist" mainline adherents remain solidly Republican, having cast 75 percent of their votes for George W. Bush in 2000. On the other hand, there are the "modernist" mainline Protestants, of whom barely half preferred Bush over Gore. This split is evident in congressional voting patterns as well.[34]

Church attendance is an increasingly important part of this gap between traditionalists and modernists. Though self-reporting may inflate actual attendance at religious services, the relative differences between groups are huge and the political implications are very real. White evangelicals attend services most frequently, followed by white Catholics and African American Christians. Trailing far behind are white mainline Protestants and Jews. Frequent attendees who are white, whether Catholic, mainline Protestant, or evangelical, are more likely to vote Republican than their counterparts

TABLE 4.5 Presidential Votes of White Mainline Protestants, 1968–2000

	Democrat	Republican	Independent
1968	26.8	64.6	8.6
1972	27.7	71.9	0.4
1976	37.7	61.2	1.1
1980	30.0	61.5	8.5
1984	28.1	70.4	1.5
1988	36.4	63.3	0.4
1992	35.5	40.7	23.8
1996	45.9	47.1	6.9
2000	47.7	49.8	2.5

SOURCE: National Elections Studies, 1968–2000. Analysis courtesy of John C. Green, University of Akron (via personal communication).

who attend religious services less frequently. They are also more likely to call themselves conservative. These differences have led many commentators to note a "new religion gap" defined not by traditional religious affiliations but rather by high levels of religious observance.[35]

Even so, attitudinal differences can be observed among different religious traditions on key political issues. On abortion, for example, mainline Protestants as a whole are more liberal than evangelicals and Roman Catholics. On the other hand, mainline Protestants take a more conservative position on universal government healthcare than do either Catholics or African American Protestants. Thus, whereas the Democrats reflect mainline sentiments on abortion, Republicans embrace their position on health care. In short, mainline Protestants are cross-pressured in almost exactly the opposite direction as white Catholics, who tend to be conservative on abortion but liberal on healthcare and the environment.

THE SECULAR VOTE: A GROWING DEMOCRATIC STRONGHOLD

In 1960, Americans were decidedly a society of churchgoers. The Democrats depended on churchgoing Catholics and some evangelicals (especially in the South) to offset Republican strength among most Protestant faithful. Only a small percentage of the population claimed no religious preference, and this group's voting rates were relatively low compared to those of the church-based population. Thus secular citizens had a negligible influence on American elections.

By the 2000s, however, an increasing number of Americans were claiming no religious affiliation. They combine with infrequent attendees to create a sizable secular and near-secular portion of the voting population. The size and nature of this secular group are not entirely clear, though analysts agree that it has grown substantially over the past three decades. Estimates of its size today range from 15 to 30 percent of the electorate; differences are dependent upon how one defines the term "secular." In the past, survey researchers included only the 10 percent of the electorate who indicated they embrace no religion. Yet there are also voters who list a religious affiliation but never attend church and otherwise show little indication of religious commitment; they are only nominally religious. Many scholars, therefore, believe that such people should be counted as part of the secular group along with those who list no religious preference. Others resist conflating weak religionists with nonreligionists. Andrew Greeley, for example, argues that lapsed Catholics retain something of the Catholic culture and are therefore distinct from truly secular voters. Mainline Protestant leaders, similarly, might claim that attending at childhood Sunday school classes will continue to influence the values of adults who have nevertheless stopped going to church.

It is not necessary for us to sort all of this out. Instead, we can suggest a profile of secular voters, however defined, as socially liberal and economically moderate voters who lean Democratic, but are also diverse and volatile as a group. Some secularists are libertarian in their political inclinations and would vote for Republican candidates who emphasize limited government and who would shy away from social conservatism on issues such as abortion. Many other secularists have moved toward the Democrats in the past several years.

With the apparent growth in its size, the secular portion of the electorate is likely to be courted more assiduously in the future. Unlike any religious group in the United States, however, secularists have no shared institution or tradition tying them together. As such they may be a difficult portion of the electorate for candidates to reach. Still, the Democratic Party has been attracting more of the secularist electorate than the Republicans have since at least the 1970s. Indeed, one recent study suggests that party loyalists at Democratic conventions since 1972 have been remarkably secularist compared to their Republican counterparts.[36] In addition, the voting gap between white secularists and traditional religionists in the 2000 election was larger than differences in education, gender, income, age, and numerous other factors.[37]

Even so, do secularists present a coherent and cohesive religion-oriented political agenda? Or are they simply indifferent to religion and thus have little to tell us about the relationship between religion and politics? The evidence suggests that there may be some unity among secularists, at least in terms of their opposition to a public role for certain forms of traditional religion. Surveys of voters in the 2000 elections, for example, indicated secularist disapproval of Christian fundamentalists at much higher levels than any other group, leading Louis Bolce and Gerald De Maio to observe that such "antipathy" toward a religious group has not been witnessed since the Catholic-Protestant conflicts of the pre-New Deal era.[38] And nearly three-quarters of these secularists voted for Al Gore, suggesting a strong link between the Democratic Party and the secular electorate.

These trends have raised some concerns among Democrats itself, many of whom fear that secularism within the party may alienate the important religious vote.[39] Some religious elites have voiced similar concerns.[40] In any event, the emergence of a discernable secular voting bloc within the Democratic Party, coupled with the increasing integration of conservative white evangelicals and other religionists into the Republican Party, might portend greater polarization along partisan lines in the future.

JEWS, LIBERALISM, AND DEMOCRATIC LOYALTY

In one sense American Jews have always been in the vanguard of a secular vision of American politics. The vast majority of Jews in the United States are liberals who celebrate the Enlightenment ideal of the nonsectarian state. Thus most behave like secular voters, are very socially liberal, and show loyalty to the Democratic Party. Their commitment to liberalism extends beyond the social realm to encompass civil rights, the welfare state, and economic issues.

Jewish voters remain one of the true paradoxes of American politics. It is only a slight exaggeration to say that, although they look like Episcopalian Republicans in socioeconomic status, they vote more like African American Democrats. Here we see the impact of a kind of value-based voting that is independent of social class. And in this case, the values are liberal ones, since, as Lee Sigelman puts it, liberalism constitutes a kind of lay religion among American Jews.[41] Jews are among the most liberal of all American voting groups and are far more likely than other citizens to describe themselves as liberals, despite the fact that the "L-word" has taken on such negative connotations that many Democrats now shun it.

This commitment to liberal ideals helps explain the loyalty of many Jews to the Democratic Party. Jewish Democratic loyalty solidified during the New Deal (during which Roosevelt received an estimated 85 percent of the Jewish vote),[42] continued through the 1960s (when Kennedy, Johnson, and Humphrey each also received over 80 percent), and remains to this day. In 2000, Al Gore received 77 percent of the votes of Jewish Americans, percentages that were even higher among rabbis.[43]

Beginning in the mid–1970s, however, Republicans began to see opportunities for making inroads into the Jewish community and attempted to co-opt some of the Jewish activism and financial support that have been mainstays of the Democratic Party. As we see in Table 4.6, these hopes sometimes were realized. Republican hopes for further gains among Jewish voters in the 1980s were buoyed by Ronald Reagan's strong pro-Israel outlook and the rise of Rev. Jesse Jackson in the Democratic Party, which produced a good deal of anxiety among Jews who believed him to be hostile to the cause of Jews in Israel and elsewhere.

But these Republican hopes proved futile in the long run. One reason was that Jackson did not receive the Democratic nomination in 1984 or 1988, which allayed Jewish fears. Moreover, no clear partisan lines were ever drawn on support for Israel. The Reagan and Bush administrations were not always uncritical of Israel, and many Democratic leaders, in spite of Jackson's efforts, remained steadfast in their support for it. But most important, the increasingly evident Republican ties to evangelical Protestants activated ever-present Jewish fears of anti-Semitism, as did Patrick Buchanan's campaigns for the Republican nomination in the 1990s.

TABLE 4.6 Presidential Votes of Jews, 1976–2000

	Democrat	Republican	Independent
1976	64	36	--
1980	45	39	15 (Anderson)
1984	67	31	--
1988	64	35	--
1992	80	11	9 (Perot)
1996	78	16	3 (Perot)
2000	79	19	1 (Nader)

Source: Ira N. Forman, "The Politics of Minority Consciousness: The Historical Voting Behavior of American Jews," in L. Sandy Maisel, *Jews in American Politics* (Lanham, MD: Rowman and Littlefield, 2001), 153.

Bill Clinton, on the other hand, skillfully touched on issues that lie close to Jewish concerns—tolerance, civil rights, an activist welfare system—and he did better among Jews than had any Democratic presidential candidate since 1968. In 1992 George Bush won a paltry 11 percent of the Jewish vote, and Bob Dole netted 16 percent in 1996. George W. Bush received 19 percent in the 2000 presidential election against Al Gore. Evidence of the continuing Democratic loyalty among Jewish voters was also present in the 1994, 1998, and 2002 midterm congressional elections. Jewish voting in those elections ran strongly against the national Republican tide, though the GOP did manage to garner 35 percent of the Jewish vote in 2002, significantly better than its past performance.[44]

Contemporary politics, however, may present other opportunities for Republican gains within the Jewish electorate. The concern of Jewish Americans over Israel's security has been heightened since the attacks of September 11, 2001, and some Jews have begun to see the GOP as more responsive to this concern than the Democratic Party.[45] Moreover, some Jews, especially some adherents of Orthodox Judaism, share the moral attitudes of traditional Christians and have already been voting Republican in the past few elections.

But past Republican efforts suggest that such opportunities can be overstated. The Orthodox, for example, compose only a small portion of the Jewish population. In addition, despite vigorous attempts by Republican leaders to court the broader Jewish community in the 1980s, and despite a sustained effort by vocal Jewish neoconservatives to dismantle traditional Jewish liberalism, Jewish voters have not abandoned the Democratic Party. They remain firmly on one side of the cultural divide.

AFRICAN AMERICAN AND LATINO CHRISTIANS

African Americans in the United States are overwhelmingly Christian and mostly evangelical. Well over half of all African Americans, for example, consider themselves born-again Christians and biblical literalists.[46] Moreover, religious salience is quite high in the African American community. Nine out of ten (more than in any other demographic or ethnic group) say that religion is important in their lives and a majority say they attend worship services weekly.[47]

Though a great many African Americans are evangelicals, they are also decidedly Democratic in their voting behavior. As is the case with the voting behavior of American Jews, African American voters are paradoxical. Their paradox differs substantively from that of their Jewish counterparts, however. Part of the African American paradox may be explained by the uniquely American tradition of black Christianity, which blends evangelical pietism with prophetic and liberationist messages. African American churches were, and are, infused with a keenly visceral understanding of the biblical narratives of captivity and freedom, of God's judgment on oppressors, and succor for the downtrodden. Many African American Christians, and especially their clergy, see themselves as chosen carriers of God's prophetic message of justice to a troubled land. What this means is that black voters often combine religious and moral traditionalism with decided support for government welfare policies. Thus black voters surpass white voters in their support for school choice and school prayer and are less liberal than Jews, secularists, and mainline white Protestants on abortion. Yet they are far more liberal than other groups in their support for government jobs programs, health care, civil rights, and affirmative action.

This blend of issue positions often receives little attention in voting studies of African Americans because what really seems to matter most is their almost monolithic (90 percent or so) support for the Democratic Party. African Americans have been loyal to the Democratic Party because of its support for the civil rights revolution of the 1960s and also because it remains committed to state-sponsored welfare and affirmative action.

Black church life, however, is also important for political behavior in ways that aggregate voting studies cannot capture. First, because the church is the central social institution in the African American community, it has traditionally been a focus for political organizing, voter registration drives, and overt campaigning. Unlike most white clergy, some African American pastors invite political candidates to speak to their congregations from the pulpit. Some also endorse specific candidates at election time. The church is, in a sense, often the precinct for black politics. Rev. Jesse Jackson's two presidential drives were church-based, with leadership, mobilization, and fundraising centered in church and congregational networks. Other Democrats now routinely campaign in black churches. No wonder that in the African American community, church membership connects people to politics, and it also increases voter turnout.[48] Black church members are far more likely to vote than nonmembers. And contrary to the pattern for whites, higher church attendance is correlated with increased identification with the Democratic Party. Thus church life is positively linked to Democratic support.

Another important development has been the expansion of the black portion of the electorate. From the 1970s through the early 2000s, African Americans cast about 90 percent of their ballots for Democratic presidential candidates, with Al Gore receiving an astounding 97 percent of the black Protestant vote in the 2000 election.[49] But this tells us nothing about the relative size of that portion of the electorate and its impact on national politics. Though the Voting Rights Act of 1965 officially ended the systematic disenfranchisement of African American voters, its promise was not fully realized until the mid–1980s, when black registration figures mushroomed, especially in the South. Though many organizations played a part in the registration effort, African American churches were crucial to the galvanizing of the black portion of the electorate. The growing number of African American voters profoundly altered the political calculi of numerous political figures. It has also enhanced the clout of black leaders in the Democratic Party.[50]

There is a final sense in which African American religious conviction has implications for politics. Because of their views on certain issues—

school prayer, abortion, gay rights, school vouchers—African American evangelicals are being courted by white religious conservatives as potential allies in their culture war against "secular elites." These efforts are based on the premise that even though African Americans vote for Democrats, alienation from secular trends may lead more African Americans to the Republican Party. Even increasing the Republican share of African Americans' votes from 10 percent to 20 percent would change the fortunes of many Republican congressional candidates. But Republican inroads have been hampered not just by the continued temptation of candidates and consultants from both parties to activate issues that play on racial fears. Also important have been the tight connections between African American religious—and secular—elites and the Democratic Party.

Like African Americans, Latinos in the United States combine a deep consciousness of racial and ethnic identity with high levels of religiosity. Ninety-five percent claim a religious affiliation; nearly 40 percent say they are "born-again" (including nearly a quarter of Catholic Latinos); and three-quarters find religion a significant source of guidance in their lives. Religious affiliation and commitment among Latinos account for a certain degree of social conservatism, with large majorities supporting school vouchers and school prayer, for example. But, as we might expect, on many issues related to immigration and economics, Latinos lean to the left of the ideological spectrum .[51]

The most important religious distinction within the Latino community is, on the surface, a familiar one: Catholic and Protestant. Seventy percent of Latinos are Catholics, but the high percentage is due in part to recent immigration from Mexico and other traditionally Catholic countries. Some second- and third-generation Latino Americans are leaving the Catholic Church and finding new church homes within Pentecostalism and other branches of Protestant evangelicalism. Within the Catholic Church itself, nearly a quarter of all Latinos claim to be charismatics.

The distinction between Protestant and Catholic Latinos appears to explain some significant differences in partisan voting. In the 2000 presidential election, Gore received nearly 70 percent of the Latino Catholic vote, but only 50 percent of Latino Protestants gave him the nod. The gap is even more pronounced in the 2002 congressional elections, in which GOP candidates received 56 percent of the total Latino Protestant vote, while garnering only 28 percent from Latino Catholics.[52]

These percentages can be misleading. They may simply reflect changes as Latinos have become established in American society. As their socioeconomic status has improved, some Latinos have gravitated toward the Republican Party—and perhaps toward Protestantism as well. But even when we account for income and education of voters in recent elections, religion is a key guide to Latino voting behavior.

CONCLUSION

Our analysis in this chapter suggests that, although conflict over religious values clearly exists within the American electorate, it is not always so divisive, nor so neatly defined, as some commentators suggest. To be sure, some voters consciously view themselves as combatants in a war over the culture, with religious traditionalists pitted against a coalition of liberal Christians, Jews, and secularists.[53] But most voters do not see the world in ideological terms, nor do they vote that way. Many mainline Protestants still vote Republican, even though they are strongly prochoice on abortion, and many Catholics still vote Democratic, even though they are prolife. And the majority of African Americans are born-again Christians, yet they remain loyal Democrats. The cultural divide is not neat.

Still, religious belief and commitment clearly foster value conflict in the electorate and, under some circumstances, it can shape ideological and partisan alignments as well. Among whites, for example, as church attendance increases, the Republican advantage increases, regardless of tradition. Moreover, orthodox religionists—whether Protestant or Catholic, Jewish or African American—tend to be more conservative on social issues than are their theologically liberal counterparts. And with the notable exception of African Americans, they are more Republican than their liberal sisters and brothers.

The increasing role of church attendance as a guide to partisan attachments has led some observers to wonder if a European-style party alignment is emerging in the United States, pitting a Christian conservative party (the Republicans) against a more secular, liberal party (the Democrats).[54] There are some problems, however, with such speculation. Many voters, such as socially liberal mainline Republicans and culturally conservative Catholic Democrats, do not fit this paradigm. Moreover, the most loyally Democratic constituency, African Americans, is strongly Christian and church-rooted. The same pattern holds for many Hispanic Catholics.

What does emerge from this analysis is that value-based voting occurs in American politics, and religious beliefs play a vital role in producing those values. At the beginning of the twenty-first century, there is no doubt that religion remains a defining characteristic in how we participate in American political life.

FURTHER READING

Guth, James, Lyman A. Kellstedt, John C. Green, and Corwin E. Smidt. "America Fifty/Fifty," *First Things* (October 2001), 19–26. A stimulating reflection on the place of religion in the controversial 2000 presidential elections.

Layman, Geoffrey. *The Great Divide: Religious and Cultural Conflict in American Party Politics* (New York: Columbia University Press, 2001). A provocative examination of the changing role of religion and culture in American voting patterns.

Menendez, Albert. *Religion at the Polls*. Philadelphia: Westminster, 1977. The classic study of religious voting in American politics.

Pew Research Center for the People and the Press, *Evenly Divided and Increasingly Polarized: 2004 Political Landscape*. Washington, D.C.: Pew Research Center, 2003. A premier polling organization looks at contemporary partisan divisions, with attention to the role of religion.

Reichley, A. James. *Faith in Politics*. Washington, D.C.: Brookings Institution, 2002. In a rich book, a good discussion of the voting behaviors of various religious groupings in historical perspective.

NOTES

1. Allen D. Hertzke, *Echoes of Discontent: Jesse Jackson, Pat Robertson, and the Resurgence of Populism* (Washington, D.C.: CQ Press, 1993), 3.

2. On the subject of Catholics and the Republican Party during this period, see A. James Reichley, *Faith in Politics* (Washington, D.C.: Brookings Institution, 2002).

3. See Paul Kleppner, *Continuity and Change in Electoral Politics, 1893–1928* (Westport, CT: Greenwood, 1987), and *The Cross of Culture: A Social Analysis of Midwestern Politics, 1850–1900* (New York: Free Press, 1970).

4. Robert Booth Fowler, *Religion and Politics in America* (Metuchen, NJ: Scarecrow Press, 1985), chap. 3.

5. For an excellent summary of the New Deal coalition, see Everett Ladd Jr. with Charles D. Hadley, *Transformations of the American Party System: Political Coalitions from the New Deal to the 1970s*, 2d ed. (New York: W. W. Norton, 1975).

6. Lyman A. Kellstedt, John C. Green, James L. Guth, and Corwin E. Smidt, "Has Godot Finally Arrived? Religion and Realignment," in John C. Green, James L. Guth, Corwin E. Smidt, and Lyman A. Kellstedt, eds., *Religion and the Culture Wars: Dispatches from the Front* (Lanham, MD: Rowman and Littlefield, 1996), 291–299.

7. Ladd and Hadley, *Transformations of the American Party System*.

8. Ibid, chap. 1.

9. Ronald Inglehart, *The Silent Revolution: Changing Values and Political Styles Among Western Publics* (Princeton, NJ: Princeton University Press, 1977).

10. See Jeffrey M. Berry, *The New Liberalism: The Rising Power of Citizen Groups* (Washington, D.C.: Brookings, 1999).

11. James L. Guth, Lyman A. Kellstedt, John C. Green, and Corwin E. Smidt, "America Fifty/Fifty," *First Things* 116 (October 2001), 19–26.

12. Robert Axelrod, "Presidential Election Coalitions in 1984," *American Political Science Review* 80 (1986), 281–284.

13. Albert Menendez, *Religion at the Polls* (Philadelphia: Westminster, 1977).

14. Ibid., chap. 7.

15. Phillip E. Converse, *Religion and Politics: The 1960 Elections* (Ann Arbor: University of Michigan Survey Research Center, 1961).

16. The CBS News–*New York Times* exit poll had all Catholics regardless of race giving 52 percent of their votes to Bush, whereas the ABC News exit poll reported 51 percent for Dukakis. These results suggest the need for caution in interpreting close margins. Though news organizations often note that their surveys should be accurate within certain confidence limits—usually plus or minus 3 percentage points—commentators are tempted to treat the results of surveys as hard, cold facts.

17. Guth et al., "America Fifty/Fifty."

18. Ibid.

19. Ted G. Jelen, "Catholic Priests and the Political Order: The Political Behavior of Catholic Pastors," *Journal for the Scientific Study of Religion* 42 (2003), 595–596.

20. Guth et al., "America Fifty/Fifty"; David C. Leege, "Divining the Electorate," *Commonweal* (October 20, 2000), 16–20.

21. See John C. Green and Mark Silk, "The New Religion Gap," *Religion in the News* 6 (Fall 2003), 3.

22. See also David C. Leege, "The Catholic Vote in '96: Can It Be Found In the Church?" *Commonweal* (September 27, 1996), 11–18.

23. Geoffrey Layman, *The Great Divide: Religious and Cultural Conflict in American Party Politics* (New York: Columbia University Press, 2001); Albert J. Menendez, *Evangelicals at the Ballot Box* (New York: Prometheus, 1995).

24. Layman, *The Great Divide*; Louis Bolce and Gerald De Maio, "Our Secularist Democratic Party," *The Public Interest* (Fall 2002).

25. Paul Lopatto, *Religion and the Presidential Election* (New York: Praeger, 1985). Lopatto concluded that Carter split the theologically conservative (or evangelical) vote with Ford, but lost among Protestants more generally. See also Albert Menendez, *Religion at the Polls* (Philadelphia: Westminster, 1977). Menendez gave the evangelical edge to Ford, but also concluded that Carter did better with evangelicals than mainline Protestants (who backed Ford by a wide margin).

26. Guth et al., "America Fifty/Fifty"; Corwin Smidt, "Marching to Different Tunes? Religious Groups and the 2000 Election," *Henry Institute Newsletter* (Fall 2001), 3–4.

27. Kellstedt et al., "Has Godot Finally Arrived?"; Mark J. Rozell and Clyde Wilcox, eds., *God at the Grassroots: The Christian Right in the 1994 Elections* (Lanham, MD: Rowman and Littlefield, 1995).

28. James L Guth et al., "The Political Activity of Evangelical Clergy in the Election of 2000: A Case Study of Five Denominations," *Journal for the Scientific Study of Religion* 42 (2003), 501–514.

29. For a fuller discussion of the issues important to evangelicals and other religious groups, see Andrew Kohut, John C. Green, Scott Keeter, and Robert C. Toth, *The Diminishing Divide: Religion's Changing Role in American Politics* (Washington, D.C.: Brookings, 2000), chap. 4.

30. Katharine Q. Seelye, "Conservatives Mobilize Against Ruling on Gay Marriage," *New York Times* (November 20, 2003); Adam Nagourney, "Decision on Gay Marriage Creates a Thorny Issue for 2004 Race," *New York Times* (November 19, 2003).

31. For trends over time, see Center for Political Studies, *National Election Studies 2002* (Ann Arbor: University of Michigan / Center for Political Studies, 2002). Data are available at http://www.umich.edu/~nes/.

32. Layman, *The Great Divide*; Louis Bolce and Gerald De Maio, "Our Secularist Democratic Party," *The Public Interest* (Fall 2002).

33. Corwin Smidt et al., "The Political Attitudes and Activities of Mainline Protestant Clergy in the Election of 2000: A Study of Six Denominations," *Journal for the Scientific Study of Religion* 42 (2003), 515–532.

34. Guth et al., "American Fifty/Fifty"; Green, "The Undetected Tide."

35. For a discussion in light of the 2000 and 2002 elections, see especially Green and Silk, "The New Religion Gap."

36. "Secularist" here is defined by relatively low regularity of prayer and church-attendance as well as belief measures that indicate religion is not important in a person's everyday life. See Bolce and DeMaio, "Our Secularist Democratic Party."

37. Ibid.

38. Ibid. See also Green and Silk, "The New Religion Gap."

39. Tony Carnes, "Swing Evangelicals," *Christianity Today* (January 9, 2004).

40. Jim Wallis, "Putting God Back in Politics," *New York Times* (December 28, 2003), 4.9.

41. Lee Sigelman, "Jews and the 1988 Election: More of the Same?" in James L. Guth and John C. Green, eds., *The Bible and the Ballot Box: Religion and Politics in the 1988 Election* (Boulder, CO: Westview Press, 1991); see also Anna Greenberg and Kenneth D. Wald, "Still Liberal After All These Years: The Contemporary Political Behavior of American Jewry," in Sandy Maisel, ed., *Jews in American Politics* (Lanham, MD: Rowman and Littlefield, 2001), 161–193.

42. Sigelman, "Jews and the 1998 Elections."

43. Guth et al., "America Fifty/Fifty"; Paul A. Djupe and Anand E. Sokhey, "American Rabbis in the 2000 Elections," *Journal for the Scientific Study of Religion* 42 (2003), 563–576.

44. Green, "The Undetected Tide," 5.

45. Laura Blumenfeld, "Terrorism Jars Jewish, Arab Party Loyalties," *Washington Post* (December 7, 2003), A1.

46. Pew Research Center, *Evenly Divided and Increasingly Polarized: 2004 Political Landscape* (Washington, D.C.: Pew Research Center, 2003), 66.

47. Center for Political Studies, *National Election Studies 2002*.

48. Fredrick C. Harris, *Something Within: Religion in African-American Political Activism* (New York: Oxford University Press, 1999), chaps. 6 and 7; see also Steven Peterson, "Church Participation and Political Participation: The Spillover Effect," *American Politics Quarterly* 20 (1992), 123–139.

49. Guth et al., "America Fifty/Fifty."

50. This development is elaborated in Hertzke, *Echoes of Discontent*.

51. Gaston Espinosa, Virgilio Elizondo, and Jesse Miranda, "Hispanic Churches in American Public Life: Summary of Findings," *Interim Reports* 2 (January 2002).

52. Green and Silk, "The New Religion Gap."

53. Most notable is James Davidson Hunter, *Culture Wars: The Struggle to Define America* (New York: Basic Books, 1991).

54. Lyman Kellstedt, John C. Green, James L. Guth, and Corwin Smidt, "It's the Culture, Stupid! 1992 and Our Political Future," *First Things* (April 1994), 28–33.

THE POLITICS OF
ORGANIZED RELIGIOUS GROUPS

Though Americans love individualism and celebrate the heroic individual in literature and history, political power in the United States flows mostly from collective action. Organizing is a key to success in American politics. In this chapter we examine organized religious groups by tracing their roots and exploring their responses to issues of the day. Religious leaders tend not to like the term "lobbying" because of its overtones of shady dealings and corruption. We use the term neutrally to describe any organized effort to influence the direction of public policy.

Our emphasis will be on the key religious players in America and how they play the political game. Religious interest groups are often associated with some of the larger Christian traditions in the United States, so we give special attention to these groups. But we also discuss Jewish groups to illustrate that relatively small size does not necessarily destine a religious tradition to political ineffectiveness. Throughout the chapter, we focus on efforts in Washington, D.C., but we also note that increasing state and local activism often emulates national efforts.

One of our central themes is (again) the diversity of religious groups and its effect of preventing any single group from becoming dominant—despite sometimes overheated claims by one group or another. Up to this point, no single religious group has proven politically dominant over a long period of time, and continued pluralism makes such dominance unlikely in the future as well. The fortunes of religious groups, like many others, rise and fall with the times as some play the political game better than others.

THE EVOLUTION OF NATIONAL RELIGIOUS LOBBIES

Religious advocacy, as we saw in Chapter 1, is as old as the republic. At first, this advocacy was episodic and restricted to state and local government, largely because the federal government's role in the lives of American citizens was limited. Issues important to religious people, such as child welfare, prison reform, education, temperance, and gambling, were state and local matters, and the common pattern was that temporary coalitions of religious groups would come together when issues arose.

In the twentieth century, however, the increasing prominence and reach of government, especially the federal government, has acted as a catalyst in the growth of ongoing church lobbying. In the past fifty years a permanent religious presence has emerged in Washington, D.C.; many religious lobby groups also have state or local affiliates. Though the growth of national lobbies occurred principally after World War II, some had precursors. The Methodist Church established a Washington office in 1916 to promote Prohibition; the National Catholic Welfare Conference set up shop in 1919; and the Quakers, who opened the first full-time registered religious lobby in 1943, began their work primarily to protect conscientious objector status. By 1950 at least sixteen religious groups had offices in Washington, mostly representing mainline Protestant, Jewish, and Catholic groups.[1]

Since then the number of religious lobbies has grown substantially. Included in this number are significant Catholic, liberal Protestant, evangelical, Jewish, and African American interest groups. Many of these groups have no formal connection to a religious denomination (they receive no funding or other resources from an organized religious body), but they are still firmly rooted in a religious tradition. Smaller lobbies range from those speaking on behalf of groups of Ultraorthodox Jews to Muslims to gay and lesbian Christians.

Why has there been all of this growth in the organized political representation of religious interest groups? It has not always been easy since, as Daniel Hofrenning has observed, many religious interest groups have a more difficult time acclimating themselves to political realities than do their secular counterparts.[2] There are many reasons for this difficulty. One is the flowering of American religious pluralism and the growing sense that such pluralism creates an imperative for religious groups to get organized to protect their collective interests. In the 1950s, Baptists established a lobby to "watch" Catholics; with the Middle East in mind, Arab Americans have co-alesced recently to counteract the influence of Jewish interest groups.

Another explanation is that as the federal government has expanded, many groups have arisen to monitor its impact on their religious organizations—hospitals, schools, charitable organizations, and development agencies—as well as on their basic religious freedom. A third reason is that many religious people have come to the conclusion that they must get organized and enter politics to promote or defend the values of their religious traditions. This realization is consistent with the greater emphasis on lifestyle and morality issues since the 1960s.[3] Whatever the reasons, the diversity, scope, and number of religious groups lobbying in Washington has never been greater (Box 5.1).

STRATEGIES FOR EFFECTIVE ADVOCACY

The politics of pressure groups has not changed fundamentally since the nineteenth century.[4] New dimensions have been added to the craft, to be sure, including advanced communication technology and the increased presence of the mass media. But effective advocacy is—and always has been—a combination of outside pressure and inside influence coalescing in favorable circumstances.

Outside Pressure

Effective interest groups must have a loyal network of members at the grassroots level who can bring pressure to bear on members of Congress and state legislators. The threat of electoral defeat remains a powerful motivator of modern politicians, and groups with many members or well-heeled contributors can make a difference in a politician's fortunes on election day. The kinds of outside pressure interest groups bring vary tremendously by group and context. Mass mobilization, a technique commonly used by conservative Protestant organizations, represents one approach. Television and radio ministry connections, computer lists of contributors, and affiliated churches can generate a sea of letters to elected officials, which can attract attention and (occasionally) affect policy. The latest trend in direct mail among religious lobbies has been the

BOX 5.1 MENNONITE CENTRAL
COMMITTEE: PACIFIST LOBBY

The story of the Mennonite Central Committee illustrates how the actions of
the federal government have spurred the growth of church lobbies. One of
the perennial issues for pacifist denominations (like the Mennonites) is how
to protect their members from compulsory military service. Thus the Mennonites were shocked in 1967 when they learned that proposed selective
service legislation during the Vietnam War would not allow the kind of broad
conscientious objector provisions that Mennonites had enjoyed during
World War II. Church leaders traveled to Washington, testified at congressional hearings, and ultimately brought about changes in the law. In the
wake of that battle, the Mennonite Central Committee established a permanent Washington office in 1968. Its first director was Deton Franz, a thirty-
six-year-old pastor who directed Mennonite lobbying until his retirement in
1994. Though small by Washington standards, the Mennonite office remains a visible player in the religious community.

SOURCE: Keith Graber Miller, *American Mennonites Engage Washington: Wise as
Serpents, Innocent as Doves?* (Knoxville: University of Tennessee Press, 1996).

use of the Internet. A variety of religious organizations now support Web
sites that allow supporters to send e-mail about issues of concern directly
to Congress (see listing in the Appendix).

Mass mobilization is necessary but rarely sufficient for success. Members of Congress often discount "artificially inseminated" constituent letters that result from mass mobilization. Effective supplements include
elite mobilization and "key contact strategies." Indeed, a few influential
community leaders and party contributors can have greater clout than a
million relatively unsophisticated supporters or newcomers to politics.

Money, though it magnifies political influence, is not everything either. Members of the liberal nuns' lobby, NETWORK, for example,
have some influence because their members are well read, knowledgeable
about politics, and hooked in to informational networks around the
globe through their religious orders.

Effective religious organizations commonly develop smaller lists of key
contact people in government who may be reached by fax, e-mail, or telephone for quick responses. For liberal Christian groups this is a way to
overcome the lack of a large grassroots following. For Jewish groups it is a
way to magnify the considerable influence they already exercise. Ideally, a
key contact is a highly committed, politically sophisticated person who

knows a member of Congress personally. Religious interest groups attempt to identify such individuals in every state and congressional district.

The key contact approach represents the perfect marriage of the Washington lobbyist and the grassroots following. To appreciate the effectiveness of this strategy, imagine a member of Congress at a hearing. At one point the member expresses skepticism about a bill's provisions. A lobbyist in the room notices this lack of support and immediately communicates with contact people from the member's home district. The contact people receive a fax or call at their workplace asking that they register their concern immediately. They respond by calling or sending a fax or e-mail to the member. Stories circulate in Washington about groups that are able to deliver faxed protests to members of Congress even before a day's hearing is over. Whether or not that happens, members of Congress know that their moves are being watched and being communicated at the speed of light to influential contributors, community leaders, or even their personal friends back in the district. And because most members of Congress want to be re-elected, they have to care deeply about what people in their district think.

Money, of course, speaks loudly in contemporary politics. Most religious groups, however, do not form political action committees (PACs), organizations that donate money to candidates. Nor are clergy normally in the position to make substantial individual contributions. Thus religious groups are not major players in the money game, with a few exceptions. Jewish organizations, especially pro-Israel groups, do support PACs; they constitute important sources of money for both individual members of Congress and political parties. Some Jewish citizens are also major contributors and fund-raisers—particularly for the Democrats—and this provides access. Like other religious bodies, African American churches are tax-exempt institutions and thus cannot form PACs or make direct financial contributions, but they do sometimes allow their property to be used for political fundraisers. They also frequently invite candidates to speak during services. Since overt political involvement is more accepted in the African American religious community than in the rest of organized religion in the United States, favored candidates are sometimes able to raise money through direct appeals made in churches.

Rev. Jesse Jackson raised healthy sums of money through such church appeals, and other politicians have also done so. Conservative evangelical organizations, such as the Christian Coalition, have raised large amounts of money for registration and voting drives. Such efforts may aid specific candidates supported by the Christian Coalition just as much as if cash contributions were made directly to candidates.

By and large, however, religious actors are not big players in the political money game. Some argue that this protects them from the corrupting influences of fund-raising and allows them to present a clearer moral message to leaders. Sometimes that may be true; religious leaders, at their best, present politicians with visions of the public good undiluted by narrow self-interest. But money does speak, and religious leaders often resign themselves to the fact that they will not have that tool at their disposal.

Finally, outside pressure involves efforts by religious actors to shape public opinion on key issues of the day. When a religious interest group demonstrates the ability to shape public opinion, it brings indirect pressure on politicians. Strategies and success rates for this activity, however, vary. Events staged for media coverage have become common. Demonstrations, dramatic testimony, publicized fact-finding reports, and statements by bishops are all aimed at the mass media and the broader public. Here it is crucial that the religious group enjoy the sympathies of the elite press. Conservative evangelicals and prolife activists complain bitterly that they are not given a fair hearing in the mass media and that they are either ignored or stereotyped. As surveys of elite journalists show, there is some truth to this analysis.[5] By contrast, in the past liberal church groups have received publicity that exaggerated their grassroots support. Though surveys show that the majority of Americans favor school prayer, mainline Protestant denominations oppose it, and they have received publicity when they announced this opposition on the steps of the U.S. Capitol.[6] The strong opposition of many mainline, Jewish, and Catholic leaders to the Iraq War in 2003 also attracted extensive press coverage, despite the majority of ordinary citizens who supported military action, often by explicitly rejecting the counsel of their own clergy.[7]

Inside Influence

No matter how much outside pressure one can mount, it means little if interest-group leaders are not skilled at gaining and keeping elite access. To have any measure of political success, a group needs the chance to tell sympathetic policy makers about their agenda. Here, too, not all religious groups are equal. Some enjoy excellent access; others have to fight for every bit. During the 1980s, for example, when so much was made of the rise of the Christian Right, the Moral Majority actually suffered because they had poor access. What mattered was how many congressional offices were open and how many executive officials would listen, not how many millions of citizens heard—or agreed with—political TV evangelists. It is a lesson evangelical conservatives learned, and today their influence is greater in large measure because they have cultivated contacts within Congress and the Bush administration. This access paid off most recently when evangelicals successfully lobbied President Bush to focus on religious persecution and other human rights abuses abroad, as we discuss more fully in Chapter 7.[8]

The quality of interest-group leadership matters greatly. Some groups employ lobbyists with years of experience and strong reputations; others suffer from lack of experience and have no reputation at all. Good interest-group leaders have a strong strategic sense: They develop a clear, limited set of attainable objectives on the basis of the current political climate. One of the recurrent problems faced by mainline Protestant lobbies is a lack of sharp focus and a tendency to take on too many issues at the same time.[9] For example, in early 2004 the agenda of the National Council of Churches (NCC) included urban initiatives, racial justice, justice for women, economic and environmental justice, public funding of religious social services, migrant labor, international peace, and the battle against religious persecution.[10]

Political fortunes can also change. Republican control of the White House after 2001 meant that mainline Protestant lobbyists lost some of the access they had enjoyed during the Clinton years. Similarly, Democratic dominance of Congress, especially the House of Representatives, was a huge impediment to the agenda of conservative evangelicals from the late 1970s through the early 1990s. When the Republicans gained control of Congress in 1994, however, evangelical access rose, in part because evangelicals had played a significant role in the Republican electoral victory.

A national lobby's effectiveness is also governed by the total quality of its operation, its resources, staff, research facilities, and technological ability to reach members. All of that takes money and institutional support. Jewish organizations are well funded and well staffed, as are such conservative Christian groups as the Christian Coalition, the Family

Research Council, Focus on the Family, and Concerned Women for America. Catholic lobbies benefit from the institutional strength of the Catholic Church, its schools, hospitals, charities, and universities. In contrast, mainline Protestant churches have met with declining financial and institutional backing as national denominational offices have cut back on their Washington operations.[11]

In spite of the growing presence and diversity of religious lobbies, however, most are small affairs compared to such giants as the National Education Association, the American Association for Retired Persons, or the National Association of Manufacturers. A large religious lobby may have thirty staff people, but a major secular lobby generally has 300 or more. This is part of the reason that religious organizations generally exercise only modest political influence in the grand scheme of Washington, or statehouse, politics.

THE LEGISLATIVE PROCESS AND THE IMPERATIVE OF COMPROMISE

At the heart of the legislative process—whether in Congress or statehouses—is compromise. Though compromise is a dubious concept to some religious activists, legislators themselves view it as the key to action. They know it is the only way to build the coalitions that are necessary to get political goals accomplished. In order to understand why compromise is so vital, it is important to recall that the American system of government frustrates swift action. The framers of the Constitution wanted to limit power because they feared tyranny. The checks and balances they built into the system are there to delay proposals and allow many groups the chance to block proposed legislation. Political insiders know this, so they work to build the strongest possible coalition of supporters. Indeed, Washington politics is renowned for its frequent "strange bedfellows" alliances. There are no permanent friends or enemies, so the saying goes, just shifting coalitions.

This need to build coalitions is especially pressing for those organizations seeking major change. It is far easier to defend the status quo than it is to pass major new legislation. Christian conservatives, for example, are often in need of allies because they seek so many major changes in policy. Sometimes they are able to forge new partnerships but they have not been able to fashion a majority coalition as they have sought to enact a school prayer amendment, to change abortion policy, or to alter what they view as a secular atmosphere in public schools.

Mainline Protestant and Catholic groups, too, have enjoyed mixed success in playing the coalition-building game. In the 1980s they built a broad coalition to expand international food programs and development aid and to enforce sanctions against South Africa under apartheid. More recently, they joined together in 2000 in a successful effort called "Jubilee 2000" that led to the forgiving of millions of dollars of debt owed by impoverished developing countries. On numerous other issues, however, they have failed to change policy.

A dramatic example of an alliance occurred during the lobbying for the Religious Freedom Restoration Act (RFRA), which Congress enacted in 1993 to uphold the view that any burden on a citizen's right to practice the religion of his or her choice must be justified by a "compelling state interest." RFRA enjoyed support from an unusual coalition of mainline Protestant denominations, conservative evangelical organizations, Jewish and Muslim groups, Native American representatives, and civil liberties advocates. This was a true political coalition: Concerned Women for America joined the United Methodist Church, Catholics joined Baptists, and evangelicals joined the American Civil Liberties Union (ACLU) in supporting the measure. They were united in the desire to protect religious liberty.[12]

One liberal Jewish lobbyist noted with amazement how he found himself making joint lobby appearances with the head of the fundamentalist homeschooling legal defense group in support of RFRA. In signing the new law on November 16, 1993, President Bill Clinton acknowledged the remarkable nature of the coalition by saying that with God's power miracles can happen "even in the legislative process."[13]

Though the U.S. Supreme Court ruled RFRA unconstitutional in 1997 in *City of Boerne v. Flores* (for more on the case, see the discussion in Chapter 9), the passage of RFRA still reflects the fact that in modern pluralist America few religious organizations see themselves representing the majority. Each, however, can conceive of itself as a potentially persecuted minority and desire protection as a result. Thus fundamentalist homeschoolers seek grounds to protect themselves from persecution by public school authorities, just as Orthodox Jews or Muslims seek to protect the broadest possible range of religious freedoms. Perhaps in that sense the bedfellows were not so strange after all.

A MODEL OF RELIGIOUS GROUP EFFECTIVENESS

What makes for religious group effectiveness?[14] Five factors contribute to success: amenable traditions and theological beliefs; internal strength and unity; strategic location; constraints and opposition from other groups; and the "spirit of the times—that is, whether the political culture is open to a group's political advocacy.

Traditions and Theological Beliefs

Historical traditions and theological beliefs influence whether a religious group will enter politics at all, and if so, how it will approach that task. Some religions are so otherworldly that they eschew politics altogether; others get involved only when they feel threatened directly. The Jehovah's Witnesses are a group that generally stays out of politics, with the exception of occasional forays into the courts to protect their religious freedom. Others, such as Lutherans, have a deep tradition of teaching civic responsibility for the individual but resisting corporate political witness by the church, a tendency that frustrates Lutheran activists.[15]

Other religious traditions lend themselves to political action more readily. The American Catholic Church has long been at ease with politics. Many Jewish groups approach public action with enthusiasm. More than any other American religious group, African American Protestantism has long been deeply involved in political activism. The civil rights movement was organizationally based in black churches. Many African American clergy say they would not be able to imagine their pastoral role without a political component. These proclivities are not etched in stone, however, and change does occur. For example, for at least a generation evangelical Protestant churches taught that politics was not for them; now they have become more politicized. Tradition and theological beliefs also structure the political agendas of religious groups and their clergy; certain theological orientations are associated with different types of issue concerns.[16]

Internal Strength and Unity

No religious group will be able to make much of a political impact without supportive lay members. It is strategically important to have a large and unified membership. At the same time, the existence of internal dissent, disputes among leaders, and resistance from members all detract from political clout. Equally important is the intensity of members' commitment. Are lay members only willing to write an occasional letter to Congress? Or are they ready to sacrifice hours of their time building the organization, participating in telephone trees, and attending endless meetings? Are they willing to speak, vote, demonstrate, or even go to jail for their convictions?

Even the most committed participants need effective leaders. Strong leaders must exhibit energy, drive, and conviction. They also must have the ability to think strategically, form alliances, and articulate their messages in an appealing manner—often to elites who do not share their religious values. As in any organization, however, there is a risk that leaders may become overbearing and, in the case of membership organizations, inattentive to the members themselves. Indeed, Theda Skocpol suggests that leadership of many advocacy organizations has become highly professionalized and that ordinary members today make fewer decisions about the direction of organizations than they did just a few decades ago.[17] Because this can diminish members' sense of having a stake in the organization, the best leaders try to balance the inevitable need for management at the top with an attentiveness to the goals and energies of members at the grassroots. Some religious groups, as we shall see, have been highly successful at doing just that, while others have largely failed.

Finally, resources, especially financial resources, are an absolute necessity for any political organization. Are members affluent, and are they willing to make financial contributions? Do they have time for politics? Are they well connected already, as contributors to political parties, as personal friends of members of Congress, or as leaders in their communities? Do they have expertise that the organization might need, perhaps in legal advocacy, policy analysis, or marketing? Many Jewish groups, for example, combine all of these components of internal strength and unity and are therefore politically effective. Even religious groups without such advantages may stand a good chance to build a reasonable degree of political effectiveness. A recent major study shows that when people are deeply involved in any of a religious group's activities (such as serving on a church council), they learn valuable "civic skills" such as organizing and letter writing. These civic skills make people better equipped and more willing to participate in politics.[18]

Strategic Location

Another factor that is crucial to political success is the group's "strategic location." Does the group enjoy natural access to elites in government? Or does it have to beat down the door just to get noticed? Meaningful access does not just involve securing one meeting with a few members of Congress or their staffs. It means getting serious hearings with congressional leaders and committee chairs, top White House officials, high-ranking bureaucrats and administrators (who formulate much policy), and the courts. Meaningful access also involves working with the assorted network of think tanks, law firms, foundations, and influence peddlers in Washington who know how the game is played. It is useful to have connections to state and local officials, some of whom retain enormous influence over the federal government as well. The best access of all is to the elite national press. In a town where the words of the *Washington Post*—and more recently the *Washington Times*—often matter a good deal, the ability to gain favorable media exposure is crucial.

Constraints and Opposition

The power, intensity, and access of a group's opponents matter. Some groups, of course, ignite more opposition than others. Some face a tougher struggle against opposition within their own ranks. Such opposition is sometimes based in policy disputes. In other instances, members simply see political involvement of any kind as a divisive diversion from their view of the church's mission: providing meaning, spiritual comfort, forgiveness, or conciliation. Moreover, suspicion of religious activism is endemic in American culture. The tradition of church-state separation in the United States encourages skepticism about church involvement in politics. How effectively a group overcomes these hurdles often determines how far it can go politically.

Interest groups seeking influence in Washington also benefit when they pool their resources. When a conservative evangelical organization can work productively with a liberal Catholic or Jewish group, for example, the individual voice of each will be magnified and they will be able to attract more attention than they could have on their own. The remarkably broad-based coalition that advanced RFRA through Congress illustrates the point. Some religious groups, however, resist ecumenical (interreligious) coalitions at all costs. In most instances such groups are not interested in working with people of other religious backgrounds because of theological incompatibility. A willingness to work with other groups rather than labeling them as enemies, then, can translate into substantial political influence.

Zeitgeist: Spirit of the Times

The fortunes of a religious group are governed in part by how well its agenda conforms to the spirit of the times. A spirit of political activism in the 1960s aided mainline Protestant churches, just as a more conservative tone since the 1980s gave a lift to evangelicals. Religious groups cannot often affect the prevailing zeitgeist, but they can recognize it and adapt their strategies accordingly. To show how these factors influence the actions and effectiveness of different American religious groups, we now turn to some examples.

MAINLINE PROTESTANT GROUPS

As we noted in Chapter 2, mainline Protestants enjoyed a strategic location in American society through much of the twentieth century. Moreover, beginning with the Social Gospel movement of the early twentieth century, mainline church leaders came to share a liberal theology that was encouraged, and even expected, their involvement in "this world," which would include the political realm. They were thus receptive to political action and in a position to have some influence.

The movement to end segregation and discrimination against African Americans that burst on the scene in the late 1950s energized liberal white religious people. Though many had participated in early civil rights demonstrations in the South, the real opportunity for liberal Christians presented itself when the landmark Civil Rights Act of 1964 was proposed. Intense and effective lobbying by religious groups, especially by African American and mainline Protestants but also by Jews and Catholics, helped it pass. [19]

Ministers flocked to Washington to lobby members of Congress. And legislators were not accustomed to being lobbied by ministers. One civil rights veteran, Joe Rauh of Americans for Democratic Action, noted how powerful this novelty was:

> Standing outside the Committee Room was the most beautiful sight I had ever seen—twenty Episcopal priests, fully garbed, all beautiful young WASPS. I used to think that the only two people out in front for civil rights were a Negro and a Jew—Mitchell of the NAACP and myself. But this was something the committee membership had never seen before. I knew then we really were in business.[20]

Summing up the role of churches, Hubert Humphrey wrote that without them "this bill could never have become law."[21]

Church leaders successfully mobilized their grassroots membership. Though the churches were by no means perfectly unified, there was sufficient lay support that the pro-civil rights message reached undecided members of Congress. The issue was relatively clear-cut, and religious arguments were compellingly persuasive. How could one really be a Christian and sanction discriminatory laws and the brutal treatment of fellow human beings?

The mid–1960s represented the high-water mark for mainline Protestant politics in Washington and elsewhere. Weakened by declining church memberships and diminishing financial support from the pews, and criticized for being out of touch with lay members, mainline church lobbies now struggle to maintain their previous clout.[22] Nonetheless, the experience of 1960s political activism led to a proliferation of liberal church interest groups. Thus mainline Protestants remain active players, often allying themselves with Catholics, Jews, and secular liberals.

The main liberal Protestant groups active in Washington today include the following:

- The government-relations offices of the mainline denominations, particularly the Episcopal Church, the Evangelical Lutheran

Church in America, the Presbyterian Church (U.S.A.), the United Church of Christ, and the United Methodist Church;

- the National Council of Churches, the key coalition of theologically liberal denominations;
- government-relations offices representing small but active pacifist churches (Quakers, Mennonites, and the Church of the Brethren), along with the Unitarian-Universalist Association;
- membership groups, such as Bread for the World, a Christian hunger lobby;
- the Interfaith Alliance, which presents itself as a direct opponent of the religious Right;
- international relief agencies, such as Church World Service and Lutheran World Relief, which lobby on foreign aid, trade, and U.S. international policies;
- issue-specific coalitions including the Religious Coalition for Reproductive Choice, the Washington Office on Africa, and the Washington Office on Latin America;
- church groups allied with the major African American denominations (such as the National Baptist Convention, U.S.A., Inc.); and
- allied groups on church-state issues, including the Baptist Joint Committee and Americans United for Separation of Church and State (which arose to combat Catholic influence and today advocates strict church-state separation).

The political agenda of mainline Protestants is wide-ranging and it is also decidedly liberal, though there are differences among the many groups. The National Council of Churches and many of its congregational leaders, for example, took a turn to the left on foreign policy in the late 1960s and early 1970s, and it has continued this stance into the twenty-first century, repeatedly objecting to U.S. military activities abroad. On domestic affairs mainline Protestants have embraced a broad agenda of women's equality, environmental protection, affirmative action, and, in some cases, abortion rights and gay rights. For example, the latest organized effort of some mainline Protestant clergy, together with a few leaders from other traditions, is the Clergy Leadership Network, which was created explicitly as a liberal alternative to Bush administration policies (foreign and domestic) and religious conservatism in politics.[23]

One of the challenges facing mainline Protestant groups, however, is that for a variety of reasons it is difficult for them to convince lay members of the value and urgency of their agenda. Sometimes this reflects an ideological gap between clergy and laity, and sometimes it demonstrates a lack of effort by leaders to persuade and mobilize members. It also reflects the fact that mainline Protestant theology is not authoritarian by nature. Lay members are accustomed to interpreting scripture as they please, so it can be difficult for clergy and other church leaders to offer prophetic pronouncements that result in mass mobilization of laity.

These challenges notwithstanding, mainline Protestant political activism is by no means a thing of the past. For example, Bread for the World has built a list of members who do support the organization's advocacy on behalf of the hungry. The Friends Committee on National Legislation and the Mennonite Central Committee have good links with their member churches. And most mainline Protestant denominations have developed lists of contacts in congregations across the country.[24] Moreover, there is some evidence to suggest that the "clergy-laity gap" may not be as salient in central city or low-income mainline congregations, where economic hardship presents incentives for political action through churches as well as heightened resonance of the social justice message.[25]

Many mainline clergy are in fact very involved in political and social issues in their local communities. This too is part of the organizational dynamics of liberal Protestantism but until recently has been less studied than the national organized efforts. What we do know is that the relationship between local clergy's political and social involvement and that of their denominations' national organizations is often tenuous.[26]

ROMAN CATHOLIC GROUPS

Catholic interest groups enjoy an advantageous strategic location in the configuration of American pressure groups. On the one hand, Catholic groups have been allied with the Democratic Party throughout much of American history and were strongly supportive of the New Deal. They are generally comfortable with the liberal Democratic agenda on such issues as welfare spending, labor laws, civil rights, and the death penalty.

On the other hand, they join with Republican conservatives in opposing abortion, promoting parental choice options in day care and education, and criticizing some elements of pop culture. Thus religio-political activists from across the spectrum—from conservative evangelicals to ecumenical liberals—view Catholics as potential allies.

The American Catholic Church has maintained a Washington presence since just after World War I, when the National Catholic Welfare Conference was established. Today, the United States Conference of Catholic Bishops (USCCB) represents the official political positions of the Church. The clear Catholic organizational structure, along with a strong hierarchical tradition, allows its leaders to speak with authority for the Catholic Church. This is a distinct political advantage. Thus, even if lay opinion is divided on an issue, the "official" church position can be articulated clearly. Even since the recent sex-abuse scandals in the Church, when the bishops present their views on issues, they are guaranteed extensive press coverage.

The Catholic lobby, however, is far from monolithic. It includes a host of associations, religious orders, and membership organizations. In most cases these groups do not oppose the bishops directly, but there are large differences in emphasis and even ideology. On the left we find groups such as NETWORK, a membership organization composed mostly of activist nuns; the Maryknoll order, which is known for its support of liberation theology; and Pax Christi, a quasi-pacifist group.[27] These groups are decidedly more liberal than the USCCB, especially on foreign policy issues. Also quite liberal are Jesuit Social Ministries, Catholic Charities, and the Campaign for Human Development, which lobby on issues of poverty and welfare. A different posture emerges, however, from large associations of Catholic hospitals and parochial schools, which have tangible financial interests to protect and are generally treated with some respect by policy makers (Box 5.2).

On church-state issues we find the Catholic League for Religious Civil Rights, headed by the irrepressible William Donohue, which vigorously combats anti-Catholic bigotry in the news and entertainment media. Finally, there are organizations sustained in part by sizable Catholic memberships, including National Right to Life, the nation's oldest antiabortion group; JustLife, which lobbies for the "seamless garment" agenda articulated by Chicago's late Joseph Cardinal Bernardin

---

**BOX 5.2 THE ROMAN CATHOLIC CHURCH
AND HEALTHCARE POLICY**

The Roman Catholic Church plays a central role in the crafting of health-care policy. Its concern with this policy area is related to a variety of factors, the most central of which is the fact that the church operates 11 percent of all community hospitals in the United States. Clarke Cochran has argued, though, that there is more to the Church's involvement in healthcare policy than material concern for this network of hospitals. The Church's opposition to managed care, for example, owes much to traditional Catholic concern for the less fortunate; managed care and social justice have little in common. From the pope down, the Church views healthcare as a right that belongs to all persons, so any system that would deny this right is patently unjust in the eyes of many Catholic leaders. Thus the Catholic Health Association (CHA) lobbies not only to protect its network of hospitals—which since the beginning have been open to all persons regardless of religion or ability to pay—but to defend the poor.

SOURCES: http://www.chausa.org; Clarke E. Cochran and David C. Cochran, *Catholics, Politics, and Public Policy: Beyond Left and Right* (Maryknoll, NY: Orbis Books, 2003); Clarke E. Cochran, "Catholic Health Care and the Challenge of Civil Society," in Margaret O. Steinfels, ed., *American Catholics and Civic Engagement: A Distinctive Voice* (Lanham, MD: Rowman and Littlefield, 2004).

(opposing abortion, the death penalty, and nuclear weaponry while supporting liberal positions on social welfare); and, to a lesser extent, Bread for the World, the nondenominational Christian hunger lobby.

Among the strengths of the Catholic lobby are a theological comfort with politics, a scholastic tradition of serious reflection on issues, clear lines of leadership, and a potentially strategic position in broader political alignments. Though there are some differences in partisanship and voting behavior among Catholic clergy, there is also a remarkable degree of cohesion about both the theological reasons for political engagement and the policies the church ought to pursue.[28] Given the formal authority of clergy in the church, these attitudes provide an important resource for mobilization.

One of the weaknesses of Catholic political groups is the diversity of opinion in the pews and among Catholic politicians.[29] The recent sexual abuse scandals in the church, moreover, have diminished the authority of the church leadership, exacerbating the problem of creating a unified Catholic voice.[30] A look at Catholic involvement in several key issues illustrates the situation.

Abortion

Even before and certainly since the U.S. Supreme Court struck down restrictive state abortion statutes in *Roe v. Wade* in 1973, the Catholic Church has been at the center of prolife lobbying, both in Washington and at state legislatures.[31] No issue so clearly illustrates the constraints facing the Catholic Church. Though the Church has invested enormous political capital in the issue, its successes have been modest. Abortion law in the United States remains among the more liberal in the world, despite three decades of agitation by prolife forces.[32] In part this can be attributed to the powerful role of the courts in the American political system. Even though a more conservative Supreme Court has returned some latitude to the states, the room for variation in abortion policy is still small.

Another constraint prolife Catholics face is the partisan nature of the abortion issue. Prochoice activists have succeeded in identifying the Democratic Party with their position. Though some exceptions exist, most Democratic leaders support a solidly prochoice policy. Hence many Catholic leaders have become ambivalent or, in some cases, highly critical about the church's historical link to the Democratic Party, and some have left the party altogether.

Finally, lack of lay unity has hurt the church. Though polls on abortion are sometimes ambiguous, there is no question that a sizable number of Catholics support some level of abortion rights, and women who identify themselves as Catholic are just as likely to have abortions as are non-Catholic women. The church can take heart, however, in the fact that prolife support is strongest among those who most faithfully attend mass, while nominal Catholics are the most likely to reject the church's prolife position.[33]

Even in the face of these impediments, the church has had some success in its efforts to pass antiabortion legislation. Most prominent has been the Hyde Amendment banning federal funding for abortion. Rep. Henry Hyde, a devout Catholic Republican from Illinois, has successfully attached his amendment to myriad federal laws since 1976. One of the most dramatic struggles over the Hyde Amendment occurred in the summer of 1993, when, despite opposition from President Clinton and Democratic congressional leaders, Hyde rallied a surprisingly strong majority to support his amendment, though it was softened somewhat to allow federal funding of abortion procedures when the mother's life was at stake or the pregnancy was the result of rape or incest.

The Catholic Church has also mobilized recently against late-term abortions. It has been joined in this effort by a range of evangelical Protestant groups (such as the Christian Coalition and Focus on the Family) that share the Catholic hierarchy's outrage at the federal government's unwillingness to ban "partial-birth" abortion during the Clinton administration. The tide turned on the issue with the election of George W. Bush, who signed into law a ban passed by Congress in late 2003.[34] Though the ban met an immediate legal challenge, it nevertheless provoked many new strategic political calculations. The actions of the Bush administration and the Republican-led Congress were clearly responsive to the demands of many religious believers, and even some Democrats have used the issue as a strategic opportunity to appear moderate by opposing this form of abortion. Moreover, the mobilization over the ban illustrates that prolife groups have adopted a strategy of chipping away at the right to abortion incrementally rather than seeking a total ban on all abortion procedures.

Nuclear Arms and Peace Issues

The Catholic Church also achieved some success in its efforts to limit the nuclear arms race. In the early 1980s American Catholic bishops wrote a highly publicized "pastoral letter" on nuclear arms in which they applied just war theory in criticizing key aspects of U.S. nuclear policy.[35] Though few lay Catholics read the document itself, the enormous publicity that surrounded its release and subsequent consideration by active Catholics affected the political environment of a number of parishes.

Careful analysis suggests that the bishops achieved something quite rare through this pastoral letter: They actually shifted Catholic lay opinion—in this instance, toward a more dovish, antiwar position.[36] Moreover, this shift could not have been timed more strategically. The pastoral letter gave a boost to the nuclear freeze movement, which was lobbying Congress for a freeze resolution. Faced with a popular mass movement and a rebellious Congress, the Reagan administration shifted its own nuclear posture.[37] The bishops made a real difference here, and they gained credibility in Washington as a result.

Catholic opinion about the Gulf War of 1991 and the Iraq War of 2003 also provides lessons about the limits of Catholic (or religious) influence regarding the momentous national decision to go to war. In response to Saddam Hussein's 1990 invasion of Kuwait, the Catholic hierarchy offered conditional support for the U.S. effort to keep the Iraqis from occupying Saudi Arabia, but it opposed the Bush administration's decision to expel them from Kuwait. Daniel Pilarczyk, the president of the National Conference of Catholic Bishops (as the USCCB was called then), expressed the church's preference for allowing economic sanctions more time. When Congress voted to authorize the use of force, allowing President George Bush to begin Operation Desert Storm, Roman Catholic parishioners strongly backed the view that it was a just war, so the reservations of church leaders were ignored.[38] Roughly the same picture emerged before and during the Iraq War of 2003, with the same general result, suggesting the continued challenge the bishops face in advancing their positions on war and peace.

Church-State Partnerships in Education and Social Services

Catholics lobby about a host of domestic economic and welfare issues as well, often in an effort to secure public money to support church schools or provide help for the poor. Since the nineteenth century the American Catholic Church has battled to obtain state support for its school system. In the struggle the church has faced vigorous and effective opposition from public school teachers and administrators, civil liberties groups, and Protestant organizations such as the Baptist Joint Committee and Americans United for Separation of Church and State. While the church has recently achieved some success, including small-scale voucher programs in Milwaukee, Wisconsin; Cleveland, Ohio; and Florida, it has not realized its major educational goal of broadening parental choice through tax credits or vouchers for parochial school attendance.

Catholic groups have had much greater success is the public funding of various social service agencies associated with the church. Part of the reason Catholic organizations have had such success is their tendency to separate religion from the actual method of providing the service. Unlike evangelical "gospel missions" and other pervasively religious groups,

Catholic agencies such as Catholic Charities do not expect clients to engage in religious behavior as a condition of receiving food assistance, job training, housing, or other benefits. Consequently, public funding of these agencies, with federal and state grants worth millions of dollars, has never raised serious constitutional challenges.[39] While President George W. Bush has proposed expanding the range of grantmaking to include other religious groups as well, it appears that in the short term, Catholic groups will face relatively little competition for grants and continue to enjoy a successful church-state partnership in the provision of social services.

JEWISH GROUPS

Jews have thrived in the United States, which protects their religious freedom, after centuries of persecution elsewhere. Though the Jewish proportion of the population in the United States is small—less than 2 percent—it is also highly educated, relatively affluent, and politically active. These characteristics translate into significant resources, but other factors as well account for the success of Jewish interest groups, especially in Washington.

Jews have lived in the United States since the seventeenth century, but their first national interest group, the American Jewish Committee (AJC), was not formed until 1906, in response to a Russian pogrom. Since then, the AJC has sought to protect Jews both at home and abroad. In 1913, the Anti-Defamation League of B'nai B'rith was founded to combat domestic anti-Semitism, followed by the American Jewish Congress, which was made up at first of Jews devoted to the creation of a Jewish homeland in Palestine.[40] The Washington offices of these organizations today should not be considered strictly religious lobbies, since many of their members are not religious. Still, close ties remain between Jewish congregations and these interest groups.

Like the mainline Protestant denominations, the three major branches of Judaism—Orthodox, Conservative, and Reform—support government-relations offices in Washington, D.C., to coordinate their political activities. Of these the most active is the Union for Reform Judaism (formerly the Union of American Hebrew Congregations), which represents the largest branch of American Judaism. Though Reform and Conservative

Jews dominate the political scene, Orthodox Jews have also recently gotten into the act. Hasidic Jews also opened up their own Washington office in the early 1990s.

In a class by itself is the America Israel Public Affairs Committee, or AIPAC, one of the most formidable lobbies in Washington. Its sole aim is to coordinate American support for Israel, and it has become a model for a whole range of other interest groups that wish to influence U.S. foreign policy. For years AIPAC has been respected and even feared in Washington politics. AIPAC has combined excellent research resources in its Washington office, a grassroots network of activist members, and a host of affiliated political action committees that contribute money to pro-Israel candidates for federal office. And there is, in fact, tangible evidence of AIPAC's effectiveness in Congress. Largely because of AIPAC's efforts, the billions of dollars in foreign aid that the United States sends to Israel no longer comes in the form of loans; it is now given as outright grants.[41]

On most issues Jewish political groups are liberal. Jewish lobbies have championed abortion rights, opposed school prayer and school voucher programs, sought strict separation of church and state, and strongly backed full gender equality. They have consistently opposed evangelicals in the political realm.

On matters involving Israel, however, Jewish groups often part company with their usual religious allies. For many mainline Protestants and liberal Catholics, not to mention African American Christians and Muslims, justice for the Palestinian people demands more U.S. pressure on Israel to make concessions and to change its treatment of the Palestinians. American Jews, in contrast, remain strongly pro-Israel and united in their resolve to protect the existence of the Jewish homeland, however pained they may be from time to time about some of Israel's own actions and policies. In one of the great ironies of contemporary religious politics, evangelical Protestants have emerged as the Christian group most supportive of Israel. Their support for Israel is sometimes rooted in the belief that Jews must return to their homeland before Jesus Christ can come again. For others, support for Israel is a way to ensure God's blessing, since the Jews are described as God's chosen people in the Bible.[42] Whatever the motivations, many Jewish leaders have welcomed evangelicals' help, while others have resisted it.[43]

The growing political clout of Orthodox Jews, particularly since the 2000 vice-presidential nomination of Sen. Joseph Lieberman (D-Conn.), himself an Orthodox Jew, has increased the pluralism of Jewish political witness. On such issues as opposition to abortion and gay rights, and support for public recognition of faith, Orthodox and Ultraorthodox Jews often have the same perspective as Christian evangelicals and conservative Catholics. The Rabbinical Council—the national organization of Orthodox rabbis—has also become more politically active on such issues as public support for religious schools. Christian conservatives, of course, have leaped at the chance to build alliances here. Rev. Pat Robertson features Jews at Christian Coalition meetings; Christians and Jewish conservatives have jointly established organizations such as Stand for Israel; and Michael Horowitz, a Jewish man, now leads the fight against religious persecution in all its varieties around the world (see Chapter 7). How far such efforts can go, however, remains to be seen.

Why do Jewish groups enjoy such excellent elite access in Washington and elsewhere? First, Jewish faith and tradition promote political participation. Like mainline Protestantism, Judaism emphasizes worldly engagement. In Jewish scripture, for example, the ancient Hebrews lived under God's mercy and judgment on the basis of how faithfully they organized their communal affairs. Jewish communities in America also foster a robust public life in which people are at home with the debates and compromises of politics. Indeed, if one compares Jewish Americans with other Americans of similar economic standing, it is striking how much more interested in the world of politics Jews are. This ease with politics is, of course, a major resource. Jewish leaders do not have to spend time and energy convincing their members that politics is a legitimate activity. Often their members are already politically involved.

Second, Jewish political organizations build on many internal resources. At the local level, American Jews operate vibrant community organizations and chapters of national groups. Thus, when national leaders seek to mount political pressure, they can call upon a range of groups. Even in places with small Jewish populations, prominent Jewish citizens sometimes know their congressional representatives personally. Relative affluence is also a real resource—and one that leaders have no timidity about tapping. Jews are major contributors to a range of interest groups and to political parties, candidates, and pro-Israel PACs.

Jewish political resources are maximized by a host of strong leaders. Indeed, some of them have been legends in Washington: confidants of presidents, friends of members of Congress, quintessential insiders. One reason for this sustained access is the longevity of senior Jewish leadership, a product of stability in the Washington community. Longevity fosters not only wisdom in the ways of politics but a long view of lobbying strategy. These leaders encourage workshops to train new members and foster college clubs to bring a new generation into the fold. They help build relationships with local politicians, mayors, and state representatives, especially because years later these people may be elected to Congress.

Third, Jews enjoy excellent strategic access to political elites. In part their strategic location is a function of the presence of Jews in a variety of elite circles. It is, of course, hard to speak of this fact without promoting unfair stereotypes or feeding conspiracy theories that suggest a vast Jewish ruling cabal. The truth is that American Jews believe in strong families, education, and civic engagement. This results in a mathematical overrepresentation of Jews at elite levels of government, media, and the academy.

Jewish leaders employ resources to cultivate political elites throughout the system. Whether in a Democratic or Republican White House, a Democratic or Republican Congress, a conservative or liberal Supreme Court, Jewish leaders work to win. They also work assiduously with top bureaucrats and cabinet members. They cultivate the media, and they build alliances with the vast network of Washington lobbies and law firms.

On some issues Jews face strong opposition, and they adapt accordingly. As strict church-state separatists they have been fighting increasingly assertive evangelicals and Catholics.[44] On Israel, however, they have faced relatively weak domestic opponents. Israel has enjoyed broad popular support as the only democracy in the Middle East, with an image of David among Arabic Goliaths. Moreover, Christian support for Israel includes not only evangelicals who see its formation as a fulfillment of biblical prophecy but also mainline Protestants who identify with the "holy land." Though anti-Semitism certainly lurks in some circles, the vast majority of American Christians view Jewish neighbors with respect.[45] American Jews also benefit from their willingness and ability to form coalitions with a wide variety of political bedfellows.

This picture of robust influence, however, rests on a world situation that often changes. Suicide bombings in Israel increase public sympathy among Americans for Israel. Rigid opposition to compromise with the Palestinians, on the other hand, does not. But even when Jewish groups face events that are out of their control, they draw on a long history of expertise in responding to those events.

EVANGELICAL PROTESTANT GROUPS

In the 1980s a few evangelical Protestant organizations generated a lot of heat and received a huge amount of media attention. Moral Majority leader Rev. Jerry Falwell made frequent television appearances, Christian Voice director Gary Jarmin blanketed churches with his "Moral Report Card" of the votes of members of Congress, and Concerned Women for America mobilized thousands of women opposed to feminism and full gender equality. These and other groups reflected the early militancy of a movement that came to be known as the New Christian Right. As a movement, the Christian Right succeeded in shaping the Washington agenda and putting adversaries on the defensive, primarily through mobilization drives and media attention. On the matter of school prayer, for example, the Christian Right buried Capitol Hill in millions of pieces of mail. But despite this sound and fury, the Christian Right achieved only modest policy success. Lack of elite access hurt tremendously, as did unfavorable press coverage and financial instability. When the Moral Majority closed up shop in 1989 and the Christian Voice receded, obituaries were prematurely written for the Christian Right movement.[46]

What has happened instead is growth and increasing sophistication. One way to comprehend this movement is to list its various groups and compare their ideological hues and issue concerns. Conservative evangelical groups are a diverse lot, and they include the following:

- Organizations that work mostly through the courts but that lobby legislatures as well. These include the Christian Legal Society, an organization made up of lawyers who take on religious freedom issues; the more conservative Rutherford Institute headed by John Whitehead; and Pat Robertson's American Center for Law and Justice, headed by Jay Sekulow, a constitutional law specialist.
- The National Association of Evangelicals (NAE), the umbrella organization for the evangelical mainstream. In Washington since the early 1940s and analogous to the mainline National Council

of Churches, its approach is nonconfrontational ("cooperation without compromise" is its motto), and it has frequently parted company with more militant fundamentalists. It is conservative on social issues and a strong defender of religious liberty.

- Denominational organizations, such as the Ethics and Religious Liberty Commission of the Southern Baptist Convention (SBC) and the government-relations office of the Lutheran Church–Missouri Synod. One of the advantages these relatively new groups enjoy is a church base that can be mobilized. Thus, when the SBC launched a national campaign to block abortion funding in President Clinton's national healthcare proposal, it announced that materials on the issue would be mailed to every one of its member congregations—a powerful statement since the SBC is the largest of all American Protestant denominations with over 15 million members.

- Single-issue groups, including National Right to Life, which works closely with evangelical and Catholic groups in lobbying against abortion, euthanasia, and medical use of fetal tissue; the Home School Legal Defense Association, led by attorney Michael Farris; and Prison Fellowship, created and led by evangelical moderate Charles Colson, the former Nixon aide who went to jail for Watergate crimes. Colson's prison experience and conversion led him to create what has become a worldwide organization focused on prison reform and the spiritual rehabilitation of prisoners.

- Broad-based membership organizations, such as the Christian Coalition, Focus on the Family, Family Research Council, the Traditional Values Coalition, and Concerned Women for America.

- Groups such as Evangelicals for Social Action and Sojourners, which combine theological conservatism with a liberal political ideology.

The most influential organization to emerge in the 1990s was the Christian Coalition.[47] Formed in the wake of Pat Robertson's 1988 presidential bid, the Christian Coalition has succeeded in channeling the political energies of grassroots evangelicals in a way that the Moral Majority never achieved. In part this is because activists learned from Jerry Falwell's mistakes, and in part it reflects a changing agenda. Though the Moral Majority enjoyed enormous media exposure in the 1980s, it rested on shaky financial ground and depended on continuous emergency appeals for funds from contributors. Even those who acknowledge Falwell's pioneering role note that the Moral Majority remained what some thought to be nothing more than a mailing list and a string of television appearances by Falwell—not a sustainable organization. Robertson's presidential campaign and subsequent organizing efforts, in contrast, focused on building a real grassroots base of activists. This effort was premised on Robertson's recognition that to achieve its long-range goals the conservative Christian movement had to shift from a national focus to state and local forums, where much of the battle over American culture was being fought.

Though Robertson has always been president and spiritual leader of the Christian Coalition through his Christian Broadcasting Network (CBN), it was Ralph Reed who led the organizational effort in the 1990s. Reed combined a highly educated background (a Ph.D. in history) with extensive experience as a campaign consultant. Youthful and skilled in dealing with the media, Reed also wrote widely for opinion magazines and newspapers and published a best-selling book as the Christian Coalition's executive director.[48] By the mid–1990s he had built an organization with more than one million members, fifty state affiliates, nearly 900 local chapters, an active Washington lobby, and an annual budget of over $20 million.

One of Reed's key strategies was hosting "leadership schools" in cities across the country to train local activists to run campaigns and influence public policy. Another major focus has been identifying sympathetic voters, maintaining computer files organized by electoral districts, and getting voters to the polls. The leadership schools and member profiles exemplify the organization's grassroots strengths in the 1990s, which distinguished it from trends toward an overbearing top-down managerial style common to many other groups.[49] Ordinary members felt they had a stake in the decisions of the Christian Coalition, and they were therefore willing to commit strongly to its work.

The Christian Coalition came of age in the 1994 election cycle, when Republicans won majorities in both Houses of Congress and had success in state-level elections as well. The Christian Coalition recruited and supported sympathetic candidates in primaries, generated enormous publicity, and distributed some 30 million "voter guides" rating the records of congressional incumbents on key conservative positions at churches across the country. This effort coincided with and supported a strong conservative tide in congressional elections. Though a number of factors contributed to the huge Republican victory nationwide, the Christian Coalition could legitimately claim some credit and a legacy that is still felt in national and, perhaps more strongly, state politics today.[50]

Many changes have come upon the Christian Coalition since 1996. First, Ralph Reed resigned in June 1997 and was replaced by a leadership team consisting of Donald Hodel (a former Reagan cabinet member) and Randy Tate (a former Republican member of Congress). Since then, the organization has suffered from dramatic declines in financial contributions and visibility and cut the size of its staff, scaled back its political agenda, and phased out the glossy magazine it once sent to members.[51] In 1999 the Coalition underwent a serious reorganization after losing its tax exempt status because of aggressive electioneering. Pat Robertson took the reins for a short period of time and then passed them to Roberta Combs in 2001, who continues the restructuring process today.

As the Christian Coalition faded, other faces gained prominence in the political movement of evangelical Protestants. Gary Bauer, for example, who served as president of the Family Research Council in the late 1990s, emerged as one of the most influential moral conservatives in Washington. Under his leadership, the Family Research Council became adept at fundraising; Bauer also spun off a political action committee, the Campaign for Working Families. Though Bauer himself left the Family Research Council to run for president in 2000 (he has since returned to the Campaign for Working Families), the organization has maintained a decidedly different tack from the Christian Coalition's. Indeed, James Dobson, radio psychologist and head of FRC's parent organization, Focus on the Family, has always favored a more confrontational approach to the Republican Party than did Reed. He wants Christian conservatives to have a stronger voice in the GOP and is willing to reshuffle old alliances to accomplish this goal. So steadfast is Bauer that, because of China's human rights abuses, he alienated economic conservatives by opposing both the United States' 2000 decision to grant permanent normal trade relations status to China and China's 2001 entry into the World Trade Organization.

CONCLUSION

How effective are religious lobbies? Effectiveness is a notoriously difficult concept to measure. Most legislation involves broad coalitions of groups and members of Congress, so determining any single group's influence is difficult if not impossible. But the best evidence we have suggests that most groups enjoy only modest and periodic influence. Jewish groups have clearly made a difference on U.S. foreign aid to Israel. The religious prolife lobby has won on late term abortion, but not much else. Bread for the World and religious relief agencies have secured increased funding for hunger programs, and evangelicals have succeeded in getting religious persecution on the national policy agenda. There is some movement on increased funding for faith-based social services and educational vouchers. Though these are major accomplishments, compared to the vast amount of policymaking and budgeting that goes on in Washington and in each state capitol, they nonetheless represent modest gains. When religious groups come together, their impact can be dramatic (see Chapter 7 for case studies). But since that is rare indeed, one should be cautious about claiming too much for the religious advocacy community.

As we look to the future, a number of trends bear watching. First, rapid technological change has speeded up the lobbying process and made the links between leaders and members more sophisticated. Fax technology, the Internet and e-mail, satellite hookups, and computer phoning services facilitate rapid communication between activist citizens, Washington, and other levels of government. Groups that are able to employ the latest technology will have the edge. Some conservative Christian organizations have been quicker than their liberal counterparts to incorporate new technology into their lobbying strategies. Rapid response may also foster changes in the governing structures of organizations to allow leaders the flexibility to respond to breaking events while providing accountability to members and church bodies.

A second trend is the growing importance of intellectual discourse, including the war of ideas fought out in elite journals and magazines, think tank reports, policy institute advocacy, and academic research. Ideas clearly matter, and so does the marshaling of facts and analysis. Groups cannot depend solely upon pressure or skilled maneuvering in Washington. They must be a part of the intellectual debate. If the conservative Heritage Foundation or the liberal Brookings Institution publishes research supporting school choice (which both have done), then that research becomes grist for religious activists who have complaints about public schools. Similarly, if the Children's Defense Fund releases a well-publicized study on childhood immunization rates, then mainline Protestant lobbyists receive a boost in their efforts to immunize children. Washington today teems with this new brand of advocacy, and it seems that every day some institute is releasing a new report, calling for a new program, or presenting new facts to support a particular agenda. Similarly, such magazines as the *Weekly Standard, New Republic, The Nation, National Review, Commentary*, the *Atlantic Monthly*, and *First Things* provide venues for intellectuals to present ideas publicly and offer solutions to the problems of the day. Religious groups must be a part of this world or they will see their influence wane.

Perhaps the most important trend of all is the move toward involvement in state and local politics. Though some liberal Protestant and Catholic groups have operated in state and local politics for some time, the state and local scene has become more of a battleground for religio-political groups. Battles over school curricula, home-schooling, and vouchers, and the continuing struggle over abortion constitute the true skirmishes in the "culture wars." Since so many of these issues concern conservative evangelicals and Catholics, we expect to see even more of their efforts focused at this level. But given the pluralism of American society, strong opposition will also emerge to check such efforts.

Finally, it is clear that the struggle over American culture will produce changes in the relative strength and efficacy of national groups. Such groups, especially when they link with broader efforts, will probably see their influence grow over time. Because they seek sweeping social change, evangelical leaders have been busy founding their own secondary schools, colleges, and media companies for what they see as a long-term struggle with secular society. One can detect modest fruit from this effort. Wander the offices of Concerned Women for America, the Christian Coalition, or the Family Research Council and you will find recent graduates of such institutions as Regent University (founded by Pat Robertson) and Liberty University (founded by Jerry Falwell), as well as alumni of established evangelical institutions such as Wheaton College and Calvin College. Christian broadcasting and a growing Christian arts movement similarly seem focused on a long-term struggle, and they provide a means for new leaders to learn modern skills. More important still are the countercultural educational efforts of Christian conservatives, who aim to train a new generation of young people to move into government, academia, and the media and ultimately provide them with the elite access they now lack. Whether or not this long-term struggle over the culture will provide such access remains to be seen, but given the barriers these groups now face, it may be the only way they will ever come to exercise more than a marginal influence in the contemporary polity.

Other groups, too, understand this fact. From Orthodox Jews to Catholics, we see efforts to sustain or expand access to schools, media outlets, and other cultural institutions. Thus, if we wish to know something about the future political efficacy of a religious tradition, we should look to its present culture-building activities. Effective national advocacy ultimately rests on the vitality of the religious organizations and the constituencies they represent.

FURTHER READING

Hertzke, Allen D. *Representing God in Washington: The Role of Religious Lobbies in the American Polity.* Knoxville: University of Tennessee Press, 1988. The standard guide to religious interest groups today.

Hofrenning, Daniel J. B. *In Washington But Not of It: The Prophetic Politics of Religious Lobbyists.* Philadelphia: Temple University Press, 1995. The most recent treatment of religious lobbies, with a provocative thesis.

Olson, Laura R. "Mainline Protestant Washington Offices and the Political Lives of Clergy." In *The Quiet Hand of God: Faith-based Activism and the Public Role of Mainline Protestantism,* ed. Robert Wuthnow and John H. Evans. Berkeley: University of California Press, 2002. A new study of mainline Protestant activism.

Wood, Richard L. *Faith in Action: Religion, Race, and Democratic Organizing in America.* Chicago: University of Chicago Press, 2002. A valuable study of the role of religion in community organizing.

NOTES

1. For an account of the formative years, see Luke Eugene Ebersole, *Church Lobbying in the Nation's Capital* (New York: Macmillan, 1951).

2. Daniel J. B. Hofrenning, *In Washington But Not of It: The Prophetic Politics of Religious Lobbyists* (Philadelphia: Temple University Press, 1995).

3. Jeffrey M. Berry, *The New Liberalism: The Rising Power of Citizen Groups* (Washington, D.C.: Brookings, 1999).

4. A fuller development of strategies may be found in Allen D. Hertzke, *Representing God in Washington: The Role of Religious Lobbies in the American Polity* (Knoxville: University of Tennessee Press, 1988).

5. S. Robert Lichter, Stanley Rothman, and Linda S. Lichter, *The Media Elite* (Bethesda, MD: Adler, 1986). In this controversial work the authors argue that elite journalists are in fact highly secular in their behavior and attitudes. But see also John Schmalzbauer, *People of Faith: Religious Conviction in American Journalism and Higher Education* (Ithaca, NY: Cornell University Press, 2003).

6. Lydia Saad, "Issues Referendum Reveals Populist Leanings," *The Gallup Poll Monthly* (May 1996), 2–6. See also Hertzke, *Representing God in Washington*.

7. Elisabeth Bumiller, "Religious Leaders Ask If Antiwar Call is Heard," *New York Times* (March 10, 2003), A16; Peter Steinfels, "In a Poll, Few Say That Religion Shaped Their Views on Iraq," *New York Times* (March 22, 2003), D6.

8. Elisabeth Bumiller, "Evangelicals Sway White House on Human Rights Issues Abroad," *New York Times* (October 26, 2003), 1, 4.

9. See Laura R. Olson, "Mainline Protestant Washington Offices and the Political Lives of Clergy," in Robert Wuthnow and John H. Evans, *The Quiet Hand of God: Faith-based Activism and the Public Role of Mainline Protestantism* (Berkeley: University of California Press, 2002), 54–79.

10. http://ncccusa.org.

11. Allen D. Hertzke, "An Assessment of the Mainline Churches Since 1945," in James E. Wood Jr. and Derek Davis, eds., *The Role of Religion in the Making of Public Policy* (Waco, TX: Dawson Institute of Church-State Studies, 1991); Olson, "Mainline Protestant Washington Offices."

12. Kevin R. den Dulk and J. Mitchel Pickerill, "Bridging the Lawmaking Process: Organized Interests, Court-Congress Interaction, and Church-State Relations," *Polity,* 35 (2003), 419–440.

13. "Remarks on Signing the Religious Freedom Restoration Act of 1993," November 16, 1993, *Presidential Documents,* Administration of William J. Clinton, 2377–2378.

14. This model is a revised version of one developed by Robert Booth Fowler, *Religion and Politics in America* (Metuchen, NJ: Scarecrow Press, 1985).

15. Lawrence Kersten, *The Lutheran Ethic: The Impact of Religion on Laymen and Clergy* (Detroit, MI: Wayne State University Press, 1970).

16. James L. Guth, John C. Green, Corwin E. Smidt, Lyman A. Kellstedt, and Margaret M. Poloma, *The Bully Pulpit: The Politics of Protestant Clergy* (Lawrence: University Press of Kansas, 1997).

17. Theda Skocpol, *Diminished Democracy: From Membership to Management in American Civic Life* (Norman: University of Oklahoma Press, 2003).

18. Sidney Verba, Kay Lehman Schlozman, and Henry E. Brady, *Voice and Equality: Civic Voluntarism in American Society* (Cambridge, MA: Harvard University Press, 1995).

19. James F. Findlay Jr., *Church People in the Struggle: The National Council of Churches and the Black Freedom Movement, 1950–1970* (New York: Oxford University Press, 1993).

20. James Adams, *The Growing Church Lobby in Washington* (Grand Rapids, MI: Eerdmans, 1970), 10.

21. Findlay, *Church People in the Struggle*.

22. Hertzke, "An Assessment of the Mainline Churches Since 1945"; Olson, "Mainline Protestant Washington Offices."

23. http://www.clnnlc.org/; see Lynette Clemetson, "Clergy Group to Counter Conservatives," *New York Times* (November 17, 2003), A17.

24. Olson, "Mainline Protestant Washington Offices."

25. Laura R. Olson, *Filled with Spirit and Power: Protestant Clergy in Politics* (Albany: State University of New York Press, 2000); Sue E. S. Crawford, "Clergy at Work in the Secular City" (Ph.D. diss., Indiana University, 1995); Sue E. S. Crawford and Laura R. Olson, "Clergy as Political Actors in Urban Contexts" in Crawford and Olson, eds., *Christian Clergy in American Politics* (Baltimore: Johns Hopkins University Press, 2001), 104–119.

26. Olson, "Mainline Protestant Washington Offices."

27. Liberation theology, which originated in Latin America, teaches that churches must work to liberate those who are oppressed by economic and political inequality. See Paul E. Sigmund, *Liberation Theology at the Crossroads* (New York: Oxford University Press, 1990).

28. Ted G. Jelen, "Catholic Priests and the Political Order: The Political Behavior of Catholic Pastors," *Journal for the Scientific Study of Religion* 42 (2003), 597.

29. William D'Antonio, ed., *Laity, American and Catholic: Transforming the Church* (Kansas City, MO: Sheed and Ward, 1996).

30. NORC data, as reported in Tim O'Neil, "Scandal Rocks Church, But Faith Remains," *St. Louis Post Dispatch*, June 22, 2003, A1.

31. See Timothy A. Byrnes and Mary Segers, *The Catholic Church and Abortion Politics: A View from the States* (Boulder, CO: Westview, 1991).

32. See Mary Ann Glendon, *Abortion and Divorce in Western Law* (Cambridge, MA: Harvard University Press, 1987).

33. This point is made on the basis of national survey data as analyzed in Hertzke, *Representing God in Washington*, chap. 5. See also Chapter 4, Table 4.[x].

34. Richard W. Stevenson, "Bush Signs Ban on a Procedure for Abortions," *New York Times* (November 5, 2003), A1.

35. For an excellent overview of various aspects of just war theory, see Terry Nardin, ed., *The Ethics of War and Peace: Religious and Secular Perspectives* (Princeton, NJ: Princeton University Press, 1996).

36. Kenneth Wald notes that most Catholics had not read the document. Still, the extensive discussion surrounding it in parishes and the news media, along with the distribution of summary pamphlets, apparently succeeded in shifting Catholic opinion in a more dovish direction (if only temporarily). See Kenneth Wald, "Religious Elites and Public Opinion," *Review of Politics* 54 (Winter 1992), 112–143.

37. James McCormick, "Congressional Voting on the Nuclear Freeze Resolutions," *American Politics Quarterly* 13 (January 1985), 122–134.

38. For an excellent discussion of the churches and the Gulf War, see Andrew R. Murphy, "The Mainline Churches and Political Activism," *Soundings* (Winter 1993), 525–549; James Turner Johnson and George Weigel, *Just War and the Gulf War* (Washington, D.C.: Ethics and Public Policy Center, 1991). Johnson and Weigel argue that the Gulf War did meet just war criteria, much along the lines that Bush did in his speech to religious broadcasters. What weakened the Catholic Conference's influence, in part, was the natural ambiguity inherent in deciding whether criteria are met or not.

39. Stephen V. Monsma, *When Sacred and Secular Mix* (Lanham, MD: Rowman and Littlefield, 1996).

40. http://www.ajcongress.org/allabout.htm.

41. http://www.aipac.org.

42. Todd Hertz, "*The* Evangelical View of Israel?" *Christianity Today* (June 11, 2003); Deborah Caldwell, "Why Christians Must Keep Israel Strong: An Interview with Richard Land," available at http://www.beliefnet.com; Tatsha Robertson, "Evangelicals Flock to Israel's Banner," *Boston Globe* (October 21, 2002), A3.

43. Eun Lee Koh, "Robertson's Speech Backing Israel Gets Ovation at Temple," *Boston Globe* (April 14, 2003), B1.

44. Kevin R. den Dulk, "Prophets in Caesar's Courts: The Role of Ideas in Catholic and Evangelical Rights Advocacy" (Ph.D. Diss, University of Wisconsin, 2001).

45. Nearly three-quarters of Americans say they have either a very favorable or mostly favorable opinion of Jews, and only 9 percent have unfavorable feelings. See Pew Research Center and Pew Forum on Religion and Public Life, *2003 Religion and Public Life Survey* (June 24, 2003), available through the Roper Center, http://www.ropercenter.uconn.edu.

46. See Matthew C. Moen, *The Christian Right and Congress* (Tuscaloosa: University of Alabama Press, 1989); and Matthew C. Moen, *The Transformation of the Christian Right* (Tuscaloosa: University of Alabama Press, 1992).

47. For a good historical account of the Christian Coalition, see Justin Watson, *The Christian Coalition: Dreams of Restoration, Demands for Recognition* (New York: St. Martin's, 1997).

48. Ralph Reed, *After the Revolution* (Dallas: Word Publishing, 1996).

49. Skocpol, *Diminished Democracy*.

50. Mark J. Rozell and Clyde Wilcox, eds., *God at the Grass Roots* (Lanham, MD: Rowman and Littlefield, 1995); Kimberly Conger and John C. Green, "Spreading Out and Digging In: Christian Conservatives and State Republican Parties," *Campaigns and Elections* (February 2002), 58–65.

51. Connolly and Balz, "The Christian Coalition, Born Again," 15.

RELIGION AND
POLITICAL ELITES

Religious activism, as we have seen, can focus on shaping the culture, influencing elections, or lobbying government. To a large degree, the success or failure of these efforts hinges on the accessibility and responsiveness of the leaders of the American political system and elites in media and entertainment as well. As we explore the connections between religious politics and American elites, we must ask: How much do elites listen and respond to religious groups and activists? We ask this with the understanding that elites are not empty vessels. Their own religious backgrounds, worldviews, and biases affect how open they are to religious groups and faith-based arguments.

One might think that much is known about elite religious views, but we know less about their religious outlooks than we do about those of the general public. In part this reflects the problem of access. For example, busy members of Congress, executive branch officials, party leaders, or judges can, and often do, refuse to answer questionnaires. Rarely do they agree to provide more than the most cursory interview. Thus we have too little data on elites that can compare to standard national surveys of the religious public, such as those that the Gallup Organization or the Pew Center for the People and the Press regularly conduct. Still, we do have some information that helps us understand the various barriers religious leaders must overcome to have clout in government.

As we chart what we know of the religious perspectives of elites and the broader environment in which they work, we see that important religious differences occur among political elites, just as they do in the general public. But we also note that the religious views of elites as a group are not necessarily representative of the general public. Some perspectives are overrepresented while others are underrepresented, and this fact has political implications.

RELIGION AND THE PRESIDENCY

The outcomes of presidential elections clearly matter to religious activists. After all, the president appoints top officials in the executive branch, federal judges, U.S. Supreme Court justices, and diplomats. The president often has great influence over domestic policy and charts the nation's defense and foreign policies. Thus it matters tremendously who occupies the Oval Office, and the president can be a powerful ally or foe for activists who wish to further a political agenda based on religious principles. Presidents, for their part, realize the importance of religious constituencies and religious interest groups, and for many years they have designated White House officials to serve as liaisons to them.[1]

But every president also operates under compelling demands and a pragmatic logic that can easily override the moral pleas of religious petitioners. In the high-stakes world of *realpolitik*, religious niceties often give way to Machiavellian calculations. Moreover, the presidency is really a pluralistic office in which a host of White House aides jockey for influence, calling on religious leaders when it is expedient but ignoring them when it is not. Charles Colson recalls how he and other Nixon aides consciously used religious figures to lend legitimacy to the president and his views, or awed them with tours of the White House to mute their criticism. Religious figures, he has remarked, are often well-meaning but gullible people who understand little of the cutthroat nature of White House politics.[2] In retrospect, some evangelical leaders now suspect that they were naive about what they could get out of the Reagan White House in the 1980s. They have also raised pointed questions as to whether the Clinton White House used certain religious leaders for its own political purposes—and other critics have raised similar questions about the current Bush administration. The point is that religious influence does not flow in only one direction. Religious groups may attempt to use politics to advance their values, but political leaders might also manipulate these groups in the process.[3]

The chief executive's response to religious groups is constrained by the unique religious dimension of the Office of the President. As head of state the president serves a civil religious function.[4] Part of every president's responsibilities include offering prayers to grieving families of soldiers killed in action, invoking God's blessing on the nation on holidays like Thanksgiving and Memorial Day—and even during the presidential inauguration itself. Because of the nation's religious pluralism, presidents usually avoid clearly sectarian references on these occasions and employ the broadest, vaguest kinds of religious imagery.

The president's need to serve, in an important sense, as "pastor of the nation" can lessen the political clout of the president's own religious group. The classic illustration involves John Kennedy. His election to the presidency in 1960 brought enormous legitimacy to the Catholic population, but his presidential decisions did not advance the policy agenda of the Catholic Church (for instance, government support for parochial schools). Kennedy bent over backward to avoid the hint of favoritism, but some Catholic critics argued that this made his administration even less hospitable to the Catholic Church than previous Protestant administrations had been.

What can we make of the relationship between religion and the presidency? We should note at the outset that almost all U.S. presidents have professed to be Christians. Harry Truman was a Baptist, Eisenhower a Presbyterian, and Kennedy a Catholic. But it has only been in the last two decades or so that the issue of religion in the White House itself has become so visible and important. This is a manifestation of the growing politicization of religion. By contrasting presidents Richard Nixon, Jimmy Carter, Ronald Reagan, George Bush (the elder), Bill Clinton, and George W. Bush we will see both the scope and the limits of religious influence at 1600 Pennsylvania Avenue.

Richard Nixon, president from 1969 to 1974, offers perhaps the easiest case. Though raised a Quaker, Nixon demonstrated little personal connection between his declared Christian faith and his politics. Nixon's approach to politics was strategic, not religious or moralistic. Both his successes and his failures were closely connected to his calculating political personality. His approach produced one of the most enduring cautionary tales for would-be religious activists. That tale involved this century's most celebrated evangelist, Rev. Billy Graham.

Born in 1918, Graham emerged as the premier Protestant evangelist by mid-century, and by virtue of that role he became the unofficial pastor to presidents. Indeed, he has been invited to the White House by every president from Harry Truman to George W. Bush. It does not take a cynic to see why presidents would welcome Graham's blessing and association. Graham has relished his role, especially in the 1950s, 1960s, and early 1970s, playing golf with Ike and spending lots of time with Lyndon Johnson and even more with Nixon.

Graham got to know Nixon during the Eisenhower years, when Nixon was vice president. Graham came to count Nixon as a friend. When Kennedy opposed Nixon in the 1960 presidential election, Graham (like many evangelicals), for religious reasons, did not support Kennedy, but his sympathies also lay with Nixon as a friend. When Nixon gained the Republican nomination for a second time in 1968, Graham emerged as a visible supporter. He visited the Nixon headquarters at the Republican convention, introduced the candidate at an evangelistic crusade, and announced five days before the election that he planned to vote for Nixon (a public endorsement he repeated in Nixon's 1972 re-election campaign). After Nixon's 1968 victory, Graham was welcomed in the White House and often was included in the presidential entourage.

We now know, however, that Graham was never a member of Nixon's inner circle, nor was he privy to important decisions or secrets. Neither did Graham, as he now realizes, have a real friendship with Nixon, a man he knew much less well than he thought.[5] The Watergate scandal became the crucial moment in the Nixon-Graham relationship. When the Watergate drama unfolded, Graham initially refused to believe that Nixon had done—or could have done—anything so wrong. But as evidence piled up, and tapes revealed Nixon's personal vulgarity, meanness, and calculating manner, Graham changed his mind. The whole experience tempered Graham, leaving him more cautious about the blandishments of politicians and the temptations of power.[6]

Jimmy Carter's presidency (1977–81) provided a contrast to the Nixon years. Lauded for his strict personal morality, Carter was also criticized for his naïveté and lack of strategic ability. A born-again Southern Baptist, a Sunday school teacher, and by all accounts a devout man, Carter's faith has always mattered to him, and he draws close conscious links between his faith and his politics.[7] This was true in his view of the presidency as a trusteeship, in which he believed he should act in the public interest despite adverse political fallout.[8] It was also true, for example, in his approach to environmental politics from a framework of biblical steward-ship of God's creation. But it was most obvious in the realm of foreign policy, where Carter sought to advance what he viewed as the Christian mandates of human rights and peace. Ironically, many who later rose to prominence in the Reagan White House criticized Carter as naive and claimed that he failed to provide a robust defense of American national interests. Some critics, such as Jeane Kirkpatrick, associated the weak-nesses of Carter's foreign policy with his very Christian moralism. Carter was simply not Machiavellian enough to be a good president, they argued.

Carter's greatest triumph as president—the Camp David Accords, which sealed the peace between Egypt and Israel—reflected aspects of his faith. His belief in redemption, his stubborn determination to foster reconcilia-tion, and his embrace of both sides as religious kin of the "blood of Abra-ham" made a real difference in the delicate negotiations. Critics of Carter's international role since his presidency, which has taken him to Bosnia, Ko-rea, and Haiti, among other places—and won him the 2003 Nobel Peace Prize—claim that he seeks peace at any price and that he places too much stock in the good faith of dictators. But it is an indisputable fact that Jimmy Carter's political endeavors, which flow from his understanding of Christian faith, have made an enduring mark in the world.

An irony is that the evangelical Carter lost the support of evangelicals during the course of his presidency. In part this was because he interpreted his faith in a more liberal way than many of his fellow Southern Baptists. It was partly because the Democratic coalition he led produced liberal policies that angered and insulted many evangelicals. Carter's opponent in the 1980 election, Ronald Reagan, understood this discontent and played on it. Speaking before a convention of mostly evangelical religious broad-casters in 1980, Reagan acknowledged that as religious leaders they could not endorse him. He assured Christian evangelicals, however, that he sup-ported their policy goals. Reagan made his view clear in one succinct dec-laration: "I endorse *you*."

Many Protestant evangelicals flocked to Reagan's candidacy in 1980 and 1984, though critics complained that he was not much of a churchgoer, had been divorced, and had risen to political prominence out of Holly-wood—hardly an evangelical bastion. They also pointed out that his wife, Nancy Reagan, put some stock in astrology. Still, Reagan remained popu-lar among evangelicals because he defended "traditional values," nuclear families, patriotism, and the faith of the framers—with rhetorical skill and apparent sincerity.

This illustrates a key problem in sorting out the role that faith plays in the life of the occupant of the Oval Office. A president's electoral coalition is often formed more on the basis of his political stands than his personal practices or worldview. This is not to gainsay Reagan's religion; he did affirm orthodox beliefs and even shared in speculation about the end times prophesied in scripture. Moreover, his White House staff paid close attention to evangelicals, as well as to Jews and Catholics, while shunning most liberal religious groups. In retrospect, however, questions remain about what, if anything, evangelicals and other religious conservatives gained during the Reagan years (1981–1989). To be sure, many applauded Reagan's stand against communism, and there were new, moderate to conservative justices appointed to the U.S. Supreme Court. But most of the evangelical political agenda went nowhere during the Reagan years.[9] Abortion continued with few legal restrictions, prayer stayed out of public schools, the entertainment media became more violent, divorce remained common, and the rate of out-of-wedlock births spiraled upward. Some evangelical leaders grumbled that the Reagan administration paid only lip service to their agendas.

Reagan's vigorous denunciation of the Soviet Union—he called it the "Evil Empire"—led him to form ties with Pope John Paul II that had a global impact. Prior to his selection as pope, John Paul II had been a Polish bishop and a leader in the opposition to communist rule. Once elected, he set about using his authority and freedom to travel as a means of fostering growing opposition to communist regimes in Eastern Europe. The Reagan administration was aware of these efforts and bolstered them with initiatives of its own aimed at destabilizing Soviet rule. This alliance was a dramatic example of the power of religious and political authorities working together. What is not clear is how to disentangle President Reagan himself from his administration's motivations. Did Reagan's faith matter here? If so, how much? The answers are simply not clear.

This brings us to George Bush, Connecticut Yankee, blue blood, and president from 1989 to 1993. Here too we encounter ironies of faith versus strategic politics. Bush is a mainline Protestant, an Episcopalian, and, although he claims to be a religious man, he is uncomfortable with pietistic politics. The evangelical world of public witnessing, stories of sin and redemption, and calls for moral renewal, are as alien to Bush as they are to most mainline Protestants. And when Bush tried publicly to affirm his faith, his statements came across as strained, awkward, even humorous.

In spite of his lack of comfort with public religion, Bush worked hard to gain evangelical votes in the 1988 presidential election. He succeeded, actually garnering a greater share of the evangelical vote than Reagan had in 1984. Like his predecessor's, however, Bush's record, from the standpoint of conservative evangelicals and Catholics, turned out to be mixed. He generated considerable anger when he hosted a meeting of gay activists at the White House, and he was criticized more generally for his tepid advocacy of the Christian Right's political agenda. On the other hand, he worked to block abortion funding and fetal experimentation, and he appointed conservative Clarence Thomas to the U.S. Supreme Court. Even in defeat in 1992, Bush received more support from evangelical Protestants than from any other religious group.

In many respects, Bill Clinton, president from 1993 to 2001, was his predecessor's opposite. From an early age he was immersed in the evangelical subculture and he remained at ease with it as an adult, but his social liberalism hurt his political support among evangelicals. Clinton was raised in Bible Belt Arkansas, where he attended Baptist churches and Pentecostal summer camps as a youngster. As governor of Arkansas he joined a prominent Baptist church in Little Rock. He is fluent in the evangelical language of sin and redemption, and he is equally comfortable in black and white evangelical congregations (often joining in gospel singing from memory). His wife, Sen. Hillary Rodham Clinton (D-New York), has been an active United Methodist who embodies the social justice agenda of her denomination.

Until sexual scandal tarnished the Clinton presidency, the presence of the Clintons in Washington was a boon to the liberal religious community. From the National Council of Churches to the United Methodist Church, religious activists shut out of the White House during the Reagan-Bush years were welcomed back. Clinton also proved to be intensely popular with African Americans, but his socially liberal agenda made him equally unpopular with white evangelicals. And the sexual scandal involving Clinton and a White House intern doomed his relations with many religious leaders and groups.

Finally we consider George W. Bush, president from 2001 to the present. He grew up in west Texas, where his religious upbringing was decidedly mainline Protestant. He attended a Presbyterian church with his family until he left for his elite preparatory school and university in the Northeast. Upon returning to Texas years later, he joined his wife, Laura Bush's, United Methodist church, where he was a respected and dutiful member of the congregation. But his personal relationship to religion changed, by most accounts dramatically, when he began participating in a Bible study during a time of struggle with alcohol and family life. In 1986 he gave up drinking and embraced a more evangelical Christianity.[10]

The change became part of his public life, too, first during Bush's stint as a liaison to evangelicals during his father's 1988 presidential bid, then as governor of Texas, and finally as president.[11] During a 2000 presidential debate, for example, he famously declared that Jesus was his favorite philosopher, and he has repeatedly said that Jesus "changed my heart"—statements that resonate deeply with evangelicals. But he has also taken actions that have reinforced his religious conservative credentials. He has surrounded himself with people who share his religious commitments, including National Security Advisor Condoleezza Rice, speechwriter Michael Gerson, and old friend (and current Commerce Secretary) Donald Evans. Many of Bush's policies have also had religious overtones, from his establishment of the White House Office for Faith-based and Community Initiatives to his claims that U.S. actions against terrorism amount to a war of good versus an "axis of evil."

In light of modern presidential history, President Bush's religiosity and its connection to politics would predictably generate both criticism and support. What is less clear is how much Bush's public religion is a sincere expression of his personal faith and how much is a deliberate effort to use faith for political purposes. Sorting out religious motivations from political calculations is a difficult business. As we have seen, every president's faith matters under some circumstances, but the dynamics of political interest and advantage count for as much, if not more. Presidents are political animals, and they are in the business of making political judgments and calculations.

A different approach to the role of religion in presidential politics is to consider that what really matters is not so much presidents' own religious beliefs but rather their symbolic use of religious rhetoric. From this point of view, presidential language or rhetoric sets a national tone from the top. Adam Kradel's research on presidential rhetoric since the early 1970s shows that successive presidents have used recognizably religious language, but that Republican presidents have employed it far more often than have Democratic ones. This may surprise some observers who note that both Democratic presidents in this period were very open in their Christian religious convictions.[12] While Republican presidents, including George W. Bush, frequently used such language, Democratic presidents not only used it less, but addressed religion more in terms of specific issues (such as international human rights concerns).

These differences are real, but what is constant is the use of religious language by one American president after another. Every president knows that religion is a source of cultural influence. As political scientist David Leege and his colleagues argue, political elites have always recognized this influence and sought to exploit it.[13] In this sense, religion is very much a part of the American presidency.

RELIGION AND CONGRESS

Congress in the contemporary era reflects the religious pluralism of America more than, say, the media or Hollywood. Yet the membership of Congress does not mirror the population perfectly. Some religious groups, such as mainline Protestants and Jews, are overrepresented relative to their proportion of the U.S. population, whereas Baptists and other evangelical and fundamentalist Protestants are underrepresented. Several factors are at work here, including different religious groups' socioeconomic status, their openness to politics, and their geographic concentration.

One way to assess religion's role in Congress is to look at the patterns of religious affiliation of members over time. In the 1950s, for example, congressional membership was heavily weighted toward mainline Protestant denominations, with Catholics and evangelicals underrepresented. The first big change in this pattern occurred in 1958, when huge Democratic gains in midterm elections brought an unprecedented number of Catholics to Congress. Indeed, it was this influx of Catholics, coupled with Kennedy's presidential candidacy two years later, that motivated scholars to look seriously at the faith of members of Congress.[14]

Congressional membership since 1960 has become more religiously diverse (see Table 6.1). One striking example concerns Jewish representation. Only 2 percent of the members of the House and Senate were Jews in 1960, which was less than their share of the total population at the time. In 2002, by contrast, 6 percent of House members and 11 percent of senators were Jewish, which is considerably more than their 2 percent of the U.S. population today. Among the reasons for this change are the rise in acceptance of Jews in the country at large, strong political interest within the Jewish community, and high levels of Jewish economic status and educational attainment, which enables Jews to run for office more readily than people of lower socioeconomic status.

Catholics compose about 25 percent of the U.S. population. Though they were slightly underrepresented in Congress in 1960 (19 percent), they had achieved more than parity by 2002, when they accounted for nearly 28 percent of congressional membership. Catholic congressional representation, in fact, has consistently remained at or slightly above its proportion of the population for a number of years.

One of the notable changes in Congress in recent years has been the partisan distribution of Catholic members. In 1960, the Catholic congressional delegation was overwhelmingly Democratic. Since then, however, Republicans have made significant inroads. After the 1970 elections 35 percent of Catholics in Congress were Republicans; by the 1994 midterm elections that figure had grown to 43 percent, where it remains today. Here, at least, we see a reflection of Catholic voting patterns: the Democrats retain a slight edge, but their dominance has been greatly diminished from previous years.

Mainline Protestant denominations continue to be overrepresented relative to their share of the population. Their congressional numbers have declined since 1960, paralleling declines in mainline church membership. We see this most clearly among Presbyterians and Episcopalians. Though their membership in Congress is down from 1960 by about one-fourth, they still retain robust representation relative to their modest lay membership. This again reflects the importance of socioeconomic status. Episcopalians and Presbyterians, as a group, are part of a highly educated socioeconomic elite, so some of their members are well positioned to achieve political leadership.

Of course, congressional representation does not by definition translate into clout for the Episcopal or Presbyterian lobbies in Washington, which tend to be more liberal than Episcopalian and Presbyterian members of Congress. Members of Congress can disagree with each

TABLE 6.1 Religious Affiliations of Members of Congress, 2002

	House	Senate	Total	Percent of Congress	Percent Change Since 1960
Roman Catholic	124	25	149	27.8	+46.1
Jewish	26	11	37	6.9	+208.3
Mormon	12	5	17	3.2	+114.3
Protestant (total)	257	55	312	58.3	-25.7
Baptist	66	6	72	13.5	+12.5
Methodist	50	12	62	11.6	-39.2
Presbyterian	37	13	50	9.3	-25.4
Episcopalian	34	10	44	8.2	-31.3
Lutheran	19	4	23	6.9	+4.5
United Church of Christ	2	6	8	1.5	-70.0
Other / Unspecified Protestant	49	4	53	9.3	+121.0
Other	16	4	13	2.4	NA

Sources: Congressional Quarterly Weekly Report (January 8, 1960), 6; *Congressional Quarterly Weekly Report* (January 25, 2003), 193.

other on political issues, after all, and they also can disagree about how religious they are and thus how much religion matters in their political lives. And in some instances, it is the religious backgrounds of the constituents, rather than those of the members themselves, that bear a strong relationship to congressional voting behavior.[15] Nonetheless, having members of one's own denomination in Congress may provide at least some access.

We do not have complete data on evangelicals in Congress because they are diffused among many denominations. It is clear that their numbers have increased since 1960. Still, they remain underrepresented relative to their share of the population, in part because of the overrepresentation of mainline Protestants and growth in Catholic representation. The Baptist contingent in Congress, which contains many traditional evangelicals, illustrates this fact. Baptist representation has increased slightly since 1960, but Baptists remain slightly underrepresented. Despite the fact that they make up 16 percent of the population, Baptists compose 13.5 percent of congressional membership.[16] This should not surprise us given the historically modest economic and educational profiles of Baptists as a group. The Baptist congressional delegation is also diverse, containing a healthy share of black Baptists, whose politics often diverge from the white evangelical agenda.

The Church of Jesus Christ of Latter-day Saints is notable in that, unlike most small faith groups, Mormons have at least as great a proportion of adherents in Congress as they do in the population at large. Mormons comprised 1.5 percent of the Congress in 1960, but this share more than doubled by 2002. This proportion is larger than the Mormon share of the U.S. population, which has been steadily increasing but is still less than 2 percent. The best explanation for this phenomenon is that Mormons are concentrated in Utah and neighboring western states, the very places where most Mormons win elections. Also, Mormons are mostly middle-class people with access to the educational and financial resources that matter in politics.

Outside the Judeo-Christian orbit, the nation has experienced significant growth in the population of Hindus, Buddhists, and Muslims since 1960. While none of these groups has reached the size of the Jewish or Mormon voting populations, their share of the electorate would warrant representation in Congress. Yet currently there are no Hindu, Buddhist, or Muslim members of Congress. Muslims may have the greatest potential to fill this representational gap, but as a heavily immigrant community they will probably need to become more numerous, more strategically concentrated, and better organized to do so.

The U.S. Senate provides an interesting laboratory for discussing the representation of different religious faiths. It has a decidedly more elite religious profile than the House. The largest religious group in the Senate, comprising slightly less than half of the entire membership, is mainline Protestantism. This is true despite the fact that this group constitutes less than a quarter of the U.S. population. Next come Catholics at 25 percent, Jews at 11 percent, and Baptists at 6 percent. Evangelicals are underrepresented relative to their share of the population. Episcopalians historically have been overrepresented in the Senate, and this continues to be true. Ten senators (10 percent) are Episcopalian, even though this denomination makes up less than 2 percent of the U.S. population.

The crucial issue, however, is not about the declared affiliation of members of Congress. What matters is whether Catholic, mainline Protestant, Jewish, or Baptist members of Congress constitute distinct voting blocs. The evidence on this is mixed at best. A study of Catholic legislators in the late 1950s, for example, found some evidence of Catholic solidarity in congressional voting, but only at the margins of normal party voting.[17] Mary Hanna's study of Catholics in the 1970s showed that Catholic members of Congress were not even aware of their own sizable numbers, so they were definitely not cohesive in their votes.[18] This appears to be true today as well. It is not really surprising, since partisan differences, varying regions, specific constituencies, and personal perspectives diffuse the unity and impact of any religious group in Congress. One of the few exceptions may be unified Jewish support for Israel, but beyond that, religion-based issue cohesiveness disappears. With other groups, moreover, it is hard to find even a single unifying issue. Though one study does suggest that the most religiously committed evangelicals in Congress tend to coalesce around issues associated with the Christian Right, there is considerable partisan and ideological difference even among evangelical Protestant legislators.[19] In short, political diversity reigns within religious traditions.

Even acknowledging this diversity, we still must ask if shared religions could make a more subtle impact on congressional politics. After all, denominational affiliation can be a lot less important than *how* one experiences faith. If only we could get inside the minds of members of Congress, we might see how their religious worldviews (as opposed to their nominal religious affiliations) shape their roll call votes. Surely this would be the best guide of all as to how religion affects politics on Capitol Hill. This was exactly the premise of an ambitious study by Peter Benson and Dorothy Williams entitled *Religion on Capitol Hill*.[20]

The authors conducted in-depth interviews with a large sample of members of Congress in the 1980s. The religious themes explored in the interviews reached beyond denominational categories to personal ones. How did they experience God or religion—as comforting or challenging? As restricting or releasing? As an individual or a member of a community? What is the central demand of their religion—reverence for God or service to fellow humans? How did they view God—as a judge or loving presence?

The authors discovered that members of Congress fell into six religious types, which they labeled legalistic, self-concerned, integrated, people-concerned, nontraditional, and nominal. These categories did not correlate with particular religious denominations or political parties, but they proved widely predictive of voting behaviors. In fact, members' religious

attitudes predicted their voting patterns better than did their party affiliations. Religious worldviews clearly structured their value systems and
their political behaviors. This is not to say that some members of some
faiths do not share common attitudes. But what Benson and Williams
help us appreciate is the complexity of religious experience and its relationship with politics. Thus a "legalistic" Catholic may have more in
common with a Protestant of the same type than with a fellow Catholic
whose faith experience falls into a different category.

A number of interesting findings emerged from the Benson and Williams
study. The most politically liberal members of Congress were those whose
faith was very "people-concerned." Such members stated that their religions'
goals included promoting justice, helping the less fortunate, and other similar missions. By comparison, "legalistic" and "self-concerned" religionists
said their faith suggested a reverence for God and proper personal conduct;
they were distinctly more conservative politically. Slightly more than a fifth
of the members surveyed were "nominal" religionists; their faith seemed
weak and unconnected to politics. Many nominally religious politicians
were stymied by such questions as "What is the path to salvation?" This
most secular group was not the most liberal, however. They tended to be
liberal on social issues and conservative on economic and defense issues. By
contrast, "integrated religionists," who combined a concern for what they
understood as justice on earth and a reverence for a judging God, reversed
that pattern, taking more conservative stands on abortion and more liberal
ones on welfare and international relations.

The central finding of the Benson and Williams study remains compelling. Members of Congress are not empty vessels, they argued; rather,
they bring to their jobs years of socialization and religious experiences
that mold their worldviews. Those views, in turn, are likely to contribute, consciously and unconsciously, to their politics.

Another way to look at the study of religion and Congress is to examine particular members of Congress for whom religion matters a great
deal. As in American society, religious convictions among members of
Congress take diverse forms, sometimes even within the same religious
tradition or denomination. These expressions of religious belief and devotion often help us make sense of a member's political actions.

One illustration concerns minority faiths. Mormons in Congress, for
example, tend to mirror the conservatism on cultural and family issues

within the LDS Church as a whole. A prominent example is Senator Or-
rin Hatch (R-Utah), the conservative Chair of the Judiciary Committee,
who has been a vocal critic of the role of judicial "activism" in supporting
abortion rights and other liberal causes.

Offering a contrasting case are Jews, who tend to be liberal Democrats,
though it is often hard to sort out ethnic from the religious influences.
That is not the case, however, for the most celebrated Jewish legislator,
Senator Joseph Lieberman (D-Connecticut). He became a national figure as the result of his 2000 vice-presidential nomination and subsequent
bid for the Democratic presidential nomination in 2004. An Orthodox
Jew, Lieberman's political liberalism is tempered by his high-profile efforts to have warning labels placed on CDs featuring sexually explicit and
violent lyrics, his openness to school choice and similar policies, and his
supportive position on the war in Iraq (though not its aftermath). Each
of these positions, in fact, are reflections of his own Jewish Orthodoxy.
But his support for abortion rights, domestic partnership benefits for
same-sex couples, universal healthcare coverage, and other policies have
given him high liberal rankings among interest groups in Washington.

The Republican Party has been particularly keen on moving religiously
committed legislators into prominent roles. Rep. Eric Cantor (R-Virginia)
is the sole Jewish Republican in the House of Representatives and enjoys a
position on the leadership team of the GOP caucus. He is distinct from
most Jews in his fiscal conservatism, prolife position, and support for
school prayer. But he shares with Joe Lieberman and many other Jewish
legislators a passionate pro-Israel stance.[21] Another example is Senator
Rick Santorum (R-Pennsylvania), who quickly rose to a position of party
leadership in the Senate. A devout Catholic who attends mass every day,
he has emerged as a key spokesman for moral traditionalism. His unwa-
vering conservatism put him at the forefront of the battle to ban a late-
term abortion procedure, and he also got into a flap over his disapproving
comments about homosexuality.[22]

As with Santorum, many Republicans' religious convictions contribute
to conservativism on hot button moral issues. But for some members,
those convictions simultaneously lead them to champion causes associated with liberal groups, such as international human rights. Consider
the case of Representative Frank Wolf (R-Virginia). A conservative evangelical, he has focused attention on the spread of gambling in the United

States, which is no surprise for a religious traditionalist. But Wolf is also one of the House's leading crusaders for human rights. The *Washington Post* profiled him as the capitol's first "bleeding heart conservative," a human rights champion who "has traveled the world in search of famine, death and war, trying to find ways to help."[23] He sees his career in Congress as a response to the maxim, "To whom much is given, much is required." As co-chair of the Congressional Human Rights Caucus, he has held hearings, conducted fact finding trips (sometimes incognito), toured foreign prisons, and secured the release of dissidents. Wolf takes inspiration from the martyrdom of Dietrich Bonhoeffer, the German pastor who opposed the Nazis. For Wolf, Christian faith demands that he do all he can for the "Dietrich Bonhoeffers" around the world.[24]

A good friend of Wolf's, Rep. Chris Smith (R-NJ), presents another illustrative case. A devout Catholic, Smith traces his political convictions to his upbringing in the faith. As former director of New Jersey Right-to-Life, Smith entered Congress 1980 as a fierce opponent of abortion, which led some in the press to lump him into the new Christian Right movement. But throughout his career Smith generally has been supportive of labor unions, government aid for impoverished children, international relief programs, and global human rights. For Smith this blend of issue positions reflects his Catholicism. Describing himself as a "Matthew 25 Christian," Smith sees both his prolife and international humanitarian work as flowing from the same injunction ("whatsoever you do to the least of my brethren you do to me").[25] When Republicans took control of the House after the 1994 elections, Smith assumed the chairmanships of the International Relations Subcommittee on Human Rights. For the next six years Smith held over 150 hearings on human rights abuses and sponsored legislation on such diverse issues as promotion of religious freedom, support for victims of torture, sanctions against human trafficking, and Sudanese peace.

In the Senate Sam Brownback (R-KS) is another interesting case. He came to Congress with the new Republican class of 1994 and he lived up to its conservative profile on economic and social issues. He worked closely with a range of conservative religious groups, for example, to restrict stem-cell research and ban human cloning. But his record on international humanitarian causes has earned him respect among liberals. He was the principal Senate sponsor for major legislation on human trafficking with the late Sen. Paul Wellstone (D-Minnesota); peacemaking in Sudan; North

Korean refugees with Sen. Ted Kennedy (D-Massachusetts), and Iranian democracy. On the domestic front he cosponsored legislation with civil rights legend Rep. John Lewis (D-Georgia) to create a National Museum of African American History. To Brownback this latter act made sense because he traces his roots to antebellum evangelical abolitionists in Kansas. But he also sees his religion playing a crucial role. A United Methodist when he entered the Senate, Brownback converted to Catholicism in 2003, in part out of admiration for the humanitarian work of Mother Teresa.[26]

Among Democrats few representatives reflected the connection between faith and politics as intensely as Tony Hall (D-Ohio), who recently left Congress and now serves as ambassador to the United Nations Agencies for Food and Agriculture. A born-again Christian, he is best known as a liberal crusader against world hunger, a cause that he sees as flowing from his Christian calling. He has toured some of the worst famine-plagued regions of the world to fight for international relief. In 1993 he even undertook a personal hunger strike to pressure fellow House members to reverse plans to abolish a committee that focused on fighting hunger in the United States and abroad.

Given what we know about the heritage of the black church, we would expect many African American members of to reflect that influence. Indeed, some black members of Congress, such as former legislator Floyd Flake (D-NY), have been ministers. But sifting out religious influence from racial concerns is very difficult. Consider the case of Donald Payne (D-NJ), an influential member of the Congressional Black Caucus and ranking minority member on the Subcommittee on Africa. A devout Baptist, he circulates through black congregations to drum up support for his causes, particularly African development aid. But is this work driven by his religious convictions, or his sense of solidarity with black Africa? Probably both.

Perhaps the most celebrated liberal in Congress is Senator Hillary Rodham Clinton (D-NY), a United Methodist who sees her work as flowing from the Social Gospel heritage of the church (see profile in Chapter 11). But among the rising stars in the House of Representatives, it is another woman whose faith connects to politics in illuminating ways. As House Minority Leader Nancy Pelosi (D-CA) is the highest ranking woman in the history of Congress. In the position she holds as of this writing, she will become Speaker of the House if the Democrats regain a majority of the chamber. Strongly supportive of abortion rights, gay rights, AIDS funding, and social programs, she is tagged as a "San Francisco liberal" by Republican critics. But her religious background and identity seem to set her apart from that label. Pelosi was born Nancy D'Alesandro, daughter of a legendary politician who essentially ran Baltimore city politics. She still describes herself as a "conservative Catholic," by which she means that her strict Catholic upbringing—observant, respectful of elders—forged aspects of her character. As she said in an interview, she was taught "love of country, deep love of the Catholic Church and love of family." At a time when the old norm of the large Catholic family was becoming rare, Pelosi raised five children as a full-time mother before embarking on her political career. These experiences probably facilitate unusual alliances. She has championed the cause of persecuted Christians, a *cause celebre* of evangelicals, in part because of her concern about how Catholics are treated in China.[27]

These profiles point to the possibilities for alliances among people who are otherwise ideologically different, and that is just what we see. For years Nancy Pelosi and Frank Wolf led the fight against granting the People's Republic of China permanent normal trade relations status with the United States and admission to the World Trade Organization without human rights improvement. To promote the broader cause of human rights they have traveled abroad to investigate abuses, cosponsored legislation, and planned strategy together. We see the same kind of collaboration on the Sudan cause, in which Chris Smith and Donald Payne joined forces to back legislation that business groups opposed (see Chapter 7). In the Senate Joe Lieberman and Sam Brownback have teamed up to curb violence and misogyny in movies and rock music, while collaborating on a host of international humanitarian initiatives.

Sorting out religious motives from other factors, of course, is impossible, but probing these alliances suggests that the impact of religion in Congress is not trivial. Moreover, a testament to the importance of religion, whatever its guise, is the thriving religious culture on Capitol Hill. Full-time chaplains work for the House and Senate, spending many hours counseling harried politicians. Members of Congress also attend various area churches and religious fellowships, and Capitol Hill Bible studies have proliferated. Often these groups cross party lines and allow members of Congress to ease the frustrations and stresses of political life by praying together, sharing their stories, and offering each other solace. To be sure, such activities blend with lives that also contain plenty of strategic calculation and hardball politics. Religious practice on Capitol Hill is, like so much else, complex and mixed.

RELIGION AND OTHER POLITICAL ELITES

Outside the White House and halls of Congress are many other political elites who have a keen interest in the interaction of religion and politics. Consider the proliferating think tanks and policy institutes that contribute to the debates between partisans in Washington and elsewhere. Here, too, we see evidence of a modest religious presence that has made a difference. Important examples include the Ethics and Public Policy Center, the Center for Public Justice, and the Institute on Religion and Democracy in Washington, D.C., as well as the Institute on Religion and Public Life in New York. Many of these organizations have high-profile leaders, such as Richard John Neuhaus, George Weigel, and Eliott Abrams. They receive support from intellectuals of considerable note, including Peter Berger, Irving Kristol, and Jean Bethke Elshtain. These institutes conduct policy seminars and produce a flood of publications, including journals. Aware that religion must make its case to skeptics, these groups make a difference by offering an intellectual basis for an active role for religious faith in modern policy debates (see Box 6.1). They also provide ideas and intellectual support for their political allies.

An arena where religious influence often seems suppressed is in the upper echelons of the executive branch of the U.S. government. Bureaucratic decisions are rarely made in overtly religious contexts. Government administration often does not lend itself easily to applying faith to politics and does not often attract employees who are particularly interested in this goal. Moreover, administrative leaders often come from elite educational backgrounds, which we know to be more secular than those of the general population. Still, administrators and managers must address religion, in some instances, even if they do not do so willingly. The increasing amounts and range of grantmaking to religious social services is a case in point.

The courts play an important role in the American policymaking process, far more so than in other nations. Judicial review is a powerful

---

BOX 6.1 PATRONS OF RELIGION IN PUBLIC LIFE

Much of the public activity and discussion surrounding religion and politics today would not happen without generous funding by a small number of very large philanthropic organizations. Since the early 1980s, foundations such as Lilly, Templeton, and the Pew Charitable Trusts have provided tens of millions of dollars to the exploration of religion's role in public life. Many of the patrons who created these foundations were themselves deeply committed religious believers. The late J. Howard Pew, for example, head of the Sun Oil Company from 1912 to 1947 and a lifelong Presbyterian, established the Pew Charitable Trusts in 1948 with his siblings to support evangelical parachurch organizations and other religion-based enterprises, including the evangelical magazine *Christianity Today* and Gordon-Conwell Theological Seminary. Today the Pew Charitable Trusts actively supports academic scholarship on religion, especially work focused on evangelicals, and the Trusts also supports the Pew Forum on Religion in Public Life, which brings together a wide range of intellectuals "to promote a deeper understanding of how religion shapes the ideas and institutions of American society."

SOURCES: http://www.pewforum.org; Michael S. Hamilton and Johanna G. Yngvason, "Patrons of the Evangelical Mind," *Christianity Today* (July 8, 2002), 42.

---

tool, and many judges do not hesitate to use it to advance public policies that suit their values. At the level of the nine justices on the U.S. Supreme Court, we have little evidence about whether—or to what extent—religious convictions influence judicial decisions, partly due to a lack of access to the very private, even reclusive, justices. At least one study of lower courts, however, suggests a modest impact of faith on judicial decision-making, especially among the most religiously committed evangelicals.[28]

Finally, state and local politics, which are arenas of increasing importance, may be influenced by the religious makeup of those holding offices, whether elected or appointed. States may play larger roles in policymaking as the federal government's role diminishes in this era of budget cutting and opposition to Washington's direction of human affairs. From school board members to governors, state and local elites will increasingly make a difference. Unfortunately, we do not have much systematic information on the religious affiliations and attitudes of governors, state legislators, or local officials, much less on whether their affiliations have mattered in terms of policymaking.[29]

At the state level we do see some evidence that religion plays a role, albeit constrained, in public policymaking. One example of a religious current in state politics involves abortion, the debate over which intensified after a 1989 U.S. Supreme Court decision gave new latitude to the states to regulate abortion. Accounts of those battles reveal the importance of the attitudes of governors and state legislators. When Catholic and evangelical groups lobbied in various states for more restrictive abortion statutes, success depended in part on the views of elected officials (and the political cultures that produced them). Thus restrictive abortion statutes were passed in Idaho and Utah, where Mormons are concentrated; in Pennsylvania, with its sizable traditional Catholic population; and in Louisiana, where traditional Catholics and conservative evangelicals joined forces. Legislators in those states were sympathetic to prolife religious activists because they shared similar worldviews. On the other hand, restrictive abortion statutes were struck down in New Jersey, Florida, and Connecticut, and abortion laws remain liberal in a variety of states from New York to Colorado to California. Legislators in these and other states, which support more socially libertarian political cultures, have largely ignored antiabortion lobbying.

With increasing devolution of power from the federal government, issues from crime to welfare, education to divorce policy, and drug-abuse prevention to abortion are decided more often in state and local political arenas. The result, of course, is greater focus by religious groups on state and local politics—arenas in which they have the potential to hold substantial sway.

RELIGION AND CULTURAL ELITES

American public life involves much more, of course, than political elites. And in the realms of journalism and entertainment, too, we see varying influences of faith among elites. Despite conventional wisdom (which derives in part from the teachings of Karl Marx, who called religion "the opiate of the masses"), the wealthy and powerful in America do not all shun religion. In fact, over 40 percent of all Americans who earn more than $85,000 annually report attending religious services every week or nearly so, which represents a slightly larger proportion of the population than those who earn less than $15,000.[30] Educational attainment, another indicator of socioeconomic status, suggests the same pattern: Well over 60 percent of those Americans with college degrees claim to attend services every week compared with just under 60 percent of those with high school diplomas and 50 percent of Americans without.

One of the relative bastions of secularism, as we have noted elsewhere, is the elite press, which has great influence over how political issues are framed for the public. One matter of considerable debate is whether the elite press pays little attention to religion because its reporters and editors know little of it or because they are hostile to it.[31] A few journalists either are religious or are serious about studying the world of religion, and this is exemplified in the committed membership of the Religion Newswriters Association. *The New York Times, Washington Post, Newsweek, Time,* and the Associated Press, among others, employ serious religion journalists, even if their numbers pale in comparison to the number of sportswriters, for example. Such journalists provide access to religious activists, sometimes enabling them to articulate their message to a broader public. They are complemented by journalists who work for religious publications and write about politics, but whose work rarely reaches broader media markets. Moreover, coverage of some aspects of religion in the media is increasing, especially the status of Islam in the wake of the September 11, 2001, attacks.

Despite this evidence, however, there is still good reason to share Joan Beck's complaint that "religion is the most under-reported story of our time."[32] Although 1,500 daily newspapers operate in the United States, fewer than one hundred employ full-time religious reporters, and that number appears to be on the decline.[33] This has meant that, even though a committed and knowledgeable group of religion writers exist, the group's size is increasingly small and much reporting on religion is done by reporters with relatively little competence in the topic. Many newspapers feature weekly religion pages, but additional coverage of religious news is quite rare. Some observers have expressed dissatisfaction with this lack of coverage—and with the biases inherent in many religion stories.

Another set of elites who may have substantial influence on the American public and thus on its religious and political ideas are those who own, produce, and are involved in movies, television, popular music, and books and magazines. The role and influence of these elites in the realm of religion and politics has been little known and little studied.[34] Nevertheless, we can easily observe the content and reception of the entertainment that is produced. This gives us a portrait of commercial and artistic elites and their consumers. Some may suggest that the world of mass culture is secular and relentlessly hostile to religion and thus religion's connection to politics, but the real story is much more complicated and interesting.

Consider, first, the world of the movies, the output of Hollywood entertainment elites, some of whom have little contact with or sympathy for contemporary American religion. Hollywood has released few major movies in the past fifteen years that are explicitly religious. There have been exceptions, as recently as Mel Gibson's controversial *The Passion of the Christ* in 2004 or *Bruce Almighty* in 2003 (though the latter movie's comedic approach did not warm all religious reviewers). A few others over the years include *Sister Act*; *The Green Mile*; and *The Prince of Egypt*, an animated account of the life of Moses. A larger number of Hollywood productions contain what some consider "spiritual" themes, such as a focus on redemption (*The Shawshank Redemption*) or on the triumph of basic goodness (*Forrest Gump*). Hence some religious critics, liberal and conservative alike, assess many explicitly nonreligious movies as good quality entertainment. For example, one religious voice singled out the Holocaust film, *The Pianist*, and the fantasy tale, *The Lord of the Rings: The Fellowship of the Ring*, as recipients of his award for "faith-filled" movies of 2002.[35]

Still, only a small fraction of Hollywood movies are religious or arguably even spiritual (though in America "spirituality" is a famously elastic term), and many religious believers see little hope for greater attention to religion in an industry largely bereft of elites who are themselves religious. Nevertheless, there have been some Christian-themed television series over the years. These include the 1980s series *Highway to Heaven*, the 1990s hit *Touched by an Angel*, and the more recent shows *7th Heaven* and *Joan of Arcadia*.

Much of the debate regarding the relationship of movies and religion really turns on movies' moral messages. A tremendous amount of controversy swirls around this subject, with critics such as Michael Medved and others insisting that Hollywood elites use the movies (not to mention television and other media) to propagate values that are deeply opposed to traditional religious values. In this sense, religious critics suggest that cultural elites are knowing participants in the very political—and important—culture wars.[36]

Yet there is another side to the story and that is the growing field of religious media. The marketplace has supported a remarkable demand for Christian-sympathetic movies and videos through the large network of Christian bookstores around the country. Two popular contemporary examples are film adaptations of Tim LaHaye and his colleagues' best-selling *Left Behind* book series and "Veggie Tales," a children's video series that recounts biblical stories with a cast of animated vegetables.

These movies and videos are only a portion of the offerings of the religious, and especially Christian, subculture. Programming on religion-oriented television and especially radio stations are also important media sources. Radio is, in fact, the principal medium for religious communication today. One recent survey suggests that in any given month Americans are slightly more likely to use radio, television, and other religious mass media than they are to attend a religious service.[37] Most notably, Dr. James Dobson is perhaps better known for his top-rated radio show "Focus on the Family" than he is for the Christian conservative interest group he heads by the same name.

From all accounts these are also halcyon days for those in the Christian Booksellers Association, not least because of the Left Behind series, which has sold more than fifty million copies since 1995. Besides *The Prayer of Jabez* and *The Purpose Driven Life,* nonfiction bestsellers in 2001 and 2003, respectively, many lines of Christian fiction are now available, as well as a vast array of devotional books, and many reflections on marriage, family, and children. Scripture-filled tomes, not to mention myriad versions and forms of the Bible itself, continue to sell well. There is also much more in Christian bookstores: diet books for the pious, Last Supper jigsaw puzzles, and biblical action hero figures, among other things.

Then there is the substantial Christian magazine business, not just the "serious" magazines such as *Christianity Today, Christian Century,* or countless denominational publications, but also such magazines as *Christian Computing, Christian Motorsports,* and *Revolve,* a magazine for girls that serializes the Bible with the styling of more conventional teen-oriented publications. Add to these aspects of religious mass culture the major Christian music business, and one sees the development of alternatives to the productions of secular elites.[38]

Indeed, unlike the film industry, which remains dominated by a secular ethos despite a few religious inroads, the music scene has large and flourishing religious sectors. This takes two main forms: gospel music and contemporary Christian music . Such music does not speak to many in the pop and rock music business or even to many evangelical and religious cultural leaders, but its distinct presence rules out claims that all popular music, entertainers, and producers ignore or reject religion.

Any music store has a gospel section, as it is a distinctively American form of music with a long and distinguished history. Today there are a host of gospel groups, often African American, who make records and perform on the road.[39] An even larger, if different, audience exists for contemporary Christian music. In its innumerable forms and fashions, this music mimics every variety of secular rock music, though its lyrics, of course, are different. Some groups are explicitly Christian in their lyrics; others, such as Jars of Clay, are less so. There is also unending controversy about Christian artists and groups who appear to drift away from their Christian roots. Country singer Amy Grant's "crossover" from Christian music to a broader audience is a clear illustration. She was criticized by evangelical leaders in the early 1990s for appearing in a music video with a man who was not her husband. She attracted even more controversy when she divorced and subsequently remarried in the late 1990s. There should be no doubt, however, that there is a flourishing Christian music business that goes well beyond familiar gospel music or collections of hymns performed by the Mormon Tabernacle Choir.

Explicitly Christian music, moreover, is only a part of the story of references to religion in music today. The genre of country music has always been filled with religious references and themes, with religion generally treated in a favorable voice. Indeed, at one point in 2003 ten of the top sixty country songs expressed religious faith, and Randy Travis's "Three Wooden Crosses" became the first country single from an expressly Christian label to head the charts.

Beyond contemporary Christian music, gospel, and country music, however, lie the largest elements of contemporary popular music: "secular" rock and hip-hop. While Christopher Chapp finds that the picture here in recent decades has not been especially favorable to religion, he argues that it has not been as hostile to religion as some critics suggest. Some groups are unmistakably antagonistic toward religion, but over 10 percent of the most popular groups have at least one song that addresses religion in a sympathetic fashion—though it should be noted that the message is often vague, as in the most requested radio song of all time, Led Zeppelin's classic "Stairway to Heaven."[40]

The best description of the explicit message that most popular music offers regarding religion is indifference, not hostility. But what does occur regularly, and what represents a serious area of conflict between traditional religion and pop music, are the mores that pop music promote. Secular pop music consistently praises sexual freedom outside of marriage, often celebrates drug and alcohol abuse, demeans women, and uses obscene language. Such music contradicts values of religious people of many faiths—Christian, Jewish, Muslims, and others . The conflict takes on political tones whenever religious leaders and politicians battle with artists and elites in the music industry over CD warning labels.[41]

Nevertheless, while it is widely recognized that the messages of much pop music challenge religious values and create social and political issues, religious journals and publications devote much less attention to popular music than to movies and television.[42] This may simply reflect a widespread belief among religious traditionalists that pop music is a lost cause in the hands of entertainment elites who are relentlessly negative about religion and religious values. It may also reflect less familiarity among religious opinion leaders with a pop music scene that may seem the exclusive realm of youth. In any case it is puzzling. Music and its messages matter to an enormous number of people, certainly more so than many aspects of explicit politics, such as political speeches or the recent activities of Congress. Few areas are more influential in setting the moral and religious tone of a modern civilization than its music, films, books, and other features of mass cultural life.

CONCLUSION

It does matter what religious views elites have. For some elites, at least, faith clearly shapes worldviews and orientations to politics. But having a religious faith, much less sharing the same faith, does not necessarily engender similar political views—far from it. Moreover, even those who may belong to the same denomination will not always interpret their faith similarly, whereas people from very different faith backgrounds may share identical positions on public issues.

At the same time, religion does not matter to many political and cultural elites; even if it does, many other factors—party, constituency, the marketplace, personal experiences—may play a greater role in directing their political behaviors. The situation is not simple. Yet as the pathways of connection among elites, religion, and politics can have profound political consequences, they are worth exploring.

FURTHER READING

Benson, Peter L., and Dorothy L. Williams. *Religion on Capitol Hill: Myths and Realities.* New York: Oxford University Press, 1982. A pioneering study of how members of Congress experience their faith and connect it with politics.

Formicola, Jo Renee, and Hubert Morken. *Religious Leaders and Faith Based Politics: Ten Profiles.* Lanham, MD: Rowman and Littlefield, 2001. Biographical profiles of religious elites both within and outside of elective office.

Guth, James L., and Lyman A. Kellstedt. "Religion and Congress," in Corwin Smidt, ed., *In God We Trust: Religion and American Political Life.* Grand Rapids, MI: Baker Academic, 2001. A systematic examination of the religious composition and religion-based voting within the 105th Congress.

Leege, David C., Kenneth D. Wald, Brian S. Krueger, and Paul D. Mueller. *The Politics of Cultural Differences: Social Change and Voter Mobilization in the Post-New Deal Period.* Princeton, N.J.: Princeton University Press, 2002. An important study by astute scholars of religion in public life.

Schmalzbauer, John. *People of Faith: Religious Conviction in American Journalism and Higher Education* Ithaca, NY: Cornell University Press, 2003. An excellent introduction to its subject.

NOTES

1. Allen D. Hertzke, "Faith and Access: Religious Constituencies and the Washington Elites," in Ted G. Jelen, ed., *Religion and Political Behavior in the United States* (New York: Praeger, 1989).

2. Charles Colson, *Kingdoms in Conflict* (Grand Rapids, MI: Zondervan, 1987).

3. David C. Leege, Kenneth D. Wald, Brian S. Krueger, and Paul D. Mueller, *The Politics of Cultural Differences: Social Change and Voter Mobilization in the Post-New Deal Period* (Princeton, N.J.: Princeton University Press, 2002).

4. Richard V. Pierard and Robert D. Linder, *Civil Religion and the Presidency* (Grand Rapids, MI: Zondervan, 1988).

5. Robert Booth Fowler, *Religion and Politics in America* (Metuchen, NJ: Scarecrow Press, 1985), 113–118.

6. Ibid. See also Billy Graham, *Just As I Am: The Autobiography of Billy Graham* (New York: Walker, 1997).

7. Jimmy Carter, *Living Faith* (New York: Random House, 1996).

8. See Charles O. Jones, *The Trusteeship Presidency: Jimmy Carter and the United States Congress* (Baton Rouge: Louisiana State University Press, 1988).

9. Robert Booth Fowler, "The Failure of the Religious Right," in Michael Cromartie, ed., *The Religious New Right in American Politics* (Washington, D.C.: Ethics and Public Policy Center, 1993).

10. Stephen Mansfield, *The Faith of George W. Bush* (New York: Tarcher, 2003).

11. Howard Fineman, "Bush and God," *Newsweek* (Marh 10, 2003), 22–30.

12. Adam Kradel, "God On Our Side: Partisan Ideology and Recent Presidents' Religion Rhetoric," University of Wisconsin – Madison, unpublished paper, 2003 (on file with author).

13. Leege, Wald, Krueger, and D. Mueller, *The Politics of Cultural Differences*.

14. In January 1960, *Congressional Quarterly Weekly Report* began providing a table reflecting the religious affiliations of members of Congress.

15. John C. Green and James L. Guth, "Religion, Representatives, and Roll Calls," *Legislative Studies Quarterly* 16 (November 1991), 571–584. See also James L. Guth and Lyman A. Kellstedt, "Religion and Congress," in Corwin Smidt, ed., *In God We Trust: Religion and American Political Life* (Grand Rapids, MI: Baker Academic, 2001).

16. Center for Political Studies, *National Election Studies 2002* (Ann Arbor, MI: University of Michigan / Center for Political Studies, 2002).

17. John H. Fenton, *The Catholic Vote* (New Orleans, LA: Hauser Press, 1960).

18. Mary Hanna, *Catholics and American Politics* (Cambridge, MA: Harvard University Press, 1979).

19. Guth and Kellstedt, "Religion and Congress," 229. See also Peter L. Benson and Dorothy L. Williams, *Religion on Capitol Hill: Myths and Realities* (New York: Oxford University Press, 1982).

20. Benson and Williams, *Religion on Capitol Hill*.

21. Susan J. Crabtree, "The Chosen Republican," *The Weekly Standard* (January 27, 2003), 14–15.

22. Adam Nagourney and Sheryl Gay Stolberg, "Impolitic, Maybe, But in Character," *New York Times* (April 25, 2003), A22.

23. Lori Montgomery, "Party Lines Blur for Area Lawmakers," *The Washington Post*, Wednesday, May 24, 2000, p. A15.

24. Michael Barone and Richard E. Cohen, *Almanac of American Politics* (Washington, D.C.: National Journal, 2003).

25. Ibid.

26. Allen D. Hertzke, *Freeing God's Children: The Unlikely Alliance for Global Human Rights* (Lanham, MD: Rowman and Littlefield, 2004).

27. Joe Feuerherd, "Roots in Faith, Family, and Party Guide Pelosi's Move to Power," *National Catholic Reporter* (January 24, 2003).

28. Donald R. Songer and Susan J. Tabrizi, "The Religious Right in Court: The Decision Making of Christian Evangelicals in State Supreme Courts," *Journal of Politics* 61 (1999): 507–526.

29. But see Melissa M. Deckman, *School Board Battles: The Christian Right in Local Politics* (Washington, D.C.: Georgetown University Press, 2004).

30. Center for Political Studies, *National Election Studies 2002*. Some find a greater gap based on class, with wealthier individuals reporting much higher church attendance rates the lower earners. See Russell Shorto, "Belief by the Numbers," *New York Times Magazine* (December 7, 1997), 61.

31. For an optimistic view, see John Schmalzbauer, *People of Faith: Religious Conviction in American Journalism and Higher Education* (Ithaca, NY: Cornell University Press, 2003); John

Dart and Jimmy Allen, *Bridging the Gap: Religion and the News Media* (Nashville, TN: Freedom Forum, 1993); Mark Silk, *Unsecular Media: Making News of Religion in America* (Urbana: University of Illinois Press, 1995).

32. *Sightings*, The Public Religion Project (December 6, 1997).

33. Debra L. Mason, "Staffing for Religion Writers At Top Newsweeklies Falls to Lowest Levels in Over 50 Years," Religion Newswriters Association (2003), available at www.religionwriters.com.

34. But see the impressive pioneering work of Christopher Chapp, "Religion and Popular Culture: Examples in Music and the Cinema," University of Wisconsin-Madison, unpublished paper, 2002 (on file with author).

35. Edward McNulty, "Top 10 Faith-Filled Films of 2002," *Presbyterians Today* (March 2003), 24–25.

36. Michael Medved, *Hollywood v. America* (New York: Perennial, 1993). See also Chapp, "Religion and Popular Culture," pp. 24–42. For a religious voice that is critical yet optimistic about contemporary cinema, see William D. Romanowski, *Eyes Wide Open: Looking for God in Popular Culture* (Grand Rapids, MI: Brazos Press, 2001).

37. Barna Research Group, "Christian Mass Media Reach More Adults with Christian Message Than Do Churches," *Barna Research Online* (July 2, 2002), at www.barna.org.

38. Stephen Bates, "The Jesus Market," *The Weekly Standard* (December 16, 2002), 24–29.

39. For a history of gospel music, see James R. Goff, Jr., *Close Harmony: A History of Southern Gospel* (Chapel Hill, N.C.: University of North Carolina Press, 2002).

40. Chapp, "Religion and Popular Culture."

41. Mark Jurkowitz, "Playing Politics With Art," *Boston Globe* (August 20, 2000), M1; Steve Knopper, "Sticker Shock: 'Parental-Warning' Labels Can't Seem to Please Anyone," *Rocky Mountain News* (July 26, 2003), 1D.

42. Chapp, "Religion and Popular Culture," 71–79.

EVANGELICALS IN DOMESTIC AND INTERNATIONAL POLITICS: A CASE STUDY

The intertwining of religion and politics in American society has manifested itself in many ways and in many forms. Yet over the past several decades, it is the increasing political activism of Christian conservatives that has excited the most interest and inquiry among political and intellectual observers. Some have sought to understand this movement, often called the "Christian Right," simply as a fascinating example of the intersection of religion and politics; others have approached it with sympathy for the movement and its goals; still others regard it with fear or antagonism. But whatever the motivations that bring people to study this important movement, investigation of the political mobilization of Christian conservatives can teach us a lot about religion and politics in the United States.

The contemporary Christian conservative movement grew up primarily among evangelical Protestants in the late 1970s and early 1980s. The movement's main goal has always been to take political action in response to what it perceives to be an increasingly immoral environment in the United States, which is also disturbingly hostile to Christianity. Whether their complaint is secularized public schools, vulgar popular culture, interfering government edicts, or collapsing family values, Christian conservative activists perceive an assault on traditional standards and Christianity itself in the United States today.

The movement's leaders argue that they do not want to establish Christianity as the official religion of the United States. Instead they wish to foster an atmosphere in which devoted Christians can practice their religion and see its morality honored in the broader culture. They insist that what they see as a fraying of the cultural fabric in the United States—and its attendant increases in broken families, illegitimacy, sexual exploitation, crime, and drug abuse—can only be reversed through Christian renewal. Critics of this perspective, on the other hand, see the Christian Right as a reactionary attempt to reverse progressive social changes such as the evolution of gender roles and increased tolerance of alternative lifestyles. These critics also deny that Christianity is under fire in American culture; instead they suspect paranoia is rife among evangelicals involved in the movement.

Exactly who belongs to the Christian Right is a matter of dispute. Membership in particular organizations, whether the Moral Majority in the 1980s or the much discussed Christian Coalition in the 1990s, is too narrow a test. After all, there are a wide variety of other religious conservative organizations such as Focus on the Family, Concerned Women for America, and the Family Research Council, whose leaders and members are often involved in the cause. Second, there are many people who sympathize with the movement's agenda, especially from within the evangelical tradition of Protestantism, but do not belong to any of the movement's political organizations. Sympathizers do not always see themselves as part of a political movement, and they may not be counted on to support one or another candidate who claims to speak for it. But because they often share similar moral attitudes with Christian conservative activists, they are in some sense a part of the movement. By this definition, perhaps 15 percent of the electorate has at least been somewhat supportive of the conservative Christian political movement in recent years.[1] About 80 percent of voters who identified with the movement supported the Republican nominee for president in 1984 and 1988, as did well over 60 percent in 1992, 1996, and 2000. This is evidence of a remarkable degree of agreement within movement circles.[2]

It is important to bear in mind that the term "Christian Right" does not describe the entire evangelical population of the United States. Some evangelicals are ideologically left-of-center, and the Christian Right was and continues to be more of a self-conscious movement than can be described by lumping even all evangelical political conservatives together. Moreover, African Americans, who are overwhelmingly evangelical, rarely identify with the "Christian Right" label, while a few non-evangelicals, including some conservative Catholics, have an affinity for the movement (though that affinity is often an uneasy one). Still, most of those who might be described as members of the Christian conservative movement come from the evangelical side of Protestantism.

The main challenge faced by the Christian Right, however, is the factionalism that characterizes evangelicalism in the United States. Consider that traditional evangelicals often do not welcome Pentecostals, who focus on a spirit-filled form of worship that sometimes involves speaking in tongues. Pentecostals are also sometimes divided among themselves. Meanwhile, evangelicals and fundamentalists are divided over how inerrant (true in every regard) the Bible is and how separatist they should be from the outside world. Moreover, almost every conservative Protestant church—even those belonging to organized denominations—reserves the right of religious and political self-determination under God. Meanwhile, entire denominations, including the largest (the Southern Baptist Convention), experience significant religious division and dissent. This long tradition of religious individualism among conservative Protestants dampens the movement's hopes for political success.[3]

EVANGELICAL CONSERVATIVES AND DOMESTIC POLITICS

Statistics do not come close to telling the whole story of the recent movement of Christian conservatives into domestic politics. It is also essential to explore the culture, organization, and history of this movement. Since the 1980s, the Christian Right has been defined in part by groups such as the Moral Majority, Focus on the Family, Concerned Women for America, the Christian Coalition, and the Family Research Council. It also has been defined by its famous leaders, such as Rev. Jerry Falwell of the Moral Majority, Rev. Pat Robertson and Ralph Reed of the Christian Coalition, Beverly LaHaye of Concerned Women for America, Gary Bauer of the Family Research Council, and James Dobson of Focus on the Family. Its televangelism, Washington rallies, and crusades against such things as abortion, violent and immoral television and movies, and liberal Democrats have also served to distinguish it as a political movement.

But the evangelical conservatism that so strongly supports the political movement also has a history that did not just begin in the 1980s. The fact that scholars speak of a "*New* Christian Right" today suggests that contemporary Christian activism is only one example of many conservative Christian movements in the history of American politics.[4] Indeed, some historians have linked the Christian Right to traditions of dissent and populist protest that began even before the United States existed as a nation.[5]

In its short historical life, the contemporary Christian Right has gone through two distinct phases. The first lasted from the late 1970s until the late 1980s.[6] It might be described as the age of discovery and disappointment. The second phase began after the 1988 election and proved to be the age of realism.

The first phase of Christian Right activism built from steady growth in the numbers of evangelical Protestants in the decades after World War II (coupled with a coincident decline in the membership of mainline denominations such as the Episcopal and Presbyterian U.S.A. churches). The factors responsible for these membership dynamics are varied and controversial, but the objective fact of the growth is neither. Moreover, as many evangelical leaders observed the upswing of their tradition of Christianity, their self-confidence rose and so did their willingness to engage in public discourse on their own behalf. At the same time, the economic and educational standing of evangelicals in American society was improving. The typical conservative Protestant today belongs to the middle class.

The political origins of the movement were connected in part with discontent over a series of decisions by the U.S. Supreme Court. The Court's rulings in the 1960s declaring prayer and Bible reading in the schools unconstitutional, followed by the 1973 *Roe v. Wade* decision establishing the constitutionality of abortion, led to great dissatisfaction among many conservative evangelicals and other Christians. For them, these judgments symbolized America's retreat from Christianity. They were ominous signs that the country had fallen into the hands of secular elites who were hostile to traditional faith and its norms. As Franky Schaeffer suggested by the title of his influential book, this was *Bad News for Modern Man.*[7]

Another factor that stimulated the rise of the religious conservative movement was widespread evangelical disappointment with the presidency of Jimmy Carter. His 1976 campaign elicited strong allegiance from traditionally Democratic fundamentalists and garnered many votes from Republican evangelicals. As president, however, Carter's actions engendered bitter opposition from many parts of the conservative Protestant community. Religious conservatives increasingly came to view Carter as a traitor because he did not act decisively on behalf of their moral agenda; he did not, for example, advance the prolife cause. He was also sharply attacked for his failure to appoint conservative evangelicals to high-ranking government posts.

Opponents of religious conservatives, moreover, gave the movement a great boost in the late 1970s and early 1980s. The elite media showered what it termed, somewhat derisively, the "Christian Right" with tremendous publicity, which helped it seem a phenomenon far larger in numbers, organization, and influence than it actually was. The media may not have "made" the Moral Majority, founded in 1979 as the first major Christian conservative organization, but the media certainly helped it enormously.

On the other hand, the movement's spurt into popular awareness in the 1980s had its price—one that eventually became costly. It quickly became an inviting target and attracted many enemies. It increasingly met with vigorous opposition from an attentive liberal culture and received extensive—and highly negative—coverage in such national magazines as *Time* and *Newsweek*.[8] It also generated counterorganization (such as People for the American Way) and countermobilization by already existing groups (for example, the National Council of Churches). This was, in short, the moment when the cultural battles with which Americans are now so familiar first emerged. The Moral Majority and similar groups came to clash with liberal media, intellectual, and artistic forces.

Other troubles bedeviled this new form of conservative activism. The movement's organizations stumbled after early enthusiasm cooled and determined opponents appeared on the field. The Moral Majority, the flagship organization of the Christian Right, had collapsed entirely by 1988. It ran out of money and lost its leadership; it ultimately closed up shop with few supporters. Its leader, Jerry Falwell, quit full-time politics, and there were few who could fill his shoes.

Inexperience on the national political scene, and sometimes with lobbying in particular, proved to be damaging. So did divisive splits within the evangelical community over the effort's appropriateness, importance, leadership, and agenda. As Pat Robertson learned in his ill-fated race for the Republican nomination for president in 1988, this lack of unity among religiously and politically conservative Christians was frustrating.

In the end, great hopes were tempered and plans for national victories disappeared.

The somewhat sour conclusion of the first phase of the Christian Right in the late 1980s was speeded by a series of scandals and controversies that led to the downfall of several televangelists, some of whom, like Jim and Tammy Faye Bakker, had been allied with the movement. Throughout the 1980s Christian conservative activism and televangelism had in fact often been deeply intertwined. Jerry Falwell, for example, reached a wider audience because of his television show, *The Old Time Gospel Hour*. The use of modern broadcasting and mailing techniques to build the political movement, moreover, derived from televangelists' experience with such modern technology. No wonder that the fall of several televangelists from grace struck a major blow and provided the media and other opponents with a field day of criticism.[9]

But evangelist Pat Robertson's presidential candidacy in 1988 sowed the seeds of new life for Christian activists who wanted greater political influence. Though it failed, Robertson's candidacy demonstrated the potential strength of a grassroots Christian conservative effort. Robertson raised $41 million for his campaign. He won victories in a number of caucus states where numbers matter less than the vocal dedication of followers. He galvanized a new corps of evangelical activists who stayed in politics long after the campaign was over. Equally important, the grassroots organizational work of Robertson's campaign set the stage for the emergence in the 1990s of his more sophisticated and successful Christian Coalition.[10]

The creation of the Christian Coalition reflected a recovery from the Christian Right's deep slump of the middle to later 1980s. The movement underwent a serious organizational shake-up and has learned a great deal from its sometimes trying adventures in politics during the 1980s. It has emerged as a more experienced and more locally based movement that is now a force to be reckoned with in U.S. politics.

Evangelical conservatives, for example, have become a real force in the Republican Party. The Christian Coalition's push to get adherents trained and actively involved in Republican Party politics was successful enough that by 1994 *Campaigns and Elections*, a magazine for campaign insiders and consultants, reported that evangelical conservatives had major influence in the Republican Party in eighteen states and had significant influence in another thirteen.[11] As we discussed in Chapter 4, the Christian Coalition has recently experienced leadership changes, budget shortfalls, and staff reductions, all of which have hampered its political influence, but the group continues to play a role in American politics, especially at the state and local level.[12]

In addition to the Christian Coalition, many other "profamily" organizations emerged as influential political players in the 1990s and continue to exercise some influence today. Concerned Women for America (CWA), founded by Beverly LaHaye, focuses in particular on local issues. CWA is among the largest women's political organizations in the United States. Its stated purpose is to "protect and preserve biblical values" and to reverse what its members see as a decline in American moral values.[13] The increasingly visible Family Research Council (FRC) has a larger Washington staff than does the Christian Coalition. While the Christian Coalition has focused on voter mobilization, the FRC has emerged as a premier think tank for religious conservatives. It provides detailed policy analyses on issues such as the impact of changes in divorce laws, the increasing tax burden on parents, and the societal effects of sex and violence in the media. While FRC is clearly a political organization, it focuses more exclusively than other evangelical political groups on moral and family issues. It encourages people who are sympathetic with its agenda to participate actively in the political process by writing to members of Congress.[14]

Also noteworthy is the Focus on the Family organization and its widely known leader, James Dobson. His radio program is heard weekly on more than 3,000 radio facilities in North America, and his Colorado Springs–based operation employs 1,300 staff members to produce and distribute a vast array of publications, videos, and tapes.[15] Dobson has played a tremendous role in defining the nature of "proper family life" in evangelical circles and in bringing his opinions to bear in politics. Phones ring off the hook on Capitol Hill and in state legislatures whenever he calls for action (Box 7.1).

Chapter 8, on religious politics and the legal system, addresses the host of legal associations that are busy on behalf of the Christian conservative cause. Legal groups are springing up at the state level as well, some affiliated with national organizations, others independent. And there are many more groups that are involve themselves in school board races,[16] conflicts over public nativity scenes and gay rights ordinances, and disputes over

---

**BOX 7.1 JAMES DOBSON AND
FOCUS ON THE FAMILY**

James Dobson, a Ph.D. in child development, began his career as a professor and licensed psychologist, not as a leader of the Christian political movement. But in response to his own concerns about the effects of family breakdown, he founded Focus on the Family in 1976. Today the organization not only produces wildly popular radio programs that are heard internationally, but also innumerable books, videos, and other media that advise about parenting and family issues. Dobson's method "attempts to 'turn hearts toward home' by reasonable, biblical and empirical insights so people will be able to discover the founder of homes and the creator of families: Jesus Christ." This method often includes political efforts as well. His ability to communicate with a large group of politically active people has enhanced his political access; Dobson has consulted actively with the administrations of Presidents Carter, Reagan, George H.W. Bush, and George W. Bush on policy matters that impact the traditional family. He also helped found the Family Research Council in early 1980s, an organization that is increasingly visible in national politics. Dobson is known for taking uncompromising stances on certain policy areas, and this approach has sometimes put him at odds with allies in the Republican Party.

SOURCE: http://www.fotf.org

---

books in public libraries. Much of their effort is educational, designed to alert citizens of their view that traditional values and institutions are slipping away. These groups' larger goal is to goad others into action. In their view, America is in the midst of a culture war over values, which can be won only by the alert and committed. Dedicated foot soldiers for this war are thus at a premium.[17]

NEW EVANGELICAL ACTIVISM
IN AMERICAN FOREIGN POLICY

Until recently evangelical conservatives have focused largely on domestic policy and politics. But the evangelical impulse is not always predictable. Nowhere is this more evident than in the new engagement of evangelicals on international human rights. In alliance with those they often battle on the domestic front, evangelicals mobilized behind the successful enactment of legislation to stem global religious persecution. This success galvanized activism on other issues, from Sudanese atrocities to sex trafficking to human rights abuses in North Korea. This movement illustrates the dynamism of American religion, and the way global developments increasingly impinge on domestic religious networks.

Consider the foreign policy initiatives pressed by evangelical groups in the late 1990s and 2000s: International Religious Freedom Act of 1998; Trafficking in Victims and Protection Act of 2000; Debt Relief Appropriation in 2000; Sudan Peace Act of 2002; and the North Korean Freedom and Refugee Protection Act of 2003 (introduced). This level of international engagement is unprecedented for evangelical Christians and remarkable among American religionists generally. Surveying this picture Nicholas Kristof of *The New York Times* described evangelicals as the "newest internationalists," not only providing extensive relief and development aid but fighting against human rights abuses in numerous places around the globe.[18] Another *Times* reporter, Elisabeth Bumiller, documented how evangelical influence in the administration of George W. Bush resulted in surprising human rights achievements.[19]

What accounts for this direction in evangelical activism? Certainly the fall of the Iron Curtain brought unprecedented opportunities for international initiatives. But developments were taking place within the global Christian community that prepared the ground. In one sense, evangelical Christians have always been internationally engaged because of their commitment to the Great Commission to "make disciples of all nations." World evangelization and relief work puts denominations in touch with believers who live under harsh conditions around the globe. Mushrooming global communication and travel in turn strengthen the ties between the "suffering church" abroad and American church networks.

Decreased evangelizing by mainline Protestant churches is another part of this picture. As mainline leaders embraced more liberal theology and engaged in ecumenical enterprises, they left the missionary field to theologically traditional Protestants, who quietly went about the evangelizing in Asia, Africa, and Latin America. Thus by the mid–1990s, when the new faith-based international movement took off, mainline churches mustered less than three thousand missionaries out of a total of over 40,000 Americans sent abroad.

The crucial story is not primarily about missionary activity, however, but about the spread of Christianity outside the West. This has produced a demographic revolution, a tectonic shift of Christianity toward the developing world. Perhaps 70 percent of all Protestant evangelicals now live in Asia, Africa, and Latin America,[20] and they often suffer amidst poverty, persecution, and violence. Evangelicals in the West are naturally drawn to these besieged believers. Thus at many evangelical events one hears featured speakers from foreign countries, often treated like celebrities and role models, who share poignant testimony of how God sustained them in prison, of how the spirit worked to gain souls despite persecution.

One indication of this interest is the rapid growth of the annual event known as the International Day of Prayer for the Persecuted Church, which raises awareness about the plight of believers abroad. Conceived as a worship activity, the event is planned by a permanent evangelical organization that enlists congregations to participate and provides them with kits containing information about religious persecution and suggested activities of solidarity. Begun in 1996 with around 5,000 participating churches, organizers claim that by 2003 it enlisted an estimated 100,000 congregations. Even accounting for some exaggeration, a fifth or so of U.S. houses of worship may participate in this event in some way. This enormous grassroots reach, coupled with its potential to influence policy makers, led Richard Cizik of the National Association of Evangelicals to proclaim that "human rights is now no longer only the prerogative of the left."[21]

International Religious Freedom Act

Out of growing concern about religious persecution, Congress passed the International Religious Freedom Act of 1998, which declared that the United States would stand "with the persecuted," "condemn violations of religious freedom," and promote "the fundamental right to freedom of religion."[22] While the initial impetus for the legislation came from the Christian community, it applies to all religions around the globe.

One of the most comprehensive human rights statutes on the books, the law creates new offices at the top levels of U.S. government to promote international religious freedom. It requires the State Department to issue an annual report on the status of religious freedom around the world, which sets into motion presidential action against violating countries. The law reaches into the daily routines of foreign policy by providing better training for diplomatic personnel and fostering their ongoing contacts with vulnerable religious communities. The law also creates an independent commission, with staff and budget, to monitor violations and hold policy makers accountable for their response. The U.S. Commission on International Religious Freedom, comprised of a distinguished cross-section of religious America, has made its presence felt. Finally, the law established the nation's first Ambassador-at-Large for International Religious Freedom.[23]

The roots of evangelical engagement on this issue can be traced to the Cold War, when such organizations as Voice of the Martyrs and Open Doors with Brother Andrew formed to succor persecuted Christians in Communist countries. What has given the contemporary movement its bite and reach is the growing number and sophistication of these advocacy groups, and their ability to tap into vibrant local organizations and rich social networks of the evangelical world. From the mid–1990s onward, evangelical presses, broadcast networks, and parachurch organizations increasingly publicized the plight of believers abroad. Though much of this activity operated beneath the radar of mainstream media, the grassroots buzz was detected by politicians who have finely-tuned antenna to their district constituencies.

Ironically, evangelical activism was prodded by Jews and buoyed by Catholics. Among the most notable is Michael Horowitz, a Jew and former Reagan administration official who pushed evangelical leaders to take up the cause (Box 7.2). Horowitz also helped to enlist other prominent Jewish leaders, such as Rabbi David Saperstein, the chief Washington lobbyist for Reform Judaism, and Abe Rosenthal, former columnist of *The New York Times*, to join in initiatives with evangelicals.[24]

This Jewish-evangelical alliance defies stereotypes and suggests how profoundly the issue of international religious freedom transcends traditional ideological lines. But that was not the only example of how religious freedom produces new bedfellows. The institutional support of the United States Conference of Catholic Bishops helped legitimize the issue outside of the evangelical world, especially among Democratic legislators, as did backing by the liberal Episcopal lobby in Washington, D.C. Also intriguing was the fact that conservative evangelicals joined with such religious minorities as Tibetan Buddhists and Iranian Baha'is in the lobby campaign, suggesting a move beyond the "parochial concern" for fellow believers.

Denominational or church affiliated organizations, such as the Christian Life Commission of the Southern Baptist Convention (SBC) and the

---

BOX 7.2 MICHAEL HOROWITZ: A JEWISH ADVOCATE FOR PERSECUTED CHRISTIANS

Major credit for forcing the issue of religious persecution onto the national agenda belongs to Michael Horowitz, who attended Yeshiva school as a youth in the Bronx and thought about becoming a rabbi. A Washington think tank lawyer, he became involved in the fight against religious persecution when his Ethiopian housekeeper, who was threatened with deportation, told him of being tortured because of his Christian faith.

Horowitz launched his campaign against religious persecution with a 1995 guest editorial in the *Wall Street Journal*, followed by a letter to some 140 evangelical Christian mission boards. He later drafted a "statement of conscience" that was adopted by the National Association of Evangelicals; worked with members of Congress to write legislation; and assembled a lobby coalition that included evangelical Protestants, the United States Catholic Conference, Jewish organizations, and Tibetan Buddhists. With blunt rhetoric he argued that "Christians are the Jews of the twenty first century" and they had become the "victims of choice for thug regimes." He also "shamed Christian leaders into action" by asking "I'm a Jew, I'm interested in this, why aren't you?" Recognition of his central role in the movement came when Charles Colson presented Prison Fellowship's 1997 Wilberforce Award ("for combating injustice") to Michael Horowitz.

SOURCES: Samuel G. Freedman, "Horowitz's List," *New York* (March 31, 1997), 46; "The Jews of the Twenty First Century?" *Jubilee* (Spring 1997); Jeffrey Goldberg, "Washington Discovers Christian Persecution," *New York Times Magazine* (December 21, 1997), 46.

National Association of Evangelicals, backed the legislation. During the lobby campaign, Charles Colson and James Dobson also aired radio broadcasts urging listeners to contact Congress to register their support. Charles Colson has been the most important figure in this emerging engagement because he enjoys both wide respect in the evangelical world and credibility beyond. He not only mobilized lay evangelicals on religious persecution but actively planned strategy and personally lobbied members of Congress. Equally important, through writings, speeches, and radio commentary, Colson articulated a theological rationale for public engagement. He argues vigorously against quietism and inaction, labeling "self-indulgent" and unscriptural the view that because martyrdom is good for the church evangelicals should avoid political attempts to ameliorate persecution abroad.[25]

Questions remain about how deep into the pews lay concern for international issues reaches, and how enduring it is. Certainly, among the evangelical elite the issue is salient. Some 70 percent of the evangelical leaders surveyed in 2000 said they strongly agreed that fighting religious persecution should be a major goal of American foreign policy.[26] At the lay level, awareness and focus have probably not reached levels found among Jews during the campaign to help Soviet Jewry. But if constituent pressure has not been persistently high, it has not just been a one-shot affair either.

The Sudan Campaign

An emerging example of this human rights engagement concerns the African people of Sudan, who have suffered through twenty-year-long civil war. The conflict contains a religious dimension that drew attention in American church networks. Sudan is ruled by a Muslim regime that has attempted to subjugate or forcibly convert various southern peoples, who adhere to traditional African tribal faiths or Christianity. While only a minority of those in the South are Christians, widespread reports of atrocities and ethnic cleansing elicit strong responses within the evangelical community.

From the early 1990s onward evangelical groups such as Christian Solidarity International, Christian Solidarity Worldwide, Voice of the Martyrs, and Samaritan's Purse have publicized the massacres, slave raids, and ethnic cleansing committed by the government of Sudan. This material has been increasingly picked up by a variety of activists: from a celebrated grade school class in Colorado to producers of the popular television program *Touched by an Angel*, which ran an episode on the slave traffic in Sudan that featured actual Sudanese exiles.[27]

With the election of George W. Bush, whose electoral base was heavily evangelical, the evangelical constituency became even more pivotal to the Sudan campaign. Crucial to Bush's heightened attention to the issue is the fact that major evangelical leaders, such as Charles Colson and Franklin Graham (the son of legendary evangelist Billy Graham), not only enjoy personal relationships with the president but are deeply committed to the Sudan cause. Indeed, because Graham's Samaritan's Purse organization is heavily invested in relief and development work in Sudan, his projects have been directly hit by the Sudanese government's bombs and raids, giving him a remarkable credibility in speaking to the issue.

This engagement produced one of the most striking strange bedfellows coalitions in recent history, as key African American figures such as Kweisi Mume, Eleanor Holmes Norton, Walter Fauntroy, and Al Sharpton joined conservative evangelical leaders in calling for demonstrations, divestment, capital market sanctions, and presidential action against the regime. They gained passage of the Sudan Peace Act in 2002, which pressured the regime to negotiate a cessation of conflict. If the peace holds, this would rank as one of the signal examples of citizen diplomacy in American foreign policy.

Sex Trafficking

Another example of faith-based international involvement concerns international trafficking, mostly of women and children, into bonded slavery and forced prostitution. As many as a million women and children each year are trafficked across international boundaries into prostitution, many bought and sold until they die of disease and abuse.[28] Backed by pressure from an unlikely alliance, landmark legislation aimed at cutting this grotesque trade passed Congress in 2000. The Trafficking Victims Protection Act[29] may turn out to be among the most consequential initiatives of America's human rights leadership.[30] The law provides harsh penalties for international traffickers, equips enforcement agencies with new tools to deal with organized crime syndicates that run the traffic, penalizes countries that fail to criminalize and appropriately punish trafficking, and provides protection for victims. It also established an anti-trafficking office at the State Department, which has become one of the most aggressive human rights centers in American government.

This campaign brought together evangelical Christians and feminists. Evangelical leaders not only joined in coalition with feminist groups, but actively plotted strategy with them, indicating a willingness to work face to face with otherwise adversaries in the "culture wars." Even in a city known for odd bedfellows, this one was a sight to behold. At the pivotal last stage of the legislative campaign, members of Congress were receiving a letter from Gloria Steinem and other prominent feminist leaders at the very moment that they were being lobbied by such figures as Charles Colson of Prison Fellowship, Richard Land of the Southern Baptist Convention, Kevin Mannoia and Richard Cizik of the National Association of Evangelicals, and John Busby of the Salvation Army.[31]

A deep sense of religious mission animates the work of an emerging evangelical leader, Gary Haugen, founder and president of the Christian-based International Justice Mission (IJM). A former Justice Department lawyer and U.N. genocide investigator for Rwanda, Haugen felt called to reclaim the vocabulary of justice for the evangelical Christian community. As he wrote in a book for fellow believers, the "good news about injustice" is that "God is against it."[32] To provide a tangible way for believers to redress injustice, his organization intervenes in egregious cases of child prostitution, bonded servitude, and exploitation. In 2003 the IJM helped shut down Cambodia's most notorious brothels, freeing the captive children and placing them in the care of Christian aid workers. This dramatic event, followed by others around the world, prompted the head of the Trafficking Office to proclaim boldly that U.S. policy was now aimed at nothing less than abolishing "modern day slavery."[33]

Pivotal initiatives by evangelicals on human rights also facilitate alliances with liberal groups on humanitarian issues, such as AIDS funding for Africa and debt relief for impoverished nations. The cause of debt relief offers an especially vivid example of such interfaith coalitions. Long a cause of international development organizations, debt relief enlists such diverse actors as Pope John Paul II and Irish rock singer Bono of U2. In 2000 global activists launched what they termed a "Year of Jubilee" campaign after the biblical reference to the time when debts are forgiven and burdens lifted. Though initiatives spanned the globe, action by the United States was crucial because its financial contribution would leverage much more from international financial institutions and other nations. Thus activists were joyous when they gained a congressional appropriation of over $400 million, which passed the 106th Congress with pivotal backing from the religious community.

The religious coalition in support of this effort included Jews, Catholics, and liberal Protestants who lobbied many Democrats, along with evangelicals who took the message to conservative legislators normally skeptical of foreign aid. This produced some striking moments. When a tight-fisted Republican Senator Phil Gramm (R-Texas) threatened to filibuster the legislation, Pat Robertson went on the *700 Club* and asked viewers to contact Gramm (whose number was flashed on the screen) and demand that he remove the hold he had placed on the legislation, which he promptly did.[34] The liberal leader of the lobby coalition, Thomas Hart, director of the

Episcopal Office of Governmental Relations in Washington, credited the previous religious freedom campaign as facilitating this alliance of conservative evangelicals and liberal religionists.[35]

ASSESSMENTS OF THE EVANGELICAL SUCCESS

No one knows the limits of the conservative evangelicalism's long-term political influence at the local, national, or international level. It is clear, however, that the movement of evangelicals into politics is far from dead today.[36] Whether it will have a politically successful future is much less clear.

Consider the wave of evangelical activism on foreign affairs. It already seems to have achieved more tangible results than two decades of struggle on the domestic front. Evangelical groups continue to press for vigorous implementation of the laws they backed, and as of this writing they are publicizing the plight of North Korean refugees and pressing for congressional legislation addressing the totalitarian regime's atrocities. Still, evangelical activism on international issues could wane or be siphoned off by other concerns. Though evangelicals have often called a truce in the culture war to advance their international causes, a recrudescence of the culture war on the domestic front—perhaps this time over gay marriage—could diminish evangelical energies and undermine the strange-bedfellow alliances so essential to the faith-based international movement.

Another question of great interest is what the movement's future will be within the Republican Party. Although conservative evangelical leaders have chosen to associate with the Republican Party in order to maximize their political influence on domestic and international issues, we do not know how wise that choice will prove to be in the long run. Religious conservatives have done well within the Republican Party, but they have plenty of opponents there also. Some Republicans have argued that conservative Christians are already too powerful in the party, especially in some southern states. They see that influence as damaging the party's prospects with the larger electorate and they predict—and sometimes even favor—confrontation to weaken the movement in the party. Other Republicans have simply declared the religious conservatives in the party's ranks a "necessary annoyance."[37]

In light of the Christian conservative movement's uneasy relationship with the GOP, a key strategic question involves identifying strategies other than working through the Republican Party. The Christian Right has recently chosen to pursue a significant expansion of its emphasis on largely nonpartisan local politics, issues, and organizing.[38] Skeptics argue that this is a strategy born of defeat on domestic issues at the federal level. Yet the turn toward local politics is also a declaration of hope. Because many of the moral issues at stake in realms such as education policy, pornography, and gay rights are fought over in local settings, time and money spent elsewhere are a waste. Moreover, the local level provides the perfect setting for educating people and the ideal training ground for future leaders.

Some social scientists argue that there is yet another challenge to Christian conservatism: evangelicals are becoming more liberal in their religion, politics, and social attitudes. Such observers conclude that in the long run Christian conservative activism may be less warmly welcomed in its traditional evangelical circles. The evidence for this thesis is partial and intensely controversial, but without conservative evangelicals, the Christian Right could continue only in a shadow form. Thus the evolution of the political and social attitudes of evangelicals will be of great importance in the years ahead.[39]

Even if attitudes do not change, issues may—and with huge consequences. Shifting agendas could either strengthen or weaken the Christian conservative political movement. If modern technology makes abortion easier and public opinion makes abortion more acceptable, would this undercut the Christian conservative movement? Would changes in American views of same-sex marriage do the same thing? We doubt it. It would be unwise to underrate the movement's ability to adjust its focus with the times. It has already shown that it has the flexibility to debate whatever issues are sensitive at any given time. Moreover, the movement is not focused on any one specific issue. Its focus instead is on broad dissatisfaction with the culture in general.

IMPLICATIONS FOR RELIGION AND POLITICS

Perhaps the most important lesson to be learned from the experience of the Christian conservative political movement is about the dynamic nature of politics in the United States. After all, who predicted fifteen or twenty years ago that a vigorous, organized "Christian Right" movement would become well established on the American political scene? Who predicted what its dynamic, complex, and volatile history through the 1980s and 1990s would be like? Who would expect that the movement would push in so many directions, from the local to the international, and create a set of remarkably strange bedfellows along the way? American politics remains open and changing, and the history of evangelical conservatism demonstrates that reality.

Of course, the same point applies to religion and politics in the United States in general. Americans today are worlds away from the "settled" universe of religion and politics that characterized the United States thirty years ago. Religious conservatives changed all of that. We should expect other changes, perhaps of equal power and sweep, in the years ahead. Religion and politics in the United States, like much else, cannot for a moment be put in a bottle and set securely on a dusty shelf.

The experience of the conservative Christian movement underlines the political importance of nurturing unity—and the costs of failing to achieve it. Religious divisions among evangelicals, fundamentalists, Pentecostals, and among assorted leaders, denominations, and subcultures within conservative Protestantism have hurt its potential as a political force. So too has its failure to forge significant alliances with non-evangelicals over domestic issues. Christian conservatism's record is improving on this count, as we see in its notable success in the international arena, but it has a long way to go in its efforts to reach out to Americans who often agree with it on moral matters but are nervous about its religious and political assertiveness.

A final lesson for the movement has been the discovery of the importance of elite access. One of the greatest impediments to Christian conservative success has been the hostility of the elite media. There is no question that leading print and television news sources have been decidedly negative toward religious conservatives. Once they discovered the movement's existence in 1980, they began to attack it—and they continue to do so today.[40] Elite access is in short supply elsewhere, too. To be sure, the George W. Bush administration has been more open to evangelicals than past presidencies, but the movement still largely lacks access to top bureaucrats, most members of Congress, and the judiciary.

How does the movement overcome such a problem? Going toe-to-toe with such elites in the 1980s and 1990s did not work as well as some had hoped. Quietly building bases on the local level, often in places where such elites are not so important, would seem to be a more viable strategy. Setting aside the culture war in some instances, as evangelical conservatives have been apt to do on international matters, helps generate new contacts and may also increase access. These strategies may make sense for now, but it only postpones the larger problem of how to wring legitimacy from a hostile elite culture in the United States.

FURTHER READING

Deckman, Melissa M. *School Board Battles: The Christian Right in Local Politics.* Washington, D.C.: Georgetown University Press, 2004. A recent study of the role of evangelical conservatives in local political conflict.

Hertzke, Allen D. *Freeing God's Children: The Unlikely Alliance for Global Human Rights* Lanham, MD: Rowman & Littlefield Publishers, 2004.

Martin, William. *With God on Our Side: The Rise of the Religious Right in America.* New York: Broadway Books, 1996. A comprehensive history of the rise of the religious Right.

Moen, Matthew C. *The Transformation of the Christian Right.* Tuscaloosa: University of Alabama Press, 1992. Insightful discussion of the religious Right's movement from phase one to phase two.

Oldfield, Duane M. *The Right and the Righteous: The Christian Right Confronts the Republican Party.* Lanham, MD: Rowman and Littlefield, 1996. An excellent discussion of the past and present relationship between the Christian Right and the GOP.

Penning, James M. and Corwin Smidt. *Evangelicalism: The Next Generation.* Grand Rapids, MI: Baker, 2002. An insightful study of the religious beliefs and behaviors of young evangelicals.

Wilcox, Clyde. *Onward Christian Soldiers? The Religious Right in American Politics.* 2nd ed. Boulder, CO: Westview, 2000. A useful discussion of the identity of the Christian Right and its prospects for future success.

NOTES

1. See Mark J. Rozell, "What Christian Right?" *Religion in the News* 6 (Spring 2003), 3. There have been many efforts to measure "membership" in the Christian Right; no one has struggled harder with these issues than Clyde Wilcox. See Clyde Wilcox, *God's Warriors: The Christian Right in Twentieth-Century America* (Baltimore, MD: Johns Hopkins University Press, 1992).

2. James Guth, Lyman Kellstedt, John Green, and Corwin Smidt, "America Fifty/Fifty," *First Things* 116 (October 2001), 19–26; James Guth, John Green, Lyman Kellstedt, and Corwin Smidt, "God's Own Party: Evangelicals and Republicans in the 1992 Election," *Christian Century* (February 17, 1993), 172–176; John Green, Lyman Kellstedt, James Guth,

and Corwin Smidt, "Who Elected Clinton: A Collision of Values," *First Things* (August/September 1997), 35–40.

3. Several good works here include George Marsden, *Understanding Fundamentalism and Evangelicalism* (Grand Rapids, MI: Eerdmans, 1991); Ronald H. Nash, *Evangelicals in America: Who They Are, What They Believe* (Nashville, TN: Abingdon, 1987); and Bill Leonard, *God's Last and Only Hope: The Fragmentation of the Southern Baptist Convention* (Grand Rapids, MI: Eerdmans, 1990).

4. Robert C. Liebman and Robert Wuthnow, eds., *The New Christian Right* (New York: Aldine, 1984).

5. Two examples of this argument from rather contrasting perspectives are found in Allen D. Hertzke, *Echoes of Discontent: Jesse Jackson, Pat Robertson, and the Resurgence of Populism* (Washington, D.C.: CQ Press, 1993); and Michael Lienesch, *Redeeming America: Piety and Politics in the New Christian Right* (Chapel Hill: University of North Carolina Press, 1993).

6. See Richard J. Neuhaus and Michael J. Cromartie, eds., *Piety and Politics: Evangelicals and Fundamentalists Confront the World* (Washington, D.C.: Ethics and Public Policy Center, 1987); Corwin Smidt, ed., *Contemporary Evangelical Political Involvement* (Lanham, MD: University Press of America, 1989); Robert C. Liebman and Robert Wuthnow, *The New Christian Right* (New York: Aldine, 1984); Steve Bruce, *The Rise and Fall of the New Christian Right* (New York: Oxford University Press, 1988); David G. Bromley and Anson Shupe, eds., *New Christian Politics* (Macon, GA: Mercer University Press, 1984); Jerome Himmelstein, *To the Right: The Transformation of American Conservatism* (Berkeley: University of California Press, 1990); and Gary E. McCuen, ed., *The Religious Right* (Hudson, WI: McCuen, 1989).

7. Franky Schaeffer, *Bad News for Modern Man* (Westchester, IL: Crossway Books, 1984).

8. Classic examples include "Born Again at the Ballot Box," *Time* (April 14, 1980), 94; "Born-Again Politics," *Newsweek* (September 15, 1980), 28–36.

9. On televangelism, see Jeffrey K. Hadden, "Religious Broadcasting and the Mobilization of the New Christian Right," *Journal for the Scientific Study of Religion* 26 (March 1987), 1–24; Stewart M. Hoover, *Mass Media Religion: The Social Sources of the Electronic Church* (Newbury Park, CA: Sage Publications, 1988).

10. Matthew C. Moen, *The Transformation of the Christian Right* (Tuscaloosa: University of Alabama Press, 1992), 110–116.

11. John F. Persinos, "Has the Christian Right Taken Over the Republican Party?" *Campaigns & Elections* (September 1994), 21–29.

12. Kimberly Conger and John C. Green, "Spreading Out and Digging In: Christian Conservatives and State Republican Parties," *Campaigns and Elections* (February 2002), 58–65; Melissa M. Deckman, *School Board Battles: The Christian Right in Local Politics* (Washington, D.C.: Georgetown University Press, 2004).

13. http://www.cwfa.org.

14. http://www.frc.org.

15. David Von Drehle and Thomas B. Edsall, "The Religious Right Returns," *Washington Post National Weekly Edition* (August 29–September 4, 1994).

16. Deckman, *School Board Battles.*

17. For example, see Robert P. Dugan Jr., *Restoring America's Values: Winning the New Civil War* (Portland, OR: Multnomah Press, 1991).

18. Nicholas D. Kristof, "Following God Abroad," *The New York Times*, May 21, 2002.

19. Elisabeth Bumiller, "Evangelicals Sway White House on Human Rights Issues Abroad," *The New York Times*, October 26, 2003.

20. David B. Barrett, "Annual Statistical Table on Global Mission, 1996," *International Bulletin of Missionary Research*, January, 1996; and "A Century of Growth," *Christianity Today,*

November 16, 1998. For the most up-to-date figures see David B. Barrett, George T. Kurian, and Todd M. Johnson, eds., *World Christian Encyclopedia*, 2nd ed. (New York: Oxford University Press, 2001).

21. Laurie Goodstein, "Christians Gain Support in Fight on Persecution," *The New York Times*, November 9, 1998.

22. International Religious Freedom Act, PL 105–292, signed into law October 27, 1998.

23. International Religious Freedom Act.

24. Samuel G. Freedman, "Horowitz's List," *New York* (March 31, 1997), p. 46.

25. This particular point was made in his video taped speech to the national Campaign of Conscience on Sudan Symposium, November 6, 1998.

26. 2000 Survey of Evangelical Elites, University of Akron, John Green, principal investigator.

27. Several of the advocacy groups were, in fact, consulted by the producers of *Touched by an Angel*. The plot line involved a member of Congress pressed by her son to go to Sudan to see slave redemption taking place, against the wishes of a lobbyist concerned about the loss of gum arabic imported from Sudan.

28. William Branigin, "A Different Kind of Trade War," *The Washington Post*, Saturday, March 20, 1999.

29. Victims of Trafficking and Violence Protection Act of 2000, Public Law 106–386, October 28, 2000. The legislation is divided into two parts, each of which has its own title. So Division A is the Trafficking Victims Protection Act, which is the one cited for our purposes.

30. Elisabeth Bumiller, "Evangelicals Sway White House on Human Rights Issues Abroad," *The New York Times*, October 26, 2003.

31. This is recounted in Allen Hertzke, *Freeing God's Children: The Unlikely Alliance for Global Human Rights* (Lanham, MD: Rowman & Littlefield, 2004), chapter 8.

32. Gary A. Haugen, *Good News About Injustice* (Downers Grove, IL: InterVarsity Press, 1999).

33. John Miller, Speech delivered at Georgetown University, February 20, 2003.

34. "Religious Leaders Cheer Debt Relief," *Christian Century*, November 2000.

35. Thomas Hart, Interview with Allen Hertzke, March 2001.

36. Conger and Green, "Spreading Out and Digging In"; Deckman, *School Board Battles*; John C. Green, Mark J. Rozell, and Clyde Wilcox, eds., *The Christian Right in American Politics: Marching to the Millenium* (Washington, D.C.: Georgetown University Press, 2003).

37. Kenneth Wald and Richard K Scher, " 'A Necessary Annoyance'? The Christian Right and the Development of Republican Party Politics in Florida," in Green et al., *The Christian Right in American Politics*.

38. Conger and Green, "Spreading Out and Digging In"; Deckman, *School Board Battles*.

39. The classic, controversial, and cautious thesis of liberalization may be found in James Davison Hunter, *Evangelicalism: The Coming Generation* (Chicago: University of Chicago Press, 1987). See the response in James M. Penning and Corwin Smidt, *Evangelicalism: The Next Generation* (Grand Rapids, MI: Baker, 2002).

40. Some articles try unsuccessfully to do a better job. See Robert Sullivan, "An Army of the Faithful," *New York Times Magazine* (April 25, 1993), 32–35.

RELIGIOUS POLITICS
AND THE LEGAL SYSTEM

In this chapter and the next we enter the realm of law and the courts. We also consider policy decisions that are affected by the legal system of the United States. Legal decisions made by state and federal courts have an enormous influence on public policy in areas from aid to religious social services to prayer in public schools. Groups from all sides have become increasingly involved in legal struggles to promote their points of view. Besides being the arenas for struggles over specific policies, American courtrooms are also the setting for the airing of cultural disagreements about the general role of organized religion and the interaction between religion and politics. The stakes are high, and the legal conflicts are often intense.

No one should make the mistake of thinking that the American legal system, from the humble living room of the most rural justice of the peace to the magnificent U.S. Supreme Court building in Washington, exists independently of politics. Instead, typical political pushing and shoving are very much a part of the American legal system at all levels. This is neither shocking nor necessarily lamentable; it is simply reality. This is not to say that politics entirely defines the American legal system. It has its own internal norms, such as the principle of *stare decisis* (which means standing by previous court decisions) and concern for due process. Moreover, many judges are eminently fair and strive not to allow political prejudices to color their rulings.

In this chapter we examine the efforts of religio-political forces to affect legal outcomes. We consider some of the reasons for this development and the specific resources that help to make groups effective in the legal arena. In the process we introduce some of the most significant organizations involved in the legal struggle over religion and politics. After reflecting on the implications of this struggle, we consider broader theories of how organized religion ought to relate to government, which together form the context of various legal arguments. In Chapter 9, we examine the specific religio-political disputes that have occupied the courts—and how these disputes have been resolved.

JUDICIAL POLITICS

Most religious groups in the United States historically have ignored the courts, but in the past few decades many have become deeply involved with the legal system. It has become routine for such groups to work through the courts in order to try to achieve—or protect—objectives that they cannot accomplish in any other way. A large variety of religious legal organizations help to shepherd cases through the courts, and some bring their own lawsuits. Another common approach to judicial politics today for religious groups is the filing of amicus curiae (friend of the court) briefs. Amicus briefs are written opinions filed with a court that allow third parties (in this instance religious legal organizations) to register their views on pending cases. Even if the court does not take heed of the views of a particular group filing as amicus curiae, the group's views will nonetheless become a matter of public record, and group leaders can trumpet their efforts to their membership. And there are a host of other tactics, too: lobbying about the selection of judges to the federal courts, seeking favorable implementation of court rulings, and influencing elite and mass opinion on the meaning of law.

Why has this turn to the courts taken place? In good part, it reflects broad-based developments in the American political system as a whole. In the last half of the twentieth century the United States embraced a more centralized national political system. This trend began in the 1930s and 1940s with the emergence and success of a single leader, President Franklin Delano Roosevelt, who fought the Great Depression and World War II from the national level. In the process the size and the influence of the federal government began an expansion that has continued to the present day. Paralleling the federal government's growth has been considerable activism on the part of the federal judiciary, most notably the U.S. Supreme Court. In turn, interest groups, including religious groups, have stepped up their efforts to affect legal outcomes. They realize that the federal courts have come to exercise tremendous influence over national policy.

The First Amendment holds that "Congress shall make no law respecting an establishment of religion, or prohibiting the free exercise thereof." Before the 1940s almost all legal disputes over church and state were considered state matters and were resolved in state courts. Because the U.S. Supreme Court had interpreted the First Amendment to apply only to actions of the *national* government for 150 years, states were not forced to comply with the religion clauses of the First Amendment, so state-level church-state disputes were rarely addressed in federal courts. In the 1940s, however, the Court changed its mind about this long-standing interpretation of the First Amendment's meaning and began ruling on a wide range of religious debates from the state and local levels. The Court insisted that national standards were necessary and acceptable—and should supersede state and local norms.

The Court accomplished this goal by interpreting parts of the Fourteenth Amendment to mean that state and local laws and practices must meet with the standard of the First Amendment. The relevant part of the Fourteenth Amendment holds that: "No State shall . . . deprive any person of life, liberty, or property, without due process of law." According to the Court, this clause means that no *state* should be allowed to abridge religious freedom protected by the First Amendment, despite the fact that the amendment states that "*Congress* shall make no law," not "*Congress and the state legislatures* shall make no law." Since 1940, this interpretation has been the Court's standard—and thus the nation's—of determining the proper venue for resolving disputes about the First Amendment's religion clauses. In interpreting the Constitution this way, the Court extended the "doctrine of incorporation," its overall argument that the *states* are bound by the Fourteenth Amendment to guarantee their citizens the civil liberties set forth in the Bill of Rights.[1]

The Court first decided to incorporate the Free Exercise Clause of the First Amendment ("or prohibiting the free exercise thereof") in *Cantwell v. Connecticut* (1940). In that case the Court held that the provisions of the First Amendment regarding religious freedom should constrain the actions of state and local governments as well as those of the federal government. The state of Connecticut could not prevent Jehovah's Witnesses from proselytizing, because doing so violated their free exercise rights.

According to the Court, "The Fourteenth Amendment has rendered the legislatures of the states as incompetent as Congress to enact laws which violate the provisions of the first amendment."[2] With its judgment in *Cantwell*, the Supreme Court claimed for itself great decision-making power over state- and local-level disputes. One major consequence was that the *Cantwell* precedent sent the message that religious groups, and many others, could turn to the federal courts for the resolution of their problems with any and all governmental institutions and policies.

Other factors were also at work. The simple reality of expanding religious pluralism increased the role of the courts. The strength of minority religions can be exaggerated, but there is no doubt that every year ever more new religious movements emerge and gather strength in the United States. The growth of this pluralism began in earnest with the expansion of Roman Catholicism in the nineteenth and early twentieth centuries. As religious pluralism broadened in twentieth-century America, an increasing number of religious groups found themselves in conflict with the government or the society around them.

Some of these groups went to the federal courts to seek redress. This was particularly true of small religious groups. Their leaders often believed that Congress and the executive branch would be less likely to be responsive to a small religious minority than would the federal courts.[3] During the 1940s, the Jehovah's Witnesses pioneered this process by seeking relief in the federal courts from assorted local and state regulations limiting their door-to-door proselytizing or requiring salutes to the American flag. Such regulations severely limited Jehovah's Witnesses' freedom to practice their religion, which demands active proselytizing and prohibits the salute of any flag. In most of these instances the Witnesses succeeded in securing their free exercise rights.[4]

The success of the Jehovah's Witnesses encouraged other religious minority groups to believe that the federal courts presented both a possible and proper realm for addressing the unique problems they face. Such groups, in effect, encouraged the federal courts to take an active role in shaping the politics of religion in the United States. Since the 1940s, what was once a trickle of cases has become a flood as the conflict between religion and politics in America is increasingly played out in its courts. The federal courts have been busy since *Cantwell* was decided in 1940, with the Supreme Court alone deciding nearly 160 cases dealing with religion.[5] Some of the reason for this broader engagement is the judiciary's own preference for involvement in disputes between organized religion and the political system. Neither the lower federal courts nor the U.S. Supreme Court has shied away from this arena. This extends to the federal courts' willingness to intervene in abortion policy. For better or for worse, the Supreme Court's decision in *Roe v. Wade* (1973) that abortion was constitutional has generated an enormous amount of controversy—and legal action.

The nature of the courts' rulings, especially those of the Supreme Court, has magnified legal conflicts that are rooted in church-state disputes and other religious matters. As we note in Chapter 9, the Supreme Court's pronouncements in these areas have too often been unclear—some say contradictory—and thus have resolved little. This uncertainty ensures further litigation and more dispute. Moreover, as the federal courts have taken a more visible role in settling disputes about church-state separation and religious freedom since the 1940s, a wide variety of interest groups have entered the scene. Even religious groups that are successful in legislative and executive arenas realize that they must be participants in *every* major playing field, including the courts, if they are going make their mark on American politics.[6]

KEY PLAYERS

The legal system today bursts with activity as religious associations attempt to influence court rulings. None of these groups represents a majority of the American public. Still, many have had a significant impact on judicial politics at the federal, state, and local levels. Many of the key players are connected with what may be termed the "separationist coalition," which supports an absolute separation between church and state. Recently, however, such groups have been challenged by an emerging set of opposing groups affiliated with evangelical Protestantism.[7]

Separationist organizations come in three varieties. Some trace their roots to a separationist Protestant tradition that goes back to the Puritan leader Roger Williams in colonial Rhode Island.[8] Its members are often quite religious. Their goal is to nurture free exercise rights by keeping religion separate from government. As Roger Williams himself envisioned it in 1744, separationists believe there should be a "wall of Separation between the Garden of the Church and the Wilderness of the World."[9] One separationist organization of note is the Baptist Joint Committee. Long committed to separation of church and state, the Baptist Joint Committee is one of the most active groups in American judicial politics today. It draws support from a variety of Baptist organizations, though in 1991 it lost the support of the largest Baptist denomination, the increasingly fundamentalist Southern Baptist Convention, over disagreements regarding church-state separation and the Convention's view that BJC was leaning toward a liberal political agenda.[10]

Another major separationist organization is Americans United for Separation of Church and State, which was founded in 1947 with considerable Protestant support. Its major outlet is *Church and State*, a publication that is distinctly sympathetic to the separationist views. Though Americans United has a long history and has enjoyed a great deal of publicity since the 1940s for its zealous opposition to state aid for Catholic schools (if not Catholicism itself), it now is part of the broader separationist coalition that includes other associations that have not historically been aligned with separationist Protestantism. One example of these groups is People for the American Way (PFAW), created by Hollywood producer Norman Lear, who is famous for *All in the Family* and other television comedies (Box 8.1).

Also integral to the separationist coalition are a number of Jewish organizations and their legal arms.[11] This is most prominently true of the American Jewish Committee, but not just of them. Most Jewish groups have been involved in legal battles to promote separation of church and state as a way of protecting Jews (and other religious minorities) from the official establishment of any form of Christianity. Whenever a crèche (manger scene) appears on public property, or Christian prayers are being led by staff at public schools, or other potential violations of the separation of church and state occur, it is common to find the American Jewish Committee and its allies going to court to halt these practices.

A third, and perhaps more uneasy, partner in the separationist coalition today represents the truly secularist portion of the movement. The American Civil Liberties Union (ACLU) is the most famous and assertive member of this wing. Indeed, the ACLU gets more involved than any other organization in church-state controversies and other legal dis-

---

BOX 8.1 PEOPLE FOR THE AMERICAN WAY

People for the American Way (PFAW) was founded in 1980 by Hollywood producer Norman Lear "to monitor and counter the divisive agenda of the religious Right." It is not attached to any branch of Christianity or to any religion at all, though it steadfastly maintains that it is sympathetic to religion. It has been extremely active in taking legal action to promote separationism in church-state affairs, especially by trying to defeat or frustrate the efforts of the religious Right. Indeed, PFAW, which now claims over 300,000 members, was initially formed to combat the now-defunct Moral Majority. One of its recent tactics has been combating conservative nominees for federal judgeships—a tactic that will surely be pushed to the forefront as Supreme Court vacancies are likely in the near future.

SOURCE: http//www.pfaw.org.

---

putes involving religion. It is committed to full separation of church and state, and often to free exercise rights for small religious minorities that have been affected negatively by the state.

Though the ACLU's lack of connection with religion has not prevented it from rallying to help selected religious groups, other secular organizations exist to advance secular values and institutions only. This is a fair description of the objective of the Society of Separationists and American Atheists. American Atheists claims to be "the premier organization laboring for the civil liberties of Atheists, and the total, absolute separation of government and religion."[12] These groups have challenged all abridgments of church-state separation, including the printing of "In God We Trust" on U.S. currency and the saying of prayers before public legislative bodies.

This same principle underlies the efforts of the Freedom from Religion Foundation, whose title leaves no doubt about its objectives. Founded in Madison, Wisconsin, by Anne Gaylor and her daughter, Annie Laurie Gaylor, but now operating nationally, the Freedom from Religion Foundation has sought to make a difference in the church-state controversy by fighting in the courts to dismantle all linkages between church and state.[13] The fact that such organizations are active today is part of the reason that the courts have increasingly limited the presence of religion in public life.

Until the late 1970s, separationist groups were largely unopposed by other advocacy groups in the courts.[14] But the activity of the separationist lobby, and public perceptions of its success, has provoked a counter-reaction. Today, religious groups that are determined to fight back in court are a growth industry. Most of these are associated with evangelical Protestantism, but they often have contributors who are sympathetic with their efforts regardless of religious background.

Some religious legal organizations have existed for decades. The Christian Legal Society was founded in 1962, for example. Most, however, were born in the 1980s and 1990s when conservative groups discovered that whatever one's influence on legislatures, executives, or the people in general, the courts matter too. This sense has heightened religious groups' concern about the judicial selection process and strengthened their resolve to be involved in the politics of court decisions.

One well-known conservative religious legal organization is the Rutherford Institute, which has been involved in many high-profile cases and maintains a large and systematic national fundraising effort. The organization takes its name from a seventeenth century Scottish intellectual named Samuel Rutherford, who was among the first to reject the idea of the divine right of kings. Founded in 1982 by constitutional lawyer John Whitehead, the group is probably best known for its role in representing Paula Jones in her sexual harassment lawsuit against Bill Clinton, but its primary focus has been protecting the religious freedoms of evangelical Protestants.[15]

Another important religious legal organization is the American Center for Law and Justice (ACLJ), a creation of Rev. Pat Robertson and his associates. Under the leadership of Jay Sekulow, an effective litigator with media savvy, the ACLJ quickly became a major evangelical player in legal politics after its founding in 1990. The ACLJ has entered many legal disputes in various capacities and has been remarkably active in the Supreme Court itself, with Sekulow arguing several religious freedom and free speech cases before the justices.[16] The group has been quite adept at reaching out to the evangelical community through Robertson's media outlets and a radio show hosted by Sekulow. This exposure has helped ACLJ secure a great deal of financial support from ordinary religious conservatives, as well as from other sources (Box 8.2).

But not all religious legal groups represent evangelical Protestants and their interests. The Office of the General Counsel of the United States Conference of Catholic Bishops (USCCB) plays a significant role in church-state disputes. It represents the American Catholic Church in litigation both directly as a party and indirectly by filing amicus curiae

---

BOX 8.2 ALLIANCE DEFENSE FUND

James Dobson, D. James Kennedy, Bill Bright, and other prominent evangelicals founded the Alliance Defense Fund (ADF) in 1994 to "empower" allies such as the ACLJ through financial and other forms of support. By providing support to other organizations, ADF seeks to help coordinate evangelical efforts at legal advocacy and to channel the flow of church-state and "family values" cases on court dockets. The group has funded many notable cases, including *Rosenberger v. University of Virginia* (1995), in which several Christian college students won their challenge to a state university policy of denying certain funds to religious groups. The ADF also operates a training program for like-minded attorneys through its National Litigation Academy.

SOURCE: http://www.alliancedefensefund.org.

---

briefs.[17] Many specific denominations also undertake their own legal efforts, particularly as amicus curiae. The prolife Lutheran Church–Missouri Synod, for example, frequently files amicus briefs with the Supreme Court in abortion cases.

Some organizations are extremely specialized in their endeavors. Don Wildman's American Family Association Law Center has been particularly active in disputes over family issues and television. The Home School Legal Defense Association pursues legal issues that relate to preserving the rights of its members, who do not send their children to school outside the home. But there is rarely any neat dividing line among issues—or groups. Money and opportunity play significant roles in groups' decisions about when to go to court. What is clear is that the use of the courts is on the rise, and the increasing legal efforts by separationists have met with a parallel response from those who oppose the separationist agenda.

FACTORS FOR SUCCESS

What contributes to the success or failure of religious organizations as they enter the courts? Of course, sympathetic judges and propitious times always help, but what else matters? What are the dynamics that contribute to legal success? One crucial factor is money; litigation and other forms of legal advocacy are expensive. This painful but real fact is often an awkward matter, as there can be substantial competition among various legal action organizations for limited donors and dollars. Moreover, fundraising efforts require both time and money and leave less of both for the legal causes at hand.

Equally important, of course, are experience and expertise, both of which take time to fashion. We have already noted that in building effective lobbying organizations, people who know their way around Congress or the statehouses are indispensable. So are those who understand the concerns of the religious groups they represent, how their members think, and how they want their story told. The same applies to religious associations in the legal arena. After all, they are really just interest groups involved in legal advocacy, lobbying the courts for their self-defined interests. The lawyers who spearhead these efforts must know both the legal and religious terrain. Indeed, it helps to have lawyers with the passion that comes with being personally committed to a group's cause, especially since groups often must rely on the volunteer labor of those attorneys.[18] New groups, including those from the evangelical perspective, have sometimes neglected these resources, but they have slowly come to nurture savvy legal activists. Some groups even sponsor "litigation academies" and similar workshops to ensure that affiliated attorneys are well prepared to fight their legal battles.

A third factor for success is support for legal activism among group members and donors. If a group's members do not want their contributions to fund legal efforts, the group will find itself seriously stifled. Government support has also been of great assistance at times. This was true for many conservative Christian legal organizations during Republican presidencies, when they found themselves in the favorable position of working with Republican-appointed Justice Department lawyers on the same cases, toward the same ends. Finally, support from the larger public can help, too. Public support generates funds and favorable publicity, both of which may affect legal contests in myriad ways.

The embrace of legal strategizing by religious groups appears to be growing. This makes sense in light of the increasing religious pluralism of American society. Today less than 60 percent of the U.S. population claim to be Protestants.[19] Moreover, the fault lines within Protestantism over moral and political issues have now become as deep as any between Protestants and members of other religious traditions. In short, American society now faces an expanding religious pluralism that is accompanied by moral pluralism. Such a context is hardly a congenial one for any religious group that tries to affect politics by working only through legislatures or presidents.

This reality is sharpened in light of the fact that American religious traditions are increasingly politically organized and face organized opposition themselves. In religion, as elsewhere, the truth today is as James Madison suggested it should be in *Federalist No. 51*: Interest checks interest and ambition checks ambition. Such a situation almost compels those who seek social change into the courts, for it is often the case that judges alone make authoritative decisions that break the organized pluralist impasse that so often holds sway. The courts can render clear decisions; they can break impasses; and they can side with even the smallest religious interest if they feel that the law or the Constitution directs such a decision.

It often makes sense for religious organizations to take legal action in the current political arena. Yet we need to be clear that such a step, especially for many religious minority groups, is usually a defensive move designed to protect against domination by more powerful groups and perspectives. Indeed, in an increasingly pluralistic society, there is little else that small religious groups can do when they perceive themselves to be threatened. In times of crisis, they have only one serious recourse: the law and the courts.

Religious groups are increasingly using the courts to publicize themselves for their members and the broader society as well. When a group is involved in litigation, its members learn it is actively pursuing the group's goals. And even if the group has little actual influence over the judges' decision, it can still claim credit from its members if the case is decided in line with the group's stated agenda. Litigation can also attract the attention of people outside of the group, which attracts new members and lays the foundation for coalition-building with other groups. Coalition-building is particularly valuable because it can facilitate a division of labor. The ACLJ, for example, hires many of its lawyers from the evangelical Regent University School of Law. In its earlier years, it also received financial and research support from the Christian Coalition. None of this would have been possible if the ACLJ were shy about its engagement in judicial politics. Coalition-building can also allow religious legal organizations to pursue a wider variety of goals. Some groups may focus on education, others on abortion, and still others on pornography, but they offer mutual support for each other at the same time.

For many religious groups, the politics of legal action offers distinct advantages. Taking politics to the courts requires neither a large membership nor elite access in the powerful worlds of official Washington and the national media nor vast financial resources. Thus legal strategies make sense for small, otherwise powerless groups. For better endowed and well-connected interests that would usually lose if popularly elected legislatures had the last word on their concerns, going to court also makes sense.

For some religions, legal strategies present an additional advantage of fostering the illusion that they avoid politics, a world that many groups (such as the Jehovah's Witnesses and the Amish) dislike, fear, or oppose. They trade on the conventional wisdom that the courts are a pure, nonpolitical realm, uninvolved in the grubby world of clashing interest groups. This sometimes treasured—but inaccurate—belief attracts many religious groups to the courts to accomplish what are ultimately political ends.

For the United States as a whole, the strategy of fighting battles between religion and politics in the legal system presents mixed blessings. There is much dispute about whether religio-political controversies ought to be resolved in a democratic arena or a federal courtroom. Should religious freedom be subject to definition by the majority? Should the limits of government establishment of religion be outlined by the majority? Indeed, some participants in the church-state debates of today wonder whether democracy is an important value to begin with. Those who point out that democracy is not enshrined in the Bible or any other sacred text refuse to worry about whether the courts contribute to or hinder democracy.

For such individuals, the real issue is the need to protect rights, whether they are the rights of the Amish, strict separationists, or Mormons. By this view, if the courts serve as a setting where such questions may be addressed—and addressed without inflaming biases that often accompany religious diversity, free exercise, and official establishment—then they contribute immeasurably to a healthy society. And, one may argue, sometimes the result is a flowering of democracy, because freedom and democracy go hand in hand. After all, it is only through the courts that unpopular outlooks can be represented fully.

THE POLITICS OF CHURCH AND STATE

In the midst of the legal struggle for advantage in debates about religion and politics today lie various approaches to the relationship between church and state. There is much at stake: not simply how government relates to religious institutions, but also fundamental beliefs about the normative role of religious values in politics and society. How should the courts and those who appeal to them for recourse establish relationships between church and state, and between religion and politics? Chapter 9 will examine some of the specific church-state matters that the courts have adjudicated. Here, however, we introduce several classic perspectives on church-state relations and the extent to which the courts have embraced each in recent decades.

The Separationist Approach

For a separationist, the First Amendment's religion clauses—"Congress shall make no law respecting an establishment of religion, or prohibiting the free exercise thereof"—mean that government cannot be involved with religion *in any way*.[20] Separationists look with pride to those chapters in colonial history that were part of the journey toward separation of church and state. They honor Roger Williams, founder of Rhode Island, for his determination to separate church and state, and William Penn, founder of Pennsylvania, for his commitment to Quaker tolerance of other religious faiths. They respect the histories of colonies like New York and Pennsylvania that pioneered the tradition of separationism. Such colonies were sure that true free exercise was possible only when the state and the law were kept apart from organized religion.

Though church-state relations during the colonial era were complicated, there is no doubt that the separationist point of view united many people. Separationism formed an umbrella under which those who feared state religions and those who were skeptical of religion in any form could gather. It also accommodated those whose ardent commitment to minority and dissenting religions made them worry about how they—and thus true religion—would fare if the government were to become involved in religious matters. From these diffuse roots, ranging from the skeptical Thomas Jefferson to the earnest New England Baptists, the separationist tradition grew.[21] Sophisticated separationists, however, were and are well aware that even after the adoption of the Constitution and the Bill of Rights, the American record was hardly separationist. Religion (especially Christianity) has always been deeply connected with, and often supported by, the state.

Thus there has been much for separationists to litigate. Separationists have been concerned about the saying of prayers at the opening of sessions of state legislatures and Congress, the president's inauguration, and even the opening session of the U.S. Supreme Court itself. They worry about the employment of government-sponsored chaplains in the military and government aid for religious hospitals, religious social service agencies, and religious colleges. They note with displeasure the references to God on American currency and in the Pledge of Allegiance. They dislike seeing crèches on public land in December and hearing government officials invoke the name of God on Thanksgiving. In short, separationists argue that American culture is schizophrenic in that it is theoretically committed to the principle of separationism— yet far from separationist in practice.

Public attitudes are equally mixed. Studies consistently demonstrate that people in the United States reflexively endorse "separation of church and state" and oppose the mixing of religion and politics. But there is often considerable support for specific actions that hardly fit with such a view. Consider opinion on the role of religion in public schools: two-thirds of the American people support spoken prayer in public schools[22] and agree that religious accounts of the origin of the human species should be taught alongside evolution in public schools.[23]

Separationists hold that the absence of official sanctioning of religion by government and religious free exercise are inseparable. They believe that the more government remains separate from religion, the more citizens will be able to enjoy religious freedom. Separationists argue that this belief was held by many of the framers of the American Constitution, including James Madison, who wrote the Bill of Rights. The idea is that an activist government presents a real threat when it becomes involved with religious institutions.

Neutrality

Neutrality is a second perspective that has often enjoyed strong support from the Supreme Court. According to this view, the courts should be neutral on all religious conflicts that clog the courts and thus the courts should neither promote nor impede religion; they should just ignore it.

The Supreme Court's version of the neutrality doctrine was formulated in the classic case *Lemon v. Kurtzman* (1971). It held that if a law has a secular purpose and a secular effect, neither advances nor inhibits religion, and does not result in excessive entanglement between religion and government, then it is constitutional. By this view, it is acceptable for there to be incidental government support for religion, but only as a byproduct of some law that is secular both in intent and effect. Similarly, it is acceptable to impair religious freedom, but only as a byproduct of a law with a secular purpose and a secular effect. The goal is for the state to be neutral, and neutralists have assumed that the way to achieve neutrality is to ignore religion in any analysis as much as possible.[24]

This understanding often angers separationists. Separationists appreciate that neutrality eliminates flagrant, overt aid to organized religion and forbids any formal establishment of religion. But they want the Court to take religion into account in order to ensure that no matter what a law's main purpose or principal effect, religion does not obtain any government benefits. For separationists, neutrality can be (and has been) used by the courts as a way to turn a blind eye toward the clever ways government hides laws that aid and support religious purposes under seemingly secular objectives and language. For radical separationists, state laws that allow nonprofit groups freedom from taxation would constitute a prime example. Under the neutralist approach, such laws would be constitutional because they have a secular purpose and mainly secular effects (since they are for nonprofit groups of all types). But in practice such rules grant an enormous privilege to religious nonprofit organizations. They meet the nonprofit test and may thus receive substantial state benefits.

A modified version of the neutrality stance toward religion is "benevolent neutrality."[25] Supporters of this approach approve of neutrality as the proper stance for the courts, because they are confident that it will prevent religion and churches from becoming a more prominent factor in government decisions. At the same time, however, benevolent neutrality tries to have it both ways. Its advocates argue that there should be sympathetic acceptance from time to time of the religious effects of "secular" government actions and laws.

Supporters of the benevolent neutrality position maintain that application of the secular purpose and secular effect test avoids government sponsorship of religion, but at the same time they insist that this test must not be followed in such a rigid fashion that religious freedom is lost. Government must not sponsor religion, but it must not destroy it either. Though government should generally stay neutral, it must do so in a benevolent mood, and no fixed formula can make that happen. Judgment is therefore needed on a case-by-case basis, according to the benevolent neutrality view.

Equal Treatment

A third view is known as "equal treatment." Its supporters maintain that the courts should sanction government assistance to churches and other religious groups *as long as this is done for all of them equally* (equal treatment) and *if it would encourage free exercise of religion.* Those in favor of equal treatment declare that religion sometimes needs the state to help free exercise become a reality. Thus separationists may not necessarily be correct when they assert that free exercise expands when the separation between church and state grows.[26]

In American history this was, in effect, part of the case made by those (primarily Roman Catholics) who felt that state aid for religious schools was a good idea. From time to time they succeeded. For example, in the years after the Civil War, President Ulysses S. Grant undertook an effort to promote peace between whites and Native Americans by encouraging the assimilation of Native Americans through education. To provide such education, he turned to churches and granted them the privilege of establishing schools on reservations. For the last three decades of the nineteenth century, Congress funded a number of religious groups as part of this effort, including the Catholic Church. In 1899, however, the entire program came to an end, in part because Protestant groups objected to the funding of Catholic schools.

This education program was very much the exception rather than the rule. A portion of the traditional argument in favor of state aid for Catholic schools was practical: Catholics wanted and needed the money to keep their schools going. Another part, though, is the argument some Catholics make that access to religious school education is vital for real free exercise of religion. The only way to achieve this goal for many Catholics is through government assistance. This view has come to be shared in the present time by some evangelical Protestant "Christian school" supporters, including many proponents of state-funded educational vouchers. But it has yet to garner broader levels of public support.[27]

In other areas, equal treatment garners much support, such as widespread support for tax deductions for all nonprofit religious organizations. There is no doubt that such policies help organized religion in a material sense and may therefore encourage its existence. Recent efforts to expand public funding for "faith-based" social services have also been based explicitly on the equal treatment view. Proponents of broader funding, including leaders in the Bush administration, argue that government support of religious agencies is constitutionally permissible as long as money is available to all groups, religious and nonreligious alike.

Opponents of equal treatment contend that nontraditional forms of equal treatment (such as substantial state aid for religious schools) and in some cases all forms (including property tax forgiveness) are unconstitutional threats to religious freedom. For such opponents, to have the state involved with religion, and certainly with religious schools, raises the very real specter of state control. That, they believe, would be a disaster.

The argument goes back and forth (Box 8.3). Those who favor positive accommodation, as they might put it, sometimes suggest a case-by-case approach. They often turn back to history to make part of their case. As they read it, the historical record reveals a complex and diverse pattern in which there was once a great deal of official establishment and accommodation of religion that did not involve the sacrifice of free exercise or the establishment of a single church.

For proponents of equal treatment, sweeping historical claims about separationism and the framers simply do not work. They point out that when the First Amendment was adopted, a number of states continued to maintain official religions. Massachusetts, the last to give up its established church, did not do so until 1833. Moreover, while Congress operated in the early years as though the First Amendment prohibited all government connection with religion or churches, at other times it gave a contrary signal. The very year Congress approved the First Amendment, for example,

---

BOX 8.3 RELIGIOUS NONPROFIT ORGANIZATIONS AND PUBLIC MONEY

A paradox of American politics is that, although fierce legal battles are fought over state aid to parochial schools, billions of dollars of government funds flow annually though other religiously based nonprofit organizations. Normally this occurs without fanfare or legal challenge.

Since colonial days, all levels of American government have sought to achieve public purposes by working through nonprofit charities, hospitals, educational institutions, and relief agencies. Many of these nonprofits are faith-based and receive a substantial portion of their budgets from government contracts, grants, or patron vouchers. This system works well from the standpoints of government because nonprofit organizations are closer to the communities they serve, less bureaucratic, and more flexible. In turn, religious communities are left relatively free to provide faith-inspired services, such as succor to the needy, adoption services, refugee settlement, and health care.

Public support for faith-based nonprofits, however, has recently come under greater scrutiny. Since the welfare reforms of 1996, a greater range of religious social services than in the past have been given the opportunity to compete for public money. Unlike Catholic Charities, Lutheran Social Services, and other regular recipients of public funds, many religious groups are often more up-front about their religious identity and integrate religious practices such as prayer and worship into their provision of social services. This has begun to raise questions about the constitutionality of public funding of religious nonprofits—questions now integral to the political debate over President George W. Bush's proposal to expand even further the public financing of religious social services.

SOURCES: Stephen V. Monsma, *When Sacred and Secular Mix: Religious Nonprofit Organizations and Public Money* (Lanham, MD: Rowman and Littlefield, 1996); Amy E. Black, Douglas L. Koopman, and David K. Ryden, *Of Little Faith: The Politics of George W. Bush's Faith-Based Initiatives* (Washington, D.C.: Georgetown University Press, 2004); http://www.whitehouse.gov/government/fbci/index.html.

---

it also reenacted the Northwest Ordinance, the document governing much of the western U.S. territory (now the Midwest). Section III of the Northwest Ordinance observed that "religion, morality, and knowledge being necessary to good government and the happiness of mankind, schools and the means of learning shall forever be encouraged."[28]

Advocates of further state aid to religion also take issue with the image of such crucial constitutional framers as Thomas Jefferson and James Madison as radical separationists. They argue that neither Jefferson nor Madison believed that there needed to be dogmatic lines separating church and state, and that normatively speaking, such lines should not be drawn in a complex, diverse political order. It is no simple matter; free exercise has sometimes been harmed by the state's assistance to religious groups, but it also sometimes has required such aid.[29]

Some proponents of equal treatment openly declare that what they favor amounts to multiple establishment—the official (or semiofficial) establishment of all faiths in the United States—because of the country's enormous religious pluralism. Advocates of this approach embrace as reality exactly what their opponents believe—and fear—is the essential truth about equal treatment. For advocates of multiple establishment, the logic of equal treatment can derive from a postmodern world in which there are no shared truths, and where the necessity of pluralist tolerance is absolutely essential.[30]

CONCLUSION

More than 150 years ago Alexis de Tocqueville discussed the inclination of Americans to try to resolve policy disputes in the courts. He saw the legal system as a way for people in the United States to avoid messy and contentious political fights. Instead, they used "neutral" judges and courtrooms to work out resolutions. Today there are many more factors compelling people to turn to the legal system to address policy conflicts, including the presence in the United States of more than a million lawyers.

In any case, Tocqueville would probably be astounded today at how often policy conflicts are met and sometimes "resolved" in the courts. This is certainly true in the area of religion and politics and church and state. The legal system is, in fact, perhaps the favorite avenue for religious politics, and its terrain is contested with all the resources and political skills that can be mustered by the interested parties. Thus it is essential for any religious group entering the political realm in the United States to know how judicial politics works.

Courts are political institutions and must be so in matters of church and state and religion and politics. They can help achieve compromises that respect the past and yet acknowledge the more diverse present. The results may often be messy and short on neat logic, but few things in politics are neat and logical and, given the nature of the human being, perhaps that is just as well.

FURTHER READING

Cord, Robert L. *Separation of Church and State: Historical Fact and Current Fiction.* Cambridge, MA: Lambeth, 1982. Interesting discussion of the religious and political views of the framers.

Fisher, Louis. *Religious Liberty in American: Political Safeguards.* Lawrence, KS: University Press of Kansas, 2002. A provocative study that suggests the regular legislative process protects religious freedom as well—if not better—than courts.

Hamburger, Philip. *Separation of Church and State.* Cambridge, MA: Harvard University Press, 2002. A stimulating argument that church-state separationism has no historical foundations.

Kramnick, Isaac, and R. Laurence Moore. *The Godless Constitution: The Case Against Religious Correctness.* New York: Norton, 1996. A fascinating separationist interpretation of the founding period.

Miller, Robert T., and Ronald B. Flowers, eds. *Toward Benevolent Neutrality: Church, State, and the Supreme Court.* Waco, TX: Baylor University Press, 1987. A defense of the neutrality doctrine.

Monsma, Stephen V. *When Sacred and Secular Mix: Religious Nonprofit Organizations and Public Money.* Lanham, MD: Rowman and Littlefield, 1996. Important work on a key area of public policy and religious jurisprudence.

Monsma, Stephen V., ed. *Church-State Relations in Crisis: Debating Neutrality.* Lanham, MD: Rowman and Littlefield, 2002. An excellent collection of views on the principle of neutrality.

Pfeffer, Leo. *Religion, State and the Burger Court.* Buffalo, NY: Prometheus, 1984. The classic defense of separationism.

Segers, Mary C., and Ted G. Jelen. *A Wall of Separation? Debating the Public Role of Religion.* Lanham, MD: Rowman and Littlefield, 1996. A discussion of various perspectives of the role of religion in democratic society.

NOTES

1. The doctrine of incorporation traces its roots to the Supreme Court's decision in *Chicago, Burlington, & Quincy Railroad Company* v. *Chicago* 166 US 226 (1897).

2. *Cantwell* v. *Connecticut* 310 US 296 (1940).

3. In many instances, these beliefs may have been mistaken. See Louis Fisher, *Religious Liberty in America: Political Safeguards* (Lawrence, KS: University Press of Kansas, 2002).

4. See Shawn Francis Peters, *Judging Jehovah's Witnesses: Religious Persecution and the Dawn of the Rights Revolution* (Lawrence, KS: University Press of Kansas, 2000).

5. John Witte Jr., *Religion and the American Constitutional Experiment: Essential Rights and Liberties* (Boulder, CO: Westview Press, 2000), Appendix 3.

6. Kevin R. den Dulk and J. Mitchel Pickerill, "Bridging the Lawmaking Process: Organized Interests, Court-Congress Interaction, and Church-State Relations," *Polity,* 35 (2003), 419–440.

7. Kevin R. den Dulk, "Prophets in Caesar's Courts: The Role of Ideas in Catholic and Evangelical Rights Advocacy" (Ph.D. Diss., University of Wisconsin, 2001); Steven P. Brown, *Trumping Religion: The New Christian Right, The Free Speech Clause, and the Courts* (Tuscaloosa, AL: University of Alabama Press, 2002).

8. For an interesting separationist interpretation of the founding, see Isaac Kramnick and R. Laurence Moore, *The Godless Constitution: The Case Against Religious Correctness* (New York: Norton, 1996).

9. Roger Williams, "Mr. Cotton's Letter Lately Printed, Examined and Answered," in John E. Semonche, ed., *Religion and Constitutional Government in the United States* (Carrboro, NC: Signal Books, 1985), 77.

10. Laura Sessions Stepp, "Conservative Reelected to Lead Baptists," *The Washington Post* (June 5, 1991), A4.

11. On this topic, see Gregg Ivers, *To Build a Wall: American Jews and the Separation of Church and State* (Charlottesville: University of Virginia Press, 1995).

12. http://www.atheists.org/.

13. http://www.ffrf.org/.

14. Frank Sorauf, *The Wall of Separation: Constitutional Politics of Church and State* (Princeton, NJ: Princeton University Press, 1976).

15. John W. Whitehead, *Slaying Dragons: The Truth Behind the Man Who Defended Paula Jones* (Nashville: Thomas Nelson, 1999).

16. See, for example, *McConnell v. FEC* (2003) and *Locke v. Davey* (2004).

17. http://www.nccbuscc.org/ogc.

18. Austin Sarat and Stuart Scheingold, *Cause Lawyering* (New York: Oxford University Press, 1998).

19. Pew Research Center and Pew Forum on Religion and Public Life, "Religion and Politics: Contention and Consensus," available at www.people-press.org/reports (July 24, 2003). For a discussion, see Chapter 2.

20. Perhaps the leading writer in support of separationism has been Leo Pfeffer, former chief attorney for the American Jewish Congress. See Leo Pfeffer, *Religion, State, and the Burger Court* (Buffalo, NY: Prometheus, 1984).

21. Two interesting books on religious freedom in the founding period are Leonard Levy, *The Establishment Clause: Religion and the First Amendment*, 2nd ed. (Raleigh, NC: University of North Carolina Press, 1994) and William L. Miller, *The First Liberty and the American Republic* (New York: Knopf, 1986).

22. George Gallup, Jr., *Gallup Poll 2001* (Wilmington, DE: Scholarly Resources, 2002), 50.

23. George Gallup, Jr., *Gallup Poll 1999* (Wilmington, DE: Scholarly Resources, 2000), 207.

24. One of the most able and determined neutralist views may be found in Paul J. Weber, *Equal Separation: Understanding the Religious Clauses of the First Amendment* (Westport, CT: Greenwood, 1990).

25. Chief Justice Warren Burger explicitly argued for this position for the first time in *Walz v. Tax Commission* (1970). For approaches somewhat sympathetic to "benevolent neutrality," see A. James Reichley, *Faith in Politics* (Washington, D.C.: Brookings Institution, 2002), chap. 3; and Robert T. Miller and Ronald B. Flowers, eds., *Toward Benevolent Neutrality: Church, State, and the Supreme Court* (Waco, TX: Baylor University Press, 1987).

26. For an excellent collection of essays arguing several sides of the equal treatment approach, see Stephen V. Monsma and J. Christopher Soper, *Equal Treatment of Religion in a Pluralistic Society* (Grand Rapids, MI: Eerdmans, 1997).

27. Hubert Morken and Jo Renee Formicola, *The Politics of School Choice* (Lanham, MD: Rowman and Littlefield, 1999).

28. 1 Statute 50, 52, Article III.

29. On the historical record, several interesting discussions are Witte, *Religion and the American Constitutional Experiment*; Robert L. Cord, *Separation of Church and State: Historical Fact and Current Fiction* (New York: Lambeth, 1982); Thomas J. Curry, *The First Freedoms*

(New York: Oxford University Press, 1986); Reichley, *Faith in Politics*, chaps. 3 and 4; and Michael Malbin, *Religion and Politics: The Intentions of the Authors of the First Amendment* (Washington, D.C.: American Enterprise Institute, 1978).

30. See Robert Booth Fowler, "A Postmodern Defense of Government Aid to Religious Schools," in Jo Renee Formicola and Hubert Morken, eds., *Everson Revisited: Religion, Education, and Law at the Crossroads* (Lanham, MD: Rowman and Littlefield, 1997).

CHURCH AND
STATE IN THE COURTS

Religious liberty has been called America's "first freedom," and rightly so. The enduring religious pluralism in the United States would be impossible without wide latitude for various religious beliefs and expressions. Much of this freedom flows from the Constitution itself. The framers put religious freedom in the forefront, as embodied in the first sixteen words of the Bill of Rights' First Amendment: "Congress shall make no law respecting an establishment of religion, or prohibiting the free exercise thereof." But securing religious freedom has often been a struggle, in part because the issues that arise under the First Amendment are rarely clear cut. Political institutions, and especially courts, have been thrust into the unenviable role of defining the limits of religious freedom and the proper interaction of church and state.

The First Amendment and its religion clauses were adopted by the first Congress of the United States, under the leadership of James Madison. Congress began its work on this task in the spring of 1789 because of agitation for the inclusion of a list of guaranteed civil liberties in the Constitution during the debates about ratification. Chief among the agitators for the Bill of Rights were the Antifederalists, who feared that the expansion of the federal government would curtail personal liberty. Records of the congressional debate indicate that bargaining and compromise were vital to the eventual agreement on the content and wording of the First Amendment. James Madison introduced the proposed amendment in its first form in June 1789. It subsequently went through several revisions before a conference committee agreed on a bill that passed Congress in September 1789 and was later sent to the states, which duly ratified it.

Madison knew he had to fashion an amendment that would satisfy critics who feared that the Constitution was hostile to religion (and suspected the same of him). Madison wanted to include what he called "rights of conscience" in the First Amendment, but some critics thought that the provision of such rights might result in government neutrality between religion and atheism, so it was dropped. Madison also failed in his attempt to eliminate the official establishment of religion at the state level. The final version of the First Amendment applied only to the federal government ("*Congress* shall make no law . . . ").

From the beginning, the issues of church-state policy that have arisen from disagreements over the meaning of the First Amendment have included (1) how to balance free exercise of religion with otherwise constitutional laws that interfere with it, and (2) how to decide when government activities that somehow involve or even benefit religion amount to an unconstitutional establishment of religion. In most of this chapter we explore these two concerns separately, following the Supreme Court's own practice of fashioning precedents and complex tests that address "free exercise" of religion and "establishment" of religion as separate and independent concepts. We conclude the chapter, however, by discussing the many ways free exercise and establishment interact and at times conflict.

RELIGIOUS FREE EXERCISE

The framers of the Constitution thought governments posed a constant threat to the free exercise of religion, especially for religious minorities and dissenters. They based this view on their sometimes negative experiences with the British government and even with their own colonial governments. Thus the framers were eager to protect the free exercise of religion from government interference. For them, protecting free exercise meant curtailing or eliminating government establishment of, and interference with, religion.

Thomas Jefferson, who wrote the Declaration of Independence, and James Madison, the principal author of the Constitution and the First Amendment, were among the strongest proponents of religious free exercise. Both had been active in opposing the establishment of religion in colonial Virginia. They also helped to bring about the disestablishment of the Anglican (now Episcopal) Church there. Neither Jefferson nor Madison advocated complete separation of church and state during their subsequent presidencies, but both tried to move in that direction. Reality, however, forced them to accept some compromises to accommodate organized religion at the federal level. And they did nothing to interfere with the states, where there was sometimes very little separation between church and state. Still, both men made important contributions to the development of American free exercise rights.[1]

Historically, Americans have enjoyed broad free exercise rights. The majority of early Americans were Protestant, and free exercise rights abounded for most of them. Though Protestantism was dominant, free exercise rights were gradually extended to Catholics, Jews, and others. Of course such groups could not constitutionally be denied free exercise rights. Still, they faced varying degrees of discrimination, which in time gave way to a broad-based acceptance of the pluralist reality of American religious life. Plenty of argument occurred along the way, but free exercise has steadily expanded in the United States.

Today, the existence of an enormous degree of religious freedom—encompassing many religious persuasions, groups, and practices—is something of which Americans justifiably may be proud. This does not deny the history of conflict that paved the road to free exercise, nor that religions still struggle for their free exercise rights. There will always be religious groups that push against the margins of American society and its written and unwritten rules about the limits of acceptable religious practices.

In attempting to interpret the Framers' mandate that citizens should have the freedom to practice whatever religion they choose, the Supreme Court has distinguished between religious beliefs themselves and actions taken as a result of those beliefs. Beliefs are absolutely protected, but religiously motivated actions that the Court deems questionable may be restricted. It should be noted, however, that the Court has avoided addressing religious freedom under some circumstances. Indeed, until the 1940s federal courts often ducked religious issues altogether. They also tried to make sure that the other branches of government followed suit. For example, courts have been loath to adjudicate arguments among members of disbanded religious groups. They have understood that to get involved in these often bitter fights may be to interfere improperly with a religion and by extension deter free exercise. This standard remains today. Religious groups are allowed to resolve their own disputes, under their own rules, as much as possible. This is especially so when the basic doctrines of a religion itself are at issue.[2]

If the courts have generally avoided becoming involved in arguments within religious organizations, they have also steered away from attempting to settle disagreements over what constitutes a "religion." Judges realize that this is treacherous ground, but their policy of avoidance has, in fact, proven to be supportive of free exercise. After all, if the definition of religion were left to the government rather than to believers themselves, free exercise could be threatened.

It is not easy to resolve disputes involving religion, but the courts' standard policy has been to avoid defining religion or deciding whether the claims of a given religion are true. For example, in *United States v. Ballard* (1944), the Supreme Court was asked to decide whether a man who was using the U.S. mail to solicit funds for his "I Am Movement" was guilty of mail fraud. Ballard, who said he was a divine messenger who could communicate with Jesus Christ, had his conviction overturned. The Court stated that "Men may believe what they cannot prove. Religious experiences which are as real as life to some may be incomprehensible to others. . . . If one could be sent to jail because a jury in a hostile environment found his or her religious teachings false, little indeed would be left of religious freedom."[3]

Even so, the Court has not been wholly successful in staying out of the business of defining religion, especially when fundamental roles of government are at stake. Consider the government's policies on taxation. In *Hernandez v. Commissioner* (1989), which involved the Church of Scientology, the Supreme Court ruled that fees for specific services such as training in Scientology could not be counted as nontaxable gifts. Critics of the Court's decision in this case complained that it implied Scientology was not a serious religion, thereby setting a dangerous precedent. If Scientology is not a religion, then what are the parameters of the religious and the secular—and who sets them?

The *Hernandez* case points to the continuing controversy over what exactly constitutes a religion—and what services an organized religion may provide. The nonprofit activities of organized religions are free from taxation, a policy that has long been in place. But just what is a "religion," and what is a "nonprofit activity"? The traditional approach has been that minimizing government interference in such matters maximizes religious freedom, but it also leaves room for abuse.

Some controversial religious practices make today's headlines. Often the courts have decided cases in ways that affirm religious freedom. One example has to do with the issue of clergy malpractice (Box 9.1).[4] Another issue of great importance concerns the level of confidentiality clergy should be allowed to maintain. This is especially difficult when clergy learn, through pastoral counseling, that a member of the congregation has committed a serious crime, such as child abuse or even murder. State policies differ, but the current trend is toward requiring clergy to report violations of the law when they learn of them, though some clergy argue that this represents an erosion of their pastor-penitent privilege. Information gleaned through the seal of private confession in Roman Catholicism, however, remains sacrosanct. The confidentiality of pastoral counseling is far more controversial, all the more so in the wake of revelations of sexual abuse by some Catholic priests.[5]

Another sensitive question is the extent to which personal risk-taking should be allowed within a church. The issues almost always arise as a result of health risks incurred because of religious practices. Examples include Jehovah's Witnesses' refusal to accept blood transfusions, Christian Scientists' belief in faith healing (and their consequent rejection of modern medicine), and the practice of serpent handling in a handful of Pentecostal churches. Such issues may be approached from many directions, and of course it matters whether church groups are honest with their members about the possible consequences of any risky behaviors they practice and encourage. The limits of religious freedom become especially important when the lives and fundamental health of children are at stake.

Disputes also swirl around the question of whether there should be limits to some religious groups' perpetual search for converts. Almost all religions assert that they seek only followers who knowingly choose their faith, so they renounce the use of fraud or manipulation to trick people into embracing their faith. But what constitutes a "trick" or a "fraud"? For many atheists, to use the extreme example, every religion is in the business of fraud. How much can government regulate what it— or society—determines to be fraudulent behavior without infringing on free exercise?

BOX 9.1 THE NALLY CASE: "CLERGY MALPRACTICE"

Consider the case of Californian Ken Nally, a mentally troubled individual who repeatedly sought help from clergy but eventually committed suicide. Family and friends sued his church, charging clergy malpractice. They claimed the clergy had misadvised Nally on how to manage his mental condition, thereby not only failing to help him but also contributing to his suicide. Eventually the California state courts decreed in *Nally v. Grace Community Church of the Valley* (1998) that there was no basis for charges of clergy malpractice. And in 1989, the U.S. Supreme Court declined to review the decision. As a result, religious freedom and religious free exercise (including the right of a clergy to make mistakes) won out, but the issue of whether there is such a thing as clergy malpractice remains very much alive.

SOURCE: Margaret P. Battin, *Ethics in the Sanctuary: Examining the Practices of Organized Religion* (New Haven, CT: Yale University Press, 1990) and Mark Weitz, *Clergy Malpractice in America: Nally v. Grace Community Church of the Valley* (Lawrence: University Press of Kansas, 2001).

Some exceptions to allowing free exercise have occurred, such as the Court's decision to outlaw the Mormon practice of polygamy in *Reynolds v. United States* (1879), but broad free exercise rights generally have been permitted in the United States. The law is often murky, and even contradictory, but many rulings testify to the American commitment to free exercise, especially for mainstream religions.

Perhaps the classic Supreme Court case in which a generous range of free exercise rights was affirmed is *Cantwell v. Connecticut* (1940). In *Cantwell*, the Court invoked both religion clauses and other parts of the First Amendment to strike down local ordinances that interfered with Jehovah's Witnesses' desire to distribute literature to and request contributions from the general public. The Court's decision in *Cantwell* to allow religious groups the right to proselytize pursuant to their freedom of religion has been repeatedly reaffirmed, subject to restrictions on the setting.[6] Likewise, state attempts to penalize fundraising by unpopular religions have been rejected.[7] The Court has also ruled that neither clergy nor religious organizations may be prevented from becoming involved in politics.[8] Similarly, the Court has granted some religious freedom in federal institutions (prisons are the most controversial), but only so long as religious practices do not disrupt standard operating procedures.[9]

In public schools, the courts have created a rather narrow zone of free exercise. Still, in *Wisconsin v. Yoder* (1982), the Court defended the decision of Amish people not to attend high school, as Amish doctrine does not require or respect that sort of schooling. It also declared in *West Virginia State Board of Education v. Barnette* (1988) that Jehovah's Witnesses have the right to refuse to say the Pledge of Allegiance in school, as their religion forbids commitment to any nation-state. In *Pierce v. Society of Sisters* (1928) it supported the right of Roman Catholic schools (and thus other private and religious schools) to exist alongside public ones. All of these cases were momentous because they demonstrated that public education must be aware that it operates in an environment of religious free exercise and must therefore take the Supreme Court's limits into account.

THE LIMITS OF FREE EXERCISE

In principle, however, there is no debate about the government's ultimate authority to restrict the free exercise of religion. In the United States nothing is superior to the powers of the government—except the people from whom the state's authority derives. Even rights granted in the Constitution and the Bill of Rights are not absolute and may be limited by other constitutional provisions and by the government. Thus it is always conceivable that the free exercise of religion may be restricted.

Many of the Supreme Court's most controversial free exercise decisions in recent years have addressed disputes in which the state's authority and need for security are at stake. In *Goldman v. Weinberger* (1986) it decided to uphold military regulations providing that no Jewish person could wear a yarmulke (skullcap) while on duty in the U.S. military. At issue was not the wisdom of the regulation but whether or not the Court should defer to military rules and the reasons behind them, namely the need to maintain military order and regularity. The Court concluded that it should defer to the military. Congress later passed a law allowing Jews to wear yarmulkes in the military, but it did so without challenging the authority of the federal government to decide such matters. A similar issue arose in a New Jersey case, *O'Lone v. Estate of Shabazz* (1987), in which Muslims in state prisons claimed that prison work rules interfered with their practice of Islam. The Court held that deference to prison rules and the administrators who make them (that is, the government) must take precedence over free exercise.

Other cases have considered challenges to public health regulations or other matters that touch on community values or the common good. The view that some government provisions designed to protect the general welfare have priority over the First Amendment's guarantee of free exercise has been endorsed in the courts for some time. A long line of cases has held that such things as required vaccinations to protect public health or laws forbidding child labor supersede free exercise rights, even though some groups' religious freedoms may thereby be violated. For example, in *Braunfeld v. Brown* (1981), the Court ruled against a group of Orthodox Jews who felt that their ability to earn a living was being compromised by Pennsylvania's Sunday closing laws. Their religion forbid them to work on Saturday, and the state forbid them to work on Sunday. The Court recognized that the Pennsylvania law made Orthodox Judaism "more expensive" than Christianity, but because the law did not prevent anyone from the actual *practice* of religion—"the Sunday law simply regulates a secular activity"—it did not violate the free exercise clause.[10]

In areas such as these the crucial question centers on where to draw the line between the pursuit of government goals and the protection of religious free exercise. The fact is, the U.S. Supreme Court has never sent a clear message about where that line ought to be drawn. It has usually appeared to be more impressed with upholding government policy than with protecting some small, dissenting religious group. But no obvious and consistent pattern has emerged. From the late 1930s until the 1960s, however, it was a safe bet that most free exercise appeals would meet with defeat in court. The Supreme Court usually sided with the federal and state governments and their laws in such conflicts. Since the 1960s, however, these matters have been less clear, as the pendulum began to swing toward the expansion of free exercise rights.

In the landmark free exercise case of *Sherbert v. Verner* (1963), the Court stated that the standard of "strict scrutiny" (the most exacting level of judicial review) must apply to any law that conflicts with the free exercise of religion. By imposing this standard the justices meant to underline the importance of free exercise, though they did not mean that any laws clashing with free exercise would automatically fail the strict scrutiny test. In *Sherbert*, a Seventh-day Adventist won her claim against South Carolina for denying her unemployment benefits after she was fired from her job for refusing to work on Saturday (the Adventist Sabbath). The Court stated clearly that "the burden on the free exercise of appellant's religion must be justified by *a compelling state interest.*"[11] Thus the *Sherbert* case set a high standard, which the Court continued to use for many years in deciding a variety of free exercise disputes.

The Rehnquist Court, however, has been less congenial to free exercise claims—which usually involve the practice of minority religions. In the much-discussed 1990 case of *Employment Division v. Smith*, the Court specifically reversed the strict scrutiny doctrine that it had set forth in *Sherbert*. No longer would states be forced to demonstrate a compelling interest if their laws had the effect of restricting free exercise rights. Though the picture is complicated and the results mixed, the Court has been increasingly willing to uphold "common good" legislation despite protests of particular religious groups and individuals who have contended that such laws infringe upon their religious practices.

In the *Smith* case, the Supreme Court affirmed Oregon's drug policy. In that state, two Native American drug counselors had been fired and prevented from collecting unemployment compensation. They had been fired for violating terms of their employment that prohibited the use of peyote, an illegal hallucinogenic drug that plays a significant spiritual role in their religion as members of the Native American Church. The Court essentially held that laws that do not target religion directly, such as Oregon's generally applicable drug laws, are constitutionally valid, even if they incidentally restrict religious practice. Though the Court's ruling in *Smith* came as something of a surprise to legal observers and advocates, it was the legal doctrine upon which the ruling was based that caused a real uproar. The Court declared that it was no longer committed to automatic "strict scrutiny" of laws that restrict free exercise of religion, thereby undoing the decades-old *Sherbert* precedent. In *Sherbert*, of course, the Court had not said that laws restricting free exercise were inherently unconstitutional, but it did suggest they would find the going tough. The reversal of this precedent seemed to bring to a close an era in which the Court provided an especially protected role for religious exercise in the United States.

The Supreme Court's 1993 decision in *Church of the Lukumi Babalu Aye v. City of Hialeah* came as a relief to some critics. In this case the Court struck down an ordinance passed by the city of Hialeah, Florida, that prohibited the ritual sacrifice of animals. The court ruled that this ordinance had been designed specifically to forbid animal-killing rituals that are practiced as part of Santeria, an Afro-Caribbean religion. The Court agreed with the Santerian Church of the Lukumi that the ordinance in question was extremely selective since it did not forbid other forms of animal killing such as hunting or Jewish ritual preparation of kosher food. It was aimed instead at one group alone: practitioners of Santeria. What distinguishes the *Smith* case from the *Lukumi* case is that laws interfering with the free exercise of particular faiths that do not further a major state policy may be ruled unconstitutional. Laws pursuant to the common good that are not intended to oppress a particular religious group, however, are likely to be upheld under the *Smith* precedent.

Some critics complain that Court rulings that uphold common-good legislation actually do promote particular moral positions at the expense of pure religious free exercise. They are correct, of course, but the reverse is just as true when free exercise claims do win out. In each instance moral choices are at issue. The question becomes one of where religious free exercise ought to rank in comparison with other values. In the American legal system free exercise is not always at the top of the list.

Though the Supreme Court would no longer defend decisions in the language of Christian morality, as was the case in *Reynolds*, it often accedes to the decisions of Congress and state legislatures, even at the expense of religious free exercise. Much of the Court's recent energy for such decisions has not come from sympathy with such laws themselves, but instead from a commitment to the proposition that courts ought not to interfere with the decisions of democratically elected legislatures.

In response to the Court's decision in *Smith*, religious groups united to push the Religious Freedom Restoration Act (RFRA) through Congress. This law, which President Clinton signed in 1994, required the federal courts to return to the doctrine of strict scrutiny when reviewing any law that abridges religious free exercise rights. In essence, Congress forced the Court to return to the *Sherbert* precedent, which effectively undercut the Court's logic in the *Smith* case. In 1997, however, the Supreme Court retaliated and struck RFRA down. Congress's initial passage of RFRA actually constituted an example of the influence American religious groups can exercise when they unite. But its days were numbered.

The Supreme Court declared RFRA unconstitutional in *City of Boerne v. Flores* (1997). A Catholic parish in Boerne, Texas, wished to expand the size of its church sanctuary but was denied a building permit. The city's policies on the protection of the historic district in which the church was located prevented any further development. Buoyed by RFRA, the parish argued that the city did not have a compelling interest in preventing it from expanding. The Court supported the city's counterargument, simultaneously striking down the provision of RFRA that called for the existence of a compelling state interest for laws to restrict free exercise rights.[12]

The debate between the Court and Congress continues over the proper limits of free exercise. In August 1997 the Clinton administration outlined a plan to protect religious expression in federal government offices. The guidelines allow bureaucrats to wear religious jewelry, hold prayer meetings during lunch breaks, distribute religious literature to coworkers, and keep scriptures on their desks. In formulating the plan, the administration was assisted by a wide array of interest groups, from the conservative Christian Legal Society, to the liberal National Council of Churches, to the separationist People for the American Way.[13] A similar coalition of groups supported the Religious Land Use and Institutionalized Persons Act, which was passed in 2000. The law places limits on the ability of local governments to restrict religious groups from developing property and seeks to secure greater protection for the religious practice of people in prisons, mental hospitals, and other institutions. The law already has been invoked in several disputes over church development and prisoner worship, and it is currently the subject of several legal challenges.[14]

THE POLITICS OF RELIGIOUS ESTABLISHMENT

Whether church and state are truly separated in the United States, in theory or in practice, is a very controversial matter. Perhaps the best strategy is to say that everything depends on what the term "establishment" means. Without doubt plenty of official religious establishment has occurred throughout American history. Most of the colonies officially established one Protestant church or another and required all taxpayers to help finance that single church. Though the First Amendment of the U.S. Constitution outlawed the establishment of any single religion at *the national level*, some states continued to support their own established churches. This practice came to an end when in 1833 Massachusetts became the last state to do away with officially established religion. That marked the end of *legal* establishment (Box 9.2), but it was hardly the end of the notion of establishment. After all, throughout much of the nineteenth century the United States had established Christianity in an implicit way—and Protestantism in particular. This was most obvious in the widespread reading of the Protestant King James Bible in nineteenth-century public schools.

Separationist and antireligion lobbies have had only mixed success in attempting to dismantle these more subtle forms of establishment. For example, atheist leader Madalyn Murray O'Hair failed in her 1979 attempt to persuade the United States Court of Appeals (Fifth Circuit) to banish "In God We Trust" from the currency (*O'Hair v. Blumenthal*). Efforts in 1983 to get the Supreme Court to eliminate prayer at the beginning of legislative sessions also proved unsuccessful *(Marsh v. Chambers).* Though a U.S. Court of Appeals (Ninth Circuit) struck the phrase "under God" from the Pledge of Allegiance in a controversial 2002 ruling—a dispute now pending before the Supreme Court—the weight of the traditional establishment of what may be called *religion in general* has been substantial throughout American history. Nonetheless, pressures against the symbolic establishment of *Christianity* have grown stronger over the years—and have been increasingly successful. The coalition against official endorsements of Christianity is often broad and frequently includes the American Civil Liberties Union, Americans United for Separation of Church and State, and the legal arms of prominent Jewish groups.

On the other hand, the technique most often used by those who wish to defend symbolic establishment has been to repackage establishment and present it—for the benefit of the courts—as something that is not religious at all. In instances when these efforts succeed, courts appear to wink and go on to what they judge to be more important matters. This has been evident in arguments over public crèches (manger scenes depicting Jesus' birth). In both *Lynch v. Donnelly* (1984) and *Allegheny County v. Greater Pittsburgh ACLU* (1989), the Supreme Court allowed crèches to stand on public land or in connection with public buildings only if they are merely one element of what the Court describes as a "winter display." When crèches exist alone as a Christian symbol, however, as was the case in a Pittsburgh courthouse in *Allegheny County v. Greater Pittsburgh ACLU*, the Court has deemed them unconstitutional.

**BOX 9.2 ESTABLISHMENT IN THE COURTROOM:
JUDGE ROY MOORE AND THE TEN COMMANDMENTS**

One of the better-publicized debates over religious establishment in recent years has involved, ironically, a courthouse itself. In 2000, then Circuit Court Judge Roy Moore rode a wave of popularity to election as Alabama's chief justice. His victory was largely due to public support for his defiant battle with the ACLU throughout the late 1990s over two practices: his recitation of an explicitly Christian prayer at the opening of court sessions and his display of a handmade plaque bearing the Ten Commandments on the wall behind his bench. Upon assuming the position of chief justice in Alabama, the "Ten Commandments" judge upped the ante. In 2001, Moore placed a two-and-a-half ton granite monument topped with a sculpture of the Ten Commandments in the rotunda of Alabama's Supreme Judicial Building. A local lawyer sued with the help of the ACLU and other groups, arguing that Moore's actions represented another egregious violation of the Establishment Clause, but Moore openly defied an order by a federal judge in 2002 to remove the monument from the building. Though thousands of sympathetic citizens rushed to his aid, Moore lost his battle when the other eight justices on Alabama's Supreme Court ordered the monument taken away; the state's Court of the Judiciary then removed Moore himself from his position as chief justice, citing judicial misconduct for his refusal to acknowledge the federal court order. Moore is appealing the ruling, but whatever the outcome he will continue to be a judicial cause célèbre of many religious conservatives.

SOURCE: Jeffrey Gentleman, "Thou Shalt Not, Colleagues Tell Alabama Judge," *New York Times* (August 22, 2003), A1.

Governments in the United States—local, state, and federal—funnel tremendous amounts of financial aid to various religions. Insofar as they do so, they are sustaining an establishment of religion and undermining the principle of separation. Government aid to nonprofit organizations (which includes religious groups) for assorted public purposes constitutes the most obvious illustration. Examples of this practice, affirmed by the courts since 1899 in *Bradfield v. Roberts*, include assistance to religious hospitals and clinics, orphanages, halfway houses, retirement homes, refugee resettlement projects, and other social service endeavors and programs. The exact amounts of aid and the specific rules governing its use vary from federal to state governments, from state to state, and from one policy area to another, but the practice itself is widespread.

One of the Court's efforts to fashion a governing principle for establishment cases is the so-called *Lemon* test. Formulated in *Lemon v. Kurtzman* (1971), the *Lemon* test holds that laws are constitutional when they serve a secular legislative purpose, neither advance nor inhibit religion, and do not foster an "excessive entanglement" between government and religion.[15] In establishment cases the *Lemon* test has been used in a variety of ways, and its implementation has been a controversial undertaking even within the Supreme Court. Justice Antonin Scalia, for example, has bemoaned "the strange Establishment clause geometry of crooked lines and wavering shapes [the *Lemon* test's] intermittent use has produced."[16]

The *Lemon* test allows the constitutional provision of substantial government aid to religious organizations of all sorts. Thus if governments decide that aid to nonprofit hospitals is in the public interest, then it is constitutional because the legislation from which the hospitals would benefit may be said to have a secular purpose, neither advance nor inhibit religion, and fail to foster any excessive entanglements between church and state. It is still true, however, that in such a situation government is undeniably aiding religious groups and thus promoting some form of religious establishment. Granted, this sort of implicit establishment is by no means the same as the official establishments of the colonial era. In that age, government support was enjoyed exclusively by one church. Instead, the modern arrangement normally takes the form of "multiple establishment." Government provides aid in a particular policy area to all qualified applicants. For example, both secular and religious hospitals may receive government funds.

Contemporary establishment also occurs in the common practice of granting all nonprofit groups (again, including religious institutions) freedom from property taxes. Because churches, synagogues, and mosques often occupy extensive and highly valuable properties, this arrangement is a tremendous financial boon for them. This has been defended not as a grant to religious groups *per se*, but as a neutral law with the secular purpose of helping nonprofit (and only nonprofit) groups that benefit society. Though some separationists have argued strenuously against this arrangement as a flagrant form of establishment, they have not succeeded in the courts. Establishment in the United States is often legal if it is indirect and accomplished through "neutral" laws that stand up to the *Lemon* test.

Education policy is another arena in which many conflicts have emerged over religious establishment. The battle over religion in the schools has been waged throughout American history, and it continues unabated today. The American culture's faith in schooling ensures that struggles over education policy will continue, for Americans believe that a great deal is at stake.

All sorts of religious practices in schools, some of which have reflected the beliefs of a particular religious group, have been common throughout the history of American public education. Public prayers and Bible reading in class have been the most widespread of these practices. However, such policies began to face serious criticism after World War II when religious "release-time" education became a widespread fashion. Such programs allowed religious teachers to come into public schools during regular hours and teach religious lessons to students who had the permission of a parent or guardian. In the late 1940s and early 1950s the Supreme Court was indecisive about the constitutionality of this practice. In *McCollum v. Board of Education* (1948), release-time classes held on school grounds were ruled unconstitutional. In 1952, the Court seemed to reverse itself in *Zorach v. Clauson*, but the release-time classes at stake in that case took place off of school property.

Even though release-time programs are no longer popular in most places, the disputes surrounding them were an early sign of the courts' willingness to tackle establishment issues that related to public education. Steadily since the 1960s, courts have brought about a sweeping disestablishment of conventional religion in public schools. This is seen as a great victory by separationist and antireligious groups that argue religion has no place in the classroom.

The Court's first step was to remove state-sponsored prayer from the schools in the monumental 1962 case of *Engel v. Vitale*. One year later, the Court also put a stop to Bible reading in public schools in *Abington School District v. Schempp* (1963). In 1980, the posting of the Ten Commandments in classrooms was ruled unconstitutional *(Stone v. Graham)*. For some critics the last straw came in *Wallace v. Jaffree* (1985), in which the Court struck down an Alabama law requiring public school teachers to open each day with a moment of silence. The Court interpreted the law as Alabama's "effort to return voluntary prayer to our public schools."[17] The Court did not accept Alabama's argument that the moment of silence served the secular purpose of encouraging good student behavior. The latest issue of this nature to come before the Court has involved the constitutionality of prayer at public school graduation ceremonies and other public events. The Supreme Court rejected clergy-led graduation prayers in *Lee v. Weisman* (1992) and student-led prayers at high school sporting events in *Santa Fe Independent School District v. Doe* (2000).

Critics have sometimes lamented the exit of nondenominational religion from public schools, charging that religion has been replaced by "secular humanism" (which is actually a very small organized "religion" that places humans above all else). But in the 1987 case of *Smith v. Board of Commissioners*, the U.S. Court of Appeals (Eleventh Circuit) disagreed, apparently believing instead that it is possible to foster neutrality. Some religious groups have welcomed judicial efforts to force religion out of the public schools. They believe religion belongs at home and in church; they often have no use for vague nondenominational religion in the first place. Other observers, however, are uneasy about the need for many public schools to go to great lengths to avoid the presentation or teaching of anything religious.

Despite a long history of religious establishment in American public schools, the teaching of overtly religious lessons has now ceased in most school districts. This fact is reflected in the failure of efforts by conservative Protestants to force school districts in several southern states to provide instruction in creationism. Courts have invariably deemed such efforts a manifest establishment of religion. Instead, the Supreme Court has protected the teaching of evolution. In 1968, the Court struck down an Arkansas law forbidding the teaching of evolutionary theory in *Epperson v. Arkansas*. It is also unconstitutional for a state to require the teaching of both creationism and Darwinism, according to the Court's ruling in *Edwards v. Aguillard* (1987). In both instances the Court felt that the states in question were specifically attempting to establish Christianity.

Disputes over the judiciary's view of establishment have also raged in the context of financial aid to religious schools. Historically this meant that aid to Roman Catholic schools was denied on establishment grounds because to give such aid would be to establish a branch of Christianity, Roman Catholicism. Since public schools once were permeated by practices such as group readings from the Protestant King James Bible, skeptics have suggested that the real problem was not with establishment per se; it was rather a question of which religion would be given preference in most public schools. Though modern courts have removed much of the old Protestant establishment from public schools, their record is complicated on the matter of financial aid to religious schools. Aid for teacher salaries, which is by far the greatest portion of school budgets, repeatedly has failed on establishment grounds, as was the case in *Lemon v. Kurtzman* (1971).

At the same time, the Supreme Court has upheld state laws allowing several significant forms of assistance to religious schools. According to the Court's 1947 decision in *Everson v. Board of Education*, public school buses may be used to transport children to and from religious schools. Transportation to religious schools was not perceived to be a substantial violation of the Establishment Clause. A similar logic drove the Court's 1968 decision in *Board of Education v. Allen*, in which it upheld New York's policy of allowing religious schools to borrow secular textbooks from public school districts. In *Meek v. Pittenger* (1975), however, the Court ruled that neither state-paid staff nor instructional materials other than books could be loaned to religious schools. In *Wolman v. Walter* (1977), the Court affirmed *Meek* and further rejected state aid by declaring that public school buses could not be used to transport children from religious schools on field trips. Finally, in *Aguilar v. Felton* (1985), the Court struck down a New York law providing state-financed remedial courses and guidance services in religious schools. But just over a decade later, the Court specifically overturned *Aguilar* in *Agostini v. Felton* (1997), holding that public school teachers may provide state-mandated special services in religious schools. And following *Agostini* came the Court's decision in *Mitchell v. Helms* (2000), in which the Court upheld state aid to parochial schools in the form of computers and other instructional materials and equipment. The logic of the *Mitchell* case effectively overturned the Court's decisions in *Meek* and *Pittenger*.

In other recent cases the Court has ruled that government funds could be used to pay an interpreter to accompany a deaf student attending a religious school, as it did in *Zobrest v. Catalina Foothills School District* (1993). Proponents could see no problem with this since insignificant establishment, at most, was at issue. Opponents, however, said the policy was a serious breach of the no-establishment principle, since taxpayers would be financing translation by the interpreter of such sectarian events as mass in the school. In *Kiryas Joel Village School District v. Grumet* (1994), however, the Court held that New York could not set up a special school district for disabled children in an Orthodox Jewish town in suburban New York City.

Whereas only one student was being assisted in *Zobrest*, the Court saw the creation of an entire school district for disabled Orthodox Jewish children as another matter altogether.

Taken as a whole, Establishment Clause jurisprudence in the twentieth century amounted to nothing more than a confusing mess to many observers. As one remarks:

> Bus trips from home to religious schools are constitutional, but bus trips from religious schools to local museums are unconstitutional. . . . Standardized tests are okay, but teacher-prepared tests are not. Government can provide parochial schools with books but not maps, provoking Senator Daniel Moynihan's quip: "What about atlases?" The Court has invoked *Lemon* to strike down a nativity scene surrounded by poinsettias and to uphold a nativity scene surrounded by elephants, teddy bears, Santa's workshop, and a talking wishing well.[18]

The Court's logic has been based in its attempt to balance two goals: ensuring no establishment and benefiting children. On the one hand, the Court's reasoning has been that establishment is especially dangerous in the schools because children are much more vulnerable to inculcation than are adults; on the other hand, that very vulnerability has led the Court to avoid disadvantaging children in any fundamental way if they happen to attend religious schools. Thus the Court has been understanding if states decide that all children need textbooks and transportation to school. State-paid religious school teachers, however, would move too far toward establishment.

Obviously there is room for argument on every point. Advocates contend that if religious schools can receive only a certain amount of aid for specific government services, then families of religious school students ought also to receive some compensation for the costs they incur in sending their children to these schools. Families that send children to religious schools commonly complain that they are forced to pay twice to educate their children—once through taxes to support public schools they do not use and again in tuition to the religious school. Opponents reply that no one is forced to send their children to a religious school and that public schools enhance the common good. They question why taxpayers should have to pay for the choices of one small portion of the population, especially when those choices may involve an establishment of religion.

However, some Catholics, evangelical Protestants, Muslims, and Orthodox Jews believe today that they must send their children to religious schools in order to practice their religion freely—especially in light of what they perceive to be growing secularism in public schools. For them, state support for religious schools, if it is made available to all, does not involve much establishment. Nor, they insist, does it hinder free exercise. Critics reply that such support does constitute unacceptable religious establishment because it makes all citizens contribute to the education of children in religious schools. Such critics find allies among some supporters of religious schools who fear that the heavy hand of government regulation might come along with aid.

In the past, the courts have sided with citizens who oppose any form of financial relief for families sending children to private schools. State tuition grants, for example, have been held unconstitutional. The governing rule now, however, is not quite the same. In 1983, the Supreme Court decided in *Mueller v. Allen* that Minnesota's policy of allowing tax deductions for tuition, textbooks, and transportation to private schools—including religious ones—was permissible. The Court cast aside charges of establishment because Minnesota made such expenses deductible only if they were provided to all state-approved private schools. Minnesota has now expanded its program to allow tax deductions for *any* expense (within prescribed financial limits) for private education and introduced a $1,000 tax credit for lower-income citizens who incur expenses other than tuition costs in sending their children to private schools.

The courts have begun to weigh in on the efforts of many states and localities to adopt "school choice" plans, which permit families and students to choose between public and private schools at state expense. Still, it is not obvious what the Supreme Court's reaction would be if these plans become widespread. Several cities, including Milwaukee, Wisconsin, and Cleveland, Ohio, now have school choice plans in operation that provide grants of money (sometimes called vouchers) to low-income families that may be used at certain private schools, including religious ones. On June 27, 2002, the U.S. Supreme Court upheld Cleveland's plan in *Zelman v. Simmons-Harris*. Though 96 percent of the students participating in the program used their grants to attend religious schools, the Court decided that the program was designed to enable a purely private choice. Parents, not government, choose to send their children to religious schools under the program, and so the program did not involve unconstitutional government support for religion. The decision was clearly a victory for school choice advocates, including those who desire greater governmental accommodation of religion in public life. But the decision is unlikely to be the last word on voucher programs (Box 9.3).

The courts have consistently ruled that aid directed to religious colleges and universities raises considerably less concern about establishment. The assumption is that college students, as adults, are a good deal less vulnerable to religious propaganda than are children and young adults in K–12 schools. Thus aid may be provided to religious colleges for buildings as long as they are not used for worship or sectarian education, according to the Court's decisions in *Tilton v. Richardson* (1971) and *Roemer v. Board of Public Works* (1976).

CONCLUSION

One of the most interesting issues today in modern church-state politics is the relationship between free exercise and establishment. The framers of the Constitution took for granted that establishment of religion by definition meant restriction of free exercise rights. And they were correct in instances when establishment means state sponsorship of a single religion. At least for practitioners of minority religions, free exercise was bound to be burdened (at best) in the face of a single established religion. At worst, they would face drastic curtailment of their free exercise rights.

Much current church-state jurisprudence proceeds under the same assumption, namely that no official establishment can possibly enhance the free exercise of religion. But this assumption is not always self-evidently true; sometimes, in fact, establishment may bolster the free exercise rights of many citizens. The classic illustration is provided by the benefits that flow from state aid to religious schools. If state aid is given to all religious schools, religious free exercise may be expanded for families that desire a religious education for their children but cannot afford it—a key contention of many groups and commentators who supported the *Zelman* decision. Some critics point out that implicit in this view is the idea

BOX 9.3 THE FUTURE OF
VOUCHERS FOR RELIGIOUS SCHOOLS

While the Supreme Court's decision in *Zelman v. Simmons-Harris* was a victory for supporters of vouchers and other forms of school choice, the issue is not as settled as some observers and activists have assumed. The case has already generated new constitutional questions, as well as heightened conflict over the political and policy implications of voucher programs.

For example, at least thirty-seven states have their own constitutional provisions prohibiting government funding of religious institutions, which limits widespread use of vouchers for religious schools across the country. In *Locke v. Davey* (2004), the U.S. Supreme Court upheld this restriction in Washington state. In addition to the legal questions about school choice programs, public support for voucher experiments has varied widely and research is just beginning on vouchers' effectiveness as a means to improve educational quality. Though *Zelman* is a fresh point of departure in the ongoing debate about the role of religion in education in the United States, the debate will surely continue.

SOURCES: National School Boards Association/Zogby, "School Vouchers: What the Public Thinks and Why" (March 2002), available at http://www.nsba.org/novouchers/vsc_docs/zogby_results.pdf; Thomas Berg et al., "Joint Statement of Church-State Scholars on School Vouchers and the Constitution," Pew Forum on Religion and Public Life (August 2002), available at http://www.pewforum.org/issues/files/Voucher Package.pdf.

---

that somehow government has an obligation to promote the free exercise of religion, an assumption at which they insist the First Amendment does not even hint. They read the First Amendment to mean that government should not interfere with religious free exercise, which is far different from providing active support for religion.

Such an interpretation of the First Amendment is only one possible understanding of its protection of free exercise rights, and it is no longer consonant with the Supreme Court's approach to free exercise. The Court has defined free exercise of religion as a constitutional right that must be protected affirmatively. But does this mean that the government must promote free exercise? Even if one concludes that government must promote free exercise, it does not follow that it should also offer state aid to religious schools. The point is that it is not always obvious that an increase in establishment (of all religions) leads necessarily to a decrease in free exercise rights. In some instances, the opposite may be true. Some argue that, as a result, sweeping formulas should be replaced by more case-by-case analysis and discussion. The courts have argued for decades that some forms of religious expression in public schools constitute unacceptable establishment. To say the least, these decisions have offended many critics who contend that the resulting absence of religious expression in the public schools amounts to an establishment of secularism.

Some critics have tried to create opportunities in public schools for extracurricular student-led religious groups. The Supreme Court upheld such a policy for college campuses in 1981 by arguing that if a university offers the use of facilities to one extracurricular group, it must do so for all (*Widmar v. Vincent*). In 1984, Congress passed the Equal Access Act, which applied the same principle to public high schools. It provided that high schools had to allow student-led religious groups to meet after school if other extracurricular clubs were also permitted to do so. Many schools have resisted, but the Supreme Court affirmed the law in *Board of Education v. Mergens* (1990) by contending that granting space to an after-school Bible club did not amount to an unconstitutional establishment of religion—as long as a teacher did not lead club meetings.

The impact of the Court's decision to allow high school Bible clubs to form already has been felt, as an increasing number of schools have developed such clubs. Close to 20 percent of all American high schools now have at least one extracurricular religious club. High school ministries such as Young Life, the Fellowship of Christian Athletes, Youth for Christ, First Priority, and Student Venture (the high school ministry of Campus Crusade for Christ) have been active on campuses across the country, in some cases for many decades.[19]

Battles over such clubs and organizations continue, however. In 1993, the Court ruled that if a school district allows other community groups to use its buildings when classes are not in session, then religious groups must also be offered the same privilege *(Lamb's Chapel v. Center Moriches Union Free School District)*. The Court also held in *Rosenberger v. Rector* (1995) that because the University of Virginia provides support to a wide variety of student publications, it must as a matter of equal access do the same for a campus Christian publication. The university at first had not assisted the Christian publication for fear of violating the Establishment Clause.

It is, however, quite possible to disagree with the Court and insist that the principle of equal access is simply an invitation to establish religion.

Though school teachers may not run Bible clubs and other religious groups that meet after school, meetings do take place on public school grounds. Recent developments also constitute a form of multiple establishment because any religious group may take advantage of the policy. But establishment it remains, legally justified by the principles of free speech, free exercise of religion, and equal protection of the laws.

It is also crucial to ask whether the political issues of the day should be fought out in the courts in the first place.[20] And the issue is not only one of how elitist or democratic the courts may be, though that is certainly a subject that deserves reflection. Nor is the question as straightforward as deciding on the wisdom of removing controversial religio-political issues from the public arena. The fact is that the legal remedy, given its focus on adversarial conflict, often exacerbates tensions and thus frequently fails to encourage the compromise that is essential for the increasingly multicultural and multireligious character of American society.

The reality of the politics of church and state today is that all sides turn to the courts when they believe they will win, and to the legislatures when they desire a more sympathetic hearing. This is well illustrated by the efforts of some members of Congress who believe that the federal courts, especially the Supreme Court, do not care enough about freedom of religious expression in public settings. Led by Rep. Ernest Istook (R–Oklahoma), these congressional activists unsuccessfully sought the adoption of a constitutional amendment designed "to secure the people's right to acknowledge God according to the dictates of conscience." The amendment would also have provided that "the people's right to pray and to recognize their religious beliefs, heritage or traditions on public property, including schools, shall not be infringed." This Religious Freedom Amendment (RFA, or Istook Amendment) was endorsed by more than thirty religious organizations, most of them conservative, including the Christian Coalition, the Family Research Council, and Focus on the Family. Several denominations, such as the Southern Baptist Convention and the National Baptist Convention U.S.A., Inc., also supported the Istook Amendment. The House rejected the RFA after heated debate, however, on June 4, 1998.[21]

Certainly there is a need for a perspective on church-state politics that is much more sophisticated than that which often dominates the headlines. There are more than just two positions. There are many kinds of establishment and separationism, many degrees of free exercise and limits on free exercise. Everything is dependent upon specific circumstances. The concrete issues that shape the politics of church and state are complicated, fascinating, and always evolving.

FURTHER READING

Malbin, Michael. *Religion and Politics: The Intentions of the Authors of the First Amendment*. Washington, D.C.: American Enterprise Institute, 1978. A study of the church-state ideas of the framers.

Miller, Robert T., and Ronald B. Flowers, eds. *Toward Benevolent Neutrality: Church, State, and the Supreme Court*. Waco, TX: Baylor University Press, 1987. A defense of the neutrality doctrine.

Miller, William L. *The First Liberty and the American Republic*. New York: Knopf, 1986. A wide-ranging, interesting discussion of church and state and the founding of the American nation.

Wilson, John F., and Donald L. Drakeman. *Church and State in American History*. Boulder, CO: Westview, 2003. A wide-ranging compilation of key cases and commentaries on its subject.

Witte, John. *Religion and the American Constitutional Experiment: Essential Rights and Liberties*. Boulder, CO: Westview, 2000. A valuable introduction to the context for religious liberty in America.

NOTES

1. See, for example, Vincent Phillip Muñoz, "James Madison's Principle of Religious Liberty," *American Political Science Review* 97 (2003), 17–32; Thomas J. Curry, *The First Freedoms* (New York: Oxford University Press, 1986); William L. Miller, *The First Liberty and the American Republic* (New York: Knopf, 1986); and Michael Malbin, *Religion and Politics: The Intentions of the Authors of the First Amendment* (Washington, D.C.: American Enterprise Institute, 1978).

2. See, for example, *Watson v. Jones* 80 US 679 (1871); and *Jones v. Wolf* 443 US 595 (1979).

3. *United States v. Ballard* 322 US 78 (1944).

4. We draw much of the following discussion on clergy malpractice from Margaret P. Battin, *Ethics in the Sanctuary: Examining the Practices of Organized Religion* (New Haven, CT: Yale University Press, 1990) and Mark Weitz, *Clergy Malpractice in America: Nally v. Grace Community Church of the Valley* (Lawrence: University Press of Kansas, 2001).

5. For a discussion of the legal ramifications of the scandals, see Marc D. Stern, "Masses of Torts," *Religion in the New* (Summer 2003), 2–3, 26.

6. See *Airport Commissioners v. Jews for Jesus* 482 US 569 (1987).

7. See *Larsen v. Valente* 456 US 228 (1982).

8. See *McDaniel v. Paty* 435 US 618 (1978); *Catholic Conference v. Abortion Rights Mobilization* 487 US 72 (1988).

9. See *Cruz v. Beto* 405 US 319 (1972); and *O'Lone v. Estate of Shabazz* 482 US 342 (1987).

10. *Braunfeld v. Brown* 366 US 599 (1961). Also see *Jacobson v. Massachusetts* 197 US 11 (1905); *Prince v. Massachusetts* 321 US 158 (1944).

11. *Sherbert v. Verner* 374 US 398 (1963).

12. For extensive analysis of the *Boerne* case and its implications, see "Does Religious Freedom Have a Future? The First Amendment After *Boerne*," *Journal of the Chapman Law School* 2 (Fall 1997).

13. Peter Baker, "Workplace Religion Policy Due," *The Washington Post* (August 14, 1997), 1A.

14. "Coalition Tries to End Zoning Abuse," *Chicago Sun-Times* (August 11, 2000), 30.

15. On the matter of excessive entanglement, also see *Walz v. Tax Commission* 397 US 664 (1970).

16. Justice Scalia made this comment in his opinion in *Lamb's Chapel v. Center Moriches Union Free School District* 508 US 385 (1993).

17. *Wallace v. Jaffree* 105 S. Ct. 2479 (1985).

18. Jeffrey Rosen, "Lemon Law," *New Republic* (March 29, 1993), 17.

19. On Young Life, see http://www.younglife.org; on Fellowship of Christian Athletes, http://www.fca.org; on Youth for Christ, http://www.gospelcom.net/yfc; on Student Venture, http://www.studentventure.com.

20. Margaret Battin first got us to take this subject seriously.

21. Katharine Q. Seelye, "House Rejects School Prayer Amendment to Constitution," *New York Times* (June 5, 1998), A13. Also see http://religiousfreedom.house.gov.

LATINO AND AFRICAN AMERICAN RELIGION AND POLITICS

Throughout this book, we have often distinguished Americans not simply by the diversity of religious traditions and behaviors, but also by their race. Thus we have focused not only on evangelicals as a group, but have divided evangelicals into white and African American categories when explaining political beliefs and behaviors; similarly, we have placed Latino and non-Hispanic Catholics into separate groups. This is an acknowledgment that racial and ethnic identity is intimately linked with religion in the United States, and that fact has political significance. In this chapter we take a step back to consider this interaction of race, religion, and politics in America.

We focus on the two most prominent racial and ethnic groups in the United States: Latinos and African Americans. Religion has always been important in the African American and Latino communities. In few other racial or ethnic groups, in fact, does religion play a more central role. But the two groups have distinctive histories and diverse cultures that make them a useful comparison as we consider the impact of religion on politics within their communities. We begin with Latinos, a community that is growing rapidly in the United States and catching the attention of the political establishment as a result. We then consider the rich traditions of religion and politics within the African American community.

THE CHANGING ROLE OF LATINO RELIGION

There is no better place to begin a discussion of Latino religion than with the role of Roman Catholicism in Hispanic culture and history.[1] Hispanic

Catholicism has remarkably deep roots in North America, predating even the immigration of Puritans to the United States in the early 1600s. The Spanish brought Roman Catholicism with them during their conquest of the continent in the sixteenth century. Fueled by the efforts of Catholic missionaries, who were intimately connected with Spanish colonization, Catholicism spread through the native populations of what is now New Mexico, Texas, Arizona, California, and the fringes of bordering states. Simply looking at a map of the region, with its hundreds of cities, streets, and public spaces named in Spanish after saints and other symbols of the Catholic faith, gives a sense of the unmistakable legacy of both Catholicism and Spanish colonization in the American southwest.

Roman Catholicism continues to play a central role in the lives of Latino Americans. Today some 70 percent claim an affiliation with Catholicism, and many are intensely committed to the beliefs and practices of the institutional church.[2] Slightly more Latino than non-Hispanic whites attend religious services regularly and claim that religion is very important to them.[3] Certain aspects of Catholicism particularly resonate with Latinos, including a strong attachment to Mary as mother of God, reflecting the Latino emphasis on family.[4]

Though many Latinos share the Spanish language and other aspects of culture, worship styles and religious practices among Latino Catholics vary widely. Much of the diversity is tied to the home countries of Latino Americans: Mexican, Cuban, Puerto Rican, and Latinos with other points of origin often have different approaches and emphases in their practice of the Catholic faith. The differences are especially pronounced among foreign-born Hispanics who have had relatively little exposure to the enormous pressure of assimilation into the broader American culture.

Although expressions of Catholicism among Latino Americans are both vibrant and diverse, the relationship between the Latino community and the Catholic religious tradition has sometimes been an uneasy and ambivalent one. During the Spanish colonial period, for example, Latino converts were often suspicious that Catholic missions were complicit in the brutalities of conquest. Many others over the decades have felt an alienation from the immigrant groups that dominated Catholic leadership, most notably those with roots in Ireland, Germany, Poland, and other European countries. And today the Latino connections to the Catholic Church are diminishing, with many Latinos now maintaining a spiritual life outside the institutional church. It is a matter of increasing concern for the Catholic hierarchy.[5]

This uneasy relationship with the organized church today is partly the result of secular cultural and economic pressures beyond the church's control. As second- and third-generation Latinos assimilate into American culture and join the middle class, they often lose parts of a cultural identity, including their Catholicism, that their parents or grandparents brought from their countries of origin. But many Latinos also perceive that throughout its history the church itself has often been inattentive to the unique culture and concerns of Hispanic Catholics.[6] For example, a common complaint is a chronic shortage of Spanish-language masses or Latino-oriented youth ministries.[7] Or consider Latino participation in the Catholic hierarchy, a key feature of church life. Until the 1940s, Spaniards remained the largest group of Spanish-speaking priests in the American Catholic Church, and the first Mexican-American bishop, Patricio Flores, was not installed until 1970. Though the number of Latino bishops has risen since the 1970s, the historical lack of integration into church government simply reinforces the belief of many Latinos that they have been "second-class citizens" within the church.

It is in this milieu that a familiar, and very intense, competition has emerged between the Catholic Church and non-Catholic religious groups for Latino members. Many Protestant churches now have departments that focus entirely on Hispanic outreach, and they often offer Spanish-speaking worship services and various forms of social and economic aid to Latino communities. Though most Latino Americans remain Catholic, the high percentage has been propped up due in part to immigration from Mexico and other countries that are predominantly Catholic. The picture is quite different among the native-born. Large numbers of second- and third-generation Latino Americans have left Roman Catholicism for Pentecostal and other evangelical churches, as well as other faiths or none at all.[8] Even within Latino Catholicism itself we see evidence of Protestant influence. A quarter of all *Catholic* Latinos use words such as "born-again" and "charismatic" to describe their faith.[9]

Pentecostal and charismatic ministries, which claim as many as 5 million Latinos, have been particularly successful as an alternative to the Catholic Church. But we must be careful not to paint a picture of Latino Pentecostals as little more than disappointed ex-Catholics. Latino Pentecostalism in America is a century-old movement that has attracted many Mexicans and other immigrants with its emphasis on gifts of the Holy Spirit open to all and subordination of racial and social differences. Some Latino Pentecostals are former Catholics, but many others have been lifelong members of Latino Pentecostal churches, often within established denominations such as Assemblies of God and the Vineyard. Indeed, it is not uncommon for Pentecostalism in Latino American families to run generations deep.[10]

Nor should anyone think that Latino Protestantism has grown because the Catholic Church has wholly ignored or always taken for granted its Latino membership. Far from it. Some bishops have been keenly aware of the special character of Latinos within American Catholicism, and they have pushed the Catholic leadership to pay more attention. For example, Robert Emmett Lucey, Archbishop of San Antonio from 1941 to 1969, was particularly instrumental is raising social justice concerns on behalf of his Latino parishioners, who as immigrants are often impoverished and lacking in important economic skills. Lucey's efforts culminated in the formation of the bishop's Committee for the Spanish Speaking in 1945. Since the 1970s, the U.S. Conference of Catholic Bishops has sponsored several gatherings (called "Encuentros") of pastoral leaders to discuss plans for ministering to Latino Catholics. The USCCB also recently issued a major study that addresses the need for focus on the Latino membership.[11] And in 2004, citing an opportunity for "the faithful in this country to express solidarity with their brothers and sisters to the south whose pastoral and material needs are great," the Church launched a major initiative called "One Church, One America" to raise funds for Catholic churches throughout Mexico, the Caribbean, and Central and South America.[12]

All of these efforts suggest that the increasing religious divisions within the Latino community are real and momentous for various religious traditions in America. These divisions are also developing at the same time that political elites are becoming more aware that Latinos might provide a potential resource.

LATINOS, RELIGION, AND POLITICS

In 2003 the U.S. Census Bureau declared that the Latino population, which comprises 37 million Americans and has grown 150 percent since

1980, surpassed African Americans as the largest racial or ethnic minority in the United States. This fact alone has enormous political implications. It is no wonder that elected officials and political parties have embarked on an intense competition for the Latino electorate, though low voter turnout in past elections has diminished some of its potential influence. The Latino presence has also generated myriad policy debates, from the status of undocumented workers to affirmative action in education to "English-only" requirements. The high profile of these political and policy issues will only increase over time as the number of Latino Americans continues to grow.

The Latino population is also undergoing rapid cultural change. Some Latinos, especially those who are native-born Americans, have assimilated into American culture. Many now count English as their primary language, though a larger proportion is bilingual.[13] Others are at various stages in the process of assimilation, with foreign-born residents maintaining the strongest ties to the cultures of Cuba, Mexico, Puerto Rico, and other countries in Latin America and the Caribbean.

These dynamics account for the significant differences between foreign and native-born Latinos on a range of issues, including opinion on matters of politics and culture. When the foreign versus native-born division is combined with the diversity of religious traditions and areas of origin, it becomes difficult to identify strong cohesion in Latino perspectives on public life. There is certainly is no monolithic Latino opinion, and that has political implications too.

We can say, however, that Latinos as a group are somewhat more conservative than non-Hispanic whites on issues such as gender roles, abortion, homosexuality, and other matters that touch on family life. The role of family is a key factor in the political thinking of Latinos, and the foreign-born (who are also most likely to be devoutly Catholic) are most likely to espouse traditionalist views of family.[14] Latinos as a group are also generally conservative on matters of church and state, as illustrated in their support of organized prayer in public schools (70 percent) and providing parents with state-funded educational vouchers (60 percent).[15]

On many issues related to economics and immigration, however, Latinos move to the left of the ideological spectrum. Although they have positive views of the role of churches in providing social services, Latinos are more likely than non-Hispanic whites to accept the possibility of higher taxes in exchange for more government services. This view, which is correlated with lower socioeconomic standing of Hispanic Americans, also reflects the liberationist religious teachings on social justice and "the option for the poor," especially within Catholicism.[16] Latinos, not surprisingly, are also much more likely than other demographic groups to support providing welfare benefits to illegal immigrants.[17] The lesson is that ethnic identity and immigrant history shape how Latinos from across religious traditions think about policy issues.

It may be tempting to see in these issue positions the makings of another group of quintessential swing voters, not unlike the Catholic voting population as a whole. There may be some evidence of the emergence of a new swing electorate, but it is difficult to point to religion as a source of it [18]. To be sure, the distinction between Protestant and Catholic Latinos appears to explain some differences in partisan voting.[19] Yet despite these differences, a sizable majority of Latinos as a group has consistently voted with the Democratic Party. In addition, to the extent Latinos exist as a swing electorate, there is a host of factors other than religion, including class, generation, and country of origin, that help explain their voting patterns.

Are there other indicators of religion-based political behavior among Latinos? It is telling that, aside from myriad religious social service agencies that serve Latino populations, few distinctively religious groups engage in political advocacy on behalf of Latinos. Instead, most groups—the League of United Latin American Citizens, the Mexican American Defense and Educational Fund, and the National Council of La Raza, to name a few—are not explicitly religious in character or focus.

The existence of these groups, however, does point to the real possibilities for mobilization among Latinos—mobilization that religious institutions could foster. The example of César Chávez, the legendary farm workers organizer, is instructive. Spurred by a deep liberationist understanding of his own Roman Catholicism, Chávez helped unionize thousands of Latino farm workers in California from the 1950s until his death in 1993.[20] His work with the farm workers caught the eye of many Catholic priests and other religious leaders, who provided vocal support; he even ended one of his several hunger strikes with a special Catholic mass attended by religious elites from across traditions.

Nevertheless, there are some challenges to religion-based mobilization of Latinos as a group. For example, the rapid assimilation of many second-

and third-generation Latinos may decrease the likelihood that Latinos as a whole will emerge as a distinctive political group.[21] After all, if most Latinos become deeply acculturated into mainstream American society, there may be nothing particularly "Latino" about their political attitudes or behaviors. To the extent religion plays a role in politics, then, Latinos in the future may appear like anyone else in the religious traditions in which they have been assimilated.

Moreover, the very description of a group of Americans as "Latino" belies the many ways non-white Hispanics perceive their own ethnic identity. Some prefer to think of themselves as Cuban, Mexican, or Puerto Rican rather than Latino, and these categories matter both for religion and politics. Cuban Americans in south Florida have a very different political focus than, say, Mexican Americans in California or Puerto Ricans in New York City.[22] The nuances and syncretism of religious practices across these countries of origin reinforces differences among Latino Americans, making broad-based political mobilization less likely than if a homogeneous group could be clearly defined.[23]

In any event, there is no doubt that Latinos are becoming more visible players in American politics. As their voting turnout rates and other forms of political participation increase—and the trend is in that direction—they will become ever more important. It remains to be seen whether religion will play an significant role in defining the nature and scope of Latino political mobilization, but the rich history of Catholicism and other faiths within the Latino community gives religion strong potential as a political resource.

AFRICAN AMERICAN RELIGION AND POLITICS: TOWARD A BROADER VIEW

In his fascinating and sometimes eccentric *American Religion*, Harold Bloom argues convincingly that to understand African American expressions of Christianity in the United States one must appreciate both their evangelical side and their distinctly African American side.[24] While Roman Catholicism has had a profound influence on Latino Americans, black Christianity is rooted in American evangelicalism. Like the influence of colonization and assimilation in Hispanic history, black evangelicalism has also been profoundly shaped by the historical experience of race in the United States. It is important to remember that African American religion is overwhelmingly Protestant—and evangelical—in nature. African American Christians are keenly focused on scripture, and many affirm the Bible as literally true. In fact, about 70 percent claim that it is true in all aspects or nearly so. Moreover, like their white counterparts, about half of all African Americans report reading the Bible weekly.

Another indication of the evangelicalism of African American Christianity involves the basic format of worship services. African American services emphasize preaching and music, and often considerable expressiveness, as is also the case in some white evangelical services. There is little of the liturgy that one might find in Roman Catholic, Lutheran, or Episcopal services, whose roots are more clearly Catholic in origin. This is not to say that the typical African American worship service is indistinguishable from a white evangelical service. In African American churches, there is significantly more interaction between the congregation and the pastor during worship. Music plays a central role; there is a clear connection between the "call and response" musical motif and the typical flow of an African American service. In fact, some of the roots of jazz lie in black spirituals of the eighteenth and nineteenth centuries.

A third similarity between white and black evangelicalism involves church organization. African American and white evangelical denominations favor a loose organizational structure that tends to uphold the autonomy of the individual church. Such "conventions" (as in the Southern Baptist Convention) bring together many individual churches, but they usually do not support direction from the top of a hierarchy, big headquarters, large staffs, or formidable budgets.

Christianity in the black community, as in the white community, has experienced numerous and sometimes very contentious conflicts that produced permanent schisms, sometimes over doctrine and sometimes over personalities. Many African Americans Baptists, who comprise about 50 percent of the black population, are affiliated with the National Baptist Convention of America and the Progressive National Baptist Convention. Another 10 percent are Methodists, often in the African Methodist Episcopal (AME) Church (which is the oldest African American denomination), the African Methodist Episcopal Zion (AMEZ) Church, or the Christian Methodist Episcopal (CME) Church. The rest belong to a wide variety of other denominations and churches. The Pentecostal movement is also growing rapidly in the African American community. It is organized in several major denominations, especially the Church of God in Christ (COGIC), the fastest growing African American denomination, and numerous independent churches.[25]

In evangelical churches, whether they have white, black, or multiracial congregations, the laity normally hire the pastor directly. In many black churches the pastor (ordinarily a man) is a powerful and generally dominant figure. The pastor is almost always the center of his church and he makes the important decisions about community and political activities. His church often rises and falls with him. Recruiting a good pastor is therefore essential for every African American church.[26]

A recent study of African American clergy found that many have not completed college or advanced theological training, though some black pastors are highly educated. For financial reasons, a significant number of African American clergy find employment outside of their churches. There are plenty of exceptions, but often black pastors must confront economic struggles in their personal and family lives as well as in their churches, especially when they serve small or rural congregations. The situation is often complicated by the serious challenges faced by African American laity in the South and in the central cities of the North. African American clergy who serve in central city neighborhoods must deal with issues of drug abuse, violence, and abject poverty on a regular basis. Sometimes black pastors have to take personal action just to keep members of their congregations and residents of their church neighborhoods alive.[27] Samuel G. Freedman's powerful *Upon This Rock: The Miracle of a Black Church* describes some of these challenges in unmistakable terms.[28]

Attracting young people is a universal challenge faced by modern American religious groups. Black clergy routinely worry that they have a particularly hard time attracting young black men to church. Many African American congregations have a large majority of female members and there is a feeling in some African American circles that church, if not religion, is women's business. Moreover, some religious alternatives seem to appeal more to men than women in the African American community.

Among these alternatives is Islam; a vast majority of African American Muslims are men.[29]

It is crucial to remember that African American Christianity is inseparable from the history and shared experiences of black people in the United States. To know the history of African American Christianity is to understand its traditions of both resistance and accommodation; to appreciate its communal side and its individualism; and to recognize its prophetic dimension and its priestly focus.[30] Religion has served as a crucial refuge for African Americans for several hundred years. During slavery and beyond, the church was the one place where African Americans were usually able to be safe and free. The church remains today as the central institution of the black community and is integral to the identities of many African American citizens.[31]

But the distinctly African American side of black Christianity goes quite beyond history and values, and includes such things as popular music. African American spirituals are now widely sung by Christians of all racial and ethnic backgrounds.[32] This fact is both ironic and inspiring, because these spirituals emerged from the dim days of slavery. African slaves, stripped of freedom, invented the spirituals to bring themselves hope during long days of forced labor in such places as the cotton fields of the South. One spiritual, for example, contains the lyric "Before I'll be a slave, I'll be buried in my grave, and go home to my Father and be free." Slavery ended, but among its legacies is the black spiritual, with its stress on Christianity and the theme of liberation.

African American Christianity has always stressed the image of God as consoler as well as liberator of the oppressed. Religion can be a vehicle of hope for the weary and the downtrodden, a function that continues to be important for African Americans today as it was in the days of slavery. To this day, many religious African Americans find some comfort in the assurance of heavenly peace and salvation through a fervent and celebratory belief in a benevolent God.

There has been a self-conscious effort within some black theological circles to develop a black liberation ideology. James Cone and Cornel West have been the leading black liberation theologians. Cone played a crucial role in the late 1960s as elements of the civil rights movement turned toward more radical expressions of discontent. His seminal work, *Black Theology and Black Power*, justified the black power movement in religious terms.[33]

HISTORY AND BLACK POLITICAL ATTITUDES

What is most striking about religion and politics among African Americans is how closely the two issues are linked. Black Christianity has a major political component, and African American churches are often openly involved in politics in a variety of ways. There is simply no sharp division between religion and politics in the African American community today, which embraces the Old Testament model where the paths of religion and politics often crossed.

Religion and politics mix for African Americans despite a long historical experience before the civil rights revolution in the South that taught that involvement in politics could be dangerous and sometimes deadly for African Americans. To be sure, African American churches have long held that the gospel speaks of a just and equitable society. And even before the civil rights movement began in the 1950s, plenty of African American citizens were fighting for change—though often behind the scenes. Nonetheless, before the 1950s most African Americans, especially in the South, recognized that the public arena was a dangerous place, one that ought to be avoided.[34]

The early years of African American Christianity clearly exemplified this apolitical model. In two hundred years of slavery, many black people converted to Christianity—though American Christianity remained a distinctly white religion. Few allowances were made for black adaptations of white Christianity, though versions of Christianity developed anyway, out of the range of white vision and often involving features and practices from religions in Africa. The first black Baptist congregations were organized in the South at the end of the eighteenth century. But many slaves were not allowed to attend any services at these or other churches. Therefore clandestine worship groups formed on plantations, coming to be known collectively as "the invisible institution."[35]

The early African American Methodist churches were organized not by slaves but by free people living in the North. They saw white churches as complicit in the perpetuation of the institution of slavery, and they noted that segregation was enforced in white churches even in the North. Northern black Christians felt that by creating their own, separate churches, they would be able to assert their collective power more forcefully. The beginnings of organized, separate African American Protestant expression date to 1787, when several African Americans withdrew from St. George's Methodist Episcopal Church in Philadelphia. They met and prayed together informally for years with other African Americans. Finally in 1794 the white Methodist Bishop Francis Asbury dedicated Bethel Church of Philadelphia, the first African Methodist Episcopal church, which survives to this day and is known as Mother Bethel.[36]

The second phase of African American religion began after the Civil War. Black Christianity became more formally organized, and it no longer operated under the tutelage of whites. This period saw major expansion of black Baptist and Methodist denominations. It was also in this era that the African American Pentecostal movement was born. African American Pentecostal leaders today are proud of the fact that their religious movement does not trace its roots explicitly to European Protestantism. The result was a lively religious world, but after Reconstruction African Americans shied away from open political engagement. The vast majority of African Americans lived in the South, where the political freedom of Reconstruction proved fleeting.

During World War I, African Americans began moving north in search of jobs and a better life outside of the segregated South. This process accelerated during World War II and in the years afterward, when the mechanization of southern agriculture spurred even more northward migration. Eventually about half of all African Americans settled outside the South.

The quotient of fear among black religious people who had moved north began to diminish. Big northern cities soon developed large African American communities; this bred a comfort level that moved many African Americans to express their opinions freely and without substantial fear in and out of church. These changes did not, however, lead very much of the African American religious community toward political engagement. Old suspicions remained, and evangelical theology continued to teach what previous black experience had underlined: that politics was corrupt and dangerous. So African American churches continued to shun official political involvement. They urged their members to follow suit.[37]

Despite this legacy, everything began to change in the 1950s and the 1960s. African American churches shifted dramatically toward politics, and this choice changed history. The civil rights movement that began in the 1950s was led in its earliest and most productive years by African American Christians. Black pastors played a crucial role in this effort.

Rev. Martin Luther King Jr. was certainly the most visible, but he worked in coalition with others, such as Rev. Ralph Abernathy and Rev. Fred Shuttlesworth, through the Southern Christian Leadership Conference (SCLC).

For these pastors, the time had come to claim civil rights for all African Americans. They had few doubts that God supported this prophetic decision, and by the 1960s African American churches—particularly Baptist churches—throughout the South were transformed into organizational centers for the movement. Though African American clergy were not the only forces arrayed on behalf of the civil rights revolution, without the crucial support of black churches it would never have happened.[38] It was in church that African Americans heard the message that called them into the politics of protest. It was in church that they planned strategy. And it was in church that they found the moral inspiration to risk a great deal individually for the collective benefit of all.

The movement for civil rights, however, did not win quick support from all African American churches. Such an involvement—and confrontation—with the world did not sit well with dominant theologies, nor with the painful and sometimes terrible past experiences of those African Americans who had dared to get involved. There was a strong and active resistance to the civil rights movement from within organized black Christianity. Perhaps the most visible opponent was Rev. Joseph H. Jackson, longtime head of the National Baptist Convention, USA, Inc., and a major figure in the African American Christian community. In his retrospective account, he portrays himself and others like him as deeply committed to traditional "Christian activism" on behalf of African Americans. But he—and many other voices of African American religion—opposed Dr. King and his form of religious politics.[39]

One of the civil rights crusade's most obvious victories actually came within African American religion. The movement changed long-standing attitudes toward political involvement. This revolution produced the political church that is common—though not universal—in the African American community today. To be sure, a certain ambivalence remains. African Americans accept and often welcome political involvement by their churches and especially by their pastors. Many, but by no means all, African American pastors are deeply involved in politics. Some preach regularly about political issues. Some invite candidates for public office to address their congregations from the pulpit. Some run local political organizations and lead marches. Some speak out frequently about politics in the local media. And some even wear two hats by serving simultaneously as clergy and as elected or appointed public officials.

At the same time, African American laity expect that political activity by their clergy will not come at the expense of visiting sick members, preaching effectively, or being available to counsel those with personal crises.[40] While it is important to keep in mind that plenty of African American pastors shun politics, those who engage in political activity to the exclusion of other responsibilities are often viewed with displeasure by their congregations. Furthermore, some African American religious traditions are generally less accepting of political activism than others. Particularly skeptical are some African American pentecostals.[41]

The civil rights movement put black churches—as they slowly mobilized behind the cause—on the liberal side of American politics.[42] In the process, civil rights liberalism strengthened economic liberalism among African Americans. At that time, both forms of liberalism were firmly and increasingly coming to be associated with allegiance to the Democratic Party. Indeed, by the end of the 1960s, the Democratic presidential nominee could count on receiving about 85 percent of the vote of the expanding African American electorate.

The political attitudes of African Americans today are closely linked to perceptions of their collective treatment in American society and the conclusion that they need assistance from the government to achieve equal political and civil rights and real economic opportunities. This has led many African Americans to embrace a strongly favorable view of government and what it might do for them. Such attitudes reinforce support for the Democratic Party, which is far more sympathetic to government action than is the GOP.

CONNECTIONS BETWEEN RELIGION AND POLITICS

As we have already suggested, the most visible connections between black religion and American politics have come through the actions of various African American clergy. Especially since the 1960s, many black pastors have been deeply involved in politics. One important pioneer was Rev.

Adam Clayton Powell, pastor of the large and influential Abyssinian Baptist Church in New York City. He served as a member of Congress for years after World War II and provided both a vigorous and a controversial voice for African American civil rights.

Rev. Martin Luther King Jr. became the most famous model of the black pastor as political activist during his career as a civil rights crusader in the late 1950s and 1960s. King's activism attracted a host of other African American pastors to politics. Today Rev. Jesse Jackson is a leading symbol of African American clerical activism. Another is Rev. Al Sharpton, who has been much involved in New York City election politics and mounted a long-shot campaign for the Democratic presidential nomination in 2003–04. Today black clergy are engaged at all levels of politics, addressing local issues, serving in state legislatures, and contributing as members of Congress (one recent example was Rep. Floyd Flake [D–New York], a pastor from Brooklyn).

Jackson, for example, is involved in politics every day, in both the United States and abroad. His activity touches virtually every imaginable issue, and he gets involved at every level, from the most local to campaigns for president. It was his 1984 and 1988 races for the Democratic Party's presidential nomination, however, that brought him the most fame, a process repeated for Sharpton in 2003–04.

By no means have all African Americans rallied around Jackson—and a few have based their criticism partly on his deep affinity with religion.[43] But their voices form only a small ripple in a larger tide of sympathy and support for Jackson among African Americans. Most have not been bothered by Jackson's religious commitment nor by his status as a pastor. Indeed, such matters are perfectly routine in a politicized black community that has strongly supported political involvement by clergy in the decades since the emergence of Dr. King.

Jackson's presidential campaigns, especially the 1988 run, have been studied at length. The findings have confirmed that Jackson won massive support from African American Christians. Though racial pride was the most important single factor in rallying support to Jackson, the religious dimension was also significant. This was particularly true for African American women, who we know are more likely than men to be religious. They were absolutely central to both Jackson campaigns, from his campaign organization to the voting booth. Jackson's support network also included such established African American religious figures as Rev. T. J. Jemison, the former leader of the National Baptist Convention, USA, Inc. Much of Jackson's campaign rhetoric was distinctly Christian in its overtones and orientation. He emphasized sympathy for the suffering and a determination to build community despite the terrible wounds caused by poverty, drugs, and crime.[44]

Jackson's campaigns also illustrated another dimension of black religious politics: the tremendous importance of local churches. African American churches and their pastors were the "precincts" of his campaigns. Here rallies were held, publicity produced, and organizations formed to ensure that Jackson would receive significant support from the black community.[45]

Though the Jackson campaigns garnered great publicity and displayed the connection between black churches and national politics, we should not be distracted from the politics in which many African American churches and pastors engage every day on local, county, and state levels. Such involvement has little or nothing to do with Jesse Jackson. The bulk of African American church politics focuses on local issues and problems involving education, civil rights, and economic opportunity (Box 10.1).[46]

African American pastors and churches are convinced that political activity is a legitimate and necessary means of improving the African American lot on Earth. Ninety percent of African American clergy approve of political action, according to one study.[47] African American Christianity in the United States today is self-consciously political and increasingly comfortable with that fact. In this way it is unlike most of the rest of religion in the United States. Though organized American religion in general has become more openly political today than it was twenty-five years ago, many people have not made peace with this development. Politics has only one comfortable home in American religion, and that is in African American churches.

In many cases, there is a tight congruence between what black leaders and churches propose politically and what the African American community will support. This is definitely the case with regard to the key issue of improving economic opportunities for African American citizens. Many African Americans rally around the issue of economic improvement for pragmatism, which is underlined in black churches by the message of liberation.

But there are other issues about which many religious African Americans hold somewhat different views than their more secular counterparts.

**BOX 10.1 AFRICAN AMERICAN
CLERGY IN LOCAL POLITICS**

African American clergy have a long tradition of political involvement, particularly at the local level. In cities across the United States, African American clergy are involved in a variety of political activities, many of which lead them to work in concert with white clergy.

In Milwaukee, Wisconsin, for example, there is a ecumenical political group called the Milwaukee Intercity Congregation Allied for Hope (MICAH), MICAH was founded in 1985 as an interracial and interfaith coalition of clergy and laity dedicated to addressing the challenges of life in Milwaukee's central city through political means. It focuses its attention specifically on education, crime, drugs, housing, and economic development.

The most striking fact about MICAH is that it is an interfaith and international effort. Even though Milwaukee is one of the most radically divided of all American cities, black and white pastors work side by side in MICAH for what they see as the benefit for all Milwaukeeans. And they are extremely dedicated to their cause. In the words of one pastor, "MICAH meets all the time, at all hours . . . but when they call, I come running!"

SOURCE: Laura R. Olson, *Filled with Spirit and Power: Protestant Clergy in Politics* (Albany: State University of New York Press, 2000).

Many African American Christians are conservative on issues such as abortion and women's roles in the church. Yet at the same time African Americans as a group are more sympathetic to gay rights and economic parity for women than are white evangelicals. The picture is mixed and complicated, but noneconomic issues have not affected African American politics because the economic agenda has been the paramount priority that black religious leaders continually reinforce.[48]

Most major African American interest groups, such as the National Association for the Advancement of Colored People (NAACP) and the Urban League, are not religious. To be sure, they welcome religious leaders and laity as members. The lack of a religious orientation on the part of these groups is an artifact of their creation in the first two decades of the twentieth century. Groups like the NAACP were often intended as an alternative to black churches, which activists sometimes perceived as overly concerned with the next world—and thus not sufficiently devoted to assisting African Americans in this world. Yet there is regular contact between African American pastors and churches and branches of the NAACP and the Urban League. This is inevitable, since these organizations are as intertwined with the black middle class as are the large African American denominations.

THE MUSLIM CHALLENGE

Today a modest but growing number of African Americans are Muslims, many of them rather recent converts to the faith of the seventh-century Arabic prophet Muhammad.[49] The story of the Muslim dimension of the African American experience illustrates clearly the fluid nature of American religious culture and the unpredictable political consequences that arise from religious movements.

Though a number of Africans were followers of Islam before they were enslaved in America, only traces of that heritage survived. Modest interest in Islam existed among some nineteenth-century African Americans; certain black intellectuals saw it as an authentic African legacy that had been erased by the slave master. By the early part of the twentieth century, however, unorthodox, "proto-Islamic" movements emerged among growing African American populations in some northern cities.[50] These were tiny, isolated groups with teachings that seemed bizarre to outsiders.

Most notable among these groups was the Nation of Islam, led by Elijah Muhammad from 1934 until his death in 1975 (Box 10.2). Centered in Detroit, the Nation of Islam was a religion of the urban dispossessed, and it remained small and largely unrecognized until its most gifted disciple, Malcolm X, burst onto the scene in the 1960s.[51] In the 1990s, Malcolm X became a cultural icon, with the ubiquitous merchandising of "X" hats and sweatshirts, after the release of filmmaker Spike Lee's movie about Malcolm's life, *X*. Even those with only a vague understanding of his life and legacy have come to admire Malcolm's reputation for uncompromising militancy in the face of white American racism. During the early 1960s he helped inspire the black power movement. A popular speaker, he offered an early challenge to Dr. King's nonviolent resistance campaign. In many respects King and Malcolm represented opposite poles of African American experience. King was born to middle-class respectability; his highly educated father was a minister. Malcolm, by contrast, was a street hustler turned leader of the outcast black Muslims. While King preached nonviolent action, Malcolm threatened violence, though he was moving away from this stance at the time of his death (Box 10.3).

The black Muslim movement in the 1950s and 1960s had two appeals. On the one hand, it preached an attractive message to alienated urban blacks, especially men and prisoners, that placed their plight on the shoul-

---

BOX 10.2 ELIJAH MUHAMMAD

Born Robert Poole, Elijah Muhammad claimed to have received a fantastic theological revelation from his predecessor as head of the Nation of Islam, a mysterious Detroit silk merchant named Mr. Farad. At the heart of his revelation was the idea that whites were a race of devils and an aberration. Blacks, on the other hand, were descendants of an ancient master race whose wizards had ruled for millions of years over an empire that even included Mars. Whites were genetically created by a malcontented mad scientist. They gained ancestry through "Tricknology" and enslaved the remnant of the "Original People," the "Tribe of Shabazz."

Elijah Muhammad was quite critical of African American Christians, particularly clergy. He called black Christian clergy fools for allowing and perpetrating the religion of slave masters. During the 1960s Muhammad made inroads among African Americans, and the Nation of Islam grew. However, the rift between Muhammad and Malcolm X halted the movement's growth. Elijah Muhammad died in 1975. The Nation of Islam was ultimately taken over by the controversial Louis Farrakhan, who continues to preach Muhammad's message of racial separation.

SOURCE: Gayraud S. Wilmore, *Black Religion and Black Radicalism: An Interpretation of the Religious History of Afro-American People*, 2d ed. (Maryknoll, NY: Orbis, 1983).

---

ders of a race of white devils destined by Allah to be eradicated. The faith also emphasized education, sexual discipline, hard work, cleanliness, conservative dress, economic self-sufficiency, and rejection of the white man's welfare.

Malcolm X expressed deep concern over the growing numbers of young African Americans who lived the kind of self-destructive street life from which Islam had freed him. The patriarchal aspect of the faith appealed to black men emasculated by racist society; as a result, the membership of the Nation of Islam remained heavily male. In contrast to the matriarchal culture of the broader African American community, black Muslims taught that the man was the head of the family and the woman was to be his helpmate and homemaker. Black Muslims attained a certain stature in many cities—even among some non-Muslims—for being proud, disciplined, and militantly separatist from the white world. They had charismatic leaders, were organized around beliefs that were seen as "peculiar" by the broader society, and placed stringent demands on their members.

By 1960, the movement still had only a small membership, but it was making a serious effort to create a separate society of temple-run schools, businesses, and radio stations, as well as a well-armed militia (the Fruit of

---

BOX 10.3 MALCOLM X

Born in Omaha, Nebraska, Malcolm Little was a gifted youth whose father, an admirer of Marcus Garvey's pan-American movement, was murdered when Malcolm was just six years old. His impoverished mother migrated from city to city. By his early teens Malcolm had become a street hustler involved in theft, drugs, and prostitution. Arrested for burglary, he was sent to jail in 1946, when he was twenty-one years old. It was there that Malcolm was introduced to the teachings of the Nation of Islam, which profoundly altered his life.

Inspired by the idea that the white person was the devil, Malcolm transformed himself by reading voraciously and developing a steely discipline that would become his trademark. When he was released from prison in 1952, he took the name Malcolm X, with the X signifying his lost African name. He quickly became the most effective spokesperson for black Muslims and Elijah Muhammad's right hand.

Malcolm and Muhammad parted ways in 1964, however. At that time Malcolm founded the Muslim Mosque, Inc., which he wished to become more exclusive then Muhammad's Nation of Islam. In particular, he welcomed African American Christians, who were shunned by Muhammad. Malcolm X's assassination in 1965, which silenced one of the most influential voices in the later stage of the civil rights movement, was ultimately linked to Elijah Muhammad.

SOURCES: Malcolm X, with Alex Haley, *The Autobiography of Malcolm X* (New York: Grove, 1964); Gayraud S. Wilmore, *Black Religion and Black Radicalism: An Interpretation of the Religious History of Afro-American People*, 2d ed. (Maryknoll, NY: Orbis, 1983).

Islam) that operated in a number of cities.[52] The political importance of the movement was magnified by Malcolm's high level of visibility. He combined Elijah Muhammad's theology with a call for black consciousness, assertion, and pride. Malcolm told angry African Americans that they had every right to use "any means necessary" to defend themselves against violence by whites, and he challenged the very premises of Dr. King's nonviolent push for integration and civil rights. Like the black liberation theologians, Malcolm proposed separation from whites instead of integration. He declared: "We, the black man of the world, created the white man and we will also kill him." This rhetoric, of course, was explosive in the atmosphere of the mid–1960s.[53]

The most remarkable part of Malcolm's story, however, came toward the end of his life. Disciplined and puritanical in his behavior, Malcolm X was shocked to learn that his leader Elijah Muhammad lived a lavish and lascivious life. A rift quickly developed between them, as did political divisions. When Malcolm remarked that John Kennedy's assassination marked "the chickens coming home to roost," Elijah ostracized him. Malcolm had become too visible, too controversial, and too much of a threat to Elijah's leadership.

One of Malcolm's responses was to make the traditional pilgrimage to Mecca, an event that transformed his understanding of Islam and led him to reject the teachings of the Nation of Islam. Upon returning to America he renounced the white devil theology and announced that he had taken a new name, El-Hajj Malik El-Shabazz, an indication of his embrace of Orthodox Islam.[54] Cut off from the Nation of Islam, he formed his own Orthodox (Sunni) Islamic mosque and created the Organization of Afro-American Unity. His new vision was still incomplete when he was gunned down by Nation of Islam assassins in 1965.

Malcolm's legacy is a complex one. To the end he remained pessimistic about the possibility of eradicating white racism in America. He was also suspicious of white liberals who wanted to "help" the cause, and he continued to preach a kind of separatist doctrine that emphasized African American self-sufficiency. Thus he symbolizes black pride and assertion for those for whom integration proved less than salutary. Four decades after his death, the problems of the underclass reflect the glaring failure of integration among a segment of the African American population.

But there is another legacy that is less well appreciated. When Elijah Muhammad died in 1975, his son Wallace (who took the name Warith Deen Muhammad), assumed the leadership of the Nation of Islam and quietly and assiduously began to lead the movement toward a merger with Orthodox Islam—the very direction Malcolm X had envisioned. Like Malcolm, he rejected the racist teachings of his father. He dismantled some of the black Muslim institutions and integrated them into the mosques, which were being fed by the growing immigrant population of Muslims from the Middle East and Southeast Asia. Thus, today, the vast majority of African American Muslims worship alongside immigrants in Sunni mosques around the country.[55]

This merger has probably facilitated the conversion of more African Americans to Islam by providing them with the structure of a highly developed world religion as an alternative to the "white man's" Christianity. African Americans now make up more than 40 percent of the nation's Muslim population. However, neither the exact overall size of the Muslim population nor the size of its African American component is known with great certainty. Of more than 30 million African Americans, estimates of the Muslim population range as high as 2.5 million.[56]

A small group of African Americans remains loyal to the Nation of Islam and Elijah Muhammad's vision, including his doctrines about the origin of the races and the white devil.[57] The Nation of Islam today is led by the fiery Louis Farrakhan, who continues to preach black superiority and separation. Farrakhan has achieved an influence well beyond his core religious following (which numbers no more than 10,000) because he articulates the same kind of rage as did the young Malcolm X. His critics are uneasy, however, about what they see as Farrakhan's anti-Semitism.

Farrakhan gained prominence in 1984 when his association with Jesse Jackson (to whom he provided bodyguards) became an issue in the presidential campaign. At that time Farrakhan referred to Jews as members of a "gutter religion," and Jackson was chastised for not renouncing such talk and severing his ties with Farrakhan. The issue dogged Jackson's presidential quest in both 1984 and 1988.

Farrakhan's politics represents a mixture of militant racial separatism, self-reliance, and traditional moral values. On abortion, gay rights, and welfare his message is pointedly conservative. His actual political impact, however, is hard to measure. His organization has gotten nowhere when it has fielded candidates for local and national offices, but it has attracted broad support for its antidrug activities.[58] Farrakhan also organized the widely publicized Million Man March in 1995. There is no doubt that Farrakhan has some followers in many of America's central cities, and as a result he has been courted in the 1990s by some mainstream African American groups such as the Congressional Black Caucus and the NAACP.

CONCLUSION

Islamic influence in the United States may go in any one of a number of directions in the future. Where it will ultimately lead we do not profess to know. But the growing Muslim presence in the United States will likely make an increasingly important mark on American culture and politics. If it does, it will be following in the established tradition of African American Christianity. For in the much larger world of black Christianity, as we have seen, religion and politics are now pervasively intertwined.

The connections between religion and politics among Latinos, in contrast, are not as clear. In many respects, Latino American religious traditions that have existed for decades—even centuries—are still searching for their political voice. That search is shaped profoundly by the historical narratives of colonization, immigration, and assimilation, as well as the existence of diverse subcultures within the Latino community itself. The religious pluralism among Latino Americans reflects this history; it remains to be seen whether religion can provide some unity among the many voices that speak to Latino perspectives on American public life.

FURTHER READING

Cone, James. *A Black Theology of Liberation.* Philadelphia: Lippincott, 1970. The classic on black liberation theology.

Espinosa, Gaston, Virgilio Elizondo, and Jesse Miranda, "Hispanic Churches in American Public Life: Summary of Findings," *Interim Reports* 2 (January 2002). A brief look at the role of religion in Latino politics.

Garrow, David J. *Bearing the Cross: Martin Luther King Jr. and the Southern Leadership Conference.* New York: Morrow, 1986. The story of King's political and religious activism.

Haley, Alex, ed. *The Autobiography of Malcolm X.* New York: Grove Press, 1965. Malcolm X's account of his life.

Harris, Fredrick C. *Something Within: Religion in African-American Political Activism.* New York: Oxford University Press, 1999. An excellent examination of the role of religion in African American political mobilization.

Hertzke, Allen D. *Echoes of Discontent: Jesse Jackson, Pat Robertson, and the Resurgence of Populism.* Washington, D.C.: CQ Press, 1993. Discussion of the 1988 Jesse Jackson campaign.

Lincoln, C. Eric, and Lawrence H. Mamiya. *The Black Church in the African American Experience.* Durham, NC: Duke University Press, 1990. Superb work on African American religion.

Sanchez Walsh, Arlene M. *Latino Pentecostal Identity: Evangelical Faith, Self, and Society.* New York: Columbia University Press, 2003. A fascinating study of diverse expressions of Latino Pentecostalism.

Wood, Richard L. *Faith in Action: Religion, Race, and Democratic Organizing in America.* Chicago: University of Chicago Press, 2002. Examines the intersection of race, political organizing, and religion, especially in urban areas.

NOTES

1. In this chapter we use the terms "Latino" and "Hispanic" interchangeably, though the latter term is often used to denote a somewhat broader category of people with origins in Spain as well as Latin America and the Caribbean.

2. Pew Hispanic Center/Kaiser Family Foundation, *2002 National Survey of Latinos: Summary of Findings* (Menlo Park, CA: Kaiser/ Washington, D.C: Pew Hispanic Center, 2002), 53.

3. Ibid.

4. William V. D'Antonio, "Latino Catholics: How Different?" *National Catholic Reporter* (October 29, 1999).

5. U.S. Conference of Catholic Bishops, Committee on Hispanic Affairs, *Hispanic Ministry at the Turn of the Millenium* (Washington, D.C.: USCCB, 1999).

6. Janet Kornblum, "More Hispanic Catholics Losing Their Religion," *USA Today* (December 12, 2002), A1; Lisa Makson, "Latinos Call U.S. Culture Hostile Climate for Faith," *National Catholic Register* (March 9–15, 2003), 1, 12.

7. Jeff Guntzel, "Between Two Cultures," *National Catholic Reporter* (January 30, 2004).

8. Andrew Greeley, "Defection Among Hispanics: Updated," *America* (September 27, 1997), 12; Gaston Espinosa, Virgilio Elizondo, and Jesse Miranda, "Hispanic Churches in American Public Life: Summary of Findings," *Interim Reports* 2 (January 2002); Chris L. Jenkins, "Islam Luring More Latinos," *Washington Post* (January 7, 2001), C1.

9. Espinosa et al., "Hispanic Churches in American Public Life."

10. Arlene M. Sanchez Walsh, *Latino Pentecostal Identity: Evangelical Faith, Self, and Society* (New York: Columbia University Press, 2003).

11. Committee on Hispanic Affairs, *Hispanic Ministry at the Turn of the Millenium*.

12. http://www.nccbuscc.org/latinamerica/english/onechurch.htm.

13. Pew Hispanic Center/Kaiser Family Foundation, *2002 National Survey of Latinos: Summary of Findings*, 16.

14. Ibid, 54–60.

15. Espinosa et al., "Hispanic Churches in American Public Life: Summary of Findings," 21.

16. For data on these issues, see Pew Hispanic Center/Kaiser Family Foundation, *2002 National Survey of Latinos: Summary of Findings*, 62. For a history of Latino religion from a liberationist perspective, see Moises Sandoval, *On the Move: A History of the Hispanic Church in the United States* (Maryknoll, NY: Orbis Books, 1990).

17. Espinosa et al., "Hispanic Churches in American Public Life: Summary of Findings," 21.

18. Louis Desipio and Rudolfo O. de la Garza, eds., *Awash in the Mainstream: Latino Politics in the 1996 Election* (Boulder, CO: Westview Press, 1999).

19. Green and Silk, "The New Religion Gap." See discussion in Chapter 4.

20. For a discussion of Chavez's religiosity, see Frederick John Dalton, *The Moral Vision of Cesar Chavez* (Maryknoll, NY: Orbis Books, 2003).

21. Louis De Sipio, *Counting on the Latino Vote: Latinos as a New Electorate* (Charlottesville, VA: University of Virginia, 1996).

22. Rudolfo O. de la Garza, *Latino Voices: Mexican, Puerto Rican, and Cuban Perspectives on American Politics* (Boulder, CO: Westview Press, 1993).

23. For a broad discussion of Latino politics, see John A. Garcia, *Latino Politics in America: Community, Culture, and Interests* (Lanham, MD: Rowman and Littlefield, 2003).

24. Harold Bloom, *The American Religion* (New York: Simon and Schuster, 1992), chap. 5.

25. See Arthur Paris, *Black Pentecostalism: Southern Religion in an Urban World* (Amherst: University of Massachusetts Press, 1982).

26. The classic work is Charles Hamilton, *The Black Preacher in America* (New York: William Morrow, 1972).

27. Laura R. Olson, *Filled with Spirit and Power: Protestant Clergy in Politics* (Albany: State University of New York Press, 2001).

28. Samuel G. Freedman, *Upon This Rock: The Miracle of a Black Church* (New York: HarperCollins, 1993).

29. On this discussion and the entire subject of this chapter, see the wonderfully informative C. Eric Lincoln and Lawrence Mamiya, *The Black Church in the African American Experience* (Durham, NC: Duke University Press, 1990).

30. Lincoln and Mamiya, *The Black Church.*

31. See such works as E. Franklin Frazier, *The Negro Church in America* (New York: Schocken, 1964); and Clyde Wilcox and Leopoldo Gomez, "Religion, Group Identification, and Politics Among American Blacks," *Sociological Analysis* 51 (January 1990), 271–285.

32. See J. Wendell Mapson Jr., *The Ministry of Music in the Black Church* (Valley Forge, PA: Judson, 1984).

33. James Cone, *Black Theology and Black Power* (New York: Seabury, 1969).

34. See the interesting views in Peter J. Paris, *The Social Teaching of the Black Churches* (Philadelphia: Fortress Press, 1985); James Melvin Washington, *Frustrated Fellowship: The Black Baptist Quest for Social Power* (Macon, GA: Mercer University Press, 1982).

35. Lincoln and Mamiya, *The Black Church,* chap. 2.

36. Ibid., chap. 3.

37. For this four-phase analysis, see Robert Booth Fowler, *Religion and Politics in America* (Metuchen, NJ: Scarecrow Press, 1985), chap. 12.

38. See Aldon D. Morris, *The Origins of the Civil Rights Movement* (New York: Free Press, 1984); Martin Luther King Jr., *Why We Can't Wait* (New York: Mentor, 1964); Hart M. Nelsen and Anne Kusener Nelsen, *The Black Church in the Sixties* (Lexington: University of Kentucky Press, 1975); and David J. Garrow, *Bearing the Cross: Martin Luther King, Jr. and the Southern Christian Leadership Conference* (New York: Morrow, 1986).

39. Joseph H. Jackson, *A Story of Christian Activism: The History of the National Baptist Convention USA, Inc.* (Nashville, TN: Townsend, 1980).

40. See James H. Harris, *Black Ministers and Laity in the Urban Church* (Lanham, MD: University Press of America, 1987).

41. Allison Calhoun-Brown, "The Politics of African American Churches: The Psychological Impact of Organizational Resources," *Journal of Politics* 58 (November 1996), 935–953.

42. For an excellent discussion about the role of the church in mobilizing African Americans during the Civil Rights era and beyond, see Fredrick C. Harris, *Something Within: Religion in African-American Political Activism* (New York: Oxford University Press, 1999).

43. For example, see Adolph L. Reed Jr., *The Jesse Jackson Phenomenon* (New Haven, CT: Yale University Press, 1986).

44. Allen D. Hertzke, *Echoes of Discontent: Jesse Jackson, Pat Robertson, and the Resurgence of Populism* (Washington, D.C.: CQ Press, 1993), chaps. 3, 4, and 6; Charles P. Henry, *Culture and African-American Politics* (Bloomington: Indiana University Press, 1990).

45. Hertzke, *Echoes of Discontent.*

46. See Hertzke, *Echoes of Discontent,* chap. 4; and Lynda Wright, "Politics and the Pulpit: The Power of America's Black Churches," *Newsweek* (February 15, 1988), 28–31.

47. Lincoln and Mamiya, *The Black Church.*

48. Tod A. Baker, "Exposure to Religion and Southern Distinctiveness," (paper presented at the annual meeting of the Society for the Scientific Study of Religion, Washington, D.C., 1986).

49. The "challenge of Islam" is how one of the major studies of the black church depicts the growth of the Muslim population. See Lincoln and Mamiya, *The Black Church,* 388–391.

50. Lincoln and Mamiya, *The Black Church.*

51. For an excellent analysis of the life and times of Malcolm X, see Marshall Frady, "The Children of Malcolm," *New Yorker* (October 12, 1992). See also David Mills, "Malcolm X: The Messenger and His Message," *Washington Post Weekly Edition* (March 26–April 1, 1990).

52. An indication of how difficult it is to get a handle on small religious groups is the widely varying estimates of the black Muslim membership in the early 1960s. Frady suggests its membership was as small as 10,000; Lincoln and Mamiya suggest it was as sizable as 100,000. Even the higher figure, however, is tiny compared to the black Christian population, which numbers in the millions.

53. See Frady, "The Children of Malcolm."

54. Malcolm X, with Alex Haley, *The Autobiography of Malcolm X* (New York: Grove, 1964).

55. For an excellent look at contemporary American Muslims, see Steven Barboza, *American Jihad: Islam After Malcolm X* (New York: Doubleday, 1993).

56. Carla Power, "The New Islam," *Newsweek* (March 16, 1998), 35.

57. Don Terry, "Minister Farrakhan: Conservative Militant," *New York Times* (March 3, 1994). Shrona Foreman, "Muslims' Tentative Electoral Venture," *National Journal* (September 1, 1990).

58. Foreman, "Muslims' Tentative Electoral Venture."

11

GENDER, RELIGION,
AND POLITICS

In any consideration of religion and politics in the United States today, women merit special attention. Of course all American women do not share the same religion or politics, but at present they are more religious as a group than men. In this chapter we first consider the facts about women's involvement in religion in the United States. Next we discuss some of the ways in which female religious activists involve themselves in political life. Third, we explore the religious and political attitudes of women in the pews, who differ from religious activists.

WOMEN AND RELIGION IN AMERICAN LIFE

There is no doubt that American women as a group are more religiously observant than men. Public opinion polls have noted this discrepancy for years. Consider the following findings: Women say that religion is important to them much more frequently than men do (68 to 49 percent), and that gap is widening over time; a sizable majority of women (62 percent) say they have high levels of spiritual commitment, compared with 47 percent of men; women also overwhelmingly believe that God works miracles and that God is often with them.[1] And they believe that religion is relevant to most of life's challenges and difficulties.

Many women are also quite traditional in their religious beliefs. Two-thirds of American women hold that Christ is the only way to eternal life, as do only half of all men. Similarly, most women respect the Bible as a source of truth; only 11 percent of women judge it to be little more than fable, whereas nearly 20 percent of males hold this view.

These attitudes extend even to women who came to adulthood in the 1960s and early 1970s, the so-called baby boom generation, which is sometimes characterized as the least religious group of women in American history. In fact, boomer women have not brought about a break in the long tradition of religiosity among American women. Even in this generation of "rebels," a sizable majority of women rate religion as very important in their lives. Most of the rest say it is fairly important in their lives. About two-thirds expect that religion will become even more important to them in the future. Also, the baby boom generation was the first to benefit in large numbers from the opening of the pulpit to women. In some mainline Protestant denominations, such as the United Church of Christ and the Presbyterian Church (U.S.A.), women now account for more than 20 percent of all clergy, and their numbers are growing. In fact, women now comprise the majority of the student bodies of some major seminaries.

Women of all generations are more likely than men to be connected to and active in religious institutions. Though the data vary, it is safe to say that well over two-thirds of all American women belong to a religious congregation. This is an astounding proportion of the female population, especially in light of the fact that fewer than 60 percent of American men are congregation members. The proportions of men and women who belong to the Roman Catholic Church and to evangelical Protestant churches are about equal. But in mainline Protestant denominations, such as the United Methodist Church and the Episcopal Church, women predominate. Some estimates place the proportion of women members in the Presbyterian Church at 70 percent. In any given week almost half of all women in the United States say they attend a religious service as compared with fewer than 40 percent of men. Similarly, women are considerably more likely than men to watch religious television programming.

African American women tend to be even more religious than white women. Black churches in the United States attract and retain the support of the vast majority of black women, and they tend to be filled largely by women and children and much less by men, which has caused some concern in the black community.[2]

At the same time, as we saw in Chapter 10, African American clergy are almost exclusively male. This is not to say that women are not respected in African American churches; they are, and in some denominations elder women bear the formal honorary title of "Mother." Still, fewer than 5 percent of all black pastors are women. Most black clergywomen actually serve in largely white denominations or churches, although there are some women preachers in Pentecostal African American churches. Nonetheless, women have made some inroads toward the African American pulpit. The most visible of these advances came in 2000 when the African Methodist Episcopal (AME) Church installed its first female bishop, Vashti Murphy McKenzie. How long this tradition of female parishioners and male clergy will endure is one of the most intriguing questions facing black Christianity in the United States. It is particularly interesting given that African American women are often quite sympathetic to some aspects of feminism, including greater economic opportunities for women. At present, however, even though women are clearly the heart of African American religion, they rarely serve as clergy.

Women also play a central role in the operation of most white churches in the United States. This is particularly important in the Roman Catholic Church—despite its all-male priesthood. Today the vast majority of parish leaders and church employees are women, many of whom enjoy significant influence. The declining number of priests promises to increase the role of women within American Catholicism even more as women shoulder an increasing share of the responsibility for day-to-day parish functioning.[3] The influence of women is similarly pervasive within mainline Protestant churches.

Likewise, Jewish women exert substantial influence within American Judaism. Many Jewish women of the baby boom generation have displayed renewed interest in their faith tradition. This is so despite fierce debate and concern within the Jewish community about the continued vitality of Judaism—and the Jewish people themselves—in the United States. Yet there are clear signs that many Jewish women (in particular) have chosen to preserve Jewish traditions, sometimes religious, sometimes cultural, that their parents often did not emphasize.

The gender dynamics in American church life are not restricted to the central role of women. In recent years highly publicized men's events such as the Million Man March and the Promise Keepers' rallies have taken place. The Million Man March was organized and led by controversial Nation of Islam leader Louis Farrakhan; the Promise Keepers purvey a distinctly evangelical Protestant message. These events, now paralleled by the spread of male prayer groups, men's retreats, and even men-only reading clubs throughout organized religion in the United States, demonstrate that gender-based religion is growing among men too.

These trends among men may be an effort to reverse the decline of male interest in religion, a reaction to the dominance of women, or simply a recognition that in spiritual matters, as in other dimensions of life, men and women do not always have the same needs.[4] But the fact is clear. Men from a variety of walks of life—black and white, Protestant and Muslim—are reasserting their place in organized religion, the family, and society precisely at the time when women are becoming more prominent in these realms.

WOMEN, RELIGION, AND PERSPECTIVES ON AMERICAN POLITICS

A great many connections exist between religious women and politics in the United States today. The *political* orientations of religious women today defy easy characterization. For example, women are organized for social change in groups that range from the liberal womenchurch to the conservative Concerned Women for America.

Another significant trend in the relationships among religion, politics, and gender in the United States is the "gender gap" in voting behavior that has grown since the 1990s. In 1996, the majority of women (54 percent) voted for Bill Clinton, whereas a slight plurality of men (44 percent) voted for Bob Dole. Among all Protestants, Dole received 51 percent of the male vote versus only 44 percent of the female vote. The same pattern characterized the white Catholic vote: Dole got 46 percent of the male vote but only 37 percent of the female vote.[5] In 2000, 54 percent of women voted for Al Gore, and almost the same figure—53 percent—of men voted for George W. Bush. Among Protestants, this gender split seems to have cut across religious traditions.[6]

Women also lead the way theologically; they are active within Christianity and Judaism in both challenging and defending existing beliefs and structures. More and more women are finding ways to offer their viewpoints in their traditionally male-dominated religious traditions. More radical women have been involved in developing new (or reborn) spiritualities such as ecofeminism, witchcraft, and goddess religions that are designed to transform not only religion but every aspect of social and political life. Meanwhile, women sometimes organize in opposition to such new religions and their social agendas.

Conservative Intersections

Today it is commonplace in American religion to find women committed to conservative political causes (Box 11.1). Consider as an example the role of the interest group Concerned Women for America (CWA), which has been in existence since 1979. It is a decidedly conservative political group with a large national membership of over 500,000.[7] Its members are overwhelmingly evangelical Protestant women who affirm the literal truth of the Bible, hold conservative political beliefs, and vote Republican.

Beverly LaHaye founded Concerned Women for America (CWA) in 1989 and remained as its leader until 1998. LaHaye has written many books, including *I Am a Woman by God's Design,* in which she addresses a wide range of political issues and endorses the view that women should submit to male headship in marriage.[8] Her writings tightly interweave political conservatism and Christianity. LaHaye and CWA have been particularly interested and involved in "family" issues and lobbying on behalf of the prolife cause. CWA operates largely through state and local chapters connected to the national headquarters.[9]

Phyllis Schlafly's Eagle Forum has been involved in fighting for conservative political and moral concerns even longer than CWA has. Schlafly led the movement that defeated the Equal Rights Amendment in the 1970s. Eagle Forum is explicitly Christian, though it is interdenominational within that context. Despite a common assumption that she is an evangelical Protestant, Schlafly is actually a traditional Roman Catholic; many members of Eagle Forum, though, are evangelical and fundamentalist Protestants. Eagle Forum is less explicitly religious in its focus than CWA. It is also less consumed with questions of family and personal morality. Its newsletter typically addresses economic and foreign policy issues at least as often as it does personal and religious ones.[10]

Organizations like Concerned Women for America and Eagle Forum are important, but they do not begin to tell the entire story of religious women and conservative politics. Everywhere one looks in conservative

---

BOX 11.1 ROBERTA COMBS: LEADING "RENEWAL" AT THE CHRISTIAN COALITION

In December 2001, the Rev. Pat Robertson stepped down as president of the Christian Coalition and handed the reins to Roberta Combs, an evangelical Christian and longtime activist in religious conservative circles. A well-known—even flamboyant—figure in South Carolina political circles, Combs headed Robertson's presidential campaign in that state in 1988 and later served as the executive director of the Coalition, where she earned a reputation as a tough administrator. As president of the organization she has attempted to reinvigorate its membership by emphasizing the group's "distinctly and exclusively Christian" roots, an effort that included a series of voter registration drives in 2003 and 2004 that took place on Sundays at Christian churches across the country. Unlike one of her earlier predecessors, Ralph Reed, who tried to attract a broad audience, Combs does not avoid explicitly Christian language; she regularly quotes scripture in the media and integrates prayer and worship at Christian Coalition events. At the same time, she has reached out to persons and groups outside of the world of religious conservatism, even meeting with Senator Hillary Clinton to discuss prescription drugs and the elderly.

Sources: http://www.cc.org/vision.cfm; Deborah Solomon, "A New Moral Majority?" *New York Times Magazine* (November 16, 2003).

---

politics today, in fact, religious women are involved—especially where moral issues are at stake.

Women are the soul of conservative religious struggles at the local level over school curricula, library books, public religious ceremonies, and similar issues. Such local disputes lie at the center of religious politics in the United States. It is there that conservative women are both the generals and foot soldiers in religio-political battles.[11]

In both local and national conflicts, there is no doubt that conservative religious women lack elite access, especially in comparison with more liberal religious women. This is perhaps the single most important problem conservative women face when it comes to politics. Liberal women are able to voice their views in the media, at leading nonsectarian and mainline Protestant theological seminaries (such as the divinity schools of Harvard University and the University of Chicago), and also in numerous orders of Roman Catholic nuns. Liberal religious women in these settings are well connected and able to make a lasting impression in the public sphere. Conservative religious women have had a much harder time because their religious traditions tend to be more explicitly male-dominated.

Yet some stories are waiting to be discovered by a larger audience. Consider Kay Coles James, a conservative African American woman who propelled herself, as she says, "from public housing to the corridors of power."[12] James has moved into a life of political activism that has taken her from business to prolife campaigns, to Washington service as an Assistant Secretary in the Department of Health and Human Services, to senior vice president of the Family Research Council, to dean of the Robertson School of Government at Regent University, to her current appointment in the Bush Administration as director of the U.S. Office of Personnel Management, which oversees the federal civil service. James argues firmly that the prolife and profamily causes must be committed to racial equality and human compassion. She always makes it clear that her religion is her proverbial rock of support. She is a religious woman who has been compelled by her religious beliefs into politics.

We hasten to note, however, that even within conservative evangelicalism the role of religion is not always clear. Debbie Daniels' pioneering work on women's issues with the Protestant evangelical community illustrates the conflicting tensions and forces within American religion on the matter of gender politics. She notes the data that show a softening of opinion on the revealing issue of women's ordination. Among evangelical Protestants opinion favors women's ordination today, and even among self-described fundamentalist Christians a majority of men and women are no longer strongly opposed.

On the other hand, the majority of theologically conservative Protestants, men and women, continue to hold that the male should be the head of the household and make the major final decisions in the family. This view is slowly losing strength, however, as a strong majority of conservative Protestants agree that, in practice, they share in making these decisions. This decline is much sharper among evangelical college students, where a majority no longer agrees that a husband should have the final say.[13]

Daniels also notes the fascinating and important divisions among conservative Christian women (and men) at other levels. She reports the presence of competing organizations, for example, addressing the proper role for the Christian woman. In 1987 the Council on Biblical Manhood and Womanhood (CBMW) came into existence and developed the mediating position between patriarchy and feminism, which it calls the "complementarian" view. Its advocates insist that the Bible holds that men and women are fully equal in God's eyes, but God calls them to different and complementary roles. Women are called to serve in the home and as wife and mother, not to male roles as clergy or head of the home. Also founded in 1987, on the other hand, is Christians for Biblical Equality (CBE). Like its counterpart, this organization emphasizes its biblical grounding in the evangelical tradition, but argues that the Bible teaches equality among men and women, which includes opening roles in the church, the home, and elsewhere equally to both genders. For CBE, God puts no barriers on the possibilities for created beings, women or men. What this discussion within conservative Protestantism illustrates is the mixed views today among sincere women and men seeking to follow God's written word. The issues are difficult and controversies are real.[14]

Liberal Intersections

By no means should anyone assume that religious women are necessarily conservative. This is far from the case (Box 11.2). Tremendous diversity characterizes the many religious organizations that connect women to politics. Liberal women's groups normally concentrate on the status of women in church, society, religion, and politics.

This is true of groups such as Catholics for a Free Choice and Church Women United (whose members are mainline Protestants). Catholics for a Free Choice concerns itself primarily with "policy analysis, education, and advocacy on issues of gender equality and reproductive health."[15] Such liberal groups have encountered some problems, however, as the case of Church Women United illustrates. Church Women United was founded in 1941 and became active politically in the 1950s and 1960s on behalf of civil rights causes. It moved on in the later 1960s toward issues concerned specifically with women, their rights, and their development as people. Yet the organization has seen better days, as have many religious women's groups at the local and the national levels. Fewer middle-class women are available today who have the time to devote to such organizations than there were thirty years ago.[16]

In recent years another prominent liberal group has been womenchurch, a loosely structured organization founded by Catholic women

---

BOX 11.2 HILLARY RODHAM CLINTON:
LIBERAL METHODIST

Senator Hillary Rodham (D-NY) was born into a Methodist family with lineal roots back to England, where Methodism was born. She attended First United Methodist Church in Park Ridge, Illinois. A pious young woman, she volunteered in the 1964 campaign of Republican presidential candidate Barry Goldwater. Like many of her generation, though, she was swept up in the antiwar movement and became a McGovern Democrat. Still, she remained active in religious circles.

As a Wellesley student Hillary Rodham Clinton attended church, joined an interdenominational chapel society, and read widely among the liberal religious thinkers of the times. She took naturally to the intensifying "social gospel" activism in the United Methodist Church, which epitomized the liberal Protestant emphasis on using government to promote economic and social justice for the poor.

Throughout her adult life Hillary Rodham Clinton has remained a church going Methodist who believes in the Trinity and the anointing death and resurrection of Christ. As the wife of Arkansas Governor Bill Clinton she often attended his Baptist church, then her own Methodist congregation, where she taught Sunday school. In Washington the Clinton family attends Foundry United Methodist Church. Its pastor, Rev. J. Phillip Wogaman, is a noted ethicist who embraces the social gospel agenda. Castigated as left wing and New Age for her speeches on the "politics of meaning," Senator Clinton contends that she is actually an old-fashioned Methodist striving to build the Kingdom of God on Earth.

SOURCES: Kenneth Woodward, "Soulful Matters," *Newsweek* (October 31, 1994), 22; Laurie Goodstein, "Pastor to President Says Morality Includes One's Courage and Caring," *New York Times* (March 1, 1998), A16.

---

and strongly promoted by Rosemary Radford Ruether, an activist feminist Catholic theologian. Womenchurch has been at the forefront of the attempt to develop a feminist religion with a suitable political agenda. Womenchurch's religious politics stress a vaguely Christian God, creed, and church, all of which must be strongly egalitarian and communitarian. The group is committed to converting the larger society to the same goals.

Ruether in particular has encouraged women to form feminist communities of egalitarian worship outside of the Catholic Church and the rest of Christianity, which she deems too hierarchical and male-oriented. Participants in womenchurch share the premise of women's equality with men and sometimes with God—as well as the belief that political action must be taken to reorient society to these ends.[17]

To this point, womenchurch is merely one expression of the feminist movement within American religion. It has been most active, especially in the Roman Catholic Church, on such issues as abortion rights and the ordination of women. Its larger effort, however, has been aimed toward changing consciousness among the faithful to advance an egalitarian and communal social and religious order.

Another illustration is provided by the considerable numbers of African American women who provide most of the time and energy behind dozens of local African American political causes. Again and again, religious black women provide the muscle for many day-to-day African American political efforts. But one must be careful in generalizing about African American women and politics. For black women have also been at the forefront of efforts to create school choice in the inner cities of Cleveland and Milwaukee, among other places (Box 2.3), and to permit state aid to religiously connected social services, cases that are not fashionable among white liberal women activists.

A less mixed illustration, and one of equal importance to the activism of many African American women, is the role of many Jewish women in liberal politics. This is especially noteworthy both in the liberal wing of the Democratic Party, but also in a host of public actions and lobbying associations, including various feminist, "reproductive choice," and "peace" groups.[18]

Another example of liberal politics among religious women is evident in the emergence of explicitly feminist theologies. Generalizations about the complex subject of Christian or Jewish feminist theology are not a good idea. But the rise of feminist theology represents both an intellectual and political movement of importance. The goal of feminist theologians is to attack past and present male domination in religion and in churches. In the process they raise fundamental questions about images of God as Father and the male hierarchies of some faiths and religious institutions. Some feminist theologians seek to undermine and then abolish male (and all other) hierarchies in every part of society, including the political order.[19]

In this context, some feminist thinkers view traditional Western religions (mostly Christianity) as redeemable, whereas others have concluded that feminism requires a complete break with the Judeo-Christian tradition and the Western societies with which it is associated. This is not the only dividing line among these very political religious feminists, but it is an essential and illuminating one.[20]

FEMINISM AND THE REDEEMABILITY OF RELIGION

There is no doubt that tremendous intellectual energy has gone into the development of feminist theology, nor that it has taken a number of different directions beyond a shared attack on patriarchy. A great deal of feminist theology is seen through a historical lens and involves investigation of the Bible, early Christianity, and the struggles surrounding its early growth. The intention is to indict the patriarchal aspects of the Bible and early Christianity; or, in a more optimistic mindset, to recast the record in the light of a lost, nonpatriarchal, early Christianity. Despite its challenges to organized religion, though, many strains of feminist thought uphold religion as a positive force in human life. Feminists who hold this view argue that religion is redeemable when it takes gender-egalitarian and feminist perspectives into account.

Anne Carr is a leading feminist theologian who self-consciously locates herself within the Christian tradition. For Carr, Christianity and feminism can and should go together, so by no means should all of Christianity be discarded as hopelessly antifeminist. For Carr, God is not essentially male, but a deeply relational being who exists in association with humans. As Carr sees it, people of God must insist that women be welcomed in all roles in church and society. Women must be able to be active participants in lives of choice, human growth, and vigorous participation in relationships with God and all God's people.[21]

Sallie McFague has developed a somewhat more radical view. McFague has been a leader in developing new models of God to replace what she terms "God-he." McFague and other theorists do not deny the Christian tradition; they simply wish to offer reconceptualized images of who and what God is. Some theorists propose viewing God as an androgynous being. Others portray God as mother, friend, or lover. Their objective is to reimagine God, which may pave the way to systemic political and social change.[22]

Feminist currents have had a powerful impact within Judaism. Many Jewish feminists have concluded that Judaism as they understand it is redeemable as a religion or at least as a spiritual tradition. The effects of feminism in Judaism are most obvious in the dramatic breakthroughs of the past twenty years for women who wish to serve as rabbis. Though no woman was ordained a rabbi until 1972, that now seems ancient history within Judaism. At first only the liberal, nontraditional, and small Reconstructionist branch of Judaism allowed women rabbis, but then Reform Judaism and now Conservative Judaism abolished age-old prohibitions against women rabbis. Since every study in existence demonstrates that Jewish women as a group are more liberal—often far more liberal—than other Americans on so-called women's issues and almost all other political questions, change in the structure of Judaism proved inevitable.[23]

FEMINISM AND THE IRREDEEMABILITY OF RELIGION

Many feminist religious thinkers have given up entirely on the Christian and Jewish religions. To these women, Western faiths may have a few positive qualities, but they are at root sexist and supportive of the repression of women. Such theorists insist that Americans must rethink spirituality and society in a radical way. They believe that if religion is drastically altered, male images of God will fade, as will any sense of hierarchy or division in the universe. Radical feminist theologians prize the ideals of equality, community, and holism and believe that these ideals may be realized by developing entirely new religions, politics, and society.

Mary Daly was perhaps the most important advocate of the argument that Western religions are irredeemable and that radical shifts in both religion and politics are necessary. In 1973 she published the first of her many books, *Beyond God the Father*. In the 1970s Daly was still accepting of some aspects of the Christian tradition, though she was already arguing that the religion was too male-dominated in both theory and practice. Later she left Christianity behind.[24]

Goddess religion is an example of the spiritual directions taken by those who repudiate Christianity and Judaism altogether. The standard argument of goddess worshippers is that in ancient times, goddesses were the most common form of deity. In such a world, life was better for women—and for men as well—since society was more egalitarian, communal, and peaceful. In the eyes of goddess worshippers, such worlds sadly fell under the repression of male-dominated social orders. Defenders of goddess religion insist that old goddess models need to be rediscovered to replace the antifemale, hierarchical, and dualistic kinds of religion that have oppressed women for centuries.[25]

Some critics are skeptical of claims about the extent of past civilizations' allegiance to goddesses. Others protest casual generalizations about past goddess religions that sweep across cultures and millennia. Still others note that ancient goddesses were fertility deities, a rather dubious model for modern feminists.

Rosemary Radford Ruether approaches these dilemmas from a radical feminist perspective that is more sympathetic to Christianity. She appreciates the idea of a female deity. For her it provides an alternative conception of God that many women find attractive—even as she points to problems inherent in goddess religion. Ruether also argues that for adherents of Western religious traditions, interest in goddess religion can only create fissures. As radical as Ruether is, she is not prepared to give up Christianity for goddess worship.[26]

Another current direction in feminist spirituality is the Wiccan religion, or witchcraft. Its adherents consider the mainstream Western religions hopeless because of their historic oppression of women. Though witchcraft has long had an underground life in American society, it has recently emerged more openly. It is no longer unusual to find an advertisement for Wicca services on the religion page of the newspaper. Nor is it unusual to encounter voices of the Wiccan religion such as Starhawk or Margot Adler in public forums or on TV talk shows. Popular culture has even embraced witchcraft— for example, in the television series *Charmed*.

People are divided over what witchcraft involves. Practitioners themselves do not agree, except about their view that human consciousness can be altered through rituals and practices and that the power of the natural and spiritual worlds can have concrete effects on people and events. By this view, there are spiritual powers and forces with which people can connect if they know how. Practitioners of witchcraft use various rituals from the past, though some also embrace newer traditions. This is because witchcraft is a relatively open, pluralistic, and malleable kind of spirituality. Some forms of witchcraft are exclusively lesbian; others are self-consciously feminist; still others have no such boundaries. The lines between one version and another may be great at times, but overall the movement has been highly inclusive.

Ecofeminist spirituality is a third feminist approach that views Western religion as largely irredeemable. Though the term "ecofeminism" dates only from 1974, the ecofeminist movement has ancient roots. Many devotees of ecofeminist spirituality explicitly repudiate the Christian and Jewish religious traditions as male-centered. Under these religions, ecofeminists argue, both nature and women have been mistreated. "Reforms" can never be enough to eliminate the patriarchal structures of thought and organization that have facilitated this oppression. Thus ecofeminism involves a widespread search for alternative means of spiritual sustenance. Above all, ecofeminists search for holistic spiritualities. Sometimes they direct favorable attention to goddess and nature religions, witchcraft, Native American faiths, and Buddhism, among others. Ecofeminists who are unwilling to abandon Christianity strive to recast its traditional vocabularies and conceptions.[27]

Ecofeminism's basic premise is that both nature and women have been oppressed throughout Western history by men, male hierarchies (men over women, men over nature); male dualisms (mind over body, men over nature and women), and male-centered religions (especially Christianity and Judaism). This domination has proceeded in direct disregard for the holism that ecofeminists maintain is characteristic of both women and nature. Ecofeminists say it is obvious that both nature and women have suffered terribly under male domination. They note that women who have not cooperated with the male-dominated society have paid a high price (as did witches, for example, in the early years of American history).[28]

The political side of ecofeminism treasures the goal of the liberation of both nature and women. To accomplish this goal, ecofeminists advocate transcending hierarchy and dualism (that is, male rule in all areas of life), particularly in the realms of religion and politics. They believe that women must lead the way to a revolution to create an egalitarian community where holism, care, and healing will flourish among human beings.

The ecofeminist expectation is that in this ideal community spiritualism will also be nourished. Many, perhaps most, ecofeminists are self-consciously spiritual in their outlook; nature provides the common source of grounding and moral standard. Though ecofeminism speaks much of unity and community, its proponents often celebrate women as being especially close to nature as a result of the experiences of menstruation and childbirth. More than a few hints of female triumphalism are inherent in this view that do not mix well with the ecofeminist ideal of terminating male domination. Equally debatable has been the ecofeminist invocation of nature as the standard of value and the claim that most societies once worked better because they were closer to nature. Women critics in particular have attacked the idea that nature is the proper moral foundation for everything.[29]

WOMEN IN THE PEWS

Though political debates about feminist theology and the value of Christian and Jewish religions dominate a good deal of the intellectual discourse surrounding women, religion, and politics, these matters do not appear to have engaged many women in the pews of churches and synagogues. Indeed, the fact is that except for women clergy (who are markedly liberal in their political attitudes), the more a woman is involved in organized religion, the more likely she is to be relatively conservative on political and religious questions as compared with women who are relatively uninvolved.

Studies of the baby boom generation of women confirm this scenario. The more closely a woman who was socialized in the 1960s and early 1970s is connected to a church or other religious group, the more conservative she will be on issues such as women's ordination. On the other hand, women who are attracted to less conventional spiritual journeys—often outside of organized religion—are much more likely to have liberal religious and political attitudes, including a strong attachment to feminism.[30]

It is also instructive to consider Catholic women of all generations. They tend to favor women's rights strongly, and as a group they are considerably more feminist on a wide array of issues than are Protestant women. Whereas many Catholic women feel that their church meets women's needs, others consider the church's record only fair, and about one-fourth rate it as poor. Women's assessments of the Catholic Church improve when the question is whether it adequately addresses the individual needs of individual women themselves—as opposed to their perceptions of the church's success with women as a group. And despite the recent scandals involving the Catholic Church and sex abuse, attitudes are most positive when women assess their own particular parish's treatment of women.

The undertone of uneasiness does not mean that Catholic women favor drastic changes in the Catholic Church. This is definitely not the case. Thus, even as most Catholic women now support the idea of a married priesthood, the idea of female priests still provokes very divided opinions. How long this division will last, however, is uncertain. Among Catholic women a distinct age factor is at work. The generation of women who reached adulthood in the 1960s and early 1970s tends to form the line of demarcation. Younger Catholic women are much more liberal on matters involving the priesthood, and they express a greater overall degree of discomfort with the church.[31]

Other students of Catholic women paint a similar picture. Jane Redmont, in her book *Generous Lives: American Catholic Women Today*, found that Catholic women, activist or not, are strong in their religious faith but divided about the institution of the Catholic Church. They agreed considerably, however, that the status of women in the local church was a matter of serious concern—and that the Catholic Church needed to be more respectful of women in general. In Redmont's study, opinions differed somewhat by age, as we would expect, and by marital status.[32]

The irony here is that some antifeminist elements in the Roman Catholic Church are also growing dissatisfied and beginning to raise questions about the increasing role played by women in the church. Critics raise the specter of what they call the "feminization of the church," expressing their fears that fewer men will be interested in Roman Catholicism if it responds to every desire of feminist women. There is also some apprehension that the male leaders who remain will become "feminized."[33]

The attitudes in the pews are illuminated by opinions about abortion, a crucial issue that lies at the intersection of women, religion, and politics. As we know, much of the battle over abortion is fought by combatants whose base lies in organized religion. This is true both of some prochoice and some prolife activist women for whom religion matters—and in fact forms the underpinning of moral and political commitments.[34]

The split among women on abortion is real. The more a woman is involved in religion and the more traditional her religious views, the more likely she is to oppose abortion. This does not mean that all active Catholic or Lutheran women are prolife. This is far from the case. But it is true that religious intensity is the best single factor predicting conservative abortion attitudes.[35]

Religious (and secular) women on both sides of the abortion debate often have more in common with each other than many think. They usually share a strong belief in the intrinsic value of women and motherhood. They frequently share a certain suspicion of men and a sense that women ultimately must rely on themselves.[36] Yet the abortion debate does divide women, including religious women, despite the fact that in the most liberal and prochoice religious settings, such as the Episcopal Church, the more involved a woman is in the church, the more likely she is to be uncomfortable with abortion.

Gender has also been a major dividing point when it comes to voting behavior in recent years. Women of all faiths are more likely to claim that they identify with the Democratic Party and vote for Democratic presidential and congressional candidates (see Table 11.1). Gender even appears to have a more significant effect on partisanship and voting behavior than religion itself; mainline Protestant women were more likely than Catholic men to vote for Al Gore in 2000, for example. The Republican Party, however, has a slight edge with Catholic men, but it clearly has a long way to go with Catholic women. Gender differences within religious groups cannot be ignored, and they may grow even more pronounced in the years to come.

The final important dynamic regarding gender, religion, and politics in the twenty-first century is the increasing presence of women in pulpit ministry. It took generations of struggle before women were allowed to become clergy, but women now constitute about 10 percent of all American religious leaders, and their ranks continue to expand.[37] Women are not ordained in all religious traditions, though, and there is still no consensus in American religious circles about whether the Bible allows or prohibits women's ordination. Christian opponents of women's ordination point to scriptural passages including 1 Timothy 2:11–12, which says: "Let a woman learn in silence with all submissiveness. I permit no woman to teach or to have authority over men; she is to keep silent." However, proponents point to such passages as Galatians 3:28: "There is neither Jew nor Greek, there is neither slave nor free, there is neither male nor female; for you are all one in Christ Jesus."[38] Such controversy, and the ensuing skepticism that many people have toward clergywomen today, has the potential either to stifle— or spur—political activity among women of the cloth.

The simple fact of being a female religious leader carries political connotations. Today's clergywomen have cause to feel feminist bonds of sisterhood with the early pioneers of the political struggle for women's equality in the United States. In 1848, Seneca Falls, New York, played host to one of the first organized public discussions of women's rights.

TABLE 11.1 Presidential Vote by Religious Tradition and Gender, 2000

	Evangelical		Mainline		Black Protestant		Catholic		Jews		Secular	
	M	F	M	F	M	F	M	F	M	F	M	F
Bush	78	66	77	48	11	1	58	40	41	14	45	17
Gore	22	34	23	51	89	99	42	60	59	86	55	83

Source: University of Akron, 2000 National Survey of Religion and Politics. Analysis courtesy of John C. Green, University of Akron (via personal communication).

One of the many resolutions debated at Seneca Falls during the drafting of the *Declaration of Sentiments and Resolutions* stated "that the speedy success of our course depends upon the zealous and untiring efforts of both men and women, for the overthrow of the monopoly of the pulpit, and for the securing to women an equal participation with men in the various trades, professions, and commerce."[39] A generation after Seneca Falls, Frances Willard, founder of the Woman's Christian Temperance Union, saw fit to publish a book entitled *Woman in the Pulpit*.[40] It is telling that women's acceptance into the male-dominated ministry has been seen from the outset as an important prong of women's equality.

James Davison Hunter and Kimon Howland Sargeant have argued that as more women enter the ministry, the religious traditions that ordain them might move to the left politically.[41] There is good reason to believe that they may be correct in this assessment. Recent research shows that Protestant and Jewish clergywomen are quite consistently liberal in their political attitudes, particularly when it comes to rights issues such as gender equality and matters involving homosexuality.[42] And many clergywomen are not afraid to let their political voices be heard, both in their congregations and in their broader communities. Whether the influx of women into the ministry will profoundly transform the relationship between religion and politics in the United States, though, remains to be seen.

CONCLUSION

In spite of the many crosscurrents, women play a central role in American religion, and their importance is growing. The future of women, religion, and politics is not obvious, but the politics of religion will continue to involve women's voices—and organized religion may ultimately be led by women. Among the areas to watch most closely in the future are feminist movements within American religion and reactions to them. Feminists will tackle the theologies and practices of American religion, including ordination issues, the proper place of religious hierarchies, and much more. Women will not just affect politics within churches and religions; they will affect the stance and involvement of organized religion on issues of gender and family in the politics of the larger society.

Also important to observe will be the continuing conflict over abortion and developments regarding other moral issues on the conservative religious agenda in America. The role of conservative religious women in promoting and defending a "family agenda" may turn out to have a major impact, no matter how many books on feminist theology are published.

Relations among women in American religion will also be important in the future. We have noted that religious women are often divided in their orientations toward feminism and other issues, just like the population at large. Though many female religious leaders are liberal, this is far less true of women in the pews. Whether this gap closes or becomes wider in the years ahead, particularly as more and more women are ordained as clergy, will have major implications for the effectiveness of religious women in politics.

Finally, it will be fascinating to observe national political developments, including presidential campaigns, to see what connections they make with religious women. The more American politics focuses on issues that are important to religious women, or on candidates' positions on such issues, the more likely religious women are to be mobilized. We know that many religious women were mobilized during the 1988 presidential campaigns of Jesse Jackson and Pat Robertson, and during various state and local campaigns since then. This has not happened more recently, but we can predict that it will happen again. How or in what ways it will happen we do not know.

FURTHER READING

Chaves, Mark. *Ordaining Women: Culture and Conflict in Religious Organizations.* Cambridge, MA: Harvard University Press, 1997. An excellent study of conflict over women's ordination in religious groups.

Daly, Mary. *Beyond God the Father: Toward a Philosophy of Women's Liberation.* Boston: Beacon, 1973. Radical feminist attack on traditional religion.

Davidman, Lynn. *Tradition in a Rootless World: Women Turn to Orthodox Judaism.* Berkeley: University of California Press, 1991. Interesting exploration of women and traditional Judaism.

Diamond, Irene, and Gloria Feman Orenstein, eds. *Reweaving the World: The Emergence of Ecofeminism.* San Francisco: Sierra Club, 1990. Thorough considerations of ecofeminism.

Griffith, R. Marie. "The Generous Side of Christian Faith: The Successes and Challenges of Mainline Women's Groups," in Robert Wuthnow and John H. Evans, eds., *The Quiet Hand of God: Faith-Based Activism and the Public Role of Mainline Protestantism.* Berkeley, CA: University of California Press, 2002. An examination of women and organized groups within the mainline.

McFague, Sallie. *Models of God: Theology for an Ecological, Nuclear Age.* Philadelphia: Fortress, 1987. Reflections of an influential feminist liberal Protestant theologian.

Piper, John, and Wayne Grunden, eds. *Recovering Biblical Manhood and Womanhood: A Response to Evangelical Feminism.* Wheaton, IL: Crossway, 1992. Conservative Protestant views on women.

Ruether, Rosemary Radford. *Gaia and God: An Ecofeminist Theology of Earth Healing.* San Francisco: HarperCollins, 1992. The perspective of a leading feminist theologian.

Streichen, Donna. *Ungodly Rage: The Hidden Face of Catholic Feminism.* San Francisco: St. Ignatius, 1991. Sharp criticism of religious feminists in action.

NOTES

1. These findings are drawn from Albert L. Winseman, "Religion and Gender: A Congregation Divided, Parts I-III," *Gallup Poll Tuesday Briefing* (December 3, 10, and 17, 2003); Barna Research Group, "Women Are the Backbone of the Christian Congregations in America," *Barna Research Online* (March 6, 2000), available at http://www.barna.org; and Center for Political Studies, *National Election Studies 2000* (Ann Arbor, MI: University of Michigan / Center for Political Studies, 2000). Data from the NES' biannual surveys are available at http://www.umich.edu/~nes/.

2. The best discussion is in C. Eric Lincoln and Lawrence H. Mamiya, *The Black Church in the African American Experience* (Durham, NC: Duke University Press, 1990), chap. 10; a wonderful approach from another direction is Samuel G. Freedman, *Upon This Rock: The Miracles of a Black Church* (New York: HarperCollins, 1993).

3. Ruth Wallace, *They Call Her Pastor: A New Role for Catholic Women* (Albany: State University of New York Press, 1992).

4. Gerald L. Zelizer, "Men's Absence Undercuts Family Worship," *USA Today* (December 19, 2002), 23A. See also Rodney Stark, "Physiology and Faith: Addressing the 'Universal' Gender Difference in Religious Commitment," *Journal for the Scientific Study of Religion* 41 (September 2002), 495–507.

5. Voter Research Survey and Exit Poll, 1996.

6. http://www.cnn.com/ELECTION/2000/results.

7. http://www.cwfa.org.

8. Beverly LaHaye, *I Am a Woman by God's Design* (Old Tappan, NJ: Revell, 1980).

9. http://www.cwfa.org.

10. For some data on Concerned Women for America, see Lyman Kellstedt, "Religious Interest Groups and Political Behavior," *Evangelical Studies Bulletin* (Fall 1991); for one of Schlafly's most explicit statements, see Phyllis Schlafly, *The Power of the Christian Woman* (Cincinnati, OH: Standard, 1981).

11. Stephen Bates, *Battleground: One Mother's Crusade, the Religious Right, and the Struggle for Control of Our Classrooms* (New York: Poseidon Press, 1993).

12. Kay Coles James, with Jacqueline Cobb Fuller, *Never Forget: The Riveting Story of One Woman's Journey from Public Housing to the Corridors of Power* (Grand Rapids, MI: Zondervan, 1992).

13. Agnieszka Tennant, "Adam and Eve in the 21st Century," *Christianity Today* (March 11, 2002); James Penning and Corwin Smidt, *Evangelicalism: The Next Generation* (Grand Rapids, MI: Baker Books, 2002), 81.

14. Debbie Daniels, "Evangelical Feminism: The Equalitarian-Complementarian Debate," Ph.D. dissertation (Madison, WI: University of Wisconsin –Madison, 2003).

15. http://www.cath4choice.org.

16. R. Marie Griffith, "The Generous Side of Christian Faith: The Successes and Challenges of Mainline Women's Groups," in Robert Wuthnow and John H. Evans, ed., *The Quiet Hand of God: Faith-Based Activism and the Public Role of Mainline Protestantism* (Berkeley, CA: University of California Press, 2002); Barbara Brown Zikmund, "Women's Organizations: Centers of Denominational Loyalty and Expressions of Christian Unity," in Jackson Carroll and Wade Clark Roof, eds., *Beyond Establishment: Protestant Identity in a Post-Protestant Age* (Louisville, KY: Westminster, 1993).

17. Rosemary Radford Ruether, *Gaia and God: An Ecofeminist Theology of Earth Healing* (San Francisco: HarperCollins, 1992); Peter Steinfels, "Catholic Feminists Ask, Can We Remain Catholic?" *New York Times* (April 16, 1993), A9.

18. Joyce Antler, "Activists and Organizers: Jewish Women and American Politics," in L. Sany Maisel, ed., *Jews in American Politics* (Lanham, MD: Rowman and Littlefield, 2001), 231–249.

19. The classic is Mary Daly, *Beyond God the Father: Toward a Philosophy of Women's Liberation* (Boston: Beacon, 1973); also see Beverly Wildung Harrison, "The Power of Anger in the World of Love," in Ann Loades, ed., *Feminist Theology* (Louisville, KY: Westminster, 1990), 194–213; and Letty M. Russell, "Good Housekeeping," in Loades, *Feminist Theology*, 225–238.

20. For example, see Elaine Pagels, *Adam, Eve, and the Serpent* (New York: Random House, 1988). Also, exploration of many of the essays in Ann Loades, ed., *Feminist Theology*, is a good way to get an idea of the diversity of feminist theology and of where one might want to go to pursue it; also see Sallie McFague, *Models of God: Theology for an Ecological, Nuclear Age* (Philadelphia: Fortress, 1987).

21. Anne E. Carr, *Transforming Grace: Christian Tradition and Women's Experience* (New York: Continuum, 1996).

22. McFague, Models of God.

23. See Silberman, *A Certain People*; and Davidman, *Tradition in a Rootless World*.

24. Daly, *Beyond God the Father*, is a good place to start.

25. Some relevant works, supportive, ambivalent, and hostile: Carol Christ, *Laughter of Aphrodite: Reflections on a Journey to the Goddess* (San Francisco: Harper, 1987); Susanne Heine, *Matriarchs, Goddesses and Images of God* (Minneapolis: Augsburg, 1988); Janet Biehl, *Rethinking Ecofeminist Politics* (Boston: South End Press, 1991); Mary A. Kassian, *The Feminist Gospel: The Movement to Unite Feminism with the Church* (New York: Crossway, 1992); Ruether, *Gaia and God*; and Wade Clark Roof, *A Generation of Seekers: The Spiritual Journeys of the Baby Boom Generation* (San Francisco: Harper, 1993), 142–143.

26. For example, see Rosemary Radford Ruether, *Sexism and God-Talk: Toward a Feminist Theology* (Boston: Beacon, 1983).

27. See Charlene Spretnak, *The Politics of Women's Spirituality: Essays on the Rise of Spiritual Power Within the Feminist Movement* (Garden City, NY: Doubleday, 1982); Ruether, *Gaia and God.*

28. Some key sources include Judith Plant, ed., *Healing the Words: The Promise of Eco-feminism* (Philadelphia: New Society, 1989); Carol Merchant, *The Death of Nature* (San Francisco: Harper, 1980); and Irene Diamond and Gloria Feman Orenstein, eds., *Reweaving the World: The Emergence of Ecofeminism* (San Francisco: Sierra Club, 1990).

29. See such critics as Biehl, *Rethinking Ecofeminist Politics*; Kassian, *The Feminist Gospel*; Heine, *Matriarchs, Goddesses and Images of God.*

30. Roof, *A Generation of Seekers,* 222–223.

31. George Gallup Jr. and Jim Castelli, *The American Catholic People: Their Beliefs, Practices, and Values* (Garden City, NY: Doubleday, 1987); Roof, *A Generation of Seekers,* 231–232.

32. Jane Redmont, *Generous Lives: American Catholic Women Today* (New York: William Morrow, 1992). Redmont's personal views are hardly kept a secret in this work, but whether one agrees with her or not, it is a revealing and reflective study.

33. For an example of this controversial argument, see Leon J. Podles, "Men Not Wanted: A Controversial Protest Against the Feminization of the Church," *Crisis* (November 1991), 16–20.

34. Kristin Luker, *Abortion and the Politics of Motherhood* (Berkeley: University of California Press, 1984).

35. See here the elaborate study by Elizabeth Adell Cook, Ted. G. Jelen, and Clyde Wilcox, *Between Two Absolutes: Public Opinion and the Politics of Abortion* (Boulder, CO: Westview, 1992), chap. 7.

36. Faye D. Ginsburg, *Contested Lives: The Abortion Debate in an American Community* (Berkeley: University of California Press, 1989).

37. Patricia M.Y. Chang, "Female Clergy in the Contemporary Protestant Church: A Current Assessment," *Journal for the Scientific Study of Religion* 36 (1997): 565–573; Barbara Brown Zikmund, Adair T. Lummis, and Patricia Mei Yin Chang, *Clergy Women: An Uphill Calling* (Louisville, KY: Westminster John Knox, 1998).

38. Mark Chaves, *Ordaining Women: Culture and Conflict in Religious Organizations* (Cambridge, MA: Harvard University Press, 1997).

39. The *Declaration of Sentiments and Resolutions* was a bold assertion of women's equality modeled on the Declaration of Independence. See Elizabeth Cady Stanton, Susan B. Anthony, and Matilda Joslyn Gage, ed., *History of Woman Suffrage*, vol. 1 (Rochester, NY: Charles Mann, 1881), 73.

40. Frances E. Willard, *Woman in the Pulpit* (Chicago: Woman's Christian Temperance Publication Association, 1889).

41. James Davison Hunter and Kimon Howland Sargeant, "Religion and the Transformation of Public Culture," *Social Research* 60 (1993): 545–570.

42. Sue E. S. Crawford, Melissa M. Deckman, and Christi J. Braun, "Gender and the Political Choices of Women Clergy," Sue E. S. Crawford and Laura R. Olson ed., *Christian Clergy in American Politics* (Baltimore: Johns Hopkins University Press, 2001); Melissa M. Deckman, Sue E. S. Crawford, Laura R. Olson, and John C. Green, "Clergy and the Politics of Gender: Women and Political Opportunity in Mainline Protestant Churches," *Journal for the Scientific Study of Religion* 42 (2003), 621–631; Laura R. Olson, Sue E. S. Crawford, and James L. Guth, "Changing Issue Agendas of Women Clergy," *Journal for the Scientific Study of Religion* 39 (2000), 140–153.

THEORIES OF
RELIGION, CULTURE, AND
AMERICAN POLITICS

Now that we have studied religion in American politics in its many forms, we need to step back and obtain a broader perspective. In this concluding chapter we explore some broad interpretations that paint an overall picture of the relationships between religion, politics, and culture. These broader theories should help us put much of the previous discussion into a more meaningful context. Each of these theories is a simplification of reality, but each helps us make comprehensible a world of sometimes bewildering complexity. Some consider worldwide forces; others restrict themselves to the United States. Each has its own emphases and makes its own case—and offers illumination in the search to understand religion and political culture in the United States.

CULTURE WARS

No theory that addresses religion, politics, and culture in the United States today gets more attention than the "culture wars" thesis.[1] It argues that we can understand the contours of religion and politics in America today by recognizing the existence of deep social divisions over values and lifestyles. This thesis separates Americans, particularly elites, into two categories: conservatives and progressives. Conservatives, on the one hand, stress the importance of traditional values: religion, marriage and family, discipline, and opposition to abortion and homosexuality. On the other hand, progressives stress the importance of choice and diversity in every area of life, including religion, family, and sexuality. The culture wars thesis holds that supporters of each perspective are sharply critical of—and feel threatened by—the other point of view. Each is struggling for dominance in American culture.

This division cuts across all sorts of lines in American life, including traditional religious lines.[2] Thus some traditional Catholics today find themselves aligned with conservative evangelicals on many social and political issues. Both groups oppose abortion, support public expressions of faith, criticize secularism in public schools, and decry the lingering effects of the sexual revolution. Theological and cultural differences remain between traditional Catholics and evangelical Protestants, to be sure, but many in each group unite in rejecting what they see as a secular assault on time-honored traditions and values. Similarly, liberal Protestants find they often have more in common with liberal Catholics, Jews, and secular elites than they do with conservatives within their own denominations. They speak a common language of peace and justice, and they identify the great issues of the day as rights issues (racism, sexism, and homophobia), economic inequality, and militarism, rather than themes that resonate on the Right.

A kind of cultural alliance has formed among conservative evangelicals, traditional Catholics, and some Orthodox and Ultraorthodox Jews. Activists call this alliance an ecumenism of orthodoxy. On the other side are liberal Protestants from the mainline denominations, liberal Catholics, most Jews, and a small but highly influential secular segment of the culture, who together constitute the progressive coalition.

African American denominations often join the liberal alliance, but the fit is not always snug. For example, some leaders of African American Christian denominations helped block the gay-majority Fellowship of Metropolitan Community Churches from obtaining membership in the National Council of Churches. Similarly, black Muslims join with progressives on U.S. policy toward Israel, but on abortion, drugs, alcohol, and gay rights they agree with evangelicals and traditional Catholics.

A similar fault line also separates genders. Conservative evangelical and traditional Catholic women often see themselves deeply at odds with their more liberal sisters in mainline churches, Jewish synagogues, and even many Catholic parishes. Many female prolife activists judge feminists as adversaries, despite sharing with them a confrontational style of political engagement that feminists generally applaud. In churches and outside them, progressive women believe just as strongly that their conservative sisters are a negative force at best and a group of traitors at worst. Everywhere there seems to be a sense of deep cultural division.

Several scholars advance evidence of a culture war. James Guth and his colleagues have found strong evidence that something akin to a culture wars split does, in fact, divide Protestant clergy into two groups.[3] Robert Wuthnow concludes that a massive restructuring of American religion has occurred that has polarized religious Americans into hostile camps of conservatives and liberals. Not too long ago, he argues, denominations meant something distinctive. To be a Methodist, Presbyterian, Catholic, Lutheran, or Baptist implied that there was a shared religious and ethnic heritage with distinctive customs and beliefs. Today a theological and cultural divide cuts across Christian church bodies. It matters more, in terms of political attitudes and behaviors, whether one is a liberal Catholic or a conservative Catholic, or a liberal Methodist or an evangelical Methodist, than whether one is a Methodist or a Catholic. Thus a liberal Methodist will probably feel more comfortable with secular liberals than with fellow Christians who call themselves evangelicals.[4] We see evidence of these intradenominational cleavages in the recent debates about homosexuality in mainline Protestant denominations.[5]

This same case is made by James Davison Hunter. In two books, *Culture Wars* and *Before the Shooting Begins*, Hunter articulates the culture wars thesis clearly and then explains how it plays out in a number of areas of American life, including religion and politics.[6] Hunter notes various divisions as they manifest themselves in specific skirmishes—over school curricula, ordinances to recognize gay rights, abortion battles in the states, and the like, especially at the state and local levels.

Imagine two women who have certain things in common. Both are married, both are college graduates, both are church members, and both are economically comfortable. One woman attends an independent evangelical church, views abortion as morally offensive, and is an avid reader of the conservative religious and political literature found in many Christian bookstores. Deeply alienated by public schools, which she sees as having low academic standards and promoting secular and hedonistic values, she has chosen to homeschool her children. She is an active member of a homeschool association, which provides her with information about Christian curricula and ways to avoid being harassed by state education authorities. She sees that she is engaged in a conflict with the "dominant" culture, which includes the movie and television industries, public education, "antifamily" feminists, gay activists, and the government. She votes Republican.

The other woman, who came of age in the 1960s, sees the defining experience of her life as her participation in the civil rights and Vietnam War protests. She is now an active member of a United Methodist congregation known for its "peace and justice" activism. A strong feminist and a supporter of abortion rights, she belongs to several feminist organizations and donates to PACs that support women candidates. She dislikes television preachers such as Jerry Falwell and Pat Robertson, and she fears fundamentalist influence in school board elections. She deplores what she sees as religious attempts to censor books and art. She has gay friends and sympathizes with their struggle for equal rights. To her, the idea of a "dominant culture" equals white male businessmen who belong to country clubs. She is a liberal Democrat.

As Robert Wuthnow notes, despite talk of polarization, few people are comfortable with either side of the culture war. Many are in fact unaware of any culture war. To be sure, many parents—from moderate Catholics to conservative Protestants—view television as unhealthy and get angry when public schools uncritically embrace the latest curriculum fad. They take their children to church and otherwise attempt to counteract the messages purveyed by the pop culture. But they do not necessarily view these actions as battles in some cosmic conflict over the very soul of America. Whether more Americans will embrace the culture wars perspective in the future remains to be seen.[7]

There is also a self-fulfilling quality about discussion of the culture wars. Mutual stereotyping, polarization, and inflamed passions may help create culture wars where none previously existed. Talk of culture wars also undermines the possibility that adversaries may discover common ground. Compromise, that staple of American politics, is hard if one's opponents are enemies bent on destroying one's very way of life. The two hypothetical women described above might agree, in fact, that television is largely trash, that public schools are too lax, or that pornography has an unhealthy influence, but they miss the chance to work together to address such feelings because of the blinding rhetoric of cultural conflict.

Yet it is also true that signs of culture wars in the United States are unmistakable. At its root the question is one of the appropriate character of

American society. And there is no longer just one culture war in American society. In a society of increasing religious pluralism, many newer groups wrestle with how to preserve their old values, so often deeply intertwined with their religion, in a sometimes troubling American culture. This has been notably true for many Muslim citizens as they struggle to reconcile their religion and American popular culture. Thus some forms of Islam demand women's heads be covered, but most U.S. state laws require that they remove those coverings for pictures on driver's licenses.[8] Thus Muslim religious values insist that young women not touch or have any romantic relationship with males until marriage, while ordinary American customs are quite different. In fact, in some places all-women Muslim high school proms are held.[9]

The examples are numerous, as are the varieties and intensities of culture wars as diverse religious subgroups and U.S. culture clash. This is why the culture wars theory remains essential to any understanding of religion and politics in the United States today. By itself it is not a sufficient guide, but it is without question important.

THE SECULARIZATION THESIS

While the culture wars thesis focuses on today's struggles, the "secularization" thesis takes a somewhat longer view of religion in America. It suggests that we look away from the events directly before us to connect with broader developments that have served to condition culture, religion, and politics.

Proponents of the secularization thesis argue that religion has declined as secularism has advanced. They contend that this development is an inescapable result of modernity, which has already greatly influenced Western Europe and, to a lesser degree, the United States. As modernity spreads, secularism spreads in its wake—eroding the influence of religion. With religion's gradual decline, they conclude, we can expect to see religious involvement with politics decrease in the long run, both in the United States and elsewhere.[10]

The short-run picture can be different. There can be temporary surges in religio-political involvement. Losing out to secularism, some religious groups might try to use politics to stem the tide. Such efforts represent a sort of dying gasp on the part of religious forces. For some secularization analysts, this describes the current situation in the United States. Assorted religious groups with different—even opposing—agendas hurl themselves into American political life. But for some secularization theorists this is not a sign of the strength of religion in politics or in any other forum. Instead, it is a sign of weakness, a sign of desperate efforts to halt a decline that threatens American religion.

Some classic advocates of the secularization thesis were giants of nineteenth-century European thought. Karl Marx (1818–83) was among them. He was sure that class struggle and the triumph of communism would be the story of modern life—a tale in which religion would soon be a mercifully final chapter. Max Weber (1864–1920), the great German sociologist, was another classic secularization theorist. He believed that with modernity would come forces of rationalism and bureaucratization that would defeat organized religion, if not entirely eliminate religious people. Sigmund Freud (1856–1939), the founder of psychoanalysis, also addressed secularization. Freud was quite interested in religion and religious traditions, especially those of his fellow Jews. Though Freud knew that there was no guarantee religion would fade, he hoped that "the future of an illusion" would prove poor as people came to see that the modern world gave them a chance to be free of religion.[11]

Since secularization theorists take modernization to be the key to the decline of religion, we need to have some sense of what they mean by the term "modernization." Among the factors analysts usually include in defining this concept are the scientific way of thinking; modern technological advances; complex economic life; contemporary forms of mass communication and entertainment; and the growth of government bureaucracies and public education. Secularization theorists suggest that in modern societies, rational, scientific approaches dominate, whereas in traditional societies, religious worldviews govern life. In modern societies public policy is dominated by clashes of self-interested individuals and groups pursuing their "rational" interests. Education becomes an engine of secularization as it teaches science and denigrates supernatural explanations. The capitalist marketplace also mutes religious enthusiasms as it directs people to a consumer culture and the workaday corporate world.

There is ample support for the secularization worldview. Religion governs the United States today much less than it does, say, a traditional

African tribe (or than it did in earlier eras of American history). There is no doubt even that many religious Americans compartmentalize their faith today and do not manifest it in many areas of their lives. Moreover, many of the major institutions of the United States—giant corporations, public schools and universities, governmental bureaucracies, television networks—now operate on the basis of secular concerns and logic.[12] Often they either ignore religion and spiritual dimensions of life or are positively hostile toward them.

Yet in recent years the secularization thesis has come under fire. It has lost some of its luster, in large part because of the continuing resilience of religious faith in the face of secular forces. In recent decades there been a notable growth of evangelical commitment in the United States, a resurgence of religious practice in Russia and Eastern Europe, and a major increase in religious energy in many Islamic countries. Religion's demise, once predicted so confidently, has just not taken place in most parts of the world, nor is there evidence that religion is going to vanish anytime soon.

Moreover, in recent years religion has not always been content to remain in a narrow, compartmentalized realm. Religion has been very busy in the larger, public world, challenging secular authorities in the United States, many African countries, all over the Muslim world, and elsewhere. While religion may not be as tightly interwoven into most people's lives as it once was, it clearly has not disintegrated. Indeed, it may be that the secularization thesis has reality reversed. Perhaps the "unsecularization"—or even sacralization—of the world is one of the characteristics of our modern age.[13]

The response of those who have been impressed with the secularization view is that religion's current health is temporary. To them, religious vitality is further proof of secularization's progress through the world—no more than a temporary reaction to the inevitable. Perhaps they are right; perhaps secularization will proceed in the long run. But as of now there are many reasons for doubt, including the fact that the death of religion now seems very much overdue. Modernity has infused many corners of the world, but people often have chosen to retain their religions.

The secularization thesis also has variants that are often as intriguing as the theory itself. One is the "elite secularization thesis." In this view, even though religion continues to speak to most human beings, elites and elite institutions have become highly secular. The idea is that the larger secularization thesis applies to one (crucial) sector of the population only: elites. In the United States a number of theorists advance this analysis. Richard John Neuhaus, for example, uses the metaphor of the "naked public square" to describe how elites have largely banished faith-based, moral arguments from American politics. According to Neuhaus, the language of rights, efficiency, and practicality have crowded out considerations of moral obligation and timeless spiritual truths.[14] This view is echoed by Stephen Carter in *The Culture of Disbelief*, in which he takes elites in American media, law, and education to task for trivializing faith.[15]

As we saw in our chapter on elites and religion and politics (Chapter 6), there is evidence that some American elites, such as media elites, are far more secular than the population at large. And such gaps are especially pronounced when the popular religion of ordinary people is traditional or fundamentalist. Here the gap becomes a major chasm. Some academics, reporters, media elites, political leaders, and government bureaucrats profess a religious faith, but relatively few are comfortable with born-again evangelicalism, traditional Catholicism, Orthodox Judaism, or revivalist Islam. As the argument goes, Americans with orthodox religious beliefs must now confront hostile elites who have the power to shape the schools their children attend, the television and movies they and their children watch, and the government edicts with which they must comply.

One problem with the elite secularization thesis, however, is the unevenness of the phenomenon. To be sure, many national news media elites are highly secular. So are many of those who dominate the entertainment media, such as television, movies, and most popular music. But elected officials—members of Congress and state legislators, not to mention presidents—better reflect the religious diversity of the population at large.[16] Moreover, the remarkable growth of scholarship and intellectual discourse on religion and society belies the notion of totally hostile elites. There are now several widely cited elite journals publishing criticism of other elites for their hostility to faith.[17]

Another variant on secularization theory is sociologist David Yamane's neosecularization thesis. Yamane argues that it is erroneous to claim that religion is disappearing from American life. In this sense, the secularization thesis is simply incorrect as a description of the contemporary United States. Yet Yamane insists that secularization is occurring nonetheless in individual American lives, institutions, and the culture as a whole. The key is to understand that religion, even as it continues to be very much alive, is receding steadily into private realms of American life and culture. For Yamane, the true test of secularization is not whether religion is disappearing but whether its role is diminishing in ordinary lives and institutions, as well as in the broader culture. And Yamane argues that it is clear when one observes the United States and its culture from a historical perspective that religion's influence has declined.[18]

CULTURE SHIFT ANALYSIS

Ronald Inglehart has pioneered another approach to understanding secularization today that has gained substantial notice from a variety of scholars. His "culture shift" analysis dovetails with the secularization thesis in holding that the influence of old-time religion is dying. Inglehart explains this death by arguing that cultures, especially in the Western world, are changing in response to modernization. Old institutions, the old politics of class and economics, and old modes of thinking are receding (despite occasional revivals).[19] The result, however, is not what the standard secularization thesis would predict. Spiritual concerns have not disappeared, nor will they disappear. If anything, spiritual concerns are growing among individuals, but this concern is made manifest less through formal institutions than through individual journeys of the spirit. It follows for the culture shift analysis that formal religious involvement in politics will decline over time, but that does not mean that the spiritual concerns of individual citizens will decline in their impact on politics and elsewhere. Thus, according to this view, what looks like secularization around us may actually be a shift in the nature of spiritual life from the organized and public to the individual and private. It is not the end of the influence of spiritual concerns but rather a change in how they work.[20]

There is plenty of evidence in the United States that something like a culture shift has taken place. Wade Clark Roof has portrayed a resulting baby-boom "generation of seekers"[21] who look in a wide variety of places—some of them unconventional—for spiritual fulfillment. Robert C. Fuller describes a huge part of the United States as "spiritual, but not religious," reflecting this seeker movement. He contends that as many as

20 percent of the American public has spiritual concerns, sometimes very serious ones, which they do not pursue in traditional religious institutions or forms. All sorts of mystical, healing, holistic, feminist, Eastern, and other spiritualities are very much part of the American landscape now, as culture shift analysts would predict. For Fuller, everywhere we look we see the prevalence of this "seeker spirituality."[22]

Sociologist Phillip Hammond argues that American religion is actually undergoing a major "disestablishment" that demonstrates how widespread the culture shift has been. As Hammond describes it, American culture now honors choice, expressivism, and individualism in religion as elsewhere. Traditional religions in the United States that focus on duty, institutions, and collective practices face a tremendous challenge and are slowly losing out. Mainline Protestantism in particular is suffering, though it is far from alone in its predicament. All established churches and synagogues are threatened by the movement toward individualistic spirituality.[23]

To be sure, many "seekers" remain within the realm of traditional organized religions, where they are bringing about major change. For example, one excellent recent study of evangelical Protestant churches that reflect this "new paradigm" (and are booming as a result) notes that members of such churches insist on expressive and contemporary music and other means of worship that allow them to move beyond what they see as rather staid, traditional experiences in order to achieve a deeply felt, individualistic spirituality.[24] Such religious practitioners also stress the importance of a personal relationship with Jesus Christ, support the institution of the nuclear family, encourage participation in small groups at church, and radiate a decidedly unstuffy aura. The overall result is very different from traditional Catholic and mainline Protestant worship services. For their part, though, some Catholic and mainline Protestant congregations have been implementing aspects of evangelical worship in special "seeker" services designed for those who desire a more emotional, expressive religious experience.

It remains to be seen what the long-term consequences of the experiences of the "seeker" phenomenon will be for religion and politics. If American religion becomes an increasingly individualistic spirituality, its impact on political life might be less focused, organized, and unified. Thus the politics of religion may become less important over time, just as the secularization thesis suggests (though for quite different reasons). On the other hand, this is not self-evident. After all, if spirituality becomes more important and more deeply valued among more Americans, it is bound to affect their political outlooks and behavior, possibly more intensely—and more widely—than ever before.

CIVIL RELIGION

Another perspective that seeks to illuminate the relationship between religion and politics in America is the civil religion thesis. This view contends that the one important religion in the United States has nothing to do with specific denominations or religious traditions. Instead the important American religious dimension is a shared but vague political religion—a religion of America and its culture—the civil religion. Civil religion in the United States emphasizes America's unique, "blessed" status among the nations of the world and inspires in its followers a sense of American patriotism. The quick appearance of American flags and signs reading "God Bless America" in the days and weeks immediately following the terrorist attacks of September 11, 2001, provides evidence of the civil religion.

Those attracted to this thesis agree that the civil religion exists right along with the other religions in the United States without challenging them. Civil religion is nonsectarian in its belief that God has blessed the United States, endowed it with special opportunities, and assigned it responsibilities to do good in the world. Civil religion is important, analysts suggest, because it enhances national stability, governmental legitimacy, and a feeling of shared purpose among citizens. Every nation has a faith of sorts, a belief in itself, a civil religion—and in the United States this civil religion is profoundly infused with a sense that God has provided Americans with special blessings.

The civil religion thesis downplays the importance of various (perhaps passing) events such as culture wars or evidence of one type of secularization or another. It points us instead toward the existence of enduring connections between government and religion and warns us that the religions that matter most in political terms may not be practiced in conventional churches. The idea of the civil religion first received extensive attention in a 1967 essay by Robert Bellah. In it, he compares the inaugural addresses of Abraham Lincoln and John F. Kennedy and notes that these two seminal American leaders from different eras both affirmed that the nation had a divine purpose and called upon God to bless the country.[25] Others have since observed how presidential inauguration ceremonies are steeped in religious imagery and how often incoming presidents make reference to God. True to this tradition, and despite their political dissimilarity, both Bill Clinton and George W. Bush have included in their speeches to the nation religious phrases and invocations. It is now *de rigueur* for an American president to end all major speeches with some variant of the phrase "God bless you, and God bless the United States of America."

Historian Sidney Mead approaches the idea of civil religion by documenting how a "national religion" grew steadily through the early years of the United States until it was firmly established by time of the Civil War. As he observes, there are really two forms of faith in the United States—first, those of specific religious groups and denominations, and second, what he terms "the American faith" or the civil religion. Both forms, he realizes, are intertwined and mutually supportive. Patriotism in some churches and synagogues is palpable, as anyone who has seen the American flag in houses of worship or heard a spirited singing of "God Bless America" can attest. In turn, religious Americans gain affirmation of the importance of their faith when they hear political leaders publicly call on God, when they use currency that reads "In God We Trust," and when they repeat the Pledge of Allegiance, which proclaims the existence of one nation "under God."[26]

In the end the ultimate question is how to evaluate the civil religion thesis. Does the United States have a civil religion? Some evidence does support the assertion. From Abraham Lincoln's sublime vision of the nation as the last best hope on Earth to Ronald Reagan's invocation of the Puritan notion of a "city on a hill," civil religious images suggesting that America is an agent of the divine with special duties on Earth abound. And this is a view that many religious leaders like to echo. For decades evangelist Billy Graham has invoked God's blessing on the nation's leaders, institutions, and purposes. Many other religious leaders continue to do so.

And everywhere are signs of civil religious rituals, such as Fourth of July ceremonies, Memorial Day observances, and that most distinctly civil religious holiday, Thanksgiving. Each marks the calendar with its own blend of religion and patriotism, faith and political history. American civil religion has its own sacred places too, such as the majestic Lincoln Memorial or the hallowed ground of Gettysburg, Pennsylvania. Some documents are sacred, such as the original Declaration of Independence and the Constitution. At the National Archives in Washington, visitors wishing to view these two documents encounter an atmosphere not unlike that of a house of worship. It is softly lit and so quiet that people start whispering upon entering. They walk up a narrow, semicircular corridor until they enter the room containing glass cases, impervious even to nuclear war, that hold these documents for the faithful to venerate. Guards prevent visitors from getting too close to the glass, and the cases descend below the ground for safekeeping every night.

Finally, there are the prophets and saviors of the American civil religion. In Washington, D.C., one can read prophetic words carved in stone at the Jefferson Memorial or stare in awe at the soaring monument to George Washington. At the very center of the civil religion is Lincoln, "the martyred Christ of Democracy's passion play."[27] The story of his presidency, remarkable maturation, single-minded sense of purpose, and tragic assassination invokes religious images of Christ-like sacrifice and death for the nation's rebirth.

In short, we feel that the United States does have something of a civil religion, though this conclusion is far from universally shared.[28] It is there in the culture, however thinly it may be worn in these increasingly multicultural and fractious times. Perhaps the larger question is whether the civil religion thesis helps us understand religion and politics in the United States. Civil religion does tell us something about what still binds many Americans together politically. While it may appear to some scholars that civil religion is declining in the face of cultural pluralism and political cynicism, expressions of national unity after the September 11, 2001, attacks and even in support of the 2003 Iraq War raise doubts about this assumption. In any case, the civil religion thesis does not help us understand much about how specific religious *traditions* interact with politics. It tells us nothing about how one's religious beliefs affect voting behavior, or the agendas of religious interest groups, or church-state conflicts, or anything else in the boiling pot of religion and politics in America.

THE UNCONVENTIONAL PARTNERS THESIS

Another perspective on the relationships among culture, religion, and politics is the unconventional partners thesis. While it takes some inspiration from the civil religion thesis, the unconventional partners framework is broader, and it looks beyond the periodic rituals of civil religion to the deeper, day-to-day cultural patterns of the nation. It posits that religion plays a major political role because it helps to sustain America's individualistic political culture and its governmental institutions. Religion accomplishes this task not through active engagement in politics but by offering a source of meaning, morality, and community that the culture and government cannot provide. In doing so it relieves pressure on the culture and the government and strengthens both. In turn, the government and the culture promote broad religious freedom. But this symbiotic relationship is largely unintentional; hence the "unconventional partners" label.[29]

An early variant of this theory was put forward by the French statesman-author Alexis de Tocqueville. Observing conditions in America in the early nineteenth century, Tocqueville noted that in his native France the "spirits of religion and of freedom" marched in opposite directions. Not so in America, where he found that the spirit of liberty and the spirit of religion marched together, supporting and reinforcing each other. Tocqueville was impressed with the extent of political freedom enjoyed by American citizens (then defined as white males). But his European experience taught him that such freedom could easily degenerate into anarchy and then despotism. Moreover, even if such perils were avoided, maximum individual freedom, when left to itself, could promote a materialistic society of individual strivers isolated from their fellow citizens. To his amazement, though, this was not what Tocqueville found in the United States.

He concluded that the explanation for the symbiotic relationship between religion and politics was the crucial role that religion played in instilling moral self-restraint combined with the way religious congregations helped people overcome their isolation. When political freedom implied that a nineteenth-century man could do as he pleased, religion taught him he should not do things that were destructive to his family or the community. Thus religion made liberal democracy possible by instilling the inner mores that prevented the society from plunging into chaos. In turn, religion and churches thrived in the United States because they were relatively free from persecution and unencumbered by the debilitating government paternalism found in Europe.[30] Thus an unintentional symbiosis developed between government and religion, each sustaining the other.

Of course, the contemporary United States is a far cry from the still-developing republic Tocqueville observed in the 1830s. In many ways American culture is now far more materialistic, skeptical, and focused on individuals. But that has only sharpened the continuing partnership between religion and culture in America. In its modern form, religion helps to sustain an individualistic society in a paradoxical way: by offering a temporary refuge from the culture. Indeed, evidence abounds that people who turn to organized religion do so because they want it to be—as it sometimes is—somewhat different from the world they live in ordinarily. They want a refuge from the enormous burden of living in a society where meaning, morality, and community are often confusing or missing.

It is crucial to understand, however, that the unconventional partners thesis sees people getting involved in organized religion for temporary refuge only, not as a permanent or radical alternative to the broader society. Most people want religion to give them just enough communal sharing and spiritual sustenance to enable them to persist in the broader culture. Without this kind of refuge, the unconventional partners thesis argues, society might find itself wracked by radical challenges from both the right and the left. Thus religion sustains the social order by providing what that very order lacks.

The unconventional partners thesis identifies a number of ways in which religion aids American culture. First, for many citizens, religion provides meaning—a grounding for values in a culture in which such meaning is far from automatically available. Second, it helps provide moral values for a culture in which skepticism and cynicism are pervasive. Finally, it encourages community in a culture that often lacks it. Study after study demonstrates the extent to which people understand religion in precisely these ways, as a place to go in search of meaning, morality, or community. When a religion or a church can offer these things, it flourishes; when it cannot, people drift away.[31] Community and meaning may come in a variety of forms within the capacious realm of American religion. There is no single voice, to say the least, but this very fact is an immense plus for the culture. It means that American religion can and does serve many more people in this pluralistic age than it would were there only one religion in the land.

The other side of the partnership is, of course, how American culture and government assist religion. There are many ways in which they do so, despite illusions that church and state are somehow separate in America. Perhaps the most important form of assistance comes in the generous protection of free exercise that the majority of American religious traditions enjoy. The First Amendment is alive and well. The fact that both government and culture have some sympathy for religion makes a tremendous difference for the viability of organized religious life in the United States.

Moreover, the courts have sometimes shown a proclivity to extend the government's protective role to minority religions (some of which are controversial). Though the courts' attitudes vary from case to case and from time to time, religious pluralism is a fact in the United States. This pluralism is possible in good part only because the state and the culture both tacitly accept it and allow broad (if not limitless) religious freedom to flourish. This is a tremendous gift not only to specific religions but to religion in general throughout the nation. It confirms that religion is important, no matter what form it takes.

At another level organized religion has reaped extraordinary financial advantages from government and the culture on which government rests. As we discussed in Chapter 8, the United States demonstrates a great deal of "multiple establishment," which results in all sorts of concrete financial benefits from aid to church hospitals to freedom from property taxes for churches. No definite figures are available for how much direct or indirect aid religious institutions receive, but it is certainly many billions of dollars. This sort of help matters, but so too does the climate of broad religious freedom. It constitutes the other side of the partnership from which both religion and culture benefit.

This kind of partnership has existed for a long time in the United States. Government may provide more aid today, but that is mainly a reflection of the overall growth of government through American history. Religious freedom has a broader range than was the case in previous eras, but it is an extension of over two centuries of determination, initially expressed in the First Amendment, to guarantee religious freedom.

The unconventional partners thesis also offers some perspective on conflicts between church and state in the courts and on the activities of religious interest groups. The occasional sound and fury of conflict should not drown out the reality of a continuing partnerships between religion, government, and culture. This is not to say that the ordinary aspects of religion and politics—interest groups, voting, reform efforts, and court cases—are meaningless; far from it. They are an important part of the religion and politics story. But the unconventional partners thesis reminds us that their significance must be tempered in light of the deep affinity between religion and culture in the United States. That relationship will remain secure, for better or for worse, as long as organized religion does not transform itself from a temporary refuge into a permanent enemy of American culture, and as long as those who seek a total separation of religion and government do not fully succeed.

POPULISM

The unconventional partners thesis tends to discount the importance of direct religious participation in politics, but this view is not shared by those who are impressed with the frequency and power of religiously based populist movements in American politics. American politics has seen a great deal of religious energy through its history to the present day. Some observers stress the role of populist movements in generating much of the resulting political activism.[32]

The link between populism and religion flows in part from the nature of church life in America. Because churches operate in a highly competitive religious marketplace, they live or die on the basis of popular support. Only churches that tap into the deepest needs, frustrations, or anxieties of their members will thrive. Moreover, unlike the elite membership of most interest groups, church membership is extremely broad and diverse. There is no other institution or activity in which Americans of all socioeconomic strata participate in such large numbers. Especially in a highly individualistic and mobile society, religious institutions represent one of the few settings in which many people meet—and sometimes discover their common grievances. In spite of some skittishness about political engagement, church-based political movements have allowed segments of the population that are otherwise unable to find a political voice to register their discontent. Local churches, synagogues, and mosques become the focal point of community responses to all sorts of threats. They are a place in which to organize, develop leadership, and call upon members for sacrifice.

At the national level, the church-based political mobilization of African Americans and the political emergence of evangelical Protestants are the most prominent recent examples of this populist-religious intersection. Both are undeniably expressions of populism that have achieved a far-reaching impact on political party platforms, voter alignment, and presidential politics. That the same theory can accommodate such different movements illuminates its broad utility.

From the civil rights movement of the 1950s and 1960s to the two presidential campaigns of Jesse Jackson in 1984 and 1988, black churches have provided most of the organizational base, leadership, money, and moral support for African American political mobilization. In doing so, black congregations channeled aspirations for equal rights in the 1950s, continued the struggle in the 1960s, and voiced discontent with lingering economic disparities in the 1980s. Similarly, since the late 1970s evangelical churches have captured the growing discontent of their members with the "decaying" state of American culture, family breakup, loss of discipline in schools, legal abortion, and similar issues—and turned many of their members toward politics as a result. By 1988 these two populist movements had gained enough steam to propel the presidential candidacies of Jesse Jackson and Pat Robertson, two ministers who had never held elective office but who enjoyed a strong church base and a loyal following. Despite their ideological differences, both candidates shared much of the traditional populist view of the world. Jackson expressed prophetic outrage at what he viewed as the economic abandonment of working-class and impoverished Americans; Robertson vented his anger against cultural elites, who in his view were undermining traditional values. Both candidates used their religious charisma to champion "the people" and castigate elites. Moreover, both emphasized to some degree the historic populist blend of economic progressivism and social conservatism.

Jackson's liberal economic and civil rights platform drew on a strong dose of religious fervor and moral traditionalism. He admonished his followers to heed the Ten Commandments and to shun illegal drugs, sexual promiscuity, and laziness. Robertson's moral conservatism, on the other hand, was mixed with a populist distrust of large banks, economic conglomerates, and elite foreign policy makers. Jackson and Robertson both evoked a populist style in their politics and a characteristic populist mix of ideological perspectives.[33]

As we can see, the populist thesis emphasizes not only the ways religious traditions can vent their discontent but the ways they can infuse the political system with a politics that may not fit neatly into the left-right political spectrum. Moreover, events in other countries from Afghanistan to Northern Ireland to Sudan to the Philippines suggest that this link between religion and populist uprisings may be a global phenomenon. As such, the theory of populist religion helps us to understand the ways in which religion sometimes taps sentiments that elites do not notice or acknowledge.

Two cautions are in order. First, given the importance of charismatic leadership in mobilizing populist discontent, one must question whether such leaders reflect—or in fact create—popular concerns. Critics assert that both Jackson and Robertson exhibited a tendency to conflate their own ego needs with the aspirations of the communities they claimed to represent, a tendency that limited their ability to work within the system. Perhaps the populist style in general expresses discontent better than it fashions realistic remedies.

Second, one must resist taking the populist thesis too far. Many religious congregations are neither positioned nor inclined to sustain major political efforts. Even if individual Americans experience frustration with current politics, they may not be able to vent that frustration through their religious congregations. Finally, and perhaps most important, it is not clear how often populist sentiments define the link between religion and politics in American life.

MARKET THEORY, RELIGIOUS PLURALISM, AND POLITICS

The most controversial new theory regarding religion and society that matters for the study of religion and politics in the United States is market theory. Its proponents argue that religion's relative strength in every society is largely a function of how much competition there is among religious traditions in a society, and the degree to which that competition is unfettered. According to market theory, which obviously draws on economics, religion in the United States should remain very strong, and that has obvious implications for the continuing political force of American religion.

First, we know that there is intense competition among various religions in the United States. This competition draws people in and provides them with an almost unbelievable variety of religious niches among which to choose. And congregations advertise their services just like secular businesses do, via billboards, advertisements, Internet sites, and even free gifts. Some congregations market themselves as friendly places where it is not necessary to dress up on Sunday morning. Others promote themselves as offering a distinctive theological, social, or political outlook. Still others attempt to meet members' every need, offering everything from a range of worship experiences to small-group friendship networks to sports leagues to healthcare clinics. This diversity suits Americans' pluralist tastes. Market model analysts believe that congregations that fare poorly are just not competing hard enough.

Second, religion in the United States is characterized by almost unlimited free competition. While plenty of traditional "establishment" religion exists in the United States, the fact that there is no single official American religion means that government's relationship with it is mostly supportive—and that religious freedom is extended to all groups.

The implication for us, of course, is that because American religion is strong, competitive, and free, it is able to exert a continuing political force. Market theorists compare and contrast the enduring strength of religion in the United States with religion's role in other countries to illustrate their thesis more fully. For example, market theorists note that the intense religious competition that exists today in Latin America and much of Africa is resulting in tremendous growth among a variety of religious groups. They observe, however, that this growth has been possible only when governments have abandoned old alliances with particular religious groups; such arrangements inevitably restricted or even forbade competition.

Market analysts note that in much of Western Europe religion is weak and in serious decline; consequently, its political impact has also diminished. They explain these developments partly as the result of limited competition fostered by the existence of longstanding state-established churches. The Church of England, for example, is the United Kingdom's official state church. It is an important part of Queen Elizabeth II's role as monarch to serve as "Defender of the Faith." Yet many of England's majestic churches sit virtually empty most Sundays, and most accounts suggest that Britons are no longer a particularly religious people.

Whenever religious groups that lack the fire to compete aggressively for souls dominate, all religions pay a steep and inevitable price. Competitive evangelicalism appears to be an essential ingredient for the success of any religious group, according to market theorists. Tired, insular religions that in some countries are propped up by government face serious decline and an attending loss of political influence.[34]

TOWARD THE FUTURE

Which of these theories, alone or in combination with others, will best serve to illuminate the relationship between religion and politics in the United States in this new century remains to be seen. Perhaps none of them will prove very useful. None of them can explain everything, nor can they even begin to do so, though each offers a useful perspective. Moreover, what the future will produce in terms of the theory and practice of religion and politics in the United States may surprise all of us. After all, who predicted the rise of the Christian Right in the 1980s? Who expected that an African American minister named Martin Luther King would emerge in the 1950s to change fundamentally how we view race and civil rights in America? Who could have known in 1960 that Catholics and evangelical Protestants would one day be forming political alliances? And who thought that Mormons, Muslims, and a host of other small religious groups would have begun to emerge as important political players today? The subject of religion and politics in America, because it is so dynamic, defies any theory with which to capture its essence. But that should not deter us from trying to understand its contribution to the life and culture of the United States.

FURTHER READING

Bruce, Steve. *God is Dead: Secularization in the West.* Oxford: Blackwell, 2002. A contemporary application of secularization theory.

Finke, Roger, and Rodney Stark. *Acts of Faith: Understanding the Human Side of Religion.* Berkeley: University of California Press, 2000. A recent statement of the market model from two of its leading proponents.

Fowler, Robert Booth. *Unconventional Partners: Religion and Liberal Culture in the United States.* Grand Rapids, MI: Eerdmans, 1989. Contemporary account of unconventional partners thesis.

Hertzke, Allen. *Echoes of Discontent: Jesse Jackson, Pat Robertson, and the Resurgence of Populism.* Washington, D.C.: CQ Press, 1993. Recent account of populist thesis.

Hunter, James Davison. *Culture Wars: The Struggle to Define America.* New York: Basic Books, 1991. Leading version of culture wars argument.

Inglehart, Ronald. *Culture Shift in Advanced Industrial Society.* Princeton, NJ: Princeton University Press, 1990. Best statement of culture shift theory.

Smith, Christian, ed. *The Secular Revolution: Power, Interests, and Conflict in the Secularization of American Life.* Berkeley: University of California Press, 2003. A set of provocative arguments about the reasons for American secularization.

Richey, Russell, and Donald Jones, eds. *American Civil Religion.* New York: Harper and Row, 1974. Interesting views on civil religion theory.

Wuthnow, Robert. *The Restructuring of American Religion: Society and Faith Since World War Two.* Princeton, NJ: Princeton University Press, 1988. Valuable reflections on religion in the United States.

NOTES

1. James Davison Hunter, *Culture Wars: The Struggle to Define America* (New York: Basic Books, 1991).

2. Robert Wuthnow, *The Restructuring of American Religion: Society and Faith Since World War Two* (Princeton, NJ: Princeton University Press, 1988).

3. James L. Guth, John C. Green, Corwin E. Smidt, Lyman A. Kellstedt, and Margaret M. Poloma, *The Bully Pulpit: The Politics of Protestant Clergy* (Lawrence: University Press of Kansas, 1997). See also John C. Green, James Guth, Corwin Smidt, and Lyman Kellstedt, eds., *Religion and the Culture Wars: Dispatches from the Front* (Lanham, MD: Rowman and Littlefield, 1996).

4. Wuthnow, *The Restructuring of American Religion.*

5. Wendy Cadge, "Vital Conflicts: The Mainline Protestant Denominations Debate Homosexuality," Robert Wuthnow and John H. Evans ed., *The Quiet Hand of God: Faith-Based Activism and the Public Role of Mainline Protestantism* (Berkeley, CA: University of California Press, 2003).

6. Hunter, *Culture Wars*; James Davison Hunter, *Before the Shooting Begins: Searching for Democracy in America's Culture War* (New York: Free Press, 1994).

7. Robert Wuthnow, "Divided We Fall: America's Two Civil Religions," *Christian Century* (April 20, 1988), 395–399.

8. Susan Martin Taylor, "A Fight for Religion or Something More?" *St. Petersburg Times* (June 15, 2003), 2A.

9. Patricia Leigh Brown, "For the Muslim Prom Queen, There Are No Kings Allowed," *New York Times* (June 7, 2003), A1.

10. For a general discussion of secularization theory, see Steve Bruce, *God is Dead: Secularization in the West* (Oxford: Blackwell, 2002), ch. 1, and *Religion and Modernization* (New York: Oxford University Press, 1992) .

11. See Karl Marx's "Economic and Philosophic Manuscripts," "Critique of Hegel's Philosophy of Right," and "Critique of the Gotha Program," in Robert C. Tucker, *The Marx-Engels Readers*, 2d ed. (New York: Norton, 1978); Max Weber, *The Protestant Ethic and the Spirit of Capitalism* (New York: Scribner's, 1958); Sigmund Freud, *The Future of an Illusion* (Garden City, NY: Doubleday, 1964).

12. See, for example, Christian Smith, ed., *The Secular Revolution: Power, Interests, and Conflict in the Secularization of American Life* (Berkeley: University of California Press, 2003)

and George Marsden, *The Soul of the American University: From Protestant Establishment to Established Nonbelief* (New York: Oxford University Press, 1996).

13. See, for example, Peter Berger et al., *The Desecularization of the World: Resurgent Religion and World Politics* (Grand Rapids, MI: Eerdmans, 1999) and Samuel P. Huntington Jr., *The Clash of Civilizations and the Remaking of World Order* (New York: Simon and Schuster, 1998).

14. Richard John Neuhaus, *The Naked Public Square: Religion and Democracy in America* (Grand Rapids, MI: Eerdmans, 1984).

15. Stephen Carter, *The Culture of Disbelief: How American Law and Politics Trivialize Religious Devotion* (New York: Basic Books, 1993).

16. A description of the nature of religion among members of Congress is found in Peter L. Benson and Dorothy L. Williams, *Religion on Capitol Hill: Myths and Realities* (New York: Oxford University Press, 1982).

17. For an example, consider the journalism of Richard John Neuhaus, *First Things* senior editor.

18. David Yamane, "Secularization on Trial: In Defense of a Neosecularization Paradigm," *Journal for the Scientific Study of Religion* 36 (January 1997), 109–122. See also Mark Chaves, "Secularization as Declining Religious Authority," *Social Forces* 72 (1994), 749–74.

19. For an interesting new analysis of postmaterialism, see Geoffrey C. Layman and Edward G. Carmines, "Cultural Conflict in American Politics: Religious Traditionalism, Postmaterialism, and U.S. Political Behavior," *Journal of Politics* 59 (August 1997), 751–777.

20. Ronald Inglehart, *Culture Shift in Advanced Industrial Society* (Princeton, NJ: Princeton University Press, 1990).

21. Wade Clark Roof, *A Generation of Seekers: The Spiritual Journeys of the Baby Boom Generation* (San Francisco: Harper, 1993).

22. Robert C. Fuller, *Spiritual But Not Religious: Understanding Unchurched America* (New York: Oxford, 2001).

23. Phillip Hammond, *Religion and Personal Autonomy: The Third Disestablishment* (Columbia: University of South Carolina Press, 1992).

24. Donald E. Miller, *Reinventing Protestantism: Christianity in the New Millennium* (Berkeley: University of California Press, 1997).

25. Robert Bellah, "Civil Religion in America," in Russell Richey and Donald Jones, eds., *American Civil Religion* (New York: Harper and Row, 1974), 21–44.

26. Sidney Mead, *The Lively Experiment* (New York: Harper and Row, 1975).

27. Clinton L. Rossiter, *The American Presidency*, rev. ed. (Baltimore, MD: Johns Hopkins University Press, 1960), 102.

28. For example, see John Wilson, *Public Religion in American Culture* (Philadelphia: Temple University Press, 1979).

29. For this thesis, see Robert Booth Fowler, *Unconventional Partners: Religion and Liberal Culture in the United States* (Grand Rapids, MI: Eerdmans, 1989).

30. Alexis de Tocqueville, *Democracy in America*, (Garden City, NY: Doubleday/Anchor, 1969).

31. On these points see also Roger Finke and Rodney Stark, *The Churching of America: 1776–1990: Winners and Losers in Our Religious Economy* (New Brunswick, NJ: Rutgers University Press, 1992).

32. Allen D. Hertzke, *Echoes of Discontent: Jesse Jackson, Pat Robertson, and the Resurgence of Populism* (Washington, D.C.: CQ Press, 1993).

33. Ibid.

34. For a good introduction to the market approach, see Finke and Stark, *The Churching of America;* Lawrence A. Young, ed., *Rational Choice Theory and Religion: Summary and Assessment* (New York: Routledge, 1997).

TABLES AND BOXES

APPENDIX
SELECTED WEB SITES
ON RELIGION AND POLITICS

Roman Catholic

U.S. Conference of Catholic Bishops   http://www.nccbuscc.org/

Evangelical Protestant

Assemblies of God   http://www.ag.org/top/
Lutheran Church—Missouri Synod   http://www.lcms.org/
Seventh-day Adventists   http://www.sda.org/
Southern Baptist Convention   http://www.sbc.net/
Presbyterian Church in America   http://www.pcanet.org/

Mainline Protestants

American Baptist Churches
  in the USA   http://www.abc-usa.org/
Evangelical Lutheran Church
  in America   http://www.elca.org/
Episcopal Church   http://ecusa.anglican.org/
Presbyterian Church, USA   http://www.pcusa.org/
United Church of Christ   http://www.ucc.org/
United Methodist Church   http://www.umc.org/

Jewish

Orthodox Judaism   http://www.ou.org/
United Synagogue of
  Conservative Judaism   http://www.uscj.org/index1.html
Union for Reform Judaism   http://www.uahc.org/

Black Protestant

African Methodist Episcopal (AME)   http://www.ame-today.com/
Church of God in Christ   http://www.cogic.org/
National Baptist Convention, USA   http://www.nationalbaptist.com/

Others

Church of Jesus Christ of Latter-day Saints	http://www.lds.org/
Jehovah's Witnesses	http://www.watchtower.org/
Islamic Society of North America	http://www.isna.net/
Unitarian Universalist	http://www.uua.org/
Baha'i	http://www.us.bahai.org/
Buddhism	http://www.buddhanet.net/
Hinduism (ISCKON)	http://www.iskcon.com/

ADVOCACY GROUPS

American Center for Law and Justice	http://www.aclj.org/
American Israel Public Affairs Committee	http://www.aipac.org/
American Jewish Committee	http://www.ajc.org/
American Jewish Congress	http://www.ajcongress.org/
Americans United for the Separation of Church and State	http://americansunited.org/
Anti-Defamation League	http://www.adl.org/
Baptist Joint Committee	http://www.bjcpa.org/
Bread for the World	http://www.bread.org/
Catholic Conferences—state level	http://www.nasccd.org/
Catholic League for Religious and Civil Rights	http://www.catholicleague.org/
Catholics for Free Choice	http://www.catholicsforchoice.org/
Center for Law and Religious Freedom	http://www.clsnet.org/
Christian Coalition	http://www.cc.org/
Concerned Women for America	http://www.cwfa.org/
Eagle Forum	http://www.eagleforum.org/
Ethics and Religious Liberty Commission	http://www.erlc.com/
Evangelicals for Social Action	http://www.esa-online.org/
Family Research Council	http://www.frc.org/
Focus on the Family	http://www.fotf.org/
Freedom from Religion Foundation	http://www.ffrf.org/
National Association of Evangelicals	http://www.nae.org/
National Council of Churches	http://www.ncccusa.org/
National Right to Life Committee	http://www.nrlc.org/
People for the American Way	http://www.pfaw.org/
Religious Coalition for Reproductive Choice	http://www.rcrc.org/
Rutherford Institute	http://www.rutherford.org/

INFORMATION SOURCES

American Religion Data Archive	http://www.thearda.com
Barna Research Group	http://www.barna.org

General Social Survey   http://www.norc.org/projects/gensoc4.asp
Henry Institute   http://www.calvin.edu/henry
National Election Studies   http://www.umich.edu/~nes/
Pew Forum on Religion in Public Life   http://www.pewforum.org
Religion and Ethics Newsweekly   http://www.pbs.org/wnet/religionandethics/
Religious Movements Homepage
    Project   http://religiousmovements.lib.virginia.edu/

INDEX